The Temple of Youth

THE TEMPLE OF YOUTH

Jimmy Butterworth and Clubland

First published in 2019
by JB Club Press

British Library Cataloguing-in-Publication data
A catalogue record for this book is available from the British Library

ISBN: 978-1-5272-5017-8

Designed and typeset by
Carnegie Scotforth Book Production

Printed and bound by Jellyfish Solutions

Foreword

By Sir Michael Caine, CBE

Jimmy Butterworth as we all knew him was the reason I am the person I am today.

He ran an amazing Youth Club called Clubland in the Walworth Road, Camberwell. He was a very small man, but only in height. In every other way he was one of the tallest people I have ever met.

Michael Caine on the Clubland stage in *R.U.R.*, 1948

I was 12 years old and on my way to becoming a juvenile delinquent when a very pretty girl who I liked said she had joined a Youth Club and would I like to come with her. I didn't want to join a Youth Club but she was very pretty, so I went. It was a joyous place with loads of things to do. I wound up doing basketball, but found out none of the boys would join the drama class because it was too sissy. They said they had no boys in the class so I joined and that is how I became an actor. Jimmy was an extraordinary loving man in an era just after we had all been through the Blitz in the Second World War, and we were a generation who knew nothing but hate.

I owe my personality, my life and my career to this man. The most important person I ever met.

Michael Caine
December 2016

Acknowledgements

The current recollections of those who have been part of Clubland make a significant contribution to this book, together with the voices of past members, friends, and associates frequently captured in short extracts from letters from JB's schooldays onwards. We have been particularly fortunate in having the accounts of several members from Clubland's flourishing postwar years, although sadly very few who knew the Club in its earlier heyday have been around to share their memories in person. However, the story of Clubland reaches beyond personal recall to determine the place and provenance of such a multi-faceted project in the early twentieth century, and demands a balanced perspective and exacting historical research. As the centenary of Clubland approaches we have wished to do justice to the memory of its founder by relying upon a comprehensive survey of source material. This has been made possible by access to a great wealth of documentary information – diaries, newsletters, annual reviews, press cuttings, photographs, correspondence, and cine film – held in the JB archive at Southwark Library and elsewhere, as well as published commentaries on contemporaneous social projects. The narrative and analysis in this biography owes much to close research of these and other publications, as well as to the helpful staff of the institutions concerned. In addition many whose families were involved in JB's life and history, either in Lancashire or London, have generously been willing to share their personal recall and memorabilia with us. We would like to express our grateful thanks to:

LIBRARIES AND ARCHIVES: All Archive and Heritage officers at Southwark Local History Library, particularly Lisa Moss, Lisa Soverel, Bob Jones, and Patricia Dark; staff at the Lancashire Archive, Preston; Clive Taylor and Russ Haughton (Archivists), Cliff College, Calver, for their generosity with time and resource material; Staff of the Minet

Library (Lambeth Archives and Local Studies Library), Knatchbull Rd; Staff and Archivists at the John Rylance Library, University of Manchester; John Simpson, Accrington Library, for assistance with and permission to use old photographs of Accrington and Oswaldtwistle; Owen Roberts, Methodist Heritage Officer, who kindly facilitated our enquiries into Clubland's 'single station' status.

CLUB MEMBERS / FAMILIES: Terry and Teresa Barrett, Laurie and Daphne Williams, Allen and Sylvie Sparksman – with thanks for their 'bird's eye view' accounts of Clubland in the Fifties and Sixties; Luke Bedson, son of Les, who remembered JB as a 'little imp of a clergyman'; Jane Bainbridge, daughter of Gordon and Peggy Lyle; Juliet Dunmur, granddaughter of Sir Edward and Lady Prudence Maufe; Sir Len Neal, brother of Frank and member from the mid-Twenties; Stan Emmanuel, stalwart Clubland prop and presence over many years; Lambert Bignall, previously married to JB's niece Ruth; Ricky Elliot, long term postwar Clubland lieutenant; Bob Gray, one-time Head Senior, and JB's late son-in-law, who meticulously catalogued all JB's letters and literature after his death.

OSWALDTWISTLE / ACCRINGTON: Margaret Berry (nee Wilkinson), Margaret Wolstenholme Eric and Barbara Wolstenholme, whose families had supported and mentored JB in his youth; Peter Hargreaves of former Moscow Mill, Oswaldtwistle, whose ancestor James Hargreaves invented the Spinning Jenny; Mark Gerrard, General Manager, Vine Mill; John Horman of Topps Farm, who has kindly allowed us access to the disused Green Haworth Chapel, which stands on land he presently owns; Maurice Duckworth, son of JB's Duckworth cousins who shared his Lancashire heritage, and provided their recollections; the Staff of Helmshore Mill, Rossendale, for special access; John and Shirley Crook, whose family was closely involved with Green Haworth Chapel from JB's childhood onwards, for sharing documents and information.

Finally we must give particular thanks to:

Sir Michael Caine for the warm and personal message that he unhesitatingly provided for our foreword.

Peter Milner, contributing author, for his extensive and assiduous research into JB's early life, and the first draft of Chapter 1.

James Butterworth, contributing author, for his draft of Chapter 9, based upon his detailed and careful reading of several boxes of his grandfather's diaries of the American tours of the Fifties.

Mike and Mary Gee (nee Butterworth) for their professional organisation and production of the 120 photographs in the biography, selected from thousands available from archive albums.

Simon Gray, graphic designer, and grandson of JB, for his eloquent cover design.

Our friends **Deb Campbell** and **Linda Dean** for their painstaking hours sorting, reading, and identifying JB documents.

Reverend Paul Weary, the present minister at Walworth Methodist Church (Clubland), for his frequent generous welcome and encouragement during research for the book.

To **Lucy Frontani** and **Srishti Kadu** at Carnegie Book Production, for their skill and patience in preparing the book for publication.

Contents

Frontispiece   v

Foreword by Sir Michael Caine, CBE   vii

Acknowledgements   ix

Introduction   1

Chapter 1: Childhood and Chapel   9

    The Chapel on the Hill   9

    Butterworths and Duckworths   10

    Methodist Roots   13

    Schoolboy and Sunday School Scholar   15

    Steiner's Bleach Works   20

    The loss of Thomas   23

    The Little Piecer   29

    The Boy Preacher   34

    Cliff College   37

Chapter 2: 'The Great War For Civilisation'   43

    War is declared   43

    The Bantams   48

    Active service   49

    Arras   52

    Étaples   57

    Hospitals and huts   62

    A sort of ministry   65

Army life   72

Armistice   74

Chapter 3: Didsbury 1919–1922   77

  Candidature for the Ministry   77

  Didsbury Wesleyan Theological College, 1919–1922   82

  Beech Road Mission   88

  Holmes Chapel   94

  Moving on   97

Chapter 4: The Fight For Clubland   101

  Walworth   101

  The First Years: Six Boys in a Dug-Out   105

  The Stormy Petrel of Methodism   118

  Master Builder   126

  Going it alone 1930   134

Chapter 5: The Glory Years   141

  The Temple of Youth   141

  Honourable Members   144

  The Home of Friendship   152

  The Campaign in Print   159

  Trial and Travel   165

  'God Bless Our Club'   169

Chapter 6: Crucible, 1939–1945   177

  Exodus   177

  The Burning Furnace   183

  'The Lord of All Good Life'   193

  'Letters of a Clublander'   198

Chapter 7: Regeneration   205

  Beginning Again   205

  A New Jerusalem   210

  Restoration   216

  Back to business   221

  Return to the Channel Islands   229

The Silver Jubilee and beyond   235
Faultlines   241

Chapter 8: Clubland at the Crossroads   247
Through a Glass Darkly   247
'Youth on the Loose'   252
The Teddy Boys   255
The Writing on the Wall   259
Cabinet and Members   263
And then the Premiers   267

Chapter 9: To America With £5!   273
Fundraising tours of the fifties   273
The first American Tour: 8 June–1 October, 1950   276
The Second American Tour: 17 June–5 October, 1954   282
The Third American Tour: 16 June–30 September, 1955   288
The Fourth American Tour: 28 June–28 September, 1956   291
The Fifth American Tour: 10 June–13 October, 1959   298

Chapter 10: The Rock 'N' Roll Years   303
This is Your Life   303
Celebrity Clubland   307
Bricks and Mortar and Lord Rank   316
Growing up in Clubland   327
The Hard Question   334
The Sixties, Students, and Succession   339
Postwar Voices   348

Chapter 11: Epilogue: The Last Years   363
'It was all so much fun'   363
The Window Closes   365
This little imp of a clergyman   372
Postscripts   373

Bibliography   379

Index of Names   381

Introduction

To tell the story of James Butterworth is to tell the story of Clubland – the iconic boys' and girls' club that he built from nothing in the densely populated and deprived district of Walworth in south-east London. Founded just after the Great War, in the hey day of clubs, it grew and flourished for over fifty tumultuous years: the Twenties and Thirties, the war years, the rock and roll years. They were the Clubland Years, and for their duration thousands of boys and girls, young men and women, and visitors from all walks of life passed through its doors. For all those who knew it, Clubland made a profound difference to their lives, and in many cases shaped their futures. At the same time it helped dramatically to change public attitudes, both to young people and to the less privileged in society.

Clubland became a landmark in the history of social work in the 20th century, with a worldwide reputation and a succession of imitators. It was also a lightning rod for controversy – Its fine buildings designed by Edward Maufe, architect of Guildford Cathedral, and opened by Queen Mary in 1939, proclaimed challengingly to anyone passing or visiting that nothing was too good for the young members who peopled it, whatever their backgrounds. The internal design and furnishings were equally impressive. If its chapel, theatre, gymnasium, and 'Parliament' – arranged around a central quadrangle – seemed more in keeping with a university college than a traditional inner-city mission, that was the intention. It did not mean that the less privileged should either envy or imitate their 'betters': rather that they should have rightful access to the same quality of environment as those who took such quality as their due.

Not surprisingly such ambitions met with their fair share of scepticism and at times outright hostility, both from traditionalists in the church and in the locality. 'Butterworth's folly' was how some saw the impressive frontage and the lofty aspiration it symbolised. There were others, however, who recognised Clubland's high expectations and pursuit of excellence for what they were: an investment in the future – namely the young, but the young in particular who were growing up in inner-city neighbourhoods where investment of any sort had been in short supply. In 1933, barely ten years after JB's arrival in Walworth and the start of his work there, the Rt Hon. Lord Rochester (then Paymaster General in Ramsay MacDonald's National Government) told the House:

> My Lords – Only this morning I was reading of a government Commissioner who asked whether we should not spend our money much more advantageously on building clubs for young people than in some other ways in which it is now expended. In that connection perhaps I might mention an outstanding instance which happens to be little more than a couple of miles away from your Lordships' House. [...] Its purpose is to minister more adequately to those in the surrounding overcrowded district. This Clubland, the exact address of which is 54, Camberwell Road, is a home of friendships of boys and girls previously outside any church. With ideals of all-round fitness it trains members to realise the best in life. In clubs opened every night it provides for the development of mind, body and spirit, with emphasis on the spirit because the spiritual completes the whole. The entire premises have cost £34,000, every penny of which has been raised by voluntary contribution, and now the young people themselves, some 500 in number, ranging in ages from 10 to 25 years, are contributing no less than £1000 a year in weekly sums and varied efforts for upkeep. It is open every night, and I invite your Lordships to see the place for yourselves, for, as an example of what can be done by voluntary effort, it will well repay a visit.[1]

Clubland took a decade and a half to build, both physically and in terms of its membership. It started, in its founder's own words, 'with six boys in a bible class', with a minister's study as the clubroom, and a back yard as the sports pitch. After his first battle with the church elders, he managed to secure space in the basement rooms of the Walworth Wesleyan Chapel, where he had had been sent in September 1922 as a young probationary Methodist minister fresh from theological college in Didsbury, Manchester. He had already, as a student, set up and run a successful boys' club at Beech Road in Chorlton, a few miles to the west of Didsbury, earning from his elders and tutors the mixture of disapproval and respect that was to pursue him throughout his life and work.

He would have stayed in Manchester from choice, and built on what he had started and would later replicate in London; but Methodism assigns its ministers to their posts by invitation, and none was forthcoming from the kind of community he wished to serve – aside from the struggling outpost at Walworth. He was, by all accounts, a gifted preacher, for which reason his college Governor, Reverend T H Barratt, urged him to accept appointment to a more flourishing circuit where his talent in the pulpit would be properly celebrated. In his early writings JB expresses nothing but the deepest affection, bordering on reverence, for Rev. Barratt. Nonetheless, and entirely in character, he ignored the well-meant advice, and went to Walworth. There he would remain for the whole of his ministry, obstinately defying the dictates of the Methodist Conference that required ministers to move every few years.

Jimmy Butterworth had himself grown up in often extreme poverty, not in London but in Lancashire. Born at the tail-end of the nineteenth century, he was the eldest of five children, crowded into a tiny cottage on the edge of the moors between the mill towns of Accrington and Oswaldtwistle. He had left school to work in a factory by the age of twelve, and became breadwinner for the family just a year later on his father's tragic and premature death. He needed no lessons in what life meant for the deprived young people growing up in the vicinity of the failing Walworth chapel – an area with an approximate radius of half a mile and an estimated population of 85,000. He had experienced it in full and at first-hand.

From his disadvantaged start in life it is a mystery how he managed to educate himself to the level needed to pass the entrance exam to Theological College. His promise at elementary school had been noted, and his head teacher had expressed disappointment at his ceasing his education to support the family. But necessity prevailed, as it did for so many of his generation and social class. Just when children today are starting secondary school, he was working twelve hour shifts in a dye works. The one saving grace for him was the church, in his case the small, gaunt Methodist chapel of Green Haworth, perched on a hill overlooking Oswaldtwistle and the intervening hamlet of Bedlam where he first lived.

The Butterworths were staunch Methodists, and committed members of the tiny chapel, a short but steep walk from their home. His father and mother taught Sunday school classes, and so from the tender age of 10 did Jimmy, progressing by stages to occasional opportunities to preach. Boy preachers were not unheard of at the turn of the century, but still it was a relatively rare honour to conduct services and deliver a sermon. He impressed the circuit ministers with his evident gift for oratory. As he advanced into adolescence a tenacious ambition to enter the ministry became apparent, eventually leading him to enrol at Cliff College, an evangelical Methodist establishment based at Calver near Sheffield.

It was a short-lived interlude. The Great War had entered its second full year, and as casualties on the Western Front mounted, the call for volunteers spread wider and cut deeper. James had already been rejected once at the outset, not only for his age but also his height. He never did reach five feet, and even in his twenties, and running his first clubs, visitors often mistook him for one of the boys. But as the war of attrition ground on, and the supply of new recruits declined, details such as size ceased to be a bar. Indeed, special 'Bantam' battalions were formed for men under 5 feet 3, one of which was the 17th Lancashire Fusiliers, which Private Butterworth joined in February 1916. After a short period of training he was posted to France in the late summer, first to the Somme, then to Arras, and finally, after the Bantam battalions were disbanded, to work in the hospital and convalescent facilities at the notorious base in Étaples.

Like many of the survivors of the Great War JB was reluctant to describe his wartime experiences in any detail. Mostly, if he talked of it at all, he joked: how the Bantams were too short to see over the parapet, or how their uniforms, made for men twice their size, tripped them up when they marched. Trenches, like pulpits, are challenging for small men. What cannot be doubted, however, is the effect that the war, together with his childhood privation, had upon his later life and work. He, like the rest, returned to the 'land fit for heroes' only to find that the promises of a better life for all had been quickly forgotten. For great swathes of the population growing up in the inner-city communities of Manchester, London, and Liverpool, little had really changed since the years before 1914. This can only have added to an idealistic dream of building an oasis of friendship and opportunity for as many young people as he could, and a hope that others would follow suit.

The book recounts how the First Clubland Church, as it was formally named, became much more than simply an oasis: it was, as one ex-member put it, a 'finishing-school for working boys and girls'. By the outbreak of the next war, the range of its activities had extended to many of the major sports, to drama, art, music, debating, dance, and a spread of enterprises which reached far beyond the original programme. There was an active and effective Parliament through which the members took on responsibility for a measure of self-government. There were summer camps, matches against schools and colleges, and an internal house system serving both pastoral and competitive functions. The Club generated its own literature – reviews, magazines, newsletters – published by JB with content from the members. And throughout, Clubland was also a thriving church, its youthful congregation composed almost entirely of members and officers, many of whom would otherwise have had no association with any religious organisation. JB's dynamic leadership and charisma are strikingly evident in Clubland's internal development, as well as in his unremitting drive to fund the enterprise. The complex relation between the religious and secular aspects of Clubland, and of JB's own development, is itself a subject of much interest which features in discussion in later chapters.

What will also emerge is the intense interest shown by the outside world in the work of the Club, with celebrities and dignitaries from practically every of walk of life regularly visiting and mingling with the members. It no doubt added to the members' sense of self-assurance and self-worth to have such contacts, and many ex-members have spoken of the ability that their time in the club gave them to mix with ease and confidence in circles very different from their own. But the publicity that came with this interest also made Clubland itself – and its founder – something of a celebrity. As Clubland's fame and reputation spread JB, too, grew accustomed to mixing in circles very different from those in which he had grown up. It did not always lead to a comfortable meeting of minds, nor, as will be seen, did celebrity come without costs or unwanted compromises.

Clubland has been described as unique, and in a great many ways it was, but it was not without antecedents. Clubland belonged firmly within the tradition of the boys' club movement, the university and public school missions and settlements, and the evening institutes. These in turn had their roots in 19th century philanthropy: the ragged schools, Salvation Army, Barnardo's. But there was a striking difference. In his book, *A Cry from the Streets*, Frank Dawes writes of these institutions:

> Charities abounded, providing free dinners, free education, free nursing, free medicine, free soup, free clothing; but always with the message "Know thy place". [2]

Clubland's very special and independent interpretation of the boys' club movement – including the departure of being also a girls' club – is central to this book, but suffice to say 'knowing thy place' was never any part of it. For one thing Clubland was not charity. True, it relied entirely on voluntary adult help to provide its plethora of activities – and no less heavily on financial support from wealthy and not-so-wealthy donors to build and maintain the premises. But although much was given to ensure the existence of the club, it was not given for nothing to the members. From the start, and even for the poorest, the members were required to pay a subscription and to take on their share of fund-raising activity, and to make voluntary contributions. For many this represented a significant sacrifice – on their parents' part or their own – but the contract was non-negotiable. Beyond being needed for the club to survive, the members' obligatory subscription had another crucial function: it made the club theirs. It made them – to cite one of JB's essential principles – 'partners, not passengers'. In that sense only, they knew their place.

In 1939 the first Clubland was completed, and opened by Queen Mary. Two years later the beautiful chapel was destroyed by the Luftwaffe, and thereafter most of the surviving club rooms were requisitioned by the London County Council as a refuge for local victims of the Blitz. Large numbers of the Juniors were evacuated to the relative safety of the countryside, whilst the bulk of the Senior membership was conscripted and scattered. With his church a ruin, and the body of young people he had nurtured broken up, JB spent the war providing for evacuees, and maintaining a skeleton Club organisation. There was constant correspondence from far and wide with the conscripted Seniors, many of whom were sadly not to return home. Those who eventually did come back went on to form the nucleus of a revived Senior club, with the same recreational and cultural activity as before, especially theatre with a series of memorable postwar productions. The Guernsey camps resumed, too, and Clubland's youth revisited and enjoyed the island's wonderful facilities and hospitality. But the continuity of training, with Juniors graduating to Seniors and Seniors to Club Officers, that had characterised Clubland from the start, had been broken by the war.

The story of Clubland has two distinct halves. Like the century to which it belonged, it was punctuated in the middle by six years of war, which affected it profoundly. Many of the postwar members were returnees from armed service – adults in a changed world – whilst the new youth intake was unfamiliar with the traditional Clubland ethos and had varying ideas of what the Club should provide. As the forties gave way to the fifties, the broader equilibrium of society was broken by undercurrents of gang violence spreading among young people, and reaching into Clubland – at one point threatening its very existence.

Following a period of crisis the only viable solution was to start again, by reopening the door to juniors, and rebuilding from the bottom up. It was a huge gamble to make in already uncertain times, but the response was enormous and immediate. Within weeks over two hundred girls and two hundred boys had joined, reaching Club capacity, and requiring a small army of the older and ex-members to provide the activities and coach and supervise the youngsters. In less than two years, as the older children graduated, a flourishing new senior section, known as the Premiers, had emerged, many of whom remained part of the Club for decades, giving their time and talents to subsequent generations. In later chapters the text is interspersed with comment from Clubland members of this postwar era, confirming the continuing spirit of the 'Home of Friendship', and the place of Clubland in their lives. Together with JB's untiring efforts, they gave Clubland a new life.

JB still spent every spare night in the Club, as well as touring at home and abroad to raise finance. For him personally, fund-raising was to become a constant and debilitating burden, taking him as far afield as New York and Los Angeles, Toronto and St Louis. These travels, lasting throughout the 1950s, comprise a whole chapter of the book: his association with the world of American boxing; the connections he made with wealthy and famous patrons; and above all his fortuitous meeting with Bob Hope in Hollywood, when by some magic he was able to entice the famous comedian to the London stage and, more than once, to the Walworth Road. Gruelling as they were, the tours paid off. The Queen Mother opened the rebuilt church in 1964, and JB set about plans to extend the premises and build hostels whose residents would provide both rental income, and the crucial assistance with the Club's varied activities. During this phase Lord Arthur Rank became Clubland's greatest sponsor.

The welfare state had already begun to address many of the needs formerly left to voluntary organisations, and perceptions of youth – and of youth-work – were inevitably changing. The values for which Clubland stood were no less relevant. Walworth had not become a land of plenty: there was still considerable struggle and want facing the majority of families, but for young people there were other distractions and sources of entertainment. The demographic landscape of South London was also undergoing change – in contrast to its previous largely white working-class population Walworth became in the space of a decade home to a diverse multi-cultural population, celebrated by Clubland and welcomed into its membership. Through the sixties Clubland's officers and volunteers continued to organise its spread of activities, and young people populated the Clubs and attended the Church, but as the decade drew to a close the level of interest and commitment inevitably waned, in the face of competing attractions and changing priorities.

The final chapters of the book look at this transitional time, leading sadly into the twilight years of JB's great venture. He died, aged 80, in 1977 barely a year after enforced retirement and stubborn till the end, but defeated finally by exhaustion and ill-health. Specific youth projects have continued to play a part, though with less emphasis, in the work of the Walworth church and its wonderful adjoining premises. But boys and girls are no longer the exclusive heirs to the place JB grandly christened his 'Temple of Youth'.

A succession of Methodist ministers has given great service to the changing community in the decades since JB's death. The Walworth Methodist Church (Clubland), as it is now known, is a thriving mission, ministering to a huge and cosmopolitan congregation. It deserves a book of its own, but not this book. This one is about Clubland, and Clubland essentially ended as it had begun with JB. I started by saying that the story of JB is the story of Clubland, but the reverse is also true, and the lives of the two are inextricably bound together.

Because JB was so identified by his Clubland role, there is a danger in writing this book of overlooking the man behind the public persona. But the two were distinct, and the nature of his mission – particularly the unrelenting battle to fund and sustain the Club, sometimes forced him into a role that cost him in both authenticity and health. He was an inspirational leader, but there were also contradictions in his life and his character which are as much a part of this biography as his achievements. Nobody who worked closely with JB would claim that he was always an easy man – single-minded to his core, and impatient to reach his goals, he had little tolerance for anything short of total commitment in others. Yet the depths of compassion and generosity that he showed to youngsters who had lost their way, and fallen outside society's norms, knew no bounds. He reached out always to nurture body, mind, and spirit, and he gave his entire life wholeheartedly to the egalitarian enrichment of youth.

Notes

1 *Hansard*: Lords debate, 28 February, 1933. Lord Rochester.
2 Dawes, Frank. *A Cry From the Streets: The Boys' Club Movement in Britain from the 1850s to the Present Day*. Wayland Publishers 1975 p.22

CHAPTER ONE

Childhood and Chapel

The Chapel on the Hill

A traveller ascending from Accrington station, climbing up from the town along Willows Lane, past Rothwell Heights, and following the road as it turns a sharp right through Bedlam village, at last sees the plain outlines of a sombre stone building come into view, gaunt and dark against the moorland skyline. This is Green Haworth Wesleyan Chapel, built as its date-stone proclaims in 1836, and rebuilt in 1903. Disused since its closure in 1985, boarded up and squeezed within a narrow plot of farmland awaiting reinvention as dwellings, it stands at Cross Edge

Green Haworth Wesleyan Chapel today

at the summit of Fielding Lane, rising high over Oswaldtwistle. Sited 900 feet above sea level, the Chapel has unobstructed views over the county – Ingleborough, Longridge Fell, and Hoghton Tower appear in the distance. Its stark presence seems to symbolise the enduring hold of Methodism over this Lancashire landscape, across which it still gazes sternly. This Chapel marked and shaped the life of James Butterworth, from his baptism there by the Reverend J. Wesley Whitmore of the Accrington Wesleyan Circuit in 1897, to the day in 1977 when he was 'brought back to Top Chapel' for his funeral after his fifty-five year Ministry in youth work in Walworth, South London.[1]

Butterworths and Duckworths

The story of Clubland does not start with the Reverend James Butterworth's move from Lancashire to London in 1922, nor with his student years at Didsbury Methodist College in Manchester, nor even before that when he saw his friends die on the Somme, or lived through his father's suicide when he was thirteen. His project for youth was fired by many aspirations and ideals, driven by many griefs and traumas – and perhaps even fed by an underlying sense of personal injustice. The story begins in 1897 when Jimmy was born at 6 Rough Hey Gate, Oswaldtwistle, on 17 March, into a life of mill labour and material hardship, the first child of Thomas Butterworth and Ann (nee Duckworth) at the end of their first year of marriage. Both Butterworths and Duckworths were extensive families, long established in the area with names common in East Lancashire, and the new infant's familial roots lay in a network of workers in the agriculture and industry of the North. The township of Oswaldtwistle lies on the Leeds/Liverpool Canal, sharing boundaries with Church and Accrington. By legend it was named for Oswald, king of Northumbria, who passed across the finger of land at the meeting of two brooks – a 'twistle' in old English. The locality has produced prestigious families – the Peels, mill-owners and progenitors of prime minister Robert Peel, and the Hargreaves, whose 18th century ancestor James revolutionised the mill industry with his Spinning Jenny, and who still run Oswaldtwistle Mill, now a multi-franchise outlet.

By contrast the Butterworth family history was one of struggle to subsist, without reliable tenure in land or housing. The baby's great grandfather – also James Butterworth – had fallen foul of the stringent settlement rules, and was the subject of an order at the Lancashire Quarter Sessions in June 1825 that he should be removed from Oswaldtwistle,

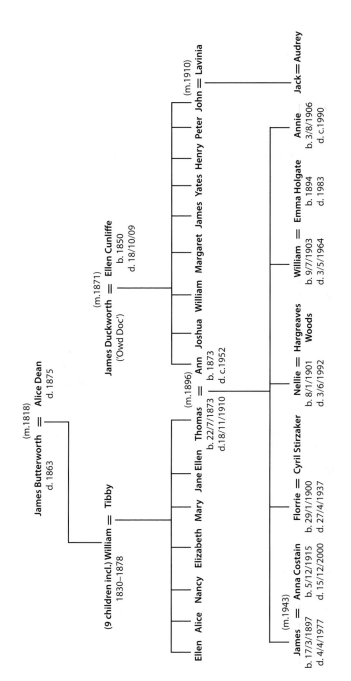

together with his wife Alice and three small children, and the family returned for its maintenance to New Accrington.[2] Green Haworth fell within the Accrington Poor Law Union, which extended as far as the Oswaldtwistle boundary – lying south-east along the brook opposite Rough Hey Gate – whilst Rough Hey was outside it and administered by Oswaldtwistle. James and Alice went on to have nine children – their son William, Baby Jimmy's grandfather was born in 1836 – and moved with their family from Green Haworth to nearby Gaulkthorn, before settling for the remainder of their lives at Rough Hey, from where they were buried in the parish churchyard at Immanuel. William Butterworth became a miner – dying from typhoid fever, which was rife in the area, at the age of 42. He left behind his wife Tibby, and six children – among whom was Jimmy's father, Thomas, who had been born in 1873. By the time of the 1891 census the family had moved into the centre of town, and Thomas, like his sisters and grandfather James, was working as a weaver.

On the Duckworth side, Jimmy's mother's relations were equally plentiful in East Lancs. A deed of 19 March 1725, relating to land at Rough Hey, contains reference to an obligation on the part of one George Duckworth to pay an annual rental of five shillings.[3] Her parents, James Duckworth and Ellen (Cunliffe), married in 1871 – Ann's half-brother Joshua Cunliffe had been born earlier that year – and went on to have ten children. Joshua's paternity is unclear, but he was certainly raised as a Duckworth with the others. James Duckworth is described as a collier on his marriage certificate, and later, in the 1891 census, as a miner working at Higher Red Walls Colliery, Oswaldtwistle – but in between, in the early eighties, the family had had a stint at farming as tenants at Westell Lot and locally at Cross Edge. James was something of a disreputable local character, and not a shining example among the abstinent Green Haworth Chapel community. Known as 'Owd Doc', he frequented the Shoulder of Mutton Public House at Cross Edge, on occasion returning home somewhat the worse for wear. Family lore recounts that on leaving this establishment late one night, without lights or name on his cart, he had the novel idea of avoiding a fine from the watchful local constable by putting his pony in the cart and getting between the shafts himself. When the policeman stepped into the road and enquired what he was up to he replied: 'Talk to t'driver'.

By 1901 James and Ellen and seven of their children were living at number 4 Rough Hey Gate, Joshua Cunliffe and his family were next door at number 5, and Thomas and Ann were at number 6 with their first three offspring. The backcloth of Jimmy's early childhood was the family web of his neighbours, and there must have been much daily interaction between the houses and family units. In 1910 James Duckworth's son John (known as Jack) got married from his parents' house to Lavinia Eustace, a cotton weaver from Huncoat, daughter of a glass blower. The new couple soon moved to Huncoat but they – and later their son Jack – remained close to Jimmy. Cousin Jack was a regular visitor to Clubland and started a youth Club in his own local Methodist chapel.

Methodist Roots

Despite family solidarity the hardship of Jimmy's early life is beyond doubt. The cottage at 6 Rough Hey Gate was a tiny four-roomed dwelling. When Jimmy was born in 1897 he was alone there with his parents for a short time only – the cramped space soon filled up with a succession of four more babies, necessitating several siblings in a bed, and containing sufficient chairs and room to allow only two of the family to sit at table at any one time.

Thomas and Ann were fortunate to be able to work and earn in the early years, although the harshness of their daily lifestyle was unremitting. In an unpublished autobiography written many years later at Clubland Jimmy recalled the sacrifices of his parents. 'My father and mother who were weavers by day, did the housework in the evenings, and stayed up most of the night if any of their five children were ill.' If the parents were ill they 'worked it off'. 'I have known my father carry me across the moors to the doctor, wait in a cold town surgery till 10 p.m. carry me back home, then up at four next morning for the same route to work. If the weft was bad the work was harder, the wage by reduced output being about 22/- (£1.20) a week.'[4] He also recalled that in addition to her house and family chores, and the weaving job, his mother took in washing which she would go out in the evenings to deliver. He relates that years afterwards on a visit to the town a mill manager described to him having once met his mother carrying him, just a month before the birth of his sister Florrie in January 1900, struggling up the hill in a blinding storm. 'My mother used to leave home at 5 a.m. carry me to a farm, call for me when the mill closed, do her washing, baking, or cleaning, then up at 4.30 next morning.'

This pressured and relentless timetable of child-rearing, mill labour, and house chores was countered by the reassurance and inspiration which sustained so very many working families in the industrialisation of the late nineteenth century – perhaps particularly in Lancashire, needful of respite from the dense presence of mills and mines. Founded in the 18th century by Charles and John Wesley, the non-conformist Methodist movement urged a return to the message of the gospels. Travelling to speak directly to agricultural and industrial workers, evangelical preachers assured them of their value and equality before the Almighty, and this message bore fruit amongst the inhabitants of the mill towns of the north of England. The chapel on the hill at Green Haworth sustained the spiritual needs and aspirations of the hard-pressed local workers, providing the balm of worship and meditation, as well as the comfort of a united community. Ultimately the Methodist Church was the medium through which Jimmy Butterworth realised his extraordinary mission to change the lives of countless young people, becoming a crusader for youth, and a pioneer of youth work – certainly within Methodism, but also on a broader national and international canvas.

For the last celebratory service at Green Haworth Chapel in 1985, prior to its closure and sale, John Crook, whose family were long-term stalwarts of the Chapel congregation, wrote a review of the Chapel's historical development. He relates how in the nineteenth century miners and weavers met in a bustling Green Haworth – usually at Owd Doc's local The Shoulder of Mutton, which was a centre for wrestling, gambling, cockfighting, and even bear-baiting. The Union Street Methodist church in Accrington had started a Sunday School, celebrating its first anniversary in a barn owned by Christopher Hindle – member of another well-known Oswaldtwistle Methodist family. From that point Green Haworth joined the Burnley Circuit and regular preaching services started. By 1835 the 25 members of the congregation had determined to build a chapel – to cost £300 and measure 39 feet by 33 feet. A year later in 1836 the building was up, drawing large crowds despite the opposition from the established church towards non-conformists. The influence of the chapel on the hill slowly calmed its pugilistic community, even enticing a congregation from the Shoulder of Mutton itself when a local preacher, Isaac Marsden, dared enter those premises and treat the drinkers to his rendering of 'Rock of Ages'.

Through the century the chapel on the hill prospered, extending its premises, providing evening classes, and building a devout and loyal community following. Butterworths and Duckworths climbed the steep half-mile up from Rough Hey Gate several times in a week, and contributed to the religious and social life of the chapel congregation – Jimmy's father played the church organ and taught Sunday School, and his mother was active on Chapel committees and in the organisation of special events. A New Year's Day celebration programme from 1915 shows the whole family participating in the proceedings, which included 'pies, buns, and entertainments'. Jimmy's sisters took part in the dramatic presentations, and his younger brother Billy provided 'songs and recitations.'[5] Billy was already showing signs of inheriting Thomas's musical talent – when grown he was possessor of a fine deep bass voice and sang with the Accrington Male Voice Choir, and the Royal Choral Society. In 1936, when the Rev. James Butterworth returned for the Chapel centenary celebrations, the local pillars of Methodism from his childhood were remembered. Influential servants of the community from his youth, such as Councillor M. Maden; Mr. Holdea Mallalieu; Farmer Jacob Crook; Mr. Mark Willan; Mr. C. Hindle; Mr. W.T. Wilkinson.

The spiritual direction and purpose offered by chapel teachings, and confirmed by the faith of his family, gripped and inspired Jimmy from an early age. Endlessly prolific in print and in the pulpit throughout his life, Jimmy was a born wordsmith and lent his early childhood fluency to the composition of sermons. Frequently these would be delivered to his many siblings and cousins in the henhouses opposite the terrace of cottages at Rough Hey. Their comments do not survive – but his enthusiasm for preaching gained strength.

Schoolboy and Sunday School Scholar

The Butterworths had little spare money for luxuries, but Jimmy's mother instilled into her children that there must always be silver for the plate at Chapel. In the Clubland Review for 1964 Jimmy – by then known at Clubland as the Head, or JB – recalled of his mother that: 'She insisted in our poverty on silver not copper in chapel collections, cleanliness in our poor home, paying our way and no debts'.[6]

In later days Jimmy quoted the 1746 exhortation of the church founder John Wesley: 'Let none ever see a ragged Methodist'. These were words which Jimmy took seriously and carried on in the lifelong principles he sought to impart to his young Clubland members of 'Pride in Premises' and 'Partners not Passengers', telling the Walworth membership that 'Clubland refuses to see any romance in raggedness.'[7] The ethical tenor and terms of living, which he was taught and absorbed in childhood from home and church, he ever afterwards taught to others. He never championed charity – the Victorian age into which he was born had been one which recognised the place of charity and maintenance for the poor, but that era was not a time of egalitarian dignity and respect. The

Victorian moralist Sam Smiles was an upholder of prudence and responsibility – the spectre of the workhouse and parish charity loomed close in the lives of the poor, and the friendly societies of the later nineteenth century instead advocated respect for thrift and independence.[8]

Ann Butterworth made sure that her children were well-presented, and when Jimmy started school, in the Summer term after his fifth birthday in 1902, he was fashionably dressed. A former classmate, Harry Godbold, in an account captured in the Lancashire Sound Archive, recalled that: '(James) wore velvet pants and a yellow blouse with one button.' This seems a curious way for a working-class boy from a mill family to dress for school, but a class photograph confirms his appearance. The children are in general neatly turned out, and it was no doubt a matter of family pride that a respectable standard was maintained.

Jimmy was sent to Hippings Lane Infants School, which was at the top of Chapel Street, around a mile from Rough Hey Gate, and had to walk this distance at least twice each day – and occasionally four times if he returned home for his dinner in the middle of the day. It was a long way

Hippings Lane Infants School, first class. Jimmy is in the 2nd row, 2nd from right.

for a five-year-old – and a very small one at that. The entire family was of small stature, and as an adult Jimmy's height remained diminutive at 4'11". Until he was in his thirties, when his face began to assume some maturity, he still looked like a young child, and was not infrequently mistaken for one. Hippings wasn't the nearest school to home – Green Haworth Church of England Primary School, just across the fields, was nearer – but Hippings Lane had the distinction of being a Wesleyan Methodist School. His family's willingness for Jimmy to make the long trek was a measure of the fierce attachment they bore to their church. The walk to Hippings and back – along an unpopulated country road in all weathers and seasonally in the dark – must have been daunting for a small boy. The stretch along Broadfield and Fielding Lane, up to the start of the terraced streets near the school, was virtually bare of buildings during that period, and would have been cold and lonely, especially on winter days.

There was just one certified teacher in the school, Miss Alice Smalley, who was assisted by three other members of staff, and the meticulously recorded school log permits readers a flavour of those long ago classrooms and the children within them. In Jimmy's first week the total average attendance in the 'Babies, First, and Second' classes was 113 children. It was particularly important to keep an exact record of the number of schooling days an individual child had received in order that the statutory minimum requirement might be recorded before the child could leave school to start work – in that era usually at twelve years of age. In Jimmy's first year at school illness was a recurrent theme – numbers were reduced to 100 at one point, due to a smallpox scare. Problems from whooping cough and scarlet fever, both potentially fatal, were also documented, and attendance was down for the 'annual poor children's treat' of an outing to Lytham.[9] More happily, special holidays were declared in May 1902, when many mills in the district closed to celebrate the news that the Boer War had ended, and again in August for the coronation of Edward Vll – the latter occasion marked by a celebratory procession through the town.

The opening of the upgraded Green Haworth Chapel in 1903 was a memorable event from which six-year-old Jimmy may unconsciously have absorbed some enduring principles. For one thing it was an object lesson in fund-raising. The original structure had been in very poor repair, and the rebuilding and extension was funded entirely by three years of local efforts. The *Methodist Recorder* retrospectively reported that the work had been completed at a cost of £1800, making it 'one of the latest and most commodious village chapels in the district.' It described the project as having been 'accomplished chiefly through the self-denying exertions of the people on the spot', which had included a final bazaar at Green Haworth which raised £550.00. It impressed upon small Jimmy the magnitude of what might be accomplished if everyone pulled together to raise the wherewithal, and must have confirmed to him the efficacy of fund-raising effort, and its appropriateness in a religious context. He grew up to be a gifted fund-raiser, with persuasive powers which inspired both community projects and major individual sponsorship – an accomplished organiser of communal efforts from pie suppers to formal ceremonies, and a master canvasser of support from the great and the good. He also absorbed the importance of paying for projects without incurring outstanding indebtedness. This was made much of in the Green Haworth Chapel refurbishment – despite the Trustees' reference to a promissory note for £300 – and ever after he would declare of Clubland enterprises that their goals must be accomplished 'free of debt.' In fact that did not always prove to be possible – and there may even sometimes have been some gloss on the figures to permit such declarations – but it remained a fundamental principle of his life that ongoing debt was to be abhorred and avoided.[10]

The Green Haworth re-opening day itself was filled with thanksgiving and celebration – well over a thousand people gathered for a public meeting, and for an address by the Rev. Richard Wilkinson, a member of a leading local Methodist family, who had returned from America to visit and preach. The new pulpit in the rebuilt chapel was dedicated to seven present or previous ladies of the congregation, one of whom was Ellen Duckworth, Jimmy's grandmother, wife of Owd Doc. Such a day was unique for the Green Haworth chapel community, but there were other regular treats for the children. Every New Year the whole Sunday School would enjoy pies of meat and fruit, and buns filled with ham, beef, or tongue – this feast cost 6d for the under-twelves and 9d for the rest – and a similar delightful plenty would be given to the children at Whitsuntide. There would also be a Whitsun walk, with a procession leaving the chapel at ten o'clock, led by men carrying banners, with the married women following, and behind them the succession of Sunday School classes, all dressed in their Sunday best and singing hymns en route. In the year of the Chapel's re-opening Farmer Jacob Crook provided a field for the enjoyment of the Scholars at the end of their walk. It is noted that not all the Scholars joined in the singing enthusiastically, causing their teachers to announce that any who did not sing in the farmyard would miss out on the buns in consequence.[11]

Our Village Chapel.

June 7th Crowd waiting for the 2nd house 7-15 pm

Village Chapel re-opening service 1903

A year after the grand re-opening of the Chapel forty-two of the erstwhile Hippings Lane primary infants, including Jimmy, were transferred to the adjacent Hippings Mixed School at Mount Pleasant. From the start the junior school had significant staffing problems. There were 286 children on the roll, but a report by His Majesty's Inspectors in November 1904 noted an unfilled vacancy. It also observed that the three youngest classes were typically too large for the qualifications of the teachers, and that the 'vocational equipment was defective.' The Headmaster, Robert Hugill, tried unsuccessfully to get the School Managers to take notice of the Report, and do something about the situation, but without success. Some of the teaching replacements lasted less than a week, and the Head generally found such staff unsatisfactory – on one occasion requiring a Mr. Fielding to explain the disappearance of 23 rulers, 10 pen holders, and several ink wells. Subsequently the unfortunate Mr. Fielding left the school permanently in January 1906 following a period of sick leave. At the end of Jimmy's first year at Mount Pleasant Mr. Hugill acknowledged the intelligent responses of the class, which suggests that the pupils were rather more satisfactory than some of the teachers. Things seem to have improved during Jimmy's third year at the school, when he was taught by Mr. Robert Hesketh. Sadly Mr. Hesketh, whose obituary reported him to have been greatly esteemed by his fellow teachers, was later killed in action in France in October 1916, leaving behind a wife and baby. Jimmy was also taught by Miss Florence Martin, a certificated teacher who remained at the school for twelve years, as well as by Miss Annie Morris.[12]

The scope of the 1910–11 curriculum was broad – stressing reading, writing and arithmetic, and encompassing science, geography, history, drawing, music, and recitation at the top of the school, with more emphasis given to the local environment at an earlier point. The quality of the teaching and education Jimmy and his peers received is, however, uncertain. There were only ever two qualified teachers for the seven classes in the school, and pupil numbers were falling during his time there. Mr. Hugill, who received a damning report from the Inspectors in February 1908 for his lack of supervision and control, and his over-assessment of the standards being reached, left the school in the Summer of 1909 – although records suggest that he had tried his best to make some difference for the better in his pupils' lives, with limited resources and a diminished staff. Barely three months later, on 30 November 1909, Jimmy himself left school aged 12 to work at Steiner's Bleach Words in Oswaldtwistle.

Steiner's Bleach Works

To twenty-first century sensibilities the fact that a bright and articulate lad would not be continuing from junior school to further education is shocking. He had started teaching Sunday School classes earlier the same year, and had been eloquent and ambitious in church pursuits from early childhood onwards. His academic level of achievement is not known, but he was not among those few children who achieved scholarships to the grammar school in his year. Everything Jimmy went on to accomplish later spoke of the ambition and intelligence that were always present, but these were either not recognised, or were considered insufficient to warrant nurturing during his schooldays. Indeed it was by no means unusual for children of 12 to leave school for the mills, and with four siblings younger than himself and money tight at home it was unavoidable. On 22 March 1909 he had been issued with a certificate under the Factory and Workshop Act 1901, enabling him to work part-time, and from 11 April 1910 a further certificate authorised him to work full-time. His father Thomas was certainly unable to afford

Fires in mills were commonplace. Five years before JB started work at Steiners a
huge blaze gutted the building

to pay fees in order to secure Jimmy a grammar school place. It is not
difficult to imagine the feelings of resentment Jimmy may have felt,
seeing his peers go off in grammar school caps whilst he rose at 4.30 to
go to Steiner's Bleach Works.

Jacob Steiner had arrived in England in 1817 – a refugee from persecution
during the Napoleonic regime – and established his bleaching and
dyeing business some years later in 1824. The bleach works was in
Church, which was contiguous with Accrington and Oswaldtwistle,
but some way from Thomas's mill employment at Perseverance Mill –
later known as Helene Mill when the Helene Company took it over in
1904 – in Grange Lane, Accrington. In the manuscript of *Letters of a
Clublander*[13] JB describes the harshness of the working day:

> He (Thomas) used to call me about 4.30 in the mornings, and walk with
> me across the fields until our paths led to two different towns. When
> we separated he used to whistle in the darkness lest I was afraid in the
> lonely lanes, and I would whistle back ... The conditions of my work

Grange Lane, leading to Perseverance Mill (Later Helene Mill)

in the bleach works were very terrible. Until the hands hardened they bled from guiding the wet cloth into caustic vats. The boiling soap and steaming dyes made everything damp, whilst foul smells and a thick fog became the natural atmosphere. The wage was 3/9 a week half time, 9/6 a week full time. We ate our meals around outside privies or on hard caked boilers. The meal time conversation and the incidents of men and boys are unprintable.

There was a very high incidence of child labour in the factories and mills of nineteenth century Lancashire, with around 40% of the two million people in the county aged under 20 years. Most working children were in the textile industry, and in Oswaldtwistle 60% of boys under 13 were employed in the mills, and adult workers often employed children as assistants. Jimmy's certificate when he left school in November 1909 was for half-time work only, and he would have been limited to this until the issue of his full-time certificate a year later. There is no indication of Parish contribution to the family's maintenance, but for those families who needed help Poor Law regulations required that children's contribution to the family income be counted in the assessment of financial assistance. Michael Winstanley states that 'an investigation into half-time rates at fifteen primary schools in Accrington Borough suggests that in the years leading up to the First World War around 10 per cent of the entire school roll, amounting to virtually all the top form in many schools, were in half time work. By the age of 13, however, the majority of children had left entirely.'[14] It is difficult to imagine that the half-time children were able to combine alert and receptive study with their long morning hours of grinding mill and factory labour. With an early education piecemeal to this degree it is unsurprising that few progressed to grammar school education and beyond.

The loss of Thomas

Jimmy's father, Thomas Butterworth, had chosen to become a weaver, rather than a miner like his own father. The available record of his life is patchy, reflected mostly in the certificate of his marriage in Blackburn in 1896 aged 23, the fact of his employment as a four-loom weaver at Perseverance Mill, and the references in the Green Haworth Sunday School papers to his Sunday School teaching and organ playing. Clearly he was musical – in his turn Thomas's younger son Billy followed him at the chapel organ, and also sang in the Accrington Male Voice Choir – and a committed Methodist like everybody in his and his wife's families. There is only one surviving photograph of Thomas – he is standing close outside the porch of 6 Rough Hey Gate, several feet apart from his wife Ann and behind his five children, who are all together in the small front garden, with Annie, the youngest, in her pram. Annie was born on 3 August 1906, so Thomas would then probably have been thirty-four years old. He gazes out from the photograph, good-looking but unsmiling.

The tenor of employment in the cotton mills of Lancashire was uneven. Lancashire was well-equipped for the industry – it had the necessary coal, climate, and flowing water to drive the mills and power the looms, and cotton had been king for a hundred years and more – but production was less stable following the American cotton famine of 1865. In 1860 there were 440,000 employees in the Lancashire cotton

Outside number 6 Rough Hey Gate: Thomas and Ann with,
left to right, Nellie, Billy, Annie, Florrie, Jimmy

24

industry, in 2650 mills, which had sprung up to mechanise and replace the earlier cottage hand-looms.[15] After the famine there were booms, strikes, lockouts, and slumps – and periods when the mill-owners found it financially expedient to delay the expensive supply of yarn to their weavers, who nonetheless were required to wait ready at their looms. In the process of weaving the warps had to be played onto the beam, and one worker could operate as many as six looms – they earned enough to support their families when the mill was in full production, but they were paid only in return for output. In a slump the weavers stood idle without pay.

On several occasions in his writings James Butterworth referred to his father's 'pain' on having to put him to work in the bleaching factory. In *Letters of a Clublander* he says that 'what hurt him most was having to send me out to work at age 12'. As the eldest child Jimmy knew his father longer and better than the other children. Not only did they trudge to work together in the early mornings, but he walked with his father on Saturday afternoons to watch Blackburn Rovers, which began his lifelong love of football – and writes that his father 'found time to take me on long rambles sometimes as far afield as Pendle Hill, over 14 miles away'. Jimmy spent a significant amount of time in his father's company, and Thomas would have been well aware of his bright chattering son's lively enthusiasm for the pursuits of childhood and chapel. Despite the work norms of the times it would be natural for a loving father to regret the dulling necessity of Jimmy's punishing occupation in the bleaching factory.

In addition to such regret there are signs that the struggle to support his family adequately was proving financially difficult for Thomas. In December 1901 Thomas promised £3.5/- from himself and his family towards the Methodists' Million Guinea Fund to build a Central Hall at Westminster. Forty members of the Green Haworth congregation signed up to the contribution – but when the sum was due Thomas was unable to pay. The amount was the equivalent of three weeks' wages and may therefore have constituted an unrealistic promise, but at the very least his failure to honour the commitment must have been a blow to his pride and self-esteem. There are also indications that all was not well in his relationship with the Green Haworth Chapel. In the Call Book for 1902 there is an entry for Thomas Butterworth as a Sunday School teacher in the infants' class, and in the same year a record of his appointment as a 'full teacher', with responsibility for teaching Testament to the male scholars. However, in October 1903 the Call Book records that Thomas was 'seen by Mr. M.J. Wilkinson about taking his class again' with the added comment that if he refused to do so the Superintendent would replace him. Mr. Wilkinson was a senior member of the congregation and Secretary to the Church Trustees. Following this meeting there are no further references to Thomas. Over time it emerged that Thomas was a deeply troubled man, and with difficulties at work, and a growing young family at home, the strain may well have been beginning to tell in those early years. It is difficult to inhabit the depth of despair which weighed so heavily on the young husband and father that he sought to give up on his life, but events showed that he could not endure his predicament any longer.

On 16 November, 1910, when Jimmy had been a year at Steiner's, Thomas left his loom in Perseverance Mill at mid-afternoon, walked up to Jacob Lodge, the mill reservoir across the field from Rough Hey Gate, and drowned himself there. He was 37 years old. The story was reported in the *Lancashire Daily Post* the next day, and the details of the inquest held at St. Helen's School, Broadfield on 18 November, before the coroner, Mr. W.H.J. Robinson, were published in the *Accrington Observer and Post* under the title 'Playing for warps: Why a weaver committed suicide.' The article continues:

> Thomas Butterworth, a weaver employed at Helene Mill, Accrington, left his looms on Wednesday afternoon; and drowned himself in a lodge known as Jacob Reservoir, which is situated on the border of Accrington and Oswaldtwistle, not far from Rough Hey Farm. The deceased lived at 6, Rough Hey, and was a married man with five children. He was well-known in the locality and the discovery of his body in the Lodge created much surprise and evoked great sympathy for the bereaved family. He was 37 years of age. The fact that he had drowned himself was traced by the finding of his overcoat and cap on a wall near the Lodge.[16]

His widow Ann told the Inquest that her husband had for some time been 'playing for beams' – standing idle waiting for yarn to enable him to weave cloth – and that this had lessened his earnings. She said that this situation had troubled him, and that he had become low in spirit as a result. On the Wednesday morning Thomas had left home at 5.15 a.m. and she had not seen him alive again.

A fellow-weaver named Crabtree, who worked near Thomas at Helene Mill, and had become friendly with him, confirmed that they had been repeatedly having to await yarn, and consequently earning little. Crabtree reported Thomas saying during the dinner break that he was sick of the situation, and being unable to earn, and that he could not keep his five children. Thomas had said nothing about intending to harm himself, and when he left the mill in the afternoon Crabtree thought nothing of it – he said it was not unusual for a weaver to leave the shed, and he assumed that Thomas would return. Later in the day John Barnes, who had previously lived at Rough Hey Gate, and knew Thomas and his family, saw a cap and overcoat as he was passing Jacob Lodge, probably on his way home from work, and informed a constable in nearby Willows Lane. The police then dragged the lodge and found Thomas' body.

Jacob Lodge lies in the land then owned by Rough Hey Farm. It is surrounded by fields which reach up to Bedlam, and to the lane to Green Haworth and the Chapel. It is only a few hundred yards from Rough Hey Gate, and within sight of Thomas' cottage at No.6. It was a further twist to the misery of that dark November afternoon that Jimmy – who had not found his father at their usual meeting place on the way home from work, and was perhaps brought to the scene by news of a drama unfolding near his home – was present when Thomas was lifted out of the lodge water. In his unpublished writing he relates: 'One freezing November night I saw a cap and coat on the reservoir banking in the plantation. As the police raised the body from the water and laid it on a door borrowed from the nearest farm, I recognised my father. It was a sad procession which crunched the snow in crossing the fields. When we stopped at the cottage I had to break the news to my mother. It was then I awakened to a sense of frustration at the uneven fight against poverty and illness, which in my father's case was intensified through lack of opportunities to express great capabilities.'[17]

The Burial Register for Immanuel Church shows that Thomas Butterworth, aged 37, of 6 Rough Hey Gate, was buried in the hallowed ground of the churchyard on 21 November, 1910 – although it always rankled with his son that because of his suicide the coffin was not allowed to rest within the church the night before the burial. In a small volume entitled *Dug out Digressions* that James wrote whilst in France, and published in 1918, he made the following Dedication:

> To one whom God permitted me to know until I reached my teens and then recalled to Himself, depriving me thereby of Love and Guidance, but giving him the Rest he sought – My Own Affectionate Father.[18]

The little that is known of Thomas seems to suggest a caring and devout father, but one frustrated by his inability to achieve the standards he wished, both in providing for his family and in his own personal attainments. There is also some indication that depressive tendencies troubled the family to some degree – life must have seemed very bleak to lead a young man, a loving husband and father, so to forsake his wife and children, and it was not the only episode of self-harm to emerge in the family through the years. Despite his outward enthusiasm and constant energetic activity Jimmy himself underwent several periods of depression – although he took pains to downplay the nature of these low intervals as 'nervous exhaustion', simply requiring rest and a change of scene. And in 1937, in an extended period of post-natal depression, his sister Florrie drowned herself in the same mill lodge in which her father had ended his life.

There can be no doubt that the loss of his father, and in such circumstances, was profoundly traumatic for Jimmy. It was already hard to be severed from school and childish pursuits, and labouring in an unwholesome and damaging bleach works from age twelve – and it was about to become immeasurably harder for the thirteen-year-old

Jacob Lodge today

upon whose shoulders now fell the needs of his younger siblings. He would also have been conscious of his obligation to assist and protect his mother, exposed to the social consequences of having a husband who had killed himself, as well as the material burden of supporting her children. In 1910, and for many years afterwards, suicide was a crime, and sinful in the eyes of the church, and there was no doubt a degree of stigma to be born. But perhaps most of all Jimmy Butterworth, raised from infancy to obedience of church precepts, and belief in the love and mercy of a heavenly father, had been forced to be privy to such despair as drives a man to drown himself, forced to see first-hand the lack of humanity which could inform church orthodoxy, and confronted with the damaging life outcomes which spring from the absence of egalitarian attitudes in society.

In the foreword to his book *Adventures in Boyland*,[19] James Butterworth acknowledges his 'obsession' with boys' club work. Of himself he wrote 'The hardships of his own boyhood, such as he believes few boys are called upon to pass through, led him to think more about boys commencing life with disadvantages, particularly fatherless boys.' Jimmy had been brought to painful awareness of the harshness of life for those who were lacking in parental protection and guidance, and whose needs were neither acknowledged nor met by any social provision.

The Little Piecer

In the immediate aftermath of Thomas's death his widow was not working, and the only breadwinner in the family was Jimmy, according to the Census of April 1911. He was still working at Steiner's – he had held a full-time certificate for a year – and was designated a 'plateing downer'. His mother Ann was a weaver, and may have returned to this work – which paid up to 25 shillings (£1.25) a week – in due course, perhaps after the family's move down the hill into Oswaldtwistle, to 27 Robert Street. This meant leaving the close society of the Duckworth clan at Rough Hey Gate, and leaving also the open fields and moorland of Jimmy's childhood years – but there were many sad memories in the cottage at Rough Hey, and also broader work prospects in the town. And Ann was not far from family support as Thomas's mother Tibby lived with her unmarried daughter Nancy a few streets away in Victoria Street.

With his father gone, and the weight of family maintenance upon him, Jimmy's prospects of advancing his education diminished further. In theory the half-timers were meant to be in continuing education – and once they became full-timers they were able to attend evening classes. In practice there was little time, energy, or inclination left over from mill work for learning. Later he wrote 'Full-time boy labour at age 13 meant rising at 4.30, at work before six, finishing at 5.30. Twice a week I called in on a night school, but often fell asleep during lessons. I heard that "nails were made in Walsall" but my mind and body were too tired to ask why, and what else.' His hindsight view of the life of unremitting drudgery was damning: 'Bodies were stunted and minds dulled as men and women, boys and girls, went to prison-like structures in darkness, left in darkness, and spent all the hours of daylight working within. The miners and weavers toiled a whole lifetime and in the end had nothing.'

In those years after his father died Jimmy's level of effort and enterprise was impressive. Not only did he continue his punishing occupation at Steiner's, but he also took on a newspaper pitch, selling the *Lancashire Daily Post* on the streets in the evenings – later expanding this to a book-lending service which he conducted by pushing a laden cart door to door – and in addition was serving in a fish and chip shop. James described himself as a 'back hole' attendant in the evenings at the fish and chip shop, and said it had given him valuable experience: 'These back kitchens were often the only meeting places for football teams, conversation, dominoes, sing songs, and much else. For the expenditure on coloured drinks or chips it was a ready-made club. I was the paid server hearing and seeing more than I ought. But it taught me much more.'[20] By 1912 seven newspapers had their branch offices in Oswaldtwistle and Accrington, and there would be Saturday late editions from some, containing the day's football results as well as match reports. Football attracted immense interest, Lancashire having dominated the setting up of the Football League in 1888, with eleven Lancashire teams playing in the League's two divisions by 1912.

An incident during the time Jimmy was selling newspapers turned out to be strangely prophetic of his future. On Wednesday 9 July 1913, when he was 16, Queen Mary visited Accrington with the King. Jimmy was watching from a doorway, where he described sheltering with a pile of unsold newspapers, when he had a strong feeling – perhaps wishful longing given the weather and his situation – that he would somehow one day build a club for unprivileged youngsters like himself, and that the grand queen passing through the teeming crowds before him in her carriage would come and open it. He even made on the wall a sketch of the frontage – which he saw repeated in the elevations that the architect Edward Maufe would propose for Clubland two decades later. JB had always a deep sense of destiny, of being called to the work of building Clubland, and he was also possessed of a strong degree of self-belief. In the years which lay ahead these qualities enabled him to overcome the considerable obstacles and opposition to his plans and ambitions which presented themselves. Whatever the explanation of his imaginings on an inclement day in Accrington in 1913, it is a fact that twenty-six years later in May 1939 Queen Mary did open the impressive complex of Clubland's completed buildings – and she also expressed generous support for James Butterworth and his youth work over many years.

At some point after the move into Oswaldtwistle Jimmy left Steiner's to work in cotton spinning at Vine Mill, on Vine Street, Oswaldtwistle, leaving the bleaching process behind for an arguably even more taxing and dangerous occupation, first as 'creeler', then as a 'little piecer.' This latter involved the repair of the threads that were broken during the mule-spinning process. The rate of breakage on a pair of 1,200 spindle mules was estimated to be five or six ends breaking every minute – and these would have to be mended in a process of twisting between the fingers by the little piecer, who would dart forward under the spinning yarn as the jenny advanced. This was why the piecer needed to be small – and many of the children of the undernourished workers were, like Jimmy, extremely diminutive. The whole carriage would roll several feet forward and back again about four times a minute, drawing and spinning the cotton fibre – or 'roving' – as it travelled outward, and winding it on to bobbins ready for weaving on the return. The spinner was assisted by two boys – a little piecer and a big piecer – whose jobs were to ensure a fresh supply for the cotton by replacing the empty roving bobbins with full ones without stopping the machine, and to mend any breaks in the thread, as well as cleaning the carriage and sweeping below and behind it.

J.R. Clynes, who worked as a little piecer in the Dowry Mill at Oldham, remembered 'rolling instinctively and in terror from beneath the gliding jennies, well aware that horrible mutilation or death would result if the advancing monsters overtook and gripped me.'[21] Needless to say, horrific accidents did occur, leaving calamitous disabilities and ruined lives. Clynes wrote how he worked barefoot, and often his feet were bloody from splinters and made the floor beneath him even more slippery and treacherous.

It is perhaps hard at such a remove to conceive of how landscape and life were dominated by the mill industry and culture in the locality. The mill chimneys and harsh brick buildings of the cotton towns of Lancashire filled the skylines, housing their many thousands of looms

Vine Mill, Oswaldtwistle

and spindles. If working life did not lie in the mills then it would be underground in the mines, extracting the coal which took over from water as the power that drove production. Child labour was a mainstay of the industry: from contributing to the domestic hand-loom weaving of a century earlier – frequently as part of a family enterprise – the children had followed the work to the factories. Factory legislation was slow to raise the minimum working age and reduce the numbers of daily hours permitted through the century – by 1899 children had to be twelve to work, and they had to have reached a stipulated standard of education to be certificated for work between 10 and 13. It was common for advertisements to be placed offering paupers and children as apprentices for employment in the North from far afield. Sometimes there was an honourable motivation to place the children where they would be fed and housed and learn a trade, but equally many would regard the endless stream of children as cheap dispensable labour, profitable in its supply. Quarry Bank Mill at Styal in Cheshire, established in 1783 and still in working order, has an apprentice house displaying the lifestyle of the child apprentices. When the Liberal Government introduced a bill to abolish the system in 1911 it was determinedly and successfully opposed by the cotton manufacturers.

The cotton masters were rich and powerful – they infiltrated the gentry and moved in aristocratic circles, becoming local dignitaries and benefactors. Frederick Steiner, a refugee immigrant in 1824, made a fortune from his Turkey Red dyeing process, for use in calico printing, and his daughter Emma Hartmann was granted Richmond Lodge for her lifetime by Edward Vll, whilst his second daughter Lena married the Marquise de Jancourt. The cotton mills were embedded in local history. The Walmsley family had farmed Rough Hey Farm, just along the lane from Jimmy's home, for more than a century, expanding towards factory process in the 19th century by employing groups of weavers on the premises. The disgruntled handloom spinners and weavers of the cottages, seeing their livelihood failing, vandalised the farm buildings, as part of the Luddite agitation in the 1820s – whereupon the Walmsley brothers promptly moved down into Oswaldtwistle, building the mill which became known as Moscow Mill, which is still in the hands of the Hargreaves family. In 1852 Benjamin and Robert Walmsley were charged with infringement of the Factory Act by putting women and young persons to work during statutory breaks.[22] The mill in Oswaldtwistle was known as Walmsleys locally for a long time, as was the mill lodge up near the farm, where Thomas Butterworth was to drown himself in 1910. Peter Hargreaves, scion of the illustrious mill family, still holds the large key which can release the waters of the lodge to tumble down, through overground channels and underground pipes, before emerging to supply the mill below.

The gradual enlightenment of the mill owners through the 20th century, driven by pressure from an expanding trades union movement and more humanitarian legislation, did much to improve the conditions for mill workers, and give them a voice in their dealings with their employers. But when Jimmy was at Steiner's such advances lay ahead. 1911 went on much as 1910 had finished, with the price of raw cotton uncomfortably high and frequent episodes of short working. In 1912 trade picked up somewhat, but the next two years saw a worldwide slump in trade and consequent disruption. In February 1914 the *Burnley Express* was claiming that the situation was worse than at any time since the American Civil War. The circumstances varied from town to town depending on the type of goods produced, but in general the outlook for the workers was grim – in Royal Oak Mill, Accrington, there was a shut down for three months until Boxing Day 1914[23] – and only after the outbreak of the war did trade begin to recover.

All this was depressing for Jimmy and his family. Ann had probably started work again by the time the family moved down to Oswaldtwistle, and Florrie and Nellie were old enough to earn, so financially some easement was to be expected. But with the markets so unreliable it is likely that money was tight as ever. That made it all the worse when Jimmy was barred from entering work at Steiner's one morning at 6 a.m. because he was a few moments late. The gatekeeper, whose name was Hindle, was still at his post, but implacable, and Jimmy had to sit out the two hours until the first break, brooding over the pay he would forfeit, and cursing the gatekeeper for his lack of charity. He had to wait fifty years for his revenge, taken whilst on a visit to his cousin Jack Duckworth, who lived in Huncoat village with his wife Audrey and son Maurice. Maurice was driving JB to Green Haworth, but relates that JB asked to stop for a few moments at the Steiner's building, by then disused and falling into disrepair. Maurice was amazed when after gazing up at the redbrick façade for a few moments, his well-known and much respected uncle – conspicuous in dark suit and clerical collar – picked up a brick and threw it through a window, shouting 'That's for Hindle', and urging his nephew to do the same. Fortunately no witnesses were about and neither of the two was arrested for vandalism.

The Boy Preacher

On 9 November 1907, when Jimmy was ten years old, it was resolved by the Green Haworth Sunday School Teachers that: 'The superintendent sees to the following persons to see if they will go on as auxiliary teachers; Messrs John Wolstenholme, W. Maden Jnr, and Master J. Butterworth.' In 1911 he became the Sunday School Librarian, following his Uncle Peter – now living with the Butterworth family at 6 Rough Hey Gate – who held the post in 1910. From there he progressed to teaching the more senior Testament Class – receiving helpful instruction from Mr. Catterns at St. Pauls, Oswaldtwistle – and in 1915, at the age of eighteen, he was appointed assistant superintendent to Christopher Hindle. The Green Haworth Wesleyan School Report for 1914 names C. Hindle, M. Maden, and J. Butterworth as Superintendents, with Messrs. Wolstenholme, Duckworth, and Crook also listed as officers. James was not the only family member committed to the chapel and Sunday school. Even after the move down into town, and the considerable climb up to Green Haworth from Robert Street, his mother and sisters, Florrie and Annie, were regular and active members of the congregation, and remained so for years to come. Peter Duckworth was an organist at the chapel, as Thomas had been and as Billy was to become, but for Jimmy the focus was words rather than music, and it was always the pulpit and not the organ which drew him.

In his address upon being honoured at a civic reception in Accrington Town Hall in February 1940 the Rev. James Butterworth related the launch of his career in the pulpit. He recalled that Christopher Hindle, the chapel Superintendent during his boyhood, used to send him to meet visiting preachers on their way up to the Green Haworth Chapel. He was always at the chapel in advance because he used to go up early and practise preaching sermons on the moors, and also in the empty church when he and his friend Dennis Rushton – the son of the caretaker Will Rushton – were lighting the lamps. One day, it might be said, Jimmy's prayers were answered when the preacher failed to show up, and he was asked to stand in at short notice. He had, at last, his congregation.

Jimmy was equal to the occasion, and it was after this that Christopher Hindle and Jacob Crook persuaded the circuit ministers to take him in hand. Mr. Hindle and Mr. Crook were Trustees of the Church, and widely known in local Wesleyan circles – both were tenant farmers, influential men whose opinions carried weight in the community, as well as the chapel. By then in his sixties, Hindle had known James Butterworth all his life, and his parents and grandparents before him. His farmhouse – a half mile down the lane from the Chapel – was open to the ministers of the district, and he was the first to welcome strangers, the one to fix the roof or the gates, to negotiate the purchase of land for the extension or to deal with the council in Oswaldtwistle. He was a good man to have as a supporter, and Jimmy was fortunate to have been able to earn that support.

The Wesleyan Church did not easily grant free access to its pulpits to any aspiring preacher, but on 30 June 1913, on the unanimous recommendation of the Local Preachers Meeting of the Accrington circuit, the Superintendent Minister, Rev. H.H. McCullough, authorised James Butterworth to be placed twice on the Circuit preaching plan, and to be 'heard' by Dr. Nuttall at Spread Eagle Street and by Mr. Crabtree at Cambridge Street. There were some provisos – Rev. John Bennetts, who had moved to the Accrington Circuit from Nelson in 1911, insisted that James change his short trousers and Eton collar for more mature dress – but even with the more grown-up clothing he quickly became widely known as 'The Boy Preacher'. Family lore relates that the first time Jimmy preached at Huncoat Methodist Church he was wearing short pants. A local mill owner – a society steward – observing tradition by saying a welcoming prayer announced on this occasion:

> We thank the Almighty for sending thy servant among us today, to preach thy holy word. We doesn't think much of what tha's sent us but I suppose tha knows what tha's doing.

He was effectively on trial, and he evidently triumphed. The addresses he had given to the two caretakers and the empty pews, and to his long suffering sisters and cousins in the hen house opposite the cottages, had finally paid off. His reputation as the boy preacher spread to nearby towns and villages – his sermons were reported in local papers, and the powerful effect his preaching had on congregations is documented in some of the letters that have survived from those who heard him.

Sadly there is no record of the content of those early sermons, but there is an obvious question around what a lad of sixteen – especially one whose formal education had been so curtailed – might preach about to these seasoned church-goers. To an extent, of course, James was himself seasoned by years of chapel and Sunday School attendance. There was

Scene of Jimmy's early practice sermons to a captive audience of siblings and cousins

no formal lay minister training in place at that time, but the need for instruction was recognised unofficially, and James was a frequent guest at the homes of local ministers and his chapel mentors, and profited from their teaching and guidance.[24] His childhood friend Jack Blundell remembered that during those years James would 'sit up until midnight studying Greek against the day he would be a minister having done his stint in the spinning room at the mill.' He was also a frequent attendant at Willow Cottage, Accrington, where the Dewhurst family maintained a meeting place for all the local Methodist clergy, and James received advice and encouragement.[25] As he listened to preachers at Green Haworth James no doubt saw himself in their place, and strove to imitate their language and mannerisms, and preach on the same themes – but the content of his boyhood sermons remains a matter of speculation.

Later, as the cause and mission which informed his life's preaching clarified, what he had to say developed its critical edge and its challenge to comfortable assumptions and orthodoxies – but in pre-Great War Green Haworth James' focus was still traditional as he sought to impress the circuit worthies. It is likely that he would have drawn conventionally on the bible studies and testament lessons that he had attended and taught at Sunday school, as well as the prevailing moral attitudes of Wesleyan Methodism. Yet there must always have been some flashpoint in his thought, some spark of what was to come. There is little doubt that he began early in life to speak his mind; his mother and his sister Nellie both recalled that he never stopped talking, and was always 'full of ideas'. The very fact that he was ready and eager to climb into the pulpit of his local chapel, and face a large gathering of family and neighbours at a tender age, indicates an extraordinary level of self-confidence. And it also speaks of huge ambition.

Cliff College

In September 1915, aged eighteen, James left Oswaldtwistle to attend Cliff College at Calver, near Sheffield in Derbyshire. The fact that he was able to do so clearly implies that his family was able to manage without his financial contribution – Ann had returned to work, and Billy and the girls were doubtless also earning and contributing. It was his chance. In October 1915 John Holgate, an Oswaldtwistle jeweller, and Methodist mentor and friend to Jimmy, wrote expressing the hope that he would 'find the term a very helpful one in every respect.' It was the first time that he had been away from home for any significant period,

Jimmy Butterworth aged 17

and his stay at Cliff, although relatively short, represented a first step towards the realisation of his ambitions for the ministry, as well as a parting from Oswaldtwistle and his boyhood.

As a Bible college – but not one whose aim was solely to produce candidates for the Wesleyan Ministry – Cliff was evangelical in nature. It prided itself on being open to all, whether rich or poor, with students contributing financially what they could afford, and helping to maintain the college by working in the grounds and the building. James made no contribution in the Winter term (October to December 1915) and £2 in the following Spring term. Cliff College's formal title was the 'Wesleyan Lay Workers Training Home' – it was a preparatory college providing training rather than theological qualification. It offered an intensive year's course, inculcating the discipline of Methodist missionary work – after leaving many students went abroad to pursue missionary careers – but very much within the late nineteenth century philosophy of self-help, youth welfare, and co-operative endeavour. Every Whitsun, from its early days, rallies at Cliff attracted large crowds, and these Spring festivals continue to the present day, attended by thousands of people each year.

The Cliff College site opened for the training of Methodist evangelists on 3 March 1904. It had its beginnings in the zealous work of Rev. Thomas Champness, who first took young men into his home in Bolton to train them in 1883, later moving to Castleton Hall, Rochdale, as 'The Joyful News Training Home and Mission.' Thomas Cook took over this property, from the Henry Guinness institution previously known as 'Hulme Cliff College', prior to the official opening of the Calver site.

The principal of the college during Jimmy Butterworth's attendance there was Samuel Chadwick. Born in 1860 and raised in a two-bedroom house in Burnley, Chadwick's life bore remarkable similarities to James' own – at eight years of age he was rising at dawn to work alongside his father in the local mill, but by fifteen he was committed to the church and would walk miles every Sunday to preach. He studied by himself at night to obtain the education he lacked, and once he had found a clergyman to teach him Greek he attended Didsbury Theological College in 1883, afterwards taking up ministries in Edinburgh and Glasgow. Chadwick travelled to Cliff to lecture on a weekly basis – he became resident tutor in biblical and theological studies in 1907, and principal in 1913 when Cook died, remaining long term editor of its weekly paper *Joyful News*. In 1918 he was elected President of the Methodist Conference.

Samuel Chadwick was a formidable personality by anybody's reckoning, and an impressive achiever in all the fields in which Jimmy had ambition, with a particular reputation as a powerful orator. A frequent theme was his exhortation to retain sympathy with human nature, using pointed and persuasive exposition based upon bible content as authority. Students and staff would have been particularly well known to each other during Jimmy's year at Cliff, since the student population – normally between 60 and 80 strong – was reduced to a mere 21, and afterwards fell yet further, owing to the outbreak of the First World War the previous year. There are some indications that the two men did not get on particularly well together – perhaps because of similarities of temperament and background – although Chadwick was a supporter later, lending his endorsement to James' eventual admission to Didsbury College.

The course Jimmy followed operated as groundwork for a chaplaincy at one of the Methodist colleges, or alternatively as a preparation for lay preaching. The timetable shows that the daily lessons included Catechism, English Literature, Arithmetic, English Grammar, Biblical Analysis, Bible Study, Homiletics, Greek, Singing, Biblical Geography, History, Geography, Composition, and Theology. This made for a very full study spectrum. The day started at 6.45 with prayers and devotions, and lessons lasted half an hour each between 9.15 a.m. and 8 p.m. each day. There were also several sessions of Preparation – silent study – and the students regularly preached to their peers at Cliff. On Sundays they went out to spread the word at churches in the locality – borrowing college bicycles if travelling any significant distance. Then at the end of the year the students would disperse to local evangelism, or ministers' training college, with a significant percentage going overseas.

Chadwick opposed conscription, but at the end of the Easter term 1916 he was nevertheless forced to close Cliff for the duration of the war, following the Military Service Act of March 1916 and a shrinking student population due to enlistment. When the college shut its doors in March that year there were only half a dozen students who had remained in

Cliff College buildings and library

residence. For Jimmy Butterworth it was a premature ending to a year which must have begun full of hope of a path to the ministry.

Looking at this period in his life retrospectively it may be that Jimmy's nascent views on the role of the church, as an instrument for social as well as spiritual welfare, did not chime well with the evangelical emphasis of the college, and meant that his time there may well have been unsettled and in some respects unsatisfying. In later life he developed a robustly sceptical attitude to evangelism, seeing it as neglectful of the needs of mind and body. In 1915 his sights were set on becoming ordained as a Wesleyan minister, and Cliff was not a direct route towards that goal, leaving many barriers in the way of his ambitions. But as the stalemate hardened on the Western Front the questions around his immediate ministerial future became academic.

By the Spring of 2016 Jimmy was in uniform, and within a few months he had embarked for France, first to the Somme, then Arras, and finally the notorious base at Étaples. From the distant and dangerous trenches Private Butterworth wrote to the Cliff periodical 'Joyful News' – a letter published there on 4 January 1917 – confirming the sustaining value of his study at the college. In it he pays tribute to the strength given him by his time at Cliff, which he now acknowledges preserves him from the 'forces of evil' all around him. He affirms that at Cliff 'my faith in God was deepened and my desire for Christian service intensified.'

Notes

1 *North West Sound Archive.*
2 The certificate is dated 10 June, 1825 and signed by J.F. Hindle for the attention of the Overseers of the Poor of the Township of Oswaldtwistle in Lancashire.
3 Lancashire Records Office (LRO) DDX1962/acc7616/box1Deeds and Abstracts Rough Hey Estate.
4 Butterworth, James. *Letters of a Clublander*, 1942, Ch.39. Unpublished and incomplete autobiography written mostly in the 1940s. Now held at Southwark Local History Library, 211 Borough High Street, London SE1 1JA
5 Sunday School Teacher Minute Book. LRO MAC/24/3
6 Bound annuals of the *Clubland Reviews*, from the 1920s to the 1970s, can be found at Southwark Local History Library.
7 *Clubland: The Temple of Youth* (Illustrated Handbook)
8 Smiles, Samuel: *Self-Help* 1859; *Thrift* 1875.
9 *Lancashire Sound Archive.*
10 The 'Balance Sheet of Green Haworth Wesleyan Extension Scheme' from June 1901 to December 1904 shows a total expenditure of £1807.18s 5d 'For the following Objects:– Rebuilding Chapel; Building four new Class-Rooms, new Organ Chamber, Library, Heating House, new Heating Apparatus (Hot Water Pipes), new Boundary Walls and Palisading, Additional Land, and Improved Sanitary Arrangements; Painting and Decorating.' The auditor is Ahaziah Cockshut aided by Henry Maden, Mr. C. Hindle is Treasurer, and Mr. W.T. Wilkinson is Secretary.
11 *Lancashire Sound Archive.*
12 Many years later, amazed to see her pupil of fifty years earlier on *This is Your Life*, Miss Morris wrote, 'I thought "That's my Jimmy. My little pupil has climbed so high."'
13 *Letters of a Clublander*. Chapter 39, p.3.
14 Winstanley, Michael (ed.) Working Children in 19th Century Lancashire. Lancashire County Books (1995) p.52.
15 Aspin, Chris. *The Cotton Industry*. Shire Publications, 1981/2012.
16 *Accrington Observer and Post*, 19 November, 1910
17 *Letters of a Clublander*, Ch.39, p.3.
18 Butterworth, James. *Dugout Digressions*. Epworth Press, 1919. One of two small books written in France during the Great War.

19 Butterworth, James. *Adventures in Boyland*. Epworth Press, 1926.

20 *Letters of a Clublander*.

21 Winstanley, Michael(ed): *Working Children in 19th Century Lancashire*, p.57.

22 *Preston Chronicle and Lancashire Advertiser*, 13 March 1852, p.5.

23 *Burnley News*, 26 December, 2014.

24 Reverend Wilkinson's granddaughter, Margaret Berry, confirms that James was often at her grandfather's home for this purpose – so much so that her aunt was sad to leave her 'boyfriend Jimmy Butterworth' when her father returned with his family to America in 1912.

25 Jack Blundell and Mrs. Dewhurst on *This Is Your Life, James Butterworth*, 20 November, 1955.

CHAPTER TWO

'The Great War For Civilisation'

Private Butterworth,
17th Lancashire Fusiliers

JB kept an old one-pound tobacco tin containing a black jack-knife, a pocket-sized soldier's bible, a pair of name-tags, a sizeable shell fragment, a bronze service medal on a frayed rainbow ribbon, assorted badges of the Lancashire Fusiliers and one mysteriously marked 'Canadian Curlers, Scotland.' As well, there was a gold-coloured victory medal bearing the words 'The Great War for Civilisation, 1914–1919'.

War is declared

In August 1914 Britain had responded to the turbulent events in central and eastern Europe by requiring an assurance from Germany that there would be no violation of Belgium's neutrality. The stated deadline of 11 p.m. on 4 August passed without any such undertaking from Berlin, and consequently Britain was officially at war from that time. A wave of patriotic fervour immediately gripped the capital, and cheering crowds greeted the news, thronging the Mall, Whitehall and Trafalgar Square singing the national anthem and waving flags. The following day the recruiting offices were open for volunteers, and queues formed all day despite the rain, and had to be turned away in huge numbers when the offices closed.

Such may have been the mood in London and the more affluent south, or on the fabled playing fields of the English public schools and in the green shires, but in the industrial regions of the north and midlands there was a more sombre response to the announcement.[1] The mill towns of Lancashire were well used to the hardships brought about by foreign conflicts, and had less relish for a repeat. The immediate effect of the outbreak of hostilities was dire for the Lancashire textile industry, with its disruption to rail transport and coal supplies, seaports on hold, and mills closed due to the reductions in supply and demand. Much of the yarn was sourced from abroad, and much of the produce sold to overseas markets, so the paralysis in transport led immediately to depression in the industry. Accrington's main employer, Howard and Bullough's machine works, had already endured a month-long lockout following a strike, when management refused to recognise trade unions and pay a minimum wage of thirty-six shillings (£1.80) for a 53-hour week.[2]

Despite the north's more sombre response there was no shortage of volunteers when the call to arms came. The Accrington *Observer & Times* of 29 August 1914 had published letters which took the town to task in the strongest terms for its supposed tardiness in providing recruits[3] – and two days later the Mayor of Accrington offered to raise a battalion of Accrington's men and boys. In mid-September offices opened in Accrington, Church, and Oswaldtwistle, and by 24 September, barely a month after the declaration of war, the East Lancashire Regiment could field a full battalion of volunteers from Accrington and the surrounding district. This was the 7th Service Battalion (later the 11th), better known and forever engraved on Lancashire's folk-memory, as the Accrington Pals – the most revered of all the pals battalions and an icon of the War. The 'Pals' battalions were reputedly the brainchild of Lord Derby, the idea being that towns and cities, trade guilds and professional bodies, and even major employers, should raise, equip, and fund local units.

Part of the rationale for the Pals was the added sense of comradeship and identity that local recruiting would instil. Its curse, as events revealed soon enough, was that when heavy casualties were suffered the loss to the community was all the more terrible in its concentration. Tragically this was the outcome for Accrington and its neighbours when the 11th battalion attacked Serre on the first day of the Battle of the Somme, in July 1916. Out of some 720 Accrington Pals who took part in the attack, 584 were killed, wounded, or missing.[4] The commanding officer of the Brigade reported that hardly any of the men reached the German first line, such was the intensity of the shelling and machine-gun fire, adding that he 'had never seen, indeed could never have imagined such a magnificent display of gallantry, discipline and determination.' The small parties that did penetrate the lines were never heard of again.[5] The effect on the Lancashire town was devastating. The brother of one of the original Pals recalled: 'I remember when the news came through to Accrington that the Pals had been wiped out. I don't think there was a street in Accrington and district that didn't have their blinds drawn, and the bell at Christ Church tolled all the day.'[6]

Whilst patriotism was one potent force for joining Kitchener's New Army of volunteers, in East Lancashire there were also more prosaic inducements. In the summer of 1914 unemployment was rife and the number of unemployed or part-time cotton workers in Accrington alone was around seven thousand, with similar percentages in the adjoining towns of Church and Oswaldtwistle. Six hundred Accrington families were receiving relief, and over seven hundred children were being fed on a daily basis at the Town Hall under the 1906 Provision of Meals Act. In addition there were four and a half thousand Howard & Bulloughs workers and their families living on minimal strike or lockout pay, whilst those outside a union received nothing. In the face of such poverty the Army's pay and billeting allowance of twenty-one shillings provided a clear incentive to sign up.

The call was for men between 19 and 35 years of age, with a minimum height of 5ft 6ins (later reduced to 5ft 3ins) and chest measurement of 35 and a half inches – which shrank the pool of eligible recruits significantly. The lower age limit was elastic throughout the war – but a man's size was not so easily disguised or ignored. Like countless boys of his age Jimmy Butterworth had joined the queue outside the local recruitment hall. Not surprisingly he was rejected – he was 17 but at four feet eleven inches he stood no chance of enlisting in the early months of war, when huge numbers of men were clamouring to enlist and authorities could still afford to be selective. Despite the lax application of the minimum age he could simply never have passed for nineteen – in photographs taken in uniform eighteen or so months later he still looks like a child. The recruiting sergeant took one look at him and ordered him to 'go back home to his Mam'.

This dismissal can have done little for Jimmy's self-esteem or peer standing – as men marched away there was considerable disdain for those not called upon to fight, and conscientious objectors, particularly, were the targets of the most abusive treatment. Being small provided no exemption from taunts, and short men who strenuously protested their entitlement to serve their country were often mocked for their stature rather than applauded for their eagerness to enlist. William Turner, author of *Pals*, wrote:

> Generations of starving in the mills and workshops of Lancashire had hardly been conducive to the production of a race of giants. There were many disappointed men in those days, and scathing were their comments on the "Whitehall brass hats" who dare to think Lancashire patriotism could be measured in inches.[7]

Sidney Allinson recounts the tale of a coal haulier named Robertson who, when trying to join the London Scottish Regiment, was refused for being one inch below the minimum height. He was not even allowed into the recruiting hall, but jeered at through the railings, with one of the volunteers shouting 'Get away, Titch. To get in there'd have to be two of you.'[8] Jimmy Butterworth fared no better, and returned to piecing in the cotton mill at Vine Street, selling papers, waiting on table at the chip shop, and whatever other work was going. He continued with his Sunday School teaching, his attempts at self-education and visits to Willow Cottage for tuition, and his efforts to gain recognition as a preacher in the run-up to his two terms at Cliff College.

Cliff College itself – like most other colleges in the country – was seriously affected by the war, which led to swingeing reductions in the student body from September 1914 onwards. The college principal, Samuel Chadwick, had not been a supporter of conscription, but nevertheless closure of the college became inevitable on the eve of national conscription in the spring of 1916, and it did not re-open until hostilities ended. The closure of Cliff marked the end of a chapter for James, but he had already enlisted and a new and very different chapter of his life was beginning, thanks to changes in recruitment tactics on the Home Front. As the fighting entered its second year the appalling rate of casualties was becoming ever more apparent, and there was a shortage of eligible men coming forward to enlist. Lord Derby, appointed Director-General of Recruiting in October 1915, introduced his Group Scheme – which permitted men to attest their willingness to serve whilst deferring enlistment until required. Those who chose to delay their call-up were provided with an armband to demonstrate that they had provisionally volunteered – which permitted a show of patriotism and avoided the opprobrium shown to those thought to be evading their duty.

The Group Scheme ultimately failed to provide a sufficient increase in volunteer numbers, and was soon overtaken by the full call-up directed by the Military Conscription Act of 1 March 1916. By then another significant recruitment initiative, of particular relevance to James in the light of his diminutive stature, had met with considerable success. Alerted by the shortfall in enlistment numbers, and stories like that of Robertson – the rejected London coal-haulier – recruiting committees had recognised the existence of a deep well of willing and able volunteers, albeit under regulation height, but otherwise physically and temperamentally fit for military service.

During 1915 an entire division was formed consisting wholly of men under five feet three inches tall – dwarfed by their officers and by their fellows in conventional ranks. These were the *Bantams*, and their story is one of the most intriguing in the history of the Great War. Among the names of soldiers who served under Bantam colours was that of Billy Butlin, of Butlin's Holiday Camps. He enlisted in the Canadian Army during the war, and was transferred to a Bantam Battalion in France. The poet Isaac Rosenberg, author of '*Poems from the Trenches*', was also a Bantam, as was a celebrated soldier called Henry Thridgould, who at

Jimmy with his brother, sisters, and widowed mother,
before leaving for France in 1916.

4ft 9ins was the shortest corporal in the British Army.[9] And another was James Butterworth, who joined the Lancashire Fusiliers early in 1916 and was placed first in the 22nd Reserve Battalion for training, and transferred to the 17th (Bantam) Battalion, already active in France, during the Battle of the Somme in the late summer. James was technically exempt from conscription – he was still under 19, below even the Bantam height requirement of 5ft, and was also one of 'those who had offered themselves for enlistment since September 1914 but been rejected.'[10] But this time he was not rejected. In his own words, two decades later, he wrote: 'I was eventually permitted to join up in the Lancashire Fusiliers.'[11]

The Bantams

It is a common misconception that the raising of Bantam battalions was from the start a desperate measure necessitated by the toll of casualties; that the men were inferior soldiers, and the project a failure, resulting in the battalions being disbanded little more than a year after their deployment at the Front. The real story was quite different, with a central positive *raison d'etre* for their formation, and totally unrelated to scraping the barrel for canon-fodder. The first preparations were in place before the end of 1914, driven not merely by need for numbers but by the pressure from a multitude of small men who wanted to serve their country but had been turned down.

It is true that the Bantams were disbanded early in 1917, and it was also predictable that the concept of battalions and brigades composed entirely of small men would prove problematic militarily. One immediately obvious practical difficulty was the height of the steps in the trenches, which had to be adjusted between Bantams and conventional units. A captain in the Northumberland Fusiliers recalled his agitated CSM complaining crudely: 'Sir, them bloody little dwarfs have built up the step so they could see over. Now when my lads stand up, half their bodies are above the parapet.'[12] Soon after an order went out that sandbags could be used to raise height, but parapets were not to be lowered. It was also true that by the end of the Somme offensive many Bantams were less fit and less well prepared for the duress of trench warfare – but this was not due to any inherent deficiency of small men, but because as frontline troops haemhorraged through the spring and summer of 1916 recruitment standards were relaxed and training shortened.

The first wave of Bantam recruits had provided some of the toughest and most resilient soldiers in the British Army: work hardened miners from Wales and the north of England, Glaswegian dockers, steelworkers, farm labourers. To compensate for their lack of height they had to have an expanded chest measurement of 34 inches, one inch above the general army minimum – and soon proved that the will and competitiveness often attributed to small men was no empty stereotype. Nevertheless they had to face considerable stubborn and uninformed prejudice from the army hierarchy – one old-school officer, Lt. Colonel MacQuairie, stating publicly: 'It is quite impossible to expect undersized men to be useful as soldiers in the British line in Flanders. It is well-known that such little men cannot bear the physical and moral load of modern warfare.'[13]

Despite the nay-sayers Alfred Bigland, Birkenhead MP, obtained War Office sanction to raise a battalion of men below 5ft 3ins and within days 3,000 men had volunteered, many who had previously been rejected. They were recruited into the 15th and 16th Battalions of the Cheshire Regiment, but soon after, as train-loads of small, eager, men came from all over the country, other regiments began recruiting similar units – the Lancashire Fusiliers, West Yorkshires, Royal Scots, and Highland Light Infantry. Bigland identified the inspiration for his project as a Durham miner – sadly anonymous to history – who walked the width of the country in his attempts to join up, receiving no thanks for his pains from the recruiting sergeants who rejected him en route. When informed of the man's spurned attempts Bigland immediately wrote to Lord Kitchener with his proposal.

Through 1915 the Bantam Division was held in training on Salisbury Plain for an extended period, watching other soldier forces come and go, and were eventually told that they were going to Mesopotamia and kitted out with oversized shorts and helmets. A new order before they embarked directed that they be prepared instead for France. There was no going back this time, and before the end of January 1916 they were transported to the coast and across the Channel to le Havre. They were bound at last for the Western Front.

Active service

Private James Butterworth's battalion had been initially posted to the Arras Sector for five months before moving south to the Somme in July 1916. The daily War Diary[14] records an inspection at Wardrecques by Field Marshall Lord Kitchener – 'who expressed approval of the smart appearance of the men' – after which the men marched to join the Royal Welsh Fusiliers for instruction in trench warfare.

There were casualties and deaths from the beginning, the latter customarily reported and named individually in the Diary only if they were of officer rank. It shocks our modern sensibilities to see now, in their yellowing pages, a grim reminder that deaths as well as lives had relative value. It is unlikely that Private Butterworth ever saw a battalion diary – these were the property of officers – but the ranking reflected in their contents would have held little surprise for him, as it merely confirmed the social order into which he was born. It was an evaluation implicit in all aspects of his experience thus far – and now repeated in the army – which he afterwards spent his life working to change for others.

Following its induction at Arras the battalion rejoined the 104th Brigade and travelled to Bethune, spending four months either in the trenches, or on reserve. Their duties were varied, some more hazardous than others – work details, listening posts, intelligence gathering, wire repairs, small-scale raids – but in or out of the trenches there was constant bombardment to endure. Work details behind the lines were arduous, and route marches wearing.

In the same part of the line, on 30 June 1916 – the eve of the massive Somme offensive – three battalions of the Royal Sussex Regiment (the Southdowns) were ordered to 'bite off the head' of the Boar's Head German salient that protruded into the British position east of Richebourg in the Ferme du Bois sector. Unbeknownst to the men this was a diversionary action to distract German attention from the site of the main imminent attack. It was tragically ill-judged, with the loss of over 1000 officers and men. The 17th Lancashire Fusiliers were spared devastation by orders to depart from the sector a week or so earlier, and to transfer via Bethune to Happy Valley, a deep curving depression close to Bray-sur-Somme. Here they faced their own major challenge at Trones Wood on 18 July, a thousand yards east of the village of Guillemont – a key objective in a planned Anglo-French attack along a line southeast from Delville Wood to the River Somme. The Bantam units went into action on the 20th, attempting to capture German trenches, and afford cover to an expected French advance further south. In the event there was little French movement, but the Bantams were under sustained machine-gun and shell fire, suffering 450 casualties in the action. Guillemont presented a stubborn obstacle to French progress – there were two further concerted attacks, but both failed with consequent casualties, and the Battalions were subsequently relieved and withdrew to Happy Valley to rest and recover.

All indications are that Private Butterworth joined his battalion at this point, as part of a transfer of men from the 22nd Reserve Battalion undergoing training in England at Prees Heath. It meant that their preparation for active service had been dangerously brief. A letter from Kathleen Bennetts – daughter of James' Oswaldtwistle mentor Rev. John Bennetts – suggests that departure had originally been scheduled for the late summer. The date may have been advanced by the major Bantam casualties sustained at Guillemont, or in anticipation of further losses upon their return to the front. Without his individual army service record – destroyed with many others in the 1940 fire at the War Office warehouse where they were stored – it is impossible to be exact, but in later years JB often mentioned Happy Valley as a location of special significance to him as his first experience of the front. The 17th Battalion was frequently bivouacked there, but as it happens the last occasion was 15 August, 1916. This clearly places him in France during the first half of August 1916, or even earlier, since after that the battalion returned to the front for the attack on Falfemont Farm and from there they were posted directly back to Arras.

The training for the coming attack was intensive. There was a long march in hot sun on 5 August, and a day's rest before preparation began in earnest. The Diary reports: 'August 7. Commenced training of the Battalion in the attack. Operation was carried out on imaginary situation at Floxicourt. Musketry practice, Lewis gun practice; and bomb throwing from 6 p.m. to 7 p.m.' On 15 August there was a full-scale Brigade exercise, indicative of the demanding sequence of military tasks required of them – but the day's Diary entry reads: 'Before the final stages of the exercise had been completed, orders were received for the Battalion to stand by ready to move at short notice.' Its meaning was clear – sooner than they had anticipated they were on their way back up the line. Fresh orders soon arrived to move on 18 August to Talus Boise and march from there to the Dublin Trench area. This is the first and most significant occasion of Private Butterworth's front-line involvement for which any detail has remained available, and the report describes its frontal action in the Angle Wood sector, replacing the French 43rd and 127th regiments, thus slightly extending the British line south and eastwards. Water was in short supply, and the men were warned that one bottle per man would have to last the whole 24 hours.

Despite being carried out under heavy hostile shelling, the relief operation was reportedly a success. In the early hours the Battalion was concentrated for the attack in shell holes forward of the front line, northeast of Angle Wood, some 800 yards southwest of German occupied Falfemont Farm, and remained concealed there the whole day. Today the farm, though it has the same name, is lower down next to the Maurepas Road. The Battalion was ordered to push forward in tandem with the French on the immediate right, and its role was then to cover the French left flank when they attacked, digging in to establish a trench, whilst under heavy artillery bombardment. Following an encounter with a Bantam patrol at the farm the enemy placed a heavy barrage on Angle Wood and on the Bantams' advanced line. By midnight the shelling had become intermittent and a message from General Pinney congratulated the men on their 'good work'. There had been some advance on Falfemont Farm – which Generals Rawlinson and Haig wished to take as a matter of urgency – but worsening weather was proving a serious obstacle. Intense thunder storms and heavy rain engulfed the Somme area for days, reducing the already churned up trenches to seas of mud, and storage and distribution of food and water, as well as ammunition, became problematic. When the weather improved at the end of August the campaign to take Guillemont and Falfemont Farm continued – but for the 35th Brigade their stint on the Somme was over, and they were moved back to the Arras section under the command of the Third Army, 6 Corps.

Arras

Throughout September and October 1916 the 17th Battalion undertook tours of duty of six days in and six days out of the line. The Regimental Annual states that at first the sector was quiet – possibly because it was manned by German troops exhausted and depleted by brutal fighting on the Somme – but the relative lull did not lessen the work nor remove the ceaseless danger: the Battalion was fully employed in trench repair, wiring, and hut building whilst subjected to intermittent bombardment by trench mortars, rifle grenades, or heavy artillery. There was also the ever-present fear of gas, which was used in attacks by both German and British.

In November the level of hostility from both sides increased. Damage to enemy lines and wires drew retaliation in kind, including fire from 'aerial torpedoes', 'toffee apples', and heavy mortar shells known as 'rum jars' whose blast could demolish large sections of the recipient trench. The escalation meant constant night-time repair work, with the incessant bombardment taking a heavy toll on the nerves and morale of the men occupying the line.

On 25 November, during a period of atrocious weather, the pace and ferocity of the bombardment intensified sharply, causing severe damage to the structure of the trenches and shredding protective front wire. The signs all pointed to an impending German offensive but the British Command were intent upon completing their own preparations for another massive gas attack, and paid little attention to the threat. The gas attack eventually took place following postponements and conflicting signals, but in the interim a failed British raid carried out by the Bantams of the 19th Durham Light Infantry had been followed by – or perhaps provoked – a triple German raid, which inflicted serious damage and casualties.

It was a night of chaos and confusion, of raid and counter-raid, and later of infamy. The Germans had chosen the exact moment when the gas release was finally timed to make their attack – and this meant that there was a gap in the British defences which the attackers infiltrated with considerable ease, entering the line and fanning out in pursuit of its remaining defenders. The defences were stretched even further by orders given to the 17th Lancashire Fusiliers to secure the badly degraded and vacated trenches adjacent to their own. The Bantams held out stalwartly until support arrived, but by that time the damage had been done and the Germans had returned to their own lines, causing fatalities and taking a sizeable number of prisoners.

The Bantams as a whole won praise for their steadfastness through a night of close combat and confused orders. The Lancashire men had stuck to their assigned task in the face of several waves of attack despite their losses and their battered positions – but unfortunately other sectors had not matched their resolve. Further along the line in the dark and disarray – in trenches undermanned due to the gas attack – a number of men had allegedly abandoned their posts and fled when the Germans gained access. Extenuating circumstances were argued – the gross reduction in the normal number of posted sentries, the fact of intense bombardment following the DLI raid which should have alerted the commanders to the coming attack, and the distraction of the delayed gas release: but these were all ultimately disregarded. At a hurried inquiry during the night at least 26 men were committed for court-martial and subsequently sentenced to death for 'running away from key positions'. Despite the undoubted failings of organisation and communication, those in command were determined to make examples of the men, a deliberate policy made plain in the court-martial papers. By any standards it was a vengeful decision on the part of senior officers, infuriated by the loss of so many men taken prisoner. In the end only three of the men actually faced the firing squad – due to their superior rank as NCOs – but the others were shown little mercy, their death sentences being commuted to inordinately long terms of imprisonment with hard labour.

One of the men executed was a Durham Light Infantry Lance-Sergeant, Will Stones, even though five officers had spoken up for him, referring to his good conduct and courage, and the Brigadier General who signed the papers conceded that the grounds for conviction were dubious. Will Stones was not saved by these factors – but his name became a touchstone for a movement decades later to exonerate the 306 officers and men who had been executed for alleged cowardice during the Great War. A leading voice in the 'Shot At Dawn' (SAD) campaign was Tom Stone, Will's great nephew. The final decision following much debate was that too much water had passed under the bridge for individual cases to be decided, and a blanket pardon which made no distinctions was also inappropriate. The matter, anyway, poses an impossible dilemma: our norms have changed so radically that an informed evaluation of the decisions taken in those unspeakable conditions is far beyond the reach of reason or empathy, and old virtues such as patriotism and military honour are displaced in modern sensibilities. It can only be surmised how contemporaries reacted at the time to the conduct of their fellows, and the harsh treatment handed out – whether they would sympathise and support, or whether they would condemn comrades who did not observe the unfailing obedience on which all their lives might depend.

Those in Pte Butterworth's trench, further down but part of the same action, must have known more of the events of that fateful night and its aftermath than he was ever free to speak about. But for him, and for many others, there were repercussions of an unexpected and not unwelcome nature. The morning after the raid his battalion was congratulated, relieved by the 18th, and moved to the Brigade Reserve in Arras. At the start of December it was placed on 'divisional rest' and for a good number of the men it was their last experience of the Front. The Division's ranks had been considerably depleted through the Autumn, and there were misgivings concerning the sparser replacements being sent out from the depots – they lacked the physical strength and endurance of their predecessors in the first years of the war, and many had been hurriedly and inadequately trained. In preceding weeks, as the fighting had intensified, the ability of the 35th Division to hold the line had been called into question, and what had happened on 26 November confirmed some in their doubts concerning Bantam capability. The supply of small yet strong men from heavy industrial backgrounds could not last forever.

In his 1926 *History of the 35th Division in the Great War* Lt. Colonel Davson reflected of that fateful night that although the men had defended the trenches promptly and effectively, and had earned praise for having withstood a more than usually heavy bombardment through several hours, this was nevertheless the last action in which the 35th fought as a Bantam division. He confirmed the general agreement of commanding officers that the soldier quality of many of the most recent reinforcements was inadequate.[15] A communiqué was circulated to the effect that henceforth reinforcements would be drawn from men of normal infantry height, and that the 35th would no longer be known as the Bantam Division. Lt. Colonel Johnston of the 15thSuffolks wrote: 'I'm sorry, because the little men have done so well, but I suppose there are no more to be had by us, as all regiments now take small men.'[16] It was the beginning of the end of the designation 'Bantam', though not by any means of Bantam soldiers. The majority remained and fought right through to the armistice, although not as a separately identifiable unit – and the rooster no longer crowed on their badges.

During December a series of medical inspections was undertaken to establish how many men were realistically fit for trench warfare and its physical demands. Jimmy's battalion was inspected on 12 December, and 170 soldiers were deemed 'unsuitable for the work of normal infantrymen', on account of their health and general condition. The majority of these were soon after assigned to the Labour Corps, formed in January 1917 to carry out various kinds of work connected with the war, either in Britain or overseas. James Butterworth was one of those classified as unsuitable. Given his size and slight build – he was below even the Bantam minimum – this outcome is not surprising. He had an indomitable spirit, as time would tell, and a willingness to 'stick it out', as the Tommies expressed – and valued – their readiness to endure, but these qualities of mind could take a man only so far. Early in the new year he and the other 169 diminutive figures marched away.

Davson's summary of whether these men should ever have been enlisted in the first place is perceptive. His view was that the original Bantam drafts had been 'a fine body of men, whose shortness of stature was compensated for by breadth of chest and physical condition' – and he considered that if the supply of such men had continued then Bantam performance would have remained impressive. However this had not been the case and there had been a deterioration in the fitness of recruits.

Many who joined were immature, and with the laudable intention of serving their country when enlisting, became somewhat hazy about the actual date of their birth. Others, who were conscripted later, were weaklings who would never be fit for the strain of active service, and who were passed to the Division as the supply of men of the original Bantam standard had failed. These later men had not the fortitude to endure fatigue and hardship, and although possibly a long period of training might have given them the discipline which would have to some extent counterbalanced the failing, this was denied them.[17]

Davson also pointed out that although a certain number of Bantam recruits had been withdrawn during training, yet the recruiting authorities refused to have them discharged and instead sent them to the depots, from which – half-trained and unused to 'habits of automatic obedience' – they rejoined at a later critical period of the war, and took part in battles which tested their courage and endurance, with disastrous outcomes.

For Jimmy, personally, it was an escape to which he very probably owed his life. Had the inspection not taken place, and he had continued in front-line warfare, he would certainly have been more than fortunate to survive the battles that lay ahead for the rebranded Division. Instead he was assigned to 877 Area Employment Company, in the infamous Base Camp at Étaples – better known to Tommy, though with little fondness, as 'Eat-apples'. In a small book that James wrote whilst at the Base, and later published, he recounted how light-hearted they felt as they marched away from the front:

We knew that for a few weeks at any rate there would be no more fighting, listening patrols, or bombing parties. This morning we were to draw eight days rations and set off on a march of an unknown number of kilometres, to entrain for some base depot. After the usual 'hanging about it' we made a move. Few grumbled at the cold, the early parade, or the long march. Moving away from the field of action was enough to give anybody a light heart. Many changes were noticed as we marched out of the city (Arras). It seemed so different from when we entered it months ago.

He and his companions noted that the fine cathedral, churches, and other buildings had been badly damaged: 'Ruins lay on our right and on our left, and at times across our path so that it was necessary to climb over the debris to regain our track again.' But, nothing daunted, the lads proceeded despite the heavy ongoing shelling. Jimmy commented that 'Fags were lit and jokes made as if we were strolling around Piccadilly ...'

The book he wrote from the trenches was entitled *Bees Wings and Ruby Queens*, the names of the wartime issue cigarettes that he and his companions were no doubt lighting up as they walked, with optimism, towards an as yet unknown destination.

Étaples

On 13 February 1917 the Reverend John Bennetts wrote to James: 'It is a great relief that you are out of the trenches and back at Base Camp. The General who sent you back is kind-hearted.'

A relief it may have been, but it was harder to conceive of a transfer to wartime Étaples as an act of kindness. The General, Sir Aylmer Haldane, commander of VI Corps, had written in his diary: 'I am sorry for the poor little devils, for it was positively cruel to put them up against the sturdy Germans.' But Étaples was itself a match for any cruelty that the enemy could devise – the difference was that it was inflicted on the troops by their own side. The camp was a living hell, so loathed and feared for the brutality of its regime that many of the hundreds of thousands who passed through it during the course of the war recalled that leaving for the Front was actually a relief.

Étaples is around 25 kilometres south of Boulogne, a fishing port on the estuary of the River Canche over which a single bridge connected the town to the wooded promontory and seaside resorts of Le Touquet/Paris-Plage. Before the Great War it had been a pretty place, popular with artists and writers; and is attractive again today, in a faded French way. But for many years after 1914, when it was commandeered for the vast infantry base, it was remembered in rather different colours. Lady Baden-Powell, who established the scout hut at Étaples with which James was later involved, described it as a 'dirty, loathsome, smelly little town'. The war poet Wilfred Owen also had dark recollections of the place: 'I lay awake' he wrote in a letter, 'in a windy tent in the middle of a vast, dreadful encampment. It seemed neither France nor England, but a kind of paddock where the beasts were kept a few days before the shambles. I heard the revelling of the Scotch troops, who are now dead, and who knew they would be dead. I thought of the very strange look on all the faces in the camp; an incomprehensible look, which a man will never see in England; nor can it be seen in any battle. But only in Étaples. It was not despair, or terror, it was more terrible than terror, for it was a blindfold look, and without expression, like a dead rabbit's.'[18]

The Base had a range of functions. There were important road and rail links to strategic towns such as Arras and Bethune, and to the nearby ports of Dieppe and Boulogne, which made it an ideal staging post for new recruits arriving in France on their way to the Front, or those returning on leave or for periods of retraining. It was also the site of fifteen military hospitals where seriously wounded British and Commonwealth soldiers were sent to be treated, or to die. The war cemetery on the outskirts of Étaples, is one of the largest in northern France – 11,000 officers and men lie there, most of whom died in one or other of the hospitals from their dreadful injuries. Others, barely more fortunate, were patched up and returned to their regiments, but not before being given over into the often sadistic care of the cohort of non-commissioned officers charged with readying men and boys for the ordeal awaiting them at the Front. *Étaples* was also home to the infamous training ground known as the Bull Ring, where new arrivals and veterans alike were given 14 days of punitive introduction to – or re-acquaintance with – the gruesome reality of trench warfare. The programme included assault courses, bayonet charges, rifle practice, gas drills, trench digging – all conducted in a manner aimed at humiliating, terrorising, and exhausting the subjects. Day after day they were marched for miles, much of it at the double up and down the steep sand-dunes, or made to crawl in mud and through wire with live rounds being fired low over their heads. And on top of it all there were endless, pointless parades in nothing less than shining boots and polished brasses, with severe punishment for the slightest blemish. Every command or admonishment was delivered at a scream and accompanied by torrents of abuse. Many serious injuries, including fatalities, resulted from this 'training': an inexplicable waste of life and vital medical resources.

It was by any evaluation a deeply flawed and punitive system that had the inevitable consequence of antagonising the very men – a great many of them volunteers – whose good will and loyalty would soon be tested to the limit. The NCOs who conducted and oversaw the programme were known as the 'Canaries', because of the conspicuous yellow armbands that they wore. It was by no means all that they were called by the men: they were feared and hated in about equal measure, more so even than the Red Caps (the Military Police or MPs), whose work was cut out to maintain discipline. A simmering discontent pervaded the base, which more than once erupted into violence, and for one critical period, open mutiny.

The underlying causes of anger and resentment were plain to see, and the disturbances which occurred were entirely predictable. The town could not house the enormous numbers of soldiers passing through the camp, as well as the resident staff – doctors, nurses, trainers, caterers, labour units. And in addition to British troops there were Australians, New Zealanders, Canadians, and a number of Chinese working in foreign labour units. A sea of tents and huts had been erected to provide accommodation. Some personnel had billets in the town, and others – officers only – were ensconced in comfortable quarters in the adjoining resort of Le Touquet/Paris-Plage, which was out of bounds to other ranks. The Canaries and Redcaps, too, had separate barracks, for obvious reasons. The right to enjoy the local amenities, including bars, restaurants, and brothels, was not equally apportioned – for the ordinary men freedom of movement was limited to certain times, outside which they were expected to be back in camp. Military Police routinely guarded the bridge and entry points to the towns, to enforce the restrictions and control access, an obvious cause for resentment and a natural flash point if tempers were already running high.

Often men would get round police pickets by crossing the estuary at low tide to escape observation. On Sunday 9 September, 1917, according to various contemporary accounts, a New Zealand Gunner was arrested by the Red Caps on the bridge leading back to camp from Le Touquet after the tide had come in whilst he and others had been drinking. He was charged with desertion (a capital offence) and locked up – an extremely foolish overreaction that brought a large crowd onto the streets near the railway bridge known as Pont des Trois Arches. The gunner was hurriedly released but the level of anger had passed the tipping point, and the mob did not disperse. Matters went from bad to worse when a squad of MPs arrived, and amidst scuffles in a nearby street one Red Cap fired into the crowd killing a Gordon Highlander and wounding a female French civilian. Massively outnumbered, the Red Caps took to their heels and ran, pursued according to some reports, by up to thousand men.

The ensuing disorder lasted until the following Wednesday, gathering momentum and drawing forth an order from the base commander for a major show of strength. The crowd was confronted by 400 officers and men of the Honourable Artillery Company, as well as a detachment of machine gunners. Most of the men returned to camp, leaving behind only a few hundred, many of whom were arrested. In a more pragmatic approach than might have been expected, only one of them was sentenced to death, a Northumberland Fusilier named Jesse Short. He was charged with inciting the men guarding the bridge to attack their officer, with the words (recorded at the court martial) : 'That Buggar [sic] ought to have a rope tied around his neck with a stone on it and be chucked into the River.' [19] Despite his previously good disciplinary record, Short's execution was confirmed by Haig and carried out on 30 September 1917.

Accounts of the exact circumstances of riots and rebellions are by their very nature hazy, and the Étaples mutiny is no exception. Witness accounts vary in detail, though most share a core of corroborated testimony. A colourful version can be found in William Allison and John Fairley's book, *The Monocled Mutineer* (later televised as a BBC drama), where it is claimed that mutiny began when a corporal was arrested for speaking to a nurse, against regulations, and was then shot dead for resisting arrest (an account which is only roughly compatible with the events reported at Pont des Trois Arches). Scottish, Australian, and New Zealand soldiers then went on the rampage looking for Canaries and Red Caps. General Thomson, commander of the training camp, and his subordinates were actually thrown off a bridge into the river Canche, instead of just threatened. In another version still – or perhaps a separate incident – a report was received by the Censor Station that numbers of Scottish and Canadian soldiers were 'barring the bridges with machine-guns', and deserters had organized themselves into groups in the nearby woods.[20]

Jimmy was on the base at the time of the mutiny, but never mentioned it save on one occasion. In 1963, on a visit to Northern France – his first return since his army days – he recounted seeing a large group of Canadian soldiers coming down from their camp to a guarded bridge. The bridge led to a town, which he didn't name, but which could only have been Étaples. At the time of this later visit the fact of the mutiny was still being kept under wraps – from the general public at least – and was not officially acknowledged until the next decade. When they got to the bridge the Canadians were stopped by the pickets, whom JB described just as British. He said that the Canadians were fed up with being kept away from the bars and the women, and that after shooting – or shooting at – the guards they crossed the bridge and made their way into the town. He enlarged no further on the episode, and offered no judgement on its rights or wrongs, but it was one of the few times when he ever said anything explicit about his stay in Étaples. He would sometimes speak generally about what life had been like on the base, but otherwise kept his memories and experiences entirely to himself – except for this one story about the Canadians and the bridge.

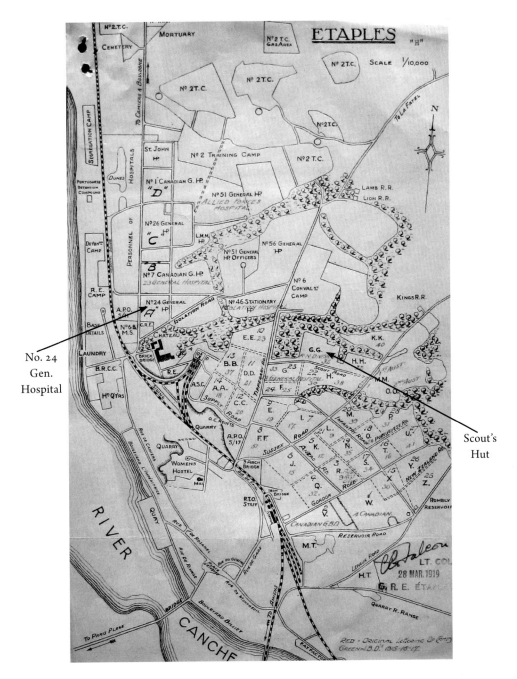

Wartime map of Étaples 1919, showing bridge over the Canche,
no.24 Hospital, and Scout Road

Hospitals and huts

Jimmy was a good deal luckier than some of the 2800 men from the 35th Division who were sent down the line from Arras to Étaples, or other depots. He was not destined for the Bull Ring but was employed, at any rate initially, as an orderly at No. 24 General Hospital on Isolation Road, in the northern part of the town near to the Chateau. The hospitals were staffed by doctors and officers from the Royal Army Medical Corps (RAMC) and nurses from the Queen Alexander's Imperial Military Nursing Service and the Territorial Nursing Service. Auxiliary support staff came from the Voluntary Aid Detachments (VAD) of the British Red Cross and the Saint John Ambulance Brigade. One of the best known VAD workers, Vera Brittain, recorded her time at No. 24 General Hospital in her book *The Testament of Youth*, describing in it how the women were locked inside the hospital for safety during the mutiny. In her own words: 'numerous drunken and dilapidated warriors from the village battle were sent to spare beds ... for slight repairs'; adding that in her personal opinion the causes of the trouble were the repressive conditions and provocation by the military police.[21]

The Labour Corps also supplied workers: orderlies, ambulance drivers, stretcher bearers, cleaners and more. The hospitals treated the military casualties of all nations and ranks throughout the war and after, and during the heaviest periods of fighting, the fifteen Étaples hospitals had to deal with over twenty thousand casualties at any one time. It was a massive and complex undertaking, employing a small army of its own. Despite its distance from the Front – and the protection supposedly afforded by various conventions covering the conduct of war, as well as the large red cross painted on each roof – the hospitals were not safe from attack from the air. No. 24 Hospital, was hit several times in the spring and summer of 1918, with numbers of patients and staff being killed or injured. James brought back photographs of the aftermath of the worst attack in August of that year, showing the ruined wards exposed to the open sky.

As well as his prescribed duties at the hospital, Jimmy Butterworth found a focus for his energies and his talents within the network of rest huts, maintained by various organisations such as the YMCA, and the Scout Movement. These were set up 'to give the men somewhere to relax and recuperate from the rigours of the Front and also, perhaps, to provide more seemly alternatives to the "estaminets" and other dubious

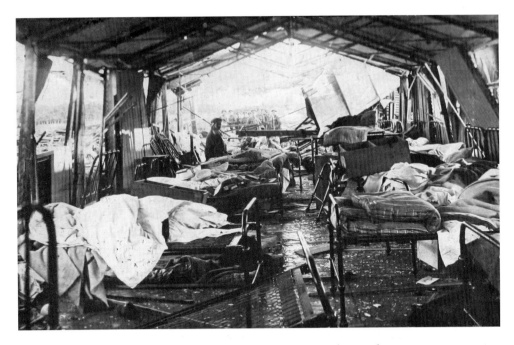

No. 24 General Hospital after aerial bombing raid

establishments to be found in most of the towns and villages in Northern France and Flanders.'[22] The Scouts Hut in Étaples was one of earliest and best known. It was opened in 1915 by Lady Baden Powell who ran it herself for a while before handing over to the Rev. Cyril Butterworth – no relation – who remained the hut-leader until it closed in 1919. At first it was no more than a canteen with a tea counter at one end, and a library at the other, but due to its popularity with the men and the numbers utilising its facilities, a large annexe and concert hall were added. The hut was sponsored and staffed by volunteers from scout troops, and YMCA members, and bore the insignias of both over the door. At some point Private Butterworth joined the team and quickly became involved in its operation, initially on a part-time basis around his shifts at the hospital, but growing over time into a full-time commitment. He also helped out at two other huts, Gordon and Walton. According to their records the huts all suffered from a chronic shortage of helpers which would have made his contributions all the more welcome, especially given his natural flare for just such work. Among the few mementos he brought back from France was the postcard shown below on which he

Scouts Hut, Scout Road

had scribbled: 'Where I was orderly to Rev. Cyril Butterworth', and 'The concert hall where I preached to 700 Tommies at Christmas'. Another arrow points to the library of which he had charge for a time – on the strength perhaps of his penny-a-loan book-trolley around the streets of Oswaldtwistle.

James was still in uniform, and only a private, and his placement at the Scouts Huts would have needed the blessing of the military authorities at some level. However, it seems that he had been befriended by an unusually enlightened officer in charge of his labour unit. It is clear, from a short correspondence between the two men, that James had put himself out to be of service to the officer, who writes to thank him for a manuscript copy of *Bees Wings and Ruby Queens*, and also for some unspecified kindness that he had apparently performed, which evidently gave his superior reason to feel indebted. In a note headed '877 Employment Company, 14.7.18', the officer wrote: 'The balance in the scale of kind action is certainly in your favour. Anything I may have done was done in an endeavour to please as many people as possible, and was in a way selfish. I can't aspire to reach the heights you express in your book – but one can do a little now and then. That's why I made it my business to put you in what I considered the right place.' The place he referred to was presumably the Scouts Hut, under the stewardship of the Rev. Cyril. If so his judgement was perceptive, for it was an environment in which James thrived personally, and in which he could do much for others. It not only gave rein to his organisational skills but also to his ability to identify and befriend the vulnerable and needy, a multitude of whom were to be found within the encampment.

A sort of ministry

James' experience in the Great War left deep and painful scars, though like so many of the survivors he never spoke about any of them in detail. He was not a natural soldier, nor a distinguished one, and whilst he took pride in having served, especially in a Lancashire regiment, there was certainly no allure for him in fighting and killing. It was an ordeal, as we might expect it was for the majority of the volunteers and conscripts who went to France at that time. Writing from England, the Rev. Bennetts sought to console him:

> No doubt you find the army life hard, but you have the satisfaction of doing your bit for your country, and the hardship you endure now will bring you a peace of mind and pride of life in the days when this awful conflict is a matter of history. If God spares you and leads you into the ministry your present experiences will be of untold value to you in the work that will lie before you.

It was a standard 'chin-up' letter. In reality there was little reason to believe that the memories being stored up from that war would bring peace of mind and pride of life to anyone – many were stricken with guilt or shame simply for having survived in one piece. John Bennetts was right however, in his prediction that James' experiences in France would be of value in the work that lay before him, though not perhaps for the reasons he had in mind. What James found in Étaples was more than just endurance of hardship: it was a positive challenge and a formative one. It infused his earlier ambition to preach the gospel with a different and far deeper urgency: to serve the needs and enrich the lives of those who belonged to no church, and often saw little reason to do so.

This turn in his thinking is plain to see in the pages of *Bees Wings and Ruby Queens*. The book opens with a chapter entitled: 'A Private's Thoughts about the Padre'. Ostensibly it is a series of observations about the feelings of the lower ranks towards the chaplains of the various denominations, in and behind the lines. But what is much more interesting about the book is the insight it gives into James's own developing philosophies of ministry and leadership arising out of his First World War experience. In the chapter he examines the complex relationship between the padre and the soldiers, and – more broadly – between the church and wider population, especially the lower classes. It was of course a relationship that was very present for him, given that he had a boot firmly planted in each camp, one thanks to his actual rank and the other reflecting his aspirations. Once or twice, in later writings and lectures, he would speak as though he had himself been a padre in the war. He never was: the padres were officers and he never rose above private. But in certain respects his work with the YMCA and other religious organisations resembled that of the padre in all but the official title. Many of their functions overlapped, including preaching appointments.

The perception of religion in a time of war, and especially that war, was inevitably complex. For some the suffering would have strengthened or even generated faith; for others, understandably, the reverse. The conflicting forces were a major challenge for chaplains of all denominations. Their primary duty was to provide for those who sought spiritual solace. As David Blake, the Curator of the Museum of Army Chaplaincy expressed it: 'They were there to minister to their adherents.'[23] Organised religion certainly occupied a more prominent place in British society at the turn of the 20th Century than it does today. It is estimated that in 1914 up to 30% of the British population attended church every Sunday, and many more than that on special occasions, so that the presence of chaplains giving spiritual guidance to the troops, and the established position of religion within the army structure, would have been regarded as the norm – as it was at home. Soldiers and seamen accepted compulsory church parades as part of their ordinary routine, and the chaplains regarded the conducting of services as their official function.

Many, though not all, saw their role as more diverse. They accompanied wounded men in the ambulances and visited them in hospital. They buried the dead; they wrote to bereaved families; they sat through the night with condemned prisoners. Clearly there was a great deal of divergence in the degree to which the chaplains mixed with the men, and endured the hardships and dangers alongside them. There were those who even went over the top with their companies when they attacked, to help bring back the wounded or simply out of solidarity. Pat Leonard, the 'Fighting Padre' was famed for his participation in action. Others took it on themselves to accompany sentries through the night to help them stay awake, since falling asleep on watch was a capital offence. Many padres were decorated for acts of individual bravery – in total 179 died during the course of the war.

Perception of the padres themselves was also sharply divided. Both Robert Graves and Siegfried Sassoon were openly disparaging in their assessments. Soldiers too had mixed opinions, with the Church of England chaplains tending to attract the poorest ratings. In his memoir *Goodbye to All That* Graves wrote: 'Anglican chaplains were remarkably out of touch with their troops'. By way of example he went on: 'The Second Battalion Chaplain [of Graves' regiment], just before the Loos fighting, had preached a violent sermon on the Battle against Sin, at which one old soldier behind me grumbled: "Christ, as if one bloody push wasn't enough to worry about at a time!" One Roman Catholic padre, on the other hand, had given his men his blessing and told them that if they died fighting in the good cause they would go straight to Heaven or, at any rate, be excused a great many years in Purgatory.'[24]

The most popular padres were those who integrated closely with their flock, often in face of censure from more traditionally minded senior officers for over-familiarity. One of the most celebrated of these was Father Geoffrey Studdert Kennedy, an Anglican priest known to the troops as 'Woodbine Willie'. He earned this nickname by distributing Woodbine cigarettes to the men – together with copies of the New Testament – on trains leaving Rouen for the front. Woodbines would have been received a lot more gratefully than the despised Bees Wings and Ruby Queens of JB's book title. But Father Geoffrey's reputation was really established in the summer of 1916, when he went with his unit to the front. A short profile of the priest, compiled by the Bible Society, recalls that

> as well as being with the troops at the front line, he marched with them, dug tunnels and trenches, shared jokes, led singing and held services. He sought out the wounded and dying in No Man's Land, often dragging them back to the trenches for treatment and prayer. He spent time at makeshift hospitals and often went for 24 hours without sleep. Later that year, he became a wandering preacher, and by the end of April 1917 had visited and preached at all the British bases in France. His ability to get alongside ordinary soldiers was frowned upon by many of the senior ranks in the Army.[25]

James Butterworth commented on Woodbine Willie on numerous occasions in the years following the war, and evidently applauded his egalitarian spirit and his readiness to reach beyond the faithful to those who did not embrace any religion. It is probable that they met, if not at the front then certainly when Kennedy visited and preached at the base in Étaples. The two men differed in respect of their backgrounds and positions, but there were also some striking resemblances in approach between them. Studdert Kennedy was a vicar and a vicar's son, an officer with a grammar school education and a university degree, whilst Jimmy was an orderly in the hospital, a private who had grown up in poverty. Geoffrey however was not unacquainted with the plight of the poor and under-privileged, and according to his biographer, Bob Holman, the Leeds parish in which his father had ministered, and he had grown up, was in one of the most run-down quarters of the city, where 17% of the wage-earning population were defined as living on incomes insufficient to meet the necessities of life.[26] In his own early ministry in Rugby and later in Worcester, he felt his duty to reside in helping the poorest elements in society, and was, Holman writes, at ease with the people in the slums. One of his parishioners recalled: 'The first thing Mr Kennedy did was visit all the poor people. He was all for the poor.'

After enlisting in the Army Chaplains' Department and arrival in France Father Geoffrey had no difficulty associating with the ordinary soldiers – he spoke their language, often colourfully, even from the pulpit, and shared their interests, especially sports. One commentator notes that when he preached 'he used the vernacular without lapsing into condescension. He cracked jokes, laughed at them, sat on the edge of the platform with his legs dangling and used salty language ...'.[27] All the same, he spoke out against the drunkenness, gambling, and sexual immorality that he found to be rife behind the lines, without losing his audience. He wrote from the base at Rouen: 'Had I a boy I would pray that he might never be long at base. He is surrounded by temptations, and has to fight every inch of the way if he wishes to live a clean life. Lord how angry it makes me this attack on men in the rear. Better the guns of the Germans than the temptations of the devil.' At that time – although later he became a pacifist following disenchantment with postwar social provision – he was also a staunch supporter of the war, for which he judged Germany wholly to blame. He thought it was every able-bodied man's patriotic duty to join up, and had no time for conscientious objectors.

Woodbine Willie's ability to engage with the lower ranks of the army earned him popularity and respect across all ranks. James Butterworth, writing in 1922, recalled that he 'said things we could understand.' That facility was one that James would strive to perfect in his own preaching and communication with his Club members, and he may well have been directly influenced by Studdert Kennedy's approach. He would also have been only too aware of the crowds the padre pulled – anywhere between 500 and 1500, according to Holman. 'At one camp', he says, 'a passer-by was puzzled by the sight of soldiers outside a large hut, climbing up to the windows and even on to the roof.'[28] By no means all of Kennedy's eager audience were members of churches, or even church-goers. James was especially struck by this, commenting that 'I used to think of [Kennedy] as the parson of all who hadn't any church. I am afraid I hadn't got such faith when this fiery little Irishman was so joyously expressing his.'[29]

There were other chaplains and ministers that James knew and admired, at the front and at the base, not all of them as colourful or as charismatic as Woodbine Willie. In *Bees Wings and Ruby Queens*, he included a chapter entitled: 'A Private's Thoughts about the Padre' although he does not mention Studdert Kennedy by name in the chapter, so we cannot be entirely sure how he viewed his idiosyncratic methods. For padres at the other extreme, who stand on their dignity and cannot, or will not, relate to the men in the ranks, he has scant respect – although he is mindful of the difficult line they have to tread.

> The chaplain is more tolerated than liked. A Sergeant Major said to me one day, "Padres are absolute failures." Major Redmond called Padres of all denominations "the prop and comfort of the men at the front". The first opinion is simply piffle, the second an exaggeration. Those who know anything about the line know what lasting good our padres have done; they also know that these men are not "the props". I am only voicing the feelings of many privates; what I say is what I hear and see daily. The padre does not know the private. Conscientious chaplains have felt very keenly the soldiers' aloofness, they are not given a chance; men with the "black braided collar" are judged too often at a distance. Few padres manage to break down the soldiers' prejudices. I have been in tents when the entry of a chaplain has changed the gay company into one of cold reserve, all seem to have the fear that this man might have heard them swear, etc. Padres' meetings are not well attended for, from both religion and the parson the soldier fights shy. What then is the stumbling block? Or are the stumbling blocks which caused this aloofness always the fault of the soldier?

In answer to these questions he concludes that it is the padre's commission that is the underlying cause. Many privates have told him that they resist going to the padre simply because he is an officer, and he quotes a chaplain saying: 'If I could succeed in making men forget my three stars, my chances of getting at men would considerably increase.' James contends that if the soldiers could only put aside such objections they would find their chaplain a valuable friend – yet he knows of many men who would never go to see a chaplain whatever their difficulties. Interestingly he considers that their reasons for reluctance are not confined to the issue of rank, but to something far deeper and older in the structure of society and the perception of the church within it.

> This objection is not a new one, but a survival of an old prejudice in a renewed form. It has always been felt that ministers had become a class of their own ... This association of ministers with a class apart, was felt more and more when the National Service Bill placed them out of the reach of the Military. It is often talked about as an injustice to see young ministers go scot-free, and men with a business, the outcome of a lifetime's toil, sacrificing all. Still stronger grew this prejudice when ministers became captains, and those who bear the name, meaning to serve, are now to be saluted.

> ... another prejudice to padres suggested itself whilst walking through a dirty French village and noticing a large house and garden belonging to the curé. My friend said, "However can these men know of the sufferings of the poor?" Those words stuck, and I am led to think that when padres preach on parade service, many privates say, "He's alright, he doesn't know all we have to put up with. He does not know what it is to line up with his mess tin, to push, rush and crush for his 'hard-tack'. His food is served neatly in a cosy mess. He had the privacy of a private tent or billet, and a servant to do his work." Irksome parades, sleeping in crowded tents, wretched fatigues, dull drills, are out of his sphere. And so, somehow, and in some way, a padre seems to be someone outside Tommy's sphere.

> The Rev. Capt. Harry Miller once said, "Men! You are saying that it's alright for me to talk like this with a private tent of my own". He was one of the most saintly and yet practical men I ever met, and was the idol of the troops at a certain base. But there in that sentence one can see that padres and privates alike are conscious of the dividing line between the Tommy and a chaplain, or in civil life between the Minister and the masses.

During his time in the army James Butterworth observed, and came to understand clearly, the reluctance of soldiers to trust the army chaplains, and the reasons for that distrust. Writing his book at barely twenty years old he was already perceptive about the nature of the distance and the obstacles it raised, and his ideas about how such barriers might be broken down are full of careful insight. The maturity of the thinking is obscured in parts by the curiously dated style, but no less interesting for that, and his words show a balanced understanding of the dilemma of leadership, not just in the military context, but in civil life too.

Whilst a padre must have some degree of authority, this can have a cost in terms of approachability. If the men cannot overlook the padre's three stars and black-braided collar, their trust and confidence will be hard if not impossible to win. James quotes approvingly a certain Padre Black from the Walton Hut for asserting that 'the true padre is the soldier in his tent who lives the true Christian life'. Yet the padre is not, and cannot be the soldier in the tent – he is the officer in the mess, and when he comes to the tent he inevitably comes *down* a level. Not only do the men close up, moderating their language and behaviour for fear of disapproval or of giving offence, they also sense the condescension. The padre in turn will always struggle to behave authentically, torn between the desire to be accepted and the need to maintain his standards and be true to his convictions. James sees the failings of the parties on both sides of the divide: the soldiers for their unwillingness to give the padre a chance to draw close, the padres for their failure to make any effective provision of comfort and support. Most of all he is contemptuous of the padre who affects to be one of the men by playing down – or of playing up for cheap approval:.

> Suffice to say that there are a few, thank God only a few, who with their pandering and playing to the gallery sort of business have brought disgust not only upon themselves and upon their sacred calling. But speaking from a private's point of view, I can only see things which will break through the reserve and overcome prejudices of the private soldier.
>
> 1. Chaplains with unmistaken convictions and an uncompromising message.
>
> 2. A minister deeply spiritual and intensely practical.
>
> There is no room for chaplains who pander, and on the other hand for those who are always looking to heaven and forgetting Earth. Whose spirituality has blinded them to practical sympathy.

These were formative years for James, in which his daily experience impressed upon him the difficulties of overcoming the divide between minister and men, and establishing a trustful communication. He had no choice but to see the church and its representatives from a private soldier's perspective – but he had been raised all his life in Chapel, and also saw the soldier from the padre's standpoint, and knew the barriers they had to climb to win hearts and minds. As he concluded: 'Breaking down old settled prejudices is ever hard work and herein lies the difficulty of the chaplain's work'. It was an early insight into the challenges he would face when in years to come he would wear the clerical collar and represent the other side.

Army life

How James related to his fellow soldiers is also an interesting question. He was one of them by rank, but not in all things – and like Studdert Kennedy he expressed disapproval for the debased behaviour that he observed on the Base. He might well have been considered priggish by many of his companions for adhering to standards of behaviour that his Methodist upbringing had inculcated in him. Others would have respected him for sticking to his guns, and some among his peers would have had the same attitudes and same Sunday-school background. At this time in his life, with the teachings of Cliff College still fresh in his ears, he continued to be influenced by its evangelical ethos. He sent a letter back from Étaples to be published in the College newsletter, *Joyful News*, entitled 'Evening Prayers in a Tent in France' writing: 'The open sins of army life astounded me ... My new life away from Church members and Christian students took me to live amongst men who cursed and gambled and drank, and whose presence was at first revolting. Interference in their habits and affairs was not "thankfully received", and I found that to live Jesus Christ is more profitable than to preach about him.' He continues on a positive note to say that in time soldiers who had never been to church save for their christening and marriage had started coming to his services.

It must be remembered that this letter was, of course, written for a Methodist college, and the writer had accordingly tailored its language and sentiments for a selective audience. In fact it is quite implausible that James had never encountered men who 'cursed, gambled and drank', given the other facet of his upbringing at the mill or in the streets of Oswaldtwistle and the 'back holes' of fish and chip shops. He would have seen it all well before he joined the army – though the conditions of war may have deepened the depravity he found there. It is true that he set high standards for himself and that he sought to encourage others to live better lives – those exacting Methodist traits were fundamental to all he had been taught. But it is equally clear that he knew better than to alienate people by aggressive moralising, and despite his own very firm beliefs he was not judgemental towards those who did not share them. For himself he kept out of the poker games, abstained from alcohol, and refrained from the coarsest language – but for others he was open-hearted. He learned early in his life that in seeking to make the world a better place, friendship and understanding of your fellow men must come first.

A far more revealing expression of how Pte Butterworth's attitudes were taking shape – very different in tone from the letter to Joyful News – appears in a later chapter of *Bees Wings*, entitled 'Imaginary Correspondence of Two Soldier Pals on "The Good and Bad Side of War".' One of the two pals has just got 'a Blighty', namely an injury that has taken him off to hospital back in London, for an extended convalescence. The other is congratulating him, enviously, and complaining of the corrupting effects of the war on young soldiers, and the coarse, dishonest, and uncharitable behaviour it brings out in men – bemoaning the fact that so many soldiers have turned their backs on religion, crowding into camp cinemas and concert halls and leaving the churches empty.[30] The reply from the other pal is both forgiving and optimistic. This pal recognises the pressures that the men are under; not condoning what they do but understanding why, and finding virtue in the sacrifice the men are making that far outweighs the forgivable lapses that his friend condemns. He also challenges the idea that the soldier is abandoning religion – giving James' lifelong refusal to equate fixed church lore with Christianity its earliest airing.

> If you judge a man's religion by how many times he goes to church, what creed he conforms to, what doctrine he holds, then I see why you are so convinced that Tommy is not religious. Churchism is not Christianity. Creed Conformity is not necessarily Religion. Yes, Tommy is showing an aversion to all these trappings of Doctrine. Religion has become too dogmatic, too exacting, too complicated. Outward conformity has taken the place of real spirituality. Religion is simply founded on Love, Brotherhood, Sacrifice. They were the characteristics of the Christ. The Cross and Calvary symbolize brotherhood and sacrifice. Look around you and see if these principles, these very essences of religion are not being practised.[31]

The answer, which is transparently the author's, is a resounding 'Yes'. The dialogue ends with the words: 'And so my dear chum … I put side by side, to your petty complaints of deterioration in character, those noble and sublime qualities, and in the light of these prove that the righteousness of many Tommies exceeds the righteousness of rigid moralists.'

What we get from this Socratic exchange is a telling glimpse of two of the motivating forces behind James Butterworth's ministry and more especially his work with youth. The first is the urgent need for the Church to extend its reach to those beyond its traditional constituency. The second is his belief in the inherent goodness in human beings, which will otherwise go unrecognised and untapped.

Armistice

His work in the hospital and at the YMCA huts was not James' only source of companionship. He formed close ties with a French family named Vigreux who lived at No.3 Rue Gabrielle, where James was billeted for a time. There are several letters on file from Mme Vigreux dating from shortly after the war that speak of a deep fondness on her part for James, urging him to come back and visit them. She was a widow, living with her two grandchildren, who also became attached to Monsieur Jim, especially the little boy, Julien who asks after him frequently, according to his grandmother's letters. There is also an extended correspondence through the late summer and autumn of 1918 from a young lady who signs herself B. Duhamel, who has evidently recently moved from Étaples to Vernon, a town south-east of Rouen. The letters, written in French, are not overtly amorous, but they are distinctly warm, and quite frequent. In his recollections he sometimes hinted at 'having been keen on a French girl' during and shortly after the war, but did not mention her by name. No copies of his replies were kept – there is just one short but interesting letter from him written earlier in the same year, also in French, and signed 'JB'. It has been written quite carefully on impressive crested Fusiliers note paper and wastes no time getting to the point: 'Cher Amie. Voulez-vous faire une recontre avec moi au coin de votre rue quelque après midi … Nous pouvons faire une promenade pour une demi-heure ou vous pourez avoir du thé chez moi dans ma chambre'. It's not clear whether or not this was intended for Mlle Duhamel, but the fact that JB still possessed the letter suggests either that it was a rough draft – or that he lost his nerve and never sent it.

Among the men he came to know well in Étaples, a significant number were Canadians – the Canadian General Base Depot (GBD) was right next to Gordon Road where the YMCA's Gordon hut was situated, and it is probable that many Canadian soldiers congregated there. Also, huge numbers of the wounded from the Battle of Vimy Ridge between 9 and 12 April 1917 were hospitalised in Étaples. Canadians made up the bulk of the combatants in that action – all told 7000 of them were wounded taking the Ridge, and half as many more were killed. Of all the great confrontations of the war, Vimy Ridge was the one James spoke about most passionately. Along with Passchendaele it symbolised the war for him. He was spared from the fighting by then, but not from witnessing the terrible suffering that was its aftermath.

In November 1918 the Armistice was signed, but there was no immediate respite for the personnel employed on the bases. The wounded and damaged still lay in their beds, needing no less care and assistance simply because a treaty had been signed. The massive infrastructure of the war needed dismantling; transport had to be organised; and as another cold Christmas approached the Labour Corps was as busy as it ever had been. Anxious to resume the struggle to gain candidacy for the Methodist ministry, James applied repeatedly to be demobilised, but he had to wait until 12 February 1919 to be granted his wish. He had found something of his vocation in Étaples, and had learned unforgettable lessons there, but he was ready now for a new battle. The country to which he eventually returned was very different from the one he had left – and he, too, was very different from the lad who had marched away three years previously.

On arrival at the Dispersal Station he was handed his 'Soldier's Demobilization Account'. Counting the balance of his army pay, 28 days 'ration' and 'plain clothes' allowances, and a War Gratuity of £15, the total came to thirty-four pounds, one shilling, and six pence.

Notes

1 See Ferguson, Niall: *The Pity of War*, p.201.
2 See webpage by Jackson, Andrew, 2002: http://www.pals.org.uk/enlistment.htm. Also: *Accrington Observer & Times*, 11 July 1914, p.8.
3 Ibid, p.4.
4 Nicholson, Cecil L., Maj. Gen., Sir: *The History of the East Lancashire Regiment in the Great War*. Lancashire Infantry Museum.(First published in 1936 and compiled by the then Colonel of the Regiment, from first-hand accounts of the men who were themselves involved.)
5 Jackson: Accrington Pals website. http://www.pals.org.uk/pals_e.htm.

6 Ibid.

7 Turner, William. *Pals: The 11th(Service) Battalion (Accrington) East Lancashire Regiment*. Pen and Sword Books (1998). First published by Wharncliffe, 1987. Turner attributes the quotation to an unpublished manuscript on the history of the Accrington Pals by H. Crossley.

8 Allinson, S. *The Bantams*, Pen & Sword Military, 2009, p.26.

9 Ibid.

10 Schedule of Exemption Clause 6, Military Service Act, March 1916.

11 *Letters of a Clublander*

12 Allinson, *The Bantams*, p.245.

13 Allinson, *The Bantams*, p.82.

14 The War Diary of the 17th Lancashire Fusiliers, 11 February, 1916. The National Archives' reference WO 95/2484/1

15 Davson, Lt Col. H.M. 1926 *The History of the 35th Division in the Great War*. London: Sifton Praed, pp.87–88.

16 Allinson, op cit p.254 – quotation from the Diary of Lt Col Harrison Johnston.

17 Davson, 1926, p.5.

18 Owen, W: *Collected Letters*. Oxford University Press. 1967.

19 Transcript of the field general court martial: http://www.nationalarchives.gov.uk/pathways/firstworldwar/service_records/p_field.htm

20 See http://www.remembrancetrails-northernfrance.com/history/armies/mutinies.html

21 Brittain, Vera: *The Testament of Youth*, first published by Victor Gollancz (1933).

22 The Scout Association Archives.

23 The Bible Society website. https://www.biblesociety.org.uk/what-we-do/england-and-wales/world-war-1/stories/soldiers/chaplains-took-christianity-to-the-front-line/ Also the Museum of Army Chaplaincy: http://www.army.mod.uk/chaplains/23363.aspx

24 Graves, R. *Goodbye to All That*, Penguin Modern Classics 2000, pp.158–59.

25 op cit. (link) https://www.biblesociety.org.uk/what-we-do/england-and-wales/world-war-1/stories/chaplains/the-man-who-stayed-with-the-troops-at-the-front/.

26 Holman, Bob: *Woodbine Willie*. Lion Books, 2012. (Kindle edition, loc. 102)

27 Ibid. Quoting Kerry Walters (ed.). *After War is Faith Possible?*' Lutterworth Press, 2008 p.12. Quoted in Holman (Kindle edition, loc. 574)

28 Ibid.

29 Butterworth, c.1922: *A Service Book of Prayers and Readings*. Jun-Aug. Southwark Local History Library (JB Clubland Archive).

30 *Bees Wings and Ruby Queens*, p.34.

31 Ibid, pp.38–9.

CHAPTER THREE

Didsbury 1919–1922

Candidature for the Ministry

Since early childhood James Butterworth had nurtured a keen desire to preach within his Church, and in the intervening years this had developed into a driving ambition for ordained ministry. The call he felt toward ministry had been intensified, rather than muted, by the traumas of his young life: the hardship in his family, the loss of his father to despair and suicide, the punishing mill work that was the lot of multitudes of children, and the end of schooling for a lad recognised as a prodigy in the pulpit for whom words were treasures. He had endured the trenches of the Somme, and the campaign at Arras, living past battles which swallowed so many of his friends and peers, including familiar faces from the past. Harry Scambler, who carried the tea urn for the 1910 New Year event at Green Haworth, and was a Sunday School teacher the following year, had emigrated to Canada with his family, but returned to perish in France on 30 October 1916, fighting with the Manitoba Regiment. Mr. Hesketh, teacher at the junior school, died in France in the same month as Harry, leaving a young wife and baby behind. And Dennis Rushton, son of the Green Haworth caretaker – fellow lamplighter, and first audience to Jimmy's' youthful preaching in the empty chapel – died on 19 May 1917 near Arras, serving with the East Lancashire Regiment whilst attached to the Royal Engineers.

His time at Cliff College before the war may have whetted James' appetite to go further, but it had come to a premature end, and had done relatively little in practical terms to advance the fulfilment of his vocation. To be ordained as a Wesleyan Minister – as opposed to practising as a local preacher, which he had already accomplished – required overcoming various obstacles. To begin with it was necessary to be put forward by his local Accrington circuit to the Bolton District Synod meeting, who would interview him and send representatives to hear him preach, before deciding whether to endorse the recommendation. Having leapt those fences his application must progress to the Annual Conference for his acceptance as a candidate for the Ministry – either before, during, or after attendance at a Wesleyan theological college – prior to entering the ministry and subsequent ordination.

Against the backcloth of the First World War this process presented several problems for candidates, and indeed for the Church – not least of which was that those serving in the armed forces could not undertake the prescribed examinations, or be heard to preach. The Annual Methodist Conference itself discussed and acknowledged these difficulties when it convened in Spring 1917, but did little to legislate their removal, and its position remained unclear – constituting an additional obstacle for many serving soldiers. Surviving letters from the Accrington Circuit ministry, and Chapel officials at Green Haworth illustrate the setbacks and frustrations which James Butterworth – now isolated in France from direct church approach and interaction – encountered in his efforts to accomplish the next step in reaching his goal of becoming an ordained Methodist minister. It was to be a testing battle in which James displayed all the persistence and determination which later became hallmarks of his life and work.

From early 1917, whilst James was stationed on the Pas de Calais coast at Étaples, he was able to pursue the matter of his candidature with greater focus. Although few of his own letters remain, the flurry of replies to him during this period demonstrates the intensity of his correspondence, and the frequency with which communications were flying to and fro across the Channel.

In February 1917 John Bennetts – previously minister at Mount Pleasant, Oswaldtwistle, and for several years Jimmy Butterworth's mentor – was able to write encouragingly that the Principal of Cliff College, Samuel Chadwick, had visited to preach in Bennetts' current West Yorkshire constituency, and had expressed admiration and support for his erstwhile student.[1] A month or so later Bennetts – who was due to move to Ossett, West Yorkshire, as Circuit Superintendent – wrote again with the news that Albert Stirzaker, James' fellow hopeful in the Oswaldtwistle church and peer at Cliff, had been recommended by the Accrington Quarterly Meeting, and would be examined in India or Mesopotamia, where he was soon bound on military service.[2] Unfortunately the Circuit recommendation proved to be no guarantee of success since the Bolton Synod – which had the Oswaldtwistle/ Accrington Circuit under its aegis along with thirty-nine others – did not favour conducting Methodist process in this way, and Albert, like James, did not reach Didsbury until 1919. However, the success of his close contemporary at this initial stage must have made it even more of a blow when in August 1917 the Reverend John Horn, one of Accrington's three current ministers, wrote to him that his request for recommendation as a candidate at the quarterly meeting was premature – many members had not heard him preach, and the vote could not be unanimous.[3] James was bitterly disappointed by Horn's brief and negative response, when he had been part of the local church since early childhood, and known to everybody within it.

The following week the Reverend Bennetts, who had long been aware of the boy preacher's abilities and ambitions, advised him to drop his candidature project until after the war, since it was difficult for Mr. Wainman – Superintendent Minister for the Accrington Circuit 1916–1918 – to nominate a candidate of whom he had sparse knowledge.[4] Reverend Thomas Wainman had been appointed to his post after James Butterworth's return from Cliff College, enlistment, and departure for army training. Bennetts, knowing his man, urged him to 'possess your soul in patience' – pointing out that time was on his side. James, however, was never noticeably possessed of great patience and chafed at the bar to his progress. Bennetts wrote again, welcoming James' evident interim assurance that he was reconciled to the situation, but nevertheless felt it appropriate to issue a gentle warning to the young man against expressing his feelings of perceived lack of support from Accrington and its Ministers. This wise and friendly caution fell upon unwilling ears and James soon wrote outside the Accrington Circuit to the Reverend Halstead, minister at Roath Park, Cardiff – whose acquaintance he had made whilst on army training in South Wales the previous year – indicating that the main obstacle was Mr. Horn, who he considered an unworthy successor to Mr. Bennetts, and a 'cold and indifferent' individual who had resisted the arguments of others seeking to intervene on his behalf. Rev. Halstead was already known to John Bennetts, with whom he had worked on the Todmorden Circuit – James was fortunate in the loyal support of several of his Methodist Seniors. Benign happenchance also led him into contact with Reverend Wilfred J. Moulton – pre-war Principal of the Methodist College at Headingley, Leeds, and later James' Principal at Didsbury – who took on the role of an army chaplain in Étaples during the War. James met and spoke with Moulton, who wrote to John Bennetts supporting him, as well as to Rev. Horn on his behalf – James was able to report to Rev. Halstead that Moulton had spoken of Horn's objections as weak and evasive, with inadequate reasons given.

It is not possible at a hundred years' distance to sort out the pros and cons of Rev. Horn's position. His dismissal of James request was undeniably both brief and curt – there was no reason for his apparent disapprobation, although James did confide to Halstead that when Horn criticised an earlier publication of his he had responded by replying that he had not known all his doings were subject to Horn's authority. It is also the case that John Horn lost his son on the Western Front early in the war, and was perhaps distracted by personal focus. The response of Reverend Wainman as Circuit Superintendent is more understandable – it would be awkward to recommend the distant and unknown (to him) Private Butterworth when the latter's own minister at Mount Pleasant was unwilling to speak for him. James himself acknowledged that Wainman had already nominated somebody who was then rejected by Conference, and that Wainman's position with the Synod would be further compromised by an unsupported recommendation and possible refusal at Conference level. The stance of Conference remained unclear – despite the support James might have hoped for from Samuel Chadwick, 1918 President of Conference as well as his old principal at Cliff College – and James reluctantly accepted that he must abandon any prospect of Candidature for March 1918. He wrote to Reverend Halstead:

> I very much feel your kindness, and the assurance of your support is indeed an inspiration to me ... I feel however that I must give up hope of Candidature for March 1918'.

The delay was a disappointing setback, but James did not have giving up in his nature, and those whose voices he had canvassed in his support continued to speak on his behalf during his absence in France. He was fighting for his future, and for the future of all those he felt he could reach through his ministry – the cause was a worthy one, and many thousands of young people in the course of his fifty-five year ministry would have reason to be grateful for his conviction and persistence. He accepted that another year must pass before his Candidature, but he was neither silent nor idle, and it was during 1918, whilst working as a hospital orderly, and organising activities and services at the Étaples YMCA, that he wrote the two small books discussed in the previous chapter, on the role of religion in army life, and the philosophy of those who live that life.

It is in these little books,[5] alongside his reflections on his comrades who are struggling with being soldiers, and the chaplains who are in their turn struggling to establish meaningful contact with the men in order to offer comfort and guidance, that James first stated his opinion of the chasm between Christianity, and the 'Churchianity' which was a poor approximation to it. Writing whilst still very young – and not always averse to sententious phrases – James nevertheless combined a light touch for observation with perceptive consideration of more abstract matters. He argued that there must be genuine communication and exchange in religious practice, since 'Reality in religion is the death blow to formality, and present formality is the death blow to churches.' James' concept of 'real' religion was one which he always championed. It meant a religion which made contact in everyday language and offered practical help in the lives of ordinary people. The books were published by the Methodist publishers Epworth Ltd. of London – the first of his many books and publications from that house – and added to his early profile and reputation within Methodism at a significant point.

By the time the 1919 Methodist Conference came around events had moved on – in February 1919 James had at last secured his demobilisation, which had been delayed after the Armistice, and returned to Lancashire. Thereafter came good news. Reverend Bennetts, by then back in Burnley, wrote in March 1919

> Our lay evangelist has resigned – could you come here temporarily –
> you are to be nominated at the Accrington 2 meeting. The Conference
> will accept you as a Candidate at the end of August, and you will be free
> to do as it directs by then. Committee members agree – salary only 30/-
> but it might tide you over. You would have every facility for going to do
> your trial sermons in the Bolton District. Come and see me in Burnley
> and we can discuss it all.

This time around his hopes were realised and the recommendation was accepted. The Wesleyan Conference of 25 July 1919 adopted James Butterworth as a candidate for the ministry. It was the door opening, and with one bound James was through and set on the trajectory of his mission for youth.

Didsbury Wesleyan Theological College, 1919–1922

The first recorded mention of Didsbury – its *origin* Diddi's Town – was of an ancient grant of land on which to build a chapel dedicated to St. Oswald, many centuries later in 1855 re-christened St. James'. In 1800 the settlement had been little more than a small rural hamlet beyond Manchester, with a couple of inns, a village green, a few handloom weavers' cottages, and the church. Larger houses such as Broome House, Didsbury House, and the Old Parsonage were built soon afterwards, as men whose wealth sprang out of the Industrial Revolution acquired sufficient funds to build themselves large rural dwellings. In the mid-nineteenth century Didsbury House – previously home to a girls' school – was extended to accommodate the Northern Branch of the Wesleyan Theological Institution, its previous premises at Hoxton Square having proven inadequate. The 1839 Conference recognised the need for increased space and withdrew £55,000 from its centenary fund to buy Didsbury House and another property in Richmond, London as joint colleges. It was purchased in 1840, opening as the first theology college in Britain for training Methodist ministers on Thursday 22 September 1842. Its satellite chapel, St. Paul's Methodist Church, was opened in 1877.

Wesleyan Theological College, Didsbury

In the early days the academic faculty was minimal – a theological tutor, a classical tutor, and an assistant tutor, teaching a theology course based on a book written by the Hoxton lecturer, John Hannah, entitled *Letter to a Junior Methodist Preacher* (1836). This split the subject into evidences, doctrines, and duties and institutions of Christianity. In addition Hannah read aloud to the students from Wesley's sermons, and there were also classes on biblical interpretation and ecclesiastical history. There was a house governor to oversee the pastoral care and domestic arrangements of the 40 students in residence, and two tutors' houses and a college chapel were soon added to the existing buildings. Importantly the students – who mostly went on to become Methodist ministers – were each allocated a district in a neighbouring village and expected to carry out weekly visits, as well as undertaking preaching engagements. This was all in accordance with the Methodist precept of itinerant preachers.

Sadly the College did not endure in Didsbury beyond its first century. It was a military hospital through World War Two, and after the war – still owned by the Methodists – was rented to Manchester Education Committee for use as an emergency teacher training establishment. Later it became a college of education, being absorbed into Manchester Polytechnic in the 1970s, and later still part of Manchester Metropolitan University. The postwar institution of Didsbury College itself was eventually transferred to Henbury Hill, Bristol, where it was renamed Wesley College, Bristol in 1967. In 2010 the Methodist Conference voted to close the College – and in Manchester the University closed the campus in 2014 selling the land to developers. The site is presently occupied by the Open College – two of the original buildings remain as Grade ll listed buildings – the Methodist Church of St. Paul, and the Methodist Theological College Building. The Old Chapel Building, originally the college chapel, and for many years afterwards the library, is also listed – and the Lodge, which was built to be a gatehouse in the 1870s, remains in place.

When Jimmy arrived back in England in February 1919, with the path to Didsbury College and the ministry at last visible before him, there remained a not inconsiderable challenge between him and the prestigious college gates. He still had to leap the hurdles of the Didsbury entrance examinations, in April and July. An aspiring Methodist clergyman was expected to be academically informed, and to have some knowledge of classical subjects – Latin, Greek, and Theology. It would be no mean feat for Jimmy Butterworth to achieve this standard in the light of his basic and curtailed formal education. The pressing time constraints of working around the clock in the Lancashire mills to support his family, and afterwards his years as a serving soldier in Northern France, had left little opportunity to fit in any significant instruction in the classics. He was reliant upon the early supervision and guidance of his Methodist mentors at Oswaldtwistle, and of his tutors during the six months at Cliff, both of which had provided a solid basis as well as encouraging him to continue to read assiduously whenever possible.

John Bennetts welcomed him back and did everything to support his study, but James was anxious for his preparation to adopt the right focus, and wrote for specific advice to the Reverend William Fiddian Moulton, for thirteen years a tutor at Cliff College.[6] Moulton wrote back with straightforward practical advice: James should read a 'good general history' and 'study earnestly the maps of Europe, Asia, Africa, and America in a good atlas.' Moulton told James that the only purpose of the examinations 'is to sort out illiterates, and your excellent writing in *Bees Wings* – for it is an excellent book – will stand you in better stead than dates of battles.'[7] Moulton was well-placed to comment as the manuscripts of *Bees Wings and Ruby Queens* and *Dug-out Digressions* had been sent on to Cliff for his appraisal by James' old headmaster Mr. Hugill the year before. Moulton's observations had been both positive and perceptive, replying to Hugill after a first reading that he found the book to have merit, even though its author tended to speak his own view through Tommy's mouth. A few months later, writing to James directly on 26 June, 1918, Moulton told him 'You have a gift.'

In the event the Didsbury Literary Paper entrance examination of July 1919 seems to go some way beyond requiring a basic general exposition of the sort anticipated by Moulton. In fact candidates were asked to provide an account of the ethical theories of Kant, Hegel, and Nietzsche, explanations of various broadly scientific terms such as 'angle of incidence', 'isotherm', 'construction of a thermometer', and 'recent modifications of Atomic Theory', as well as describing the key developments of either the Reformation or the Industrial Revolution. Moulton was certainly correct that it would exclude 'illiterates'.

James's own handwritten records of his examination results confirm that he had passed all the necessary 1919 preaching tests and committee considerations, and gone on to secure passes in the Biblical and Literary papers. In the Christmas exams at Didsbury that year his marks for New Testament, Old Testament, and Theology were in the seventies – with Greek lagging behind a bit at 48%. He also records that he won the college prize for best first year essay. Greek was his *bête noir* however, and in the 1920 examinations – when his extra-curricular Mission work had expanded to occupy most of his time – it fell even further behind his other excellent results to 35%. And then in the next summer it sank to an abysmal 15% – which James ruefully endorsed: 'bottom of the class.'

When James arrived at the college in September 1919 it had recently re-opened after functioning as a Red Cross Hospital for the duration of the war from June 1916–May 1919. The body of tutors and assistant tutors taught a broader range of academic and theological disciplines than Didsbury had offered originally, and in addition to his studies James soon became busy with the other projects of student life, undertaking several committee roles and representing his year on the Magazine Committee. The various year books of Didsbury College contain occasional traces of James' internal College activities. His first year essay award, and role on the Magazine Committee are noted, and subsequently he was nominated to make the toast to 'Our Guests' at the Didsbury Christmas party on 15 December 1920. The Minutes of the Work and Fitness Committee report of 16 June 1921 describe 'James Butterworth a preacher, good type, grand man.'

Of course it was no surprise that James was again enjoying a burgeoning reputation as a gifted preacher, and his eloquence in the pulpit led to a long list of engagements to speak at church anniversaries and celebrations. Many of the engagements necessitated travelling considerable distances, and rushing to make train connections. On one occasion when he was sent on supply to a chapel in Morecambe, James changed trains at Preston arriving at Morecambe with neither his ticket nor his sermon, but wearing a railway porter's jacket, which he had hurriedly seized up in mistake for his own at Preston. Didsbury confirmed his identity to the Morecambe station-master, he was able to proceed to his engagement, and the following Monday he returned the jacket, which he had worn to preach, to a bemused Preston porter.

Neither did he forget, or neglect to visit, his old friends and mentors at Green Haworth. The programme for the Chapel's Sunday School Anniversary Sermons on Sunday 13 June 1920 shows that two sermons were to be preached by Rev. James Butterworth that day, and bears James' endorsement, 'Preached Anniversary first time at my own village church.' Back home on family visits he also made time to participate in Circuit and Church events and contribute to organisations in Accrington and Oswaldtwistle. When he finally left Lancashire and the North, bound for South London and his great lifetime adventure, his old supporter John Holgate presented him with the Oxford Edition of the Poetical Works of William Wordsworth, inscribed 'to James Butterworth as a Token of Good Will and Appreciation in Remembrance of many Happy Hours of Christian Fellowship, from the members of Union Street Young Men's Fellowship.' The book was signed by 30 of his youthful peers and friends, and he kept it always among his most treasured possessions.

James Butterworth and his returning war comrades had not, however, found it easy to slip seamlessly back into the old settled existence they had left. Their concepts, values, and experience had been profoundly shaken by the armed conflict and their part in it. James wrote later of the disorienting strangeness of returning to a different postwar world from the one he and his comrades had left a few years previously. He described the soldier intake which entered Didsbury College that Autumn as: 'A strange crowd of students, tempered by their army days, the horrors they had witnessed, the chaos of the trenches, army discipline, and the free and wide companionship of fellow soldiers, many of whom did not return.'

James Butterworth's first year at Didsbury 1919–20

The memory of those who did not survive the conflict travelled with those who did 'as though those who came back were also coming back for those who did not.' He wrote that 'We wanted to do the things they would have done had they returned.' They were disillusioned with a country which did not seem to be delivering on its promises of a 'land fit for heroes', and unsettled by ongoing internal political upheavals in other countries – the Russian revolution, the Irish troubles. They weren't so sure quite what they believed any more, and their faith was, James said, 'a bit jumbled up. We were more mature, yet full of doubts, wise but reckless, yet the Church seemed static and untouched. It was hard to slip back into what felt unreal.' He acknowledged that 'This might have been disastrous without the understanding fellowship of our teachers. We had true fathers in God – with remarkable insight they brought to our College life a friendship of Tutors with students which must have been unusual in a theological college.'[8]

Their seniors at Didsbury were not unaware of the struggles and uncertainties facing the intake of soldier students, and gave them far greater leeway than would normally have been the case in pre-war years. These students had a need to keep contact with the realities of everyday life, feeling that they could not simply devote themselves exclusively to an academic existence and theological study. James bought a bicycle to get around the locality, and once he had re-acquired the skill – this took a while as on his first outing he collided with a lamppost outside the college gates and had to spend a few days in hospital with concussion – he explored the neighbourhood.

Cycling one day through nearby Chorlton he noticed a closed and dark chapel opposite a noisy brightly lit pub. He was immediately curious, disturbed by the contrast between the internal life of these two buildings, and struck with an instant desire to galvanise the chapel back into productive life and activity. In his endless preaching engagements he was increasingly experiencing a growing feeling of sterility of purpose, springing from an awareness of speaking to the converted, and he sensed that in this deserted chapel lay the potential challenge of making a real difference to a community of lives. On an impulse he entered the pub and asked the men around the bar whether any would be interested in helping him to set up a club for their children. After a few moments to absorb the student's unexpected offer the response was both appreciative and enthusiastic, with offers of help, furniture provision, and accommodation in the pub's upstairs room. Buoyed by this response James went immediately to the Governor of Didsbury, Reverend Thomas Hugh

Barratt, seeking permission to cancel his preaching engagement list and instead devote himself to re-invigorating the Mission at Beech Road, and spending his weekends and vacations there revitalising worship and activity. He declared to Barratt his intention of 'combing the district for a congregation.'

It was his tremendous good fortune that the wise Reverend Barratt[9], even if somewhat taken aback by the student's sudden impassioned appearance in his study, nevertheless empathised with his enthusiasm – as did the Principal of Didsbury, Reverend Moulton, when he also was made aware of the ambitious scheme. They said yes, and their enlightened and progressive attitude and support made it possible for James to pursue the project which determined the direction his entire ministry must take. It was without doubt a watershed moment in James' life, and the Beech Road Mission venture became the blueprint for the later structure and development of Clubland. It was at Beech Road that James served his apprenticeship, absorbing many lessons, and learning skills essential to his later pioneering work in South London.

Beech Road Mission

In his unfinished *Letters of a Clublander* James says of his childhood that 'clubs were always in my dreams'. He continues: 'From my father I got the idea of rambling parties or midnight hikes to Pendle Hill to watch the sun rise, and a football league of all the "back hole" gangs. A few of us published a magazine, produced a play in a barn, started a club in a boiler house from which we were kicked out.'[10] The urge to create structured associations for youthful membership was very strong in him. This club instinct – formed even before he left school for the mills, or lost his father – became inseparable from his engagement in the religious life of the Methodist church which nurtured him through childhood onwards. Rev. G.H. Simpson, a fellow student at Didsbury and later Minister at East Ham Methodist Mission, remembered that James 'never hesitated to speak of the lack of interest shown by religious bodies in the welfare of young children in towns and cities. It made him impatient. He always had a way with young people and it was clear that his greatest gift lay in this direction.'[11]

William McGillycuddy Eagar, Vice President and founding member of the National Association of Boys' Clubs, wrote in 1953 that the young James Butterworth had held to the view that the church alone had a mission to secure social justice.[12] Among the many who expressed wholehearted praise for JB's work Eagar, who was a pillar of the mainstream youth club movement, is a somewhat reluctant admirer – he advocated a more reproducible blueprint for boys clubs than JB's inspirational but idiosyncratic achievement. His brief biographical account of James Butterworth is both superficial and inaccurate, but he did note correctly James' conviction that the churches were the obvious and appropriate providers of youthful community, able to supply boys with the opportunities and assistance of which James had himself been deprived. Frank Dawes, writing in 1975, pays tribute to the men of the late 19th and early 20th centuries, including James Butterworth, who offered a 'helping hand' to boys from the streets. After documenting his early life Dawes describes what James provided for his church club membership as 'the kind of place that he had so badly needed and missed in his own early adolescence, somewhere to go in the evenings for friendship, recreation, and education.'[13]

Now, at Beech Road, James gave his prodigious energy to the task of building a community resource for the youth of the locality within a reinvigorated chapel. He cleared the decks by burning all his sermons and 'after tremendous temptations, turned my back on preaching, for I now realised that truth must enter in at lowly doors.' The Circuit officials, together with James' superiors at Didsbury, and the Beech Inn population, all proved helpful and supportive. James himself reports the Mission's progress with some degree of wonder. 'So the Beech Road Clubland was commenced, with its clubs and camps and crowded congregation. We calmly announced that we would pull down the old gallery, add a new wing, and solicit the help of the folk of the pub next door. The Governor, T.H. Barratt, and the Principal, W.J. Moulton, gave the first subs. and became trustees of the organisation, and every Sunday, and during the week, teams of students went out on this pioneering work. The Circuit gave us a free hand; most of the trustees were dead, and we just romped along.'[14] James later characterised the approach – repeated in other circuits and parishes of the era – as launching an evangelism which utilised deserted and redundant churches in order to prevent the youth which would run the future world from being otherwise absorbed into secular enterprises.

James was evidently a charismatic leader, attracting support from patrons and parents, and loyalty from the new young membership. He raised funds, ran activities and societies, started a newsletter, took the boys to camp in Yorkshire, and himself played in their football team

BEECH ROAD WESLEYAN MISSION.

CHORLTON-CUM-HARDY.   MANCHESTER.

SUNDAYS.	WEEK-DAYS.
11 a.m. Primary.	Mondays, 3 to 4, Women's Bright Hour ,, 7 p.m. Boys' Club. Tuesday, 7 p.m. Girls' Club.
2-30 p.m. Sunday School.	Wednesday, 8-15 p.m. Adult Fellow- ship Class.
6 p.m. Children's Service.	Thursday, 8-15 p.m. Boys' and Girls' Fellowship Class.
7 p.m. Preaching Service.	Saturday, 7 p.m. Concert.

We give all non-church and non-chapel goers a hearty welcome.

We stand for Love, Loyalty and Brotherhood and make strangers feel at home in our midst.

Our Sunshine Band is pleased to call on any who are sick.

Our Monthly Magazine will be delivered to you if you so wish.

Rev. J. Butterworth will be pleased to visit any home in the district.

Beech Road, blueprint for Clubland

against other teams. The life of the Beech Road Mission burgeoned for congregations of all ages. In a Souvenir Booklet which James wrote to mark the full restoration of the business of the Chapel in March 1922 it is recorded that within the previous year 12 more Sunday School teachers were put in post, and 53 more scholars – 27 attended the Mission Boys Fellowship Class, and 26 were in the Girls. There was an increase of 130 within the preaching service. Services and Fellowship Meetings had been resumed in February 1921, and in January 1922 the first Communion Service was held at which 60 people were received into membership by Rev. W.R. Cox, Superintendent Minister of the Radnor Street Circuit. On 19 March 1922 Rev. Moulton preached in the Chapel, and Rev. Barratt was principal speaker at a public meeting held a day or so later, as part of a series of services to celebrate and give thanks for the revival.

Within twelve months of James' initial overtures to the Beech Inn regulars and the Didsbury Governor a range of activities was established, and James had become known as 'the busy bee of Beech Road.' The activities ranged from rambles and cycle tours, to women's 'bright hours' and a board games club – and a flyer was produced for the Beech Road Wesleyan Chapel Renovation and Alteration Fund; the first in a very long line of fund-raising exhortations which characterised his entire ministerial career. As ever and always James Butterworth displayed an almost miraculous ability to inspire and motivate worship and activity within the church – he and his Mission Band from Didsbury brought about a great spiritual revival and an exponential increase in attendance, arranging a preachers' list, and publishing a periodical. His good work did not go without notice. In October 1920 a Mr. C.H. Perkins wrote that 'There is no telling what great things may come about through the Rev. James Butterworth (late BEF) coming to supply at Chorlton and Beech Road.' The next year Harris Martin, Treasurer and Chapel Steward, also expressed great appreciation of the Beech Road initiative, writing in June 1921 that it was 'a great experience we are having, the like of which has not been recorded for many years in this Circuit'. The Circuit Superintendent Minister, Rev. W. R. Cox, frequently expressed praise for the work James was doing – on 26 October 1921, with the end of James' student career visible on the horizon, Cox wrote somewhat plaintively, praying that 'a mantle of love for Beech Road will fall on one of your fellow students before the separation comes.'

It was foreseeable that promotional publications would follow shortly on the heels of James' arrival at Beech Road. His endless dynamic energy spilled over into words at every conceivable opportunity, words to preach, to persuade, and to put into print. He was a prolific producer, publisher, and preserver of words, binding annual copies of monthly club publications for posterity. *The Beech Road Monthly Messenger* began an occasional appearance in 1920, continuing regularly throughout 1921, and on through 1922. The pen name of the editor of the periodical is 'B' – and a young Beech Road member later writes to James as 'B' so perhaps the initial was familiarly used for him at the Mission. The *Messenger* is full of reports of engagements, celebrations, talks, money-raising ideas, descriptions of visiting preachers and speakers, bands and music – and there are presentations of cups, medals and titles for sporting achievements. A Girls Club met weekly under a Mrs. Parkinson, and put on concerts to help the Mission. In June 1921 *Bees Wings and Ruby Queens* is advertised – along with commissioned advertisements for the

Prudential – with proceeds towards the Magazine Fund, and the Boys' Camp Fund. Issue No.3 in September 1921 reports a wet but cheery camp in July at Burton-in Lonsdale. James was President of the Boys Club, arranging sports activities and giving uplifting talks to the members, exhorting them to show the same interest in Jesus' campaign as in that of Manchester City or Manchester United. He also wrote a souvenir booklet of the history of Beech Road, offering it for sale at 1/3, proceeds to the Mission.

Like most dedicated writers of words James was also a keen reader. He had made a partial livelihood from running a book-lending scheme, whilst still working at Vine Mill and serving evenings in the 'back hole' of the local fish and chip shop. It is plain from what he wrote and reported in the trenches that he was already well-read in classical literature, and it is probable that by the time he had a practical involvement in boys' club activities he would have read at least some of the material already available concerning club organisation and activity. Some years previously Charles Russell and his wife, Lilian Rigby Russell, had published their manual entitled *Working Lads' Clubs* based on their knowledge and research into early Manchester clubs.[15] The Russells cover many aspects of club management including finance, discipline, activities and sports, camps, and religious involvement. James is likely to have known about these Manchester clubs, and been aware of the development of the club movement over previous decades. The Russells were clear in their book about the necessary qualities of the club leader: 'He needs firmness of character, common-sense, and optimism' and 'will be doing very good work indeed if he will simply become the personal friend of a few boys. There is no doubt that the greatest success rests with those clubs which have on their staff at least one man who can be present every night that the doors are open ... He will be the real leader and head.'

The Russells made lots of practical suggestions for financing and arranging annual camps, stating decisively that 'in all the larger clubs of the North, and to a rapidly increasing extent in the South, a week's holiday at the seaside or in the country, under canvas or at a farmhouse, is the most important event of the year. The prior anticipation and retrospective enjoyment of such an expedition was pronounced to be every bit as valuable as the holiday itself.' James would have been keenly aware of the place of camps in club ideology, although he abhorred any element of condescension in such a provision. The June 1914 issue of *The Christian Age*[16] features a cover photograph of General and Mrs.

Bramwell Booth, and an article which pictures children riding on a gate above the Booths' caption: 'You won't forget we want to send some poor slum children into the country this summer, will you?' Whilst the wish to provide countryside visits for all was laudable, this colouring of charity, unacceptable within current norms, was already anathema to James Butterworth, whose stance, a century ago, was fiercely egalitarian. His conviction was that the youngsters of Beech Road – and all under-resourced children such as he had been – should have access to such visits as of right.

Through his visits to Morecambe as a supply preacher James became friendly with the lads of the West End Methodist Chapel, accompanying them on expeditions to scenic Wharton Craggs and Heysham Rocks. He told them of his youth club at Beech Road, and they and their parents joined his team's efforts in setting up a camp for the Manchester boys at Burton-in-Lonsdale in August 1921. This camp was the first of JB's annual club camps, which continued from Walworth until the 1960s – the earliest few returning exclusively to Yorkshire, but afterwards establishing a tradition of a parallel annual visit to Guernsey for the London boys and girls. The Beech Road lads – and later their successors from Walworth – had 'bounty and hospitality' showered on them at Burton. Freedom, singing, hearty suppers, beautiful surroundings, walks, concerts, unfamiliar mountain vistas and adventure activities, caves and waterfalls – these were all new and exciting experiences. Their first-ever view of the sea on a coach trip to Morecambe and its fairground was a very popular highlight. Before the end of their stay the food money ran out – but an unknown benefactor replenished the camp cupboards with cheeses, bacon, and ham, whilst they were out on a trip. The boys of Beech Road returned to Chorlton full of tales for those who had stayed behind, and plans to organise the next year's adventure.

Through the whole of James Butterworth's long ministerial career in youth work runs the *leitmotif* of his drawing upon a seemingly bottomless fount of internal energy and determination to achieve endless ambitious church club projects. From the early days he paid for this periodically with occasional episodes of exhaustion, mental and physical, which would necessitate a period of withdrawal and recharge, and from which he would return with renewed dynamism. He made little of these indispositions, frequently describing them in the everyday terms of familiar ailments. All those who knew him and cared about him cautioned him in their various ways against his reckless expenditure of energy. The Governor, Reverend Barratt, abjured him that he should 'Abide within your limitations with God', telling James affectionately that it is not his programme that matters, nor Barratt's own, but God's; and sharing with him 'the tale of a man called Elijah, who thought the Almighty couldn't do without Him – and the Almighty told him there were 7000 other quite decent chaps, and said "Be still, you busy little creature and learn that I am God."'[17] More prosaically his old friend and mentor in Oswaldtwistle, John Holgate, wrote reporting a letter he had received from Superintendent Cox which 'speaks volumes for the effective work you have accomplished'. He added 'I am glad to hear that you are feeling better, but I do wish you would not be so profligate with your energies even in so holy a piece of work as Beech Road ... You are not a Hercules, just take care Jim.'[18] Even a self-described 'missionite' helper, writing to James after his move to London, tells him bluntly that he should slow down for the sake of those who care about him: 'At the rate you are now living I expect you will live to be five and thirty – maybe less as you are using your vitality up quicker than it is supplied.'[19]

It was not in JB's nature to take heed of these expressions of concern and change his behaviour accordingly – he continued his habitual overspend of energy throughout his life, and his health often paid the due price. It appears that around this time James and a few friends had their horoscopes read 'for a lark'. James's says that he is a natural leader, preferring to lead than to follow, and also headstrong and impulsive, ambitious, full of enterprise and new ideas – persistent, determined, quick-tempered, but slow to hold a grudge, and most of all a great lover of justice and freedom. A few mildly entertaining sentences, with no more weight than candyfloss – and yet one feels that the caster of the horoscope must have been talking to somebody who knew its subject.

Holmes Chapel

Among the Beech Road boys was a group who originally met near the local fish and chip shop, and regularly got together to kick a football around. James befriended these boys, introducing them to the Mission. In due course he was invited to join their football team and played many times in their strip of green jerseys and blue shorts, his love of the game compensating for his diminutive height. One of their fixtures was against a reformatory school team from Holmes Chapel. Later he saw the same lads in khaki at a Cheshire chapel service, where he was reluctantly keeping a preaching engagement, and through this made contact with the Home Office head of the school, Herbert Rees. James described him as an 'outstanding headmaster, who became a great friend.' Football matches between Beech Road and Holmes Chapel were soon a regular fixture. James revealed wryly that both sides would claim his services to begin with, tossing up to have him on their side, until one match when he played in goal and his team lost 15–0. After that, he said, each side would tell the other 'you can have him.' Rees' young daughter Peggy grew up to marry Gordon Lyle, the son of a family which befriended the young minister when he moved to London, and the pair became his lifelong friends, and Trustees and Governors of Clubland. But in 1920 all that lay far away in the future.

The Training School at Holmes Chapel had moved there from Sandbach, and housed the senior group of 125 boys aged 12–16, committed there by the courts, with the Juniors at nearby Bradwall. Its origins lay in an 1854 statute under which under-16s convicted of an offence could be sent to a penal facility for children. George Latham of Bradwall Hall sponsored and managed the first reformatory school on his land from 1855. On his death Cheshire County had refused his bequest of the school, so the estate was sold privately and the school leased to new management – Bradwall merging with the Holmes Chapel premises in 1918. The school eventually closed in 1932, becoming a New Approved School in 1933.

Herbert Rees was a disciplinarian – he once reprimanded James for being inattentive during the playing of the National Anthem – but an enlightened headmaster, who ensured that his boys had the best opportunities he could offer for their futures. When James knew the school it occupied 25 acres of land, with school rooms, dormitories, a quadrangle, offices, and three cells. There were extensive gardens, amid green fields, with a cottage separate from the school buildings operating as an infirmary. The boys were prepared for a life in agricultural work – either at home or in colonial service – with activities which included a milk round, shoemaking, carpentry, a cadet corps, and competitive events such as the cricket and football matches.

In 1922 James organised a Beech Road expedition to Holmes Chapel for the Whitsun celebrations. In a newsletter to the school community later that year Superintendent Rees, amid updates on available garden plots, and other improvements to the facilities, reports a red letter day on Whit Monday when over 80 visitors arrived from Manchester.

> The party came in charabancs in charge of Rev. J. Butterworth and other students from Didsbury College, and comprised members (young and

old) of the congregation of Beech Road Wesleyan Mission, Manchester. This Mission has become a live organisation, thanks to self-sacrificing efforts of Mr. Butterworth. We had cricket and football matches, and despite the "war cry" of Mr. B. and friends we came out on top in all events. Mr. B. is now in charge of a large chapel in London and is keeping up his interest in Holmes Chapel by assisting me with after-care work. He is always glad to help our boys.

The School went each year on a fortnight's camp at Blackpool, and in 1921 James and a contingent from the Beech Road Mission accompanied them. He described his experience of Holmes Chapel – and of that summer camp in particular – as having a profound effect upon what he felt called to address during his ministry. This was brought about through separate encounters with two of the boys – Arthur, and Patrick – who had each caused problems within the school during his time there. As he walked back from the fairground to the camp with Arthur one afternoon the boy began to open his heart concerning his feelings of worthlessness, and not belonging anywhere. Seeking for some way to reach and reassure him James threw a sixpence into a bush, telling Arthur that although the sixpenny piece was presently lost, it was still silver, and had the same worth as when minted. The pair returned to the camp, and Arthur left the school soon afterwards. He kept in touch, and years later, working and with a family, Arthur told JB that it was that conversation on the sandy path back to camp that had altered his conception of himself and what he could be, and given him the will to 'go straight'.

Unfortunately the other boy, Patrick, did not manage to make his way to a better life. By coincidence his home was in Camberwell – just a few streets from James' Walworth church – and he returned there when he left Holmes Chapel. But it was not a home which had ever provided him with love and security. James wrote retrospectively that 'whether lads land in prison or college is a very thin line, and very often it all depends on whom they chance to meet around the corner. Most lads get lost on the road to goodness and to God, because they fail to creep into anybody's heart. Most of us are lucky in having met those who believe in us.'[20] Patrick came to see JB in London and told him he felt driven to commit another crime so that he could get back to Cheshire and an outdoor life, to the fields and his friends, where he could work with animals and have clean sheets on his bed. He could not be dissuaded from his plan – but Patrick's crime ended in a prison sentence rather than a return to Cheshire, and James did not hear from him again. He was convinced by his acquaintance with the Holmes Chapel community that the 'healthy young sinners' to whom the church meant nothing, must be the membership he sought to reach, in preference to any 'hardened saints' already devoted to church attendance.

Moving on

As 1922 advanced it was necessary for James to make arrangements for his next circuit posting. He wanted very much to stay on at the Beech Road Mission, where his work was making such progress, and he was so valued by the congregation, club members, and church officials. But there was no resident ministry attached to Beech Road, and he therefore had to look further afield, to those circuits which were seeking additions.

Reverend Barratt, aware of James' talents, tried to influence him to join a comfortable circuit, such as that at Lytham on the Lancashire coast, where he could develop his gift for preaching. As ever, James resisted the easy option and elected instead to begin his ministry at Walworth, in a depressed and run-down area of South London. The virtually defunct church on Camberwell Road had a dwindling congregation, and James felt that his commitment would be equal to the demands of revitalising its worship and minimal attendance. Somewhere in his mind he was no doubt already envisaging – even though it remained undeclared and undiscussed – that there would be a full quota of undirected youth in the vicinity, and that he might be able to draw them into the society of the church and there provide them with the benefits of occupation and assistance. In discussion with the Circuit contingent from Walworth, Barratt exacted a condition that James should be given the same free hand at Walworth as he had proved so worthy of at Beech Road. Disappointingly the undertaking was not honoured, and James later regretted a decade spent in fighting to have his circuit colleagues adopt an approach which had taken only months to establish in Manchester. Instead 'My best years, and energy, and time, were just wasted in fighting church and circuit on very irrelevant issues.'

It was a sad moment at the end of the Summer term of 1922 when James left Didsbury and Chorlton for London. His congregation at Beech Road gave him a full set of Shakespeare's works, and Wesley's journal – and most of all made evident their deep regret at his departure. But he had made many friends at his college and at the mission, and these ties endured. Albert Stirzaker, his contemporary at Oswaldtwistle and Cliff, and fellow protégé of John Bennetts, left Didsbury at the same time for a ministry at Cleaton Moor, Cumberland. This was certainly not a final parting however, as James' sister Florrie and Albert's younger brother Cyril were to marry a year or so afterwards.

After he left many others continued to write to express their support for the Walworth venture and to thank him again for the contribution he had made. Sidney Richardson, a stalwart youthful follower, writes of his efforts to maintain the impetus at Beech Road. On 28 October 1922, Sidney is able to report that the boys are 'sticking to the Mission' with a healthy enrolment level for the current year – but by the following July he is regretting the absence of any camp organisation, as well as a drop in attendance. He feels sorry for Mr. Martin who works so hard to keep everything going – and also tells James that there have been no recent visitors from Didsbury College. As late as 8 October 1925 Harris Martin is writing to 'My Dear Jim' to report that he has started a Guild at Beech Road, and 40 have attended – there are better congregations than the previous year, but 'we have never found anyone with dynamic force enough to fill the post you vacated.' James went back several times to spend the weekend at Chorlton, to preach at the Mission, and to see his old friends there – but the local impetus of his brief visits to Beech Road soon faded, and the demands of his struggle at Walworth limited the number of his trips north. The pathos of his absence was expressed by another Missionite, in an undated letter sometime in 1923. H. Edwards writes 'Your old friends are true to you unto death in Chorlton, but you have been gone so long now that it is like looking through the wrong end of field glasses.'

James' 'Fathers in God', Wilfred Moulton, and Thomas Barratt, remained loyal supporters of his pioneering work. Following Moulton's untimely death at the end of 1924 his sister Carrie wrote thanking James for his recent tribute to her brother in the *Methodist Recorder*, saying: 'You and your work meant so much to him. He delighted to speak about you and what you are doing.' Thomas Barratt also continued to be a good friend, writing affectionately and supportively as James faced the ailing Walworth church. Advising him not to bump into any more lamp posts, or smoke more than a pound of tobacco in his pipe per week, Barratt wrote 'God bless you my dear boy, and give you of His Best – on your first Sunday and on all the days that follow', and a few weeks afterwards, 'God keep you always in the sunshine.'

Of course Moulton and Barratt, influential and supportive in James' life as they clearly were, were not the only fatherly friends who stood behind him as pillars of encouragement and stability, when his own father was lost to him. There had also been the good men of Green Haworth and Oswaldtwistle – Christopher Hindle, Jacob Crook, Matthew Maden – who promoted his early progress in Methodism, and above all his protective friend John Holgate, and his loyal mentor John Bennetts. After these Samuel Chadwick and William Moulton at Cliff College had also played a solid part in James' early development, as had Reverend Halstead in Cardiff during James' exile at Étaples. These were not simply kind and devout individuals who wanted to lend a helping hand to a young preacher making his way – as well as this there was always that quality in James Butterworth which drew forth a response of empathy.

James' conviction was inspirational: his eloquence and enthusiasm in pursuit of youth work within his church, and the unstinting energy and drive which he brought to his calling and cause, moved others towards him. His instinctive championship of the entitlement of young people to equality of opportunity and advancement predated by a generation the oxygen of egalitarianism with which Beveridge later infused the Welfare State. James wrote that 'The Labour Movement and much else besides owed much to the Methodist class meetings and the mutual improvement societies.' But James' personal mission had little to do with party politics. He had learned lessons about the strength of social community in a religious context – in the hen houses at Rough Hey, his home church at Green Haworth, the army tents of the Somme, the YMCA hut in Étaples, the revived Beech Road Mission in Chorlton, and the Holmes Chapel Reformatory School. It was a context in which he knew how to fight for and promote the interests of young people who had been dealt a poor hand by their early lives – and he had no doubt or hesitation in devoting his own life to this end.

Notes

1 Letter from Rev. Bennetts, 13 February, 1917.
2 Letter from Rev. Bennetts, 11 April, 1917.
3 Letter from Rev. Horn, 31 August, 1917.
4 Letter from Rev. Bennetts, 7 September, 1917.
5 *Bees Wings and Ruby Queens* (March 1918) and *Dug Out Digressions* (September 1918).
6 The Rev. W.F. Moulton of Cliff College was not related to the Rev. Wilfred J. Moulton, previously head of Headingley College in Leeds, most recently army chaplain in France, and soon to become James' beloved Principal at Didsbury – although the families knew each other through their church. William Moulton's father – also William Fiddian Moulton – was Headmaster at The Leys Methodist School in Cambridge, which he had founded, and was President of Conference in 1890.

7 Letter: William Moulton, 2 April, 1919.
8 Article in *Letters of a Clublander*, 1942.
9 Pre-war Tutor at Richmond Methodist College, and later to become Principal of Didsbury following Wilfred Moulton's death in 1924.
10 *Letters of a Clublander*, ch.39.
11 These were Rev Simpson's words on 'This is Your Life James Butterworth', November, 1955.
12 Eagar, W. McG: *Making Men: The History of Boys Clubs and Related Movements in Great Britain. University* of London Press 1953.
13 Dawes, F: *A Cry From the Streets: The Boys' Club Movement in Britain from the 1850s to the Present Day* Wayland Publishers (1975) Pt.2, S.1.
14 Article by James Butterworth: 'Didsbury and Clubland'.
15 Russell, Charles E.B. and Lilian M. Rigby Working Lads' Clubs. Macmillan, 1908, pp.70, 75.
16 Document lent by Green Haworth Methodist Chapel.
17 Undated letter from Rev. T.H. Barratt, 1921.
18 Undated letter from boyhood friend John Holgate, 1921.
19 Letter 18 January, 1923 from Beech Road associate, Dorothy Griffiths.
20 *Letters of a Clublander.*

CHAPTER FOUR

The Fight For Clubland

Walworth

Walworth, in South East London, sits at the apex of the northernmost wedge of land between two old Roman roads – the Old Kent Road, and Stane Street, from Chichester – coming up from the South coast and closing on London and each other. For hundreds of years simply a quiet rural village, its ancient ground has yielded the skeletons of prehistoric creatures, as well as stone-age flints and dwelling-places. Chaucer's mediaeval Pilgrims, setting out from the Tabard Inn on Borough High Street, would have reached their first watering stop on their ride to Canterbury at the boundary stream between Walworth and Camberwell on the Old Kent Road, where the Thomas-a-Beckett pub now stands – and travellers from the South may well have paused on the road to wet their dusty throats with the ale brewed from local barley.[1]

There has always been a religious presence in Walworth: there was a Saxon Church from Domesday onwards (1086), but a century earlier there had been a royal grant of the land to a court jester who later ceded the manor to Canterbury Cathedral – in whose ownership it remained until 1862, when it passed to the Church Commissioners. Walworth Methodist Church itself had been built for a prosperous constituency in 1813, during the year of Napoleon's retreat from Moscow, but during the following century the industrial revolution changed the environment from a green residential neighbourhood to a crowded inner city slum. The elegant Georgian terraces that flanked the Walworth Road remained, but deteriorated into multi-tenanted rentals, their overcrowded inhabitants living cheek-by-jowl with disease and poverty. Earlier in the nineteenth century leading Victorian art critic John Ruskin had been familiar with Walworth as a boy, giving his name to John Ruskin School – a hundred years later attended by many Clubland members, among them Maurice Micklewhite, now better known to millions as Michael Caine. Robert Browning's parents taught Sunday School at York Street Chapel, and William Booth, founder of the Salvation Army, had worshipped at Walworth Methodist Church whilst a young man employed at the local pawnbrokers' shop.

By the time of James Butterworth's arrival in 1922 the area had fallen into disrepair and neglect, despite the number of busy shops along Walworth Road, the commerce of East Street Market – famous throughout South London – and the teeming night life of the music halls, pubs, and theatres. An overdue programme of slum clearance and provision of new housing had been abandoned by the postwar Government, and the existing buildings left to decay.

The density of the population was something of a culture shock to the new young minister, who reported that 'the thickly populated district, and whirling traffic, and great seething masses of people, are so different from the long and quiet roads of Chorlton'.[2] Rev. Walter Hawkins, an earlier incumbent at Walworth Methodist Church and still associated with the local circuit, noted, in the 1913 preface to a history of Walworth, that it would be difficult to find a busier thoroughfare than the Walworth and Camberwell Roads in all of London: 'Within a radius of half a mile it is computed that there is a population of 85,000'.[3] For a further gloomy prospect it may be noted that the Duke of York, visiting Walworth a few years later, is quoted as describing the surroundings as 'miles of squalid, vulgar, ugly, shoddy stuff, without one scrap of beauty or brightness, one touch of imagination, one memory of history.'[4]

The scale of the social challenge had yet to be broadly acknowledged or addressed, but in 1896 the social researcher Charles Booth, in his book 'Life and Labour in London', had stated his view of the locality that in this 'most miserable slum in the capital' it was likely that a high proportion of the children would grow up to be liars and thieves. The saving grace of this dismal forecast was Booth's conviction that such antisocial bravado in truth masked a strong desire for love and approval. In his history of the boys' club movement Eagar writes, of the immediate surroundings awaiting James Butterworth in Walworth, that the old Wesleyan chapel itself was 'solid and grim ... a relic of Walworth's Victorian respectability'. It was surrounded by 'a muddle of mean streets, bestridden by railway arches and coal sidings, in which a miscellany of small factories, crammed into the former garden spaces and houses ... smoked, smelt, and were noisy. Children, adolescents and adults alike ignored the grimy

Walworth rooftops, 1922

Chapel, which ignored them.'[5] The well-heeled congregation had long since moved out to the leafy suburbs, a minority dutifully returning for the Sunday services.

The situation within Walworth Church itself was scarcely more encouraging from James' point of view. In an unpublished history of Clubland he later wrote: 'The diehards administered the church from afar, the caretaker was dictator, and the hands of successive ministers were tied. The district went down, the privileged moved out and the unprivileged moved in.'[6] The Chapel had become, in his words, 'very old and weary' by the 1920s – it was run down and ill-attended, and had barely survived the struggles of previous decades against being abandoned or sold off by the Methodist church.

Methodist Ministers are appointed to circuits rather than to individual churches; they are assisted in circuit business by lay church trustees and stewards, and together with these form the circuit leadership team, led by the Superintendent Minister. Within Methodism there are many lay ministers, who share the ministry of the circuit and tend to remain within it geographically, as well as the ordained ministers – the presbyters – who are required by the Wesleyan principle of itinerancy to 'travel' from one circuit to another every few years. In the overall Methodist 'Connexion' the circuit authority is governed – along with several other local circuits – by one District Synod,[7] and all fall under the direction of the annual Conference, with a different President of Conference being appointed anew each year. There is no further hierarchy in Methodism, which structure was conceived of as promoting an egalitarian outlook. It can be seen that in consequence of it the lay constituency of trustees and stewards, remaining always attached to one circuit, and indeed to one church within that circuit, would acquire not only a continuing established authority within that particular community, but would also develop an enduring commitment to it. In many ways they might feel the church belonged more to them than to the itinerant minister, arriving and leaving within a handful of years.

Walworth Methodist Church, with its minimal Sunday attendance, and scattering of weekly group and society meetings, was a poor relation in the wealthy Mostyn Road Circuit, which included Dulwich, Herne Hill, and Brixton. The Circuit, which met on a quarterly basis, had previously referred Walworth's difficulties to the District meeting, and in May 1908 a special London District Synod Committee was appointed to attend to Walworth's problems. There had been a lengthy discussion of its future viability, but eventually it was decided not to abandon the Chapel, although a fourth ordained circuit minister had to be sacrificed and from then on Walworth attracted only a probationer appointment. Three years afterwards the crisis blew up again, with Trustee William Vogel Goad fighting virtually alone for the lease to be secured and the church preserved. In 1912 the Synod Committee again reported sympathy with Walworth's requirements, but ultimately nothing was done to address deteriorating buildings and failing congregations because the Circuit could not afford it, even taking account of personal donations which were offered.

Butterworth was a young probationer – whatever his hopes and dreams he would have to temper his ambitions for Walworth Church in the face of any entrenched and authoritative resistance from its established keepers. There were rules and expectations, especially for a new and unqualified minister – essentially he was on trial, and he needed the Circuit's annual invitation to remain at Walworth. It says much for his personal charm and restraint, and the amount of effort and energy he brought to the promotion of church interests, that for each year of his ministry there the Circuit minuted its great appreciation of his work, and continuing 'cordial' invitation for him to stay on. This remained the case despite the perpetual restrictions, rooted in bureaucracy and bias, which were simultaneously being placed upon his efforts to open the church doors to the young, and broaden the facilities offered to them within.

The First Years: Six Boys in a Dug-Out

When James Butterworth arrived in Walworth as a probationer, in the Summer of 1922, no dedicated minister's accommodation was provided by the Church, and he moved instead into Miss Hannah Gay's spacious Georgian terraced house at 14 Knatchbull Road, Camberwell. Miss Gay, a committed Methodist, proved herself a staunch supporter over many years, opening her home for meetings of the various groups which James organised, and making him a gift of a bible which he kept with him throughout all the years of his ministry. This bible, in which he wrote his sermon notes through the twenties and thirties, was one of the precious objects rescued by Club members from the smouldering ruins of the Chapel in May 1941, following its bombing in the Blitz.

James began with a Friday night bible class for six boys meeting in his study – but within weeks more joined than Miss Gay's premises could easily hold, and the boys had to be moved to some bare cellars which he located in the church basement on Walworth Road, ever afterwards designated the 'dug-outs'. Reverend Hawkins lent his support from the start – already 65 when the new minister arrived Walter Hawkins had trained at Didsbury and been ordained in 1880. Although he had served in many circuits he had always had a particular affection for the Walworth church, having first administered sacrament there as a young minister in 1887, and he often preached in the church if James was absent. He promoted sport as being of crucial value in the young lives of Methodist members, and was for many years the President of the London Wesleyan Athletics Association.[8]

Ted Bowyer, 17 when James first arrived, was one of the 'dug-outs' founder members who laboured physically with him to set up the first club premises in the disused cellars, and became a loyal and effective assistant in Clubland activities and productions through the next decade. Later Ted married another Club member in the Clubland church, and James christened their son John there in 1932.

The boys helped Jimmy clear the new underground bible class premises, Miss Gay provided furnishings, and Walter Hawkins gave counsel, and in the few months before Christmas he transformed the old church cellars into a boys' club full of welcome and opportunity. He set up the *Walworth Monthly Messenger* – essentially on the same lines as the newsy and entertaining periodical he had previously circulated at Beech Road – and organised the boys into the teams for games, sport, and other activities, which thereafter became the club houses. Nor did he neglect their spiritual requirements, preaching to his young congregation from gripping stories based on bible passages of the love of God, and the duties of loyalty and service, later emblematic of Clubland's Christian message. Self-government was central to James' wish that the club and its members learn to determine their own decisions and actions, and to understand and acknowledge their responsibility in doing so. From the first months – the original six boys having quickly grown to eighty – he established a rudimentary Parliament of twelve boys who met with

The original basement club – JB's 'Dug-outs'

him on a weekly basis to discuss the affairs of the developing club, to help organise activities, and participate in writing and producing the *Walworth Messenger* each month.

There was never any doubting Jimmy Butterworth's affinity with boys' club work, or the magic which drew lads to his leadership, but he did not dismiss the needs of the adult congregations and associations, nor his obligations towards them, as is evidenced by the flurry of church events which filled the months following his arrival. The November 1922 edition of the *Walworth Messenger*, already enjoying a stated circulation of some hundreds, devotes columns of reports to the activities of numbers of remaining groups currently within the church society organisation – the Women's Meeting, Sunday School, Wolf Cubs, Band of Hope, Camberwell Scout Group, Choir Meetings, the Temperance and Social Welfare committee – as well as local news such as the new school opening at Herne Hill, and the 'great work' which is being done by the neighbouring Cambridge University Settlement. Reverend Butterworth asks for subscriptions to purchase Christmas dinners and toys for Walworth children – with a programme of lectures to raise awareness of the poverty of local families – and in the next edition the Messenger is able to report that Christmas dinners were provided for 260 needy children, and 450 festive parcels despatched.

The Messenger also states that 'Christmas morning 1922 saw the largest congregation in thirty years.' James did his best for the existing Church, but it is also true that he encouraged the more senior congregation, who visited Walworth's Sunday services, to feel free to attend Methodist churches in the green suburbs where they now lived. There must have been some perceived gulf between these conservative weekend churchgoers and the new probationer, with his diminutive stature and childlike appearance. In a tour diary written in America thirty years later he recalled someone in his first 1922 congregation saying: 'So they have sent us just a boy this time.' And it certainly became an ongoing and increasing bone of contention between him and the local Methodist church establishment that there was little emphasis on an older presence in his burgeoning congregation. Writing of James' early days at Walworth, Frank Dawes observed that: 'The new minister at Walworth soon made it obvious that he was more interested in helping boys in the mean streets around the chapel than in leading his respectable congregation in Sunday prayers.'[9]

Many ministers of that time, and friends of the young, might have empathised with the predicament of unprivileged youth, and sought to set up schemes for them, to better their lot and increase their range of available opportunity. Many did do so through more secular projects as well as church based groups and organisations. But James Butterworth was unique in his driving vision for the club within a church that he would create and build. A difficult journey lay ahead of him, but he had no doubts about the destination – he drew from within upon energy to galvanise the venture, upon his charisma to persuade others to contribute to his endeavours, and upon his personal calibre to see the struggle through.

In many cases the men who ran the early boys' clubs – and wrote about them – were themselves from backgrounds of wealth and privileged education, or distanced by other characteristics.[10] General Robert Baden-Powell, for example, formed the Scout movement in 1908, giving it a definitive militaristic flavour, which similarly influenced the development of the Boys' Brigade. But for James no imaginative leap was necessary to empathise with the plight of lost and needy boys because somewhere inside him he always carried the needy fatherless boy he had himself been – the one who grew up in poverty, could never wear a grammar school cap, and had to risk his health and life in grinding mill labour from childhood onwards. As an army private he had witnessed at close quarters the failure of army chaplains to close the distance between themselves and ordinary young soldiers – commenting on the reasons for this breakdown of communication in the small books he wrote whilst in France. He understood very well that the lads from the surrounding streets in Walworth would not be drawn into the church by wordy sermons – these would not rival the lure of the picture palaces, dance halls, and noisy pubs of South East London, or even the street corners on which they gathered. And he recognised that there was no place for pious condescension in offering these boys the advantages which he considered to be their right. He made a deliberate and conscious choice to forego the shining oratorical path he might have taken as a gifted preacher, instead preferring to establish bonds at a level more immediate and acceptable to the street lads. Reviewing his 1932 book *Clubland* Eagar wrote 'Butterworth has triumphantly mistaken himself for a boy' – and this is not so far from the truth.

Fortunately there is little place for uncertainty in mapping out James' plan for his club since he wrote often of his aims and intentions in doing so in his books 'Byways in Boyland' (1925), 'Adventures in Boyland' (1926), and 'Clubland' (1932) – as well as in numerous articles in Clubland publications and newspaper interviews. He started from the firm ideals

Old boys' football team

that there should be 'strong Church witness' in the districts served by Methodism, that provisions parallel to those offered by settlements and clubs run by the public schools and universities should be developed, that his organisation should be self-supporting, that its own members should be trained to be officers, and that although sponsorship would always be needed 'the church's own people, however poor, must support their church'.[11] Within the Club he envisaged that there would be access to many activities. Ultimately these grew to include carpentry, chess and board games, football, cycling clubs, athletics, rambling societies, film clubs, drama groups, boxing, music, arts and crafts, pottery, annual camping trips to the countryside or seaside, debating societies, and visits to talks and exhibitions. Many of the activities were taught with professional input, and pursued to a competitive standard, and Clubland became nursery to painters and politicians, actors and athletes, journalists and musicians. The Club would establish links with schools, colleges, and universities – there would be visits from public figures from all walks of life: politics, sports, the arts and the world of entertainment, as well as royal patrons. Through their years of belonging to a church club which provided access to many skill-based social pursuits, and encouraged responsibility and loyalty, he intended that the members would acquire a sound and broad education for living a good life. This was always to be a collaborative venture – the offer of a multitude of opportunities which members would pursue to the extent of their individual ability and inclination.

In *Byways* Butterworth offers some advice for other club leaders of 'heroic age' boys (12–15 years) that they should 'remember he is a boy' and not use the sort of religious language that might be suitable for 'our saintly grandfathers'. He also cautions that 'great grace' is required in the face of 'daily despair and disappointment', but the corollary is that being their 'boyhood's friend' will always be remembered. He reports that involving the boys in church tasks has helped unite the club as well as utilise members' efforts. 'Much of my church work is done by my boys – drawing, writing, typing, errands, schedules, magazine distributing, and quite a little army rolls up on Saturdays for odd jobs.' The boys' Parliament has been a 'wonderful help' – they read and prepare speeches, and are keen in debate, proving 'very zealous for order' when they have a sense of owning the organisation. Through those early months a base of loyalty was building – returning from a football match with a club team, and still wearing their strip, the team's diminutive extra player is accused by a bus conductor of fare-dodging, and thereupon defended 'mightily' with indignant declarations of 'That's our parson.' On another occasion a vicar told the away team that Clubland was a sect and not a proper church, and their minister not a proper parson, but the boys reported back that they 'showed 'em whether they were insects and laid 'em all out by half time.'

In the text of Byways James frequently apologises for seeming to assume wisdom – and it may be that advice from a probationer in his mid-twenties could strike some as presumptuous. Yet his account of the psychology of boys in early adolescence – by then based upon several years of club experience at Walworth and Beech Road, as well as his own relatively recent personal experience – all ring true. His understanding of what works with boys, his intuitions of what will win them over and what will alienate, and his ability to hit the right note on the degree of loving care necessary, are perceptive and persuasive. He also introduces several of the approaches he instinctively favours, which later become hallmarks of his club leadership: to involve the boys in the daily work of the organisation including its creative and written output, give them a voice and authority in its running, treat them like friends and be always there without forcing any 'religious' devotion; to redirect their interests by making available a range of activities, and to join in their projects including taking them away on annual camping trips. James cherished these boys and their club associations as shaping the future of their society, and of the church within it. He considered that if they were not brought into church life, and its promotion of body, mind, and spirit in this way, then they would be lost to their communities and to themselves.

His sponsor, and strong ally against the more reactionary forces on the Mostyn Road Circuit, Sir Ernest Lamb – later Lord Rochester, Postmaster General in Ramsay MacDonald's National Government – wrote in his foreword to Byways 'He is doing pioneer work, awaking thoughts and making sunlight ways through dark and difficult paths in his district. His is the enthusiasm of youth, which sees visions and sets its hand to the plough of high adventure. Certainly he is teaching a new song to many rough untutored lips. A new time has come, with new methods and more challenging ideas.'

The 'challenging ideas' remained, however, too challenging for some for the time being. Through the early twenties the traditional mainstream church activities continued at Walworth as before, albeit alongside a much extended youth presence. For some years it was necessary for James to attempt to soft-pedal club development, and to bear with many trying restrictions imposed by his Seniors on the Circuit. The Club prospered and grew whilst remaining still very much subordinate to church identity, running alongside several disparate, virtually autonomous, groups – the prayer circles, teachers' training classes for Sunday School, women's meeting groups, the Social Welfare Group, and fellowship and bible classes. James had established the weekly envelope system, and farthing box system, whereby families raised funds for the church from small change, and the boys and girls between them contributed a total of £5 weekly towards the upkeep of their club with their envelope contributions.

The girls club had started formally in 1925 under the aegis of Lady Dorothy Lamb, wife of Sir Ernest, but owed its rapid growth and place in Clubland's history to Laurie Lowe (later Hindmarsh). Laurie was a pillar of the Club from its earliest beginnings. She was barely 15 when JB came to Walworth in 1922. Writing to him fifty years later she says: 'I was truly one of the under-privileged … one of a large family in not too happy circumstances, and your concept of Clubland was an inspiration to me, as it was to many others. You opened up to thousands of boys and girls a vision of a different kind of life from that which we knew.' Of the great many members who repaid in kind what they gained from Clubland, few can have contributed to its richness and originality as much as Laurie. At a time when youth clubs predominantly meant boys' clubs, she not only pioneered a girls' section but helped to lay the foundations for a truly mixed membership. Not that JB needed to be persuaded of the need for like provision of girls' and boys' amenities. He had already introduced a girls' club at the Beech Road Mission in Manchester before ever coming to Clubland. With Laurie's irrepressible enthusiasm Clubland followed the same path. From the mid-1920s she was organising a full range of girls' activities, camps, chapel, and parliaments, and led a talented team of officers. She continued to serve the Club in various capacities throughout the war and well into the 1950's, by which time her son Peter was a member of the Junior Club, and went on into the Seniors.

At an early point links had been forged with the Methodist schools at Kingswood, Queenswood, the Leys, and Rydal, as well as the Methodist colleges of Richmond, Handsworth, Didsbury, and Cambridge – which gave their names to the four houses of Clubland – and James established regular exchange visits and talks from these august and established institutions.

The January 1923 *Messenger* sets the pattern for those that follow with a round-up of the various club activities, each written up by its leader. At this point the minister writes much of the periodical himself – with additional articles from Reverend Hawkins. The editorial comment often contains a moral message, but there are short whimsical stories for small children, and a humorous column on 'Office Boy's Reflections', as well as an occasional correspondence between 'Samuel Inksplash' and 'Bertie Bluebottle'. In the serious articles the language of the churchmen is sometimes flowery, in accordance with the style of the time, with expressions such as 'wretched squalor of public houses' and 'tragic sight of dishevelled parents', which might raise some eyebrows in a later politically correct era, yet probably accords with the expectations of the boy readers of the time. But there is plenty written in lighter tone, and there are writing and poetry competitions, alongside announcements of various awards and successes, and of major and minor forthcoming events – Reverend F.L. Wiseman, President elect of the Methodist Conference, is to visit for Walworth's 110th Anniversary Service, Mr. Edwin Conisbee has now retired as choirmaster and become a church steward – and there is always an exhortation to ensure the Messenger's distribution to everybody associated with the Club. The next month the editor – sometimes now signing himself 'JB' – reports that £1000 is needed for 'complete renovation' and the Church Trust is already £300 in debt from the previous year. In the Spring the Messenger announces that 50 boys are to go on camp to Burton-in-Lonsdale, Yorkshire, for ten days in August, and arrangements for this adventure, and anticipation of it, fill the month ahead of the trip. It was followed by the members' written accounts and reminiscences of their exploits the month afterwards: the tasks and jobs, the many mishaps, the thrill of riding on the Flying Scotsman, the hospitality of the villagers and their generosity in bringing eggs, cheese, milk, and hot pasties unbidden to the camp kitchen. In December the *Messenger* is written around the refurbishment of the Boys' Club underground premises, with 'A Garden Party in the Backyard' on Saturday 23 December, and a sale of donated articles on the fair stalls. James later reports his dismay at realising that enterprising members of the carpentry class are selling sections of old church doors to the trustees as household items – trouser presses and iron rests.

The next year continues in the same fashion with celebration of club achievements, calls for donations, and support for particular events. It is a great occasion when Reverend Wilfred Moulton of Didsbury visits in March 1924 to inaugurate the Walworth Boys' Club and address the membership, with 100 boys singing in the choir, and Reverend Hawkins declaring that his young friend had moved Walworth from its middle-aged congregation to a church for youth. There are away games and matches, and talks for the boys from local sportsmen, and as the year advances the Club focus moves once more to the Summer Camp at Burton. Alongside, in other items, Mr. S. Panther, Senior Steward, reports on the progress of the Temperance and Social Welfare Group, and Mr. William Vogel Goad, Trustee, warns that the chapel is worse for wear and there is a deficit balance in the account.

In between the Club events – reported enthusiastically, and reflecting energetic activity – all the humdrum meetings of the separate church groups are dutifully included and covered by the ministerial editor, and it may have seemed to an outsider reading through the pages, that during these years James was merely marking time with routine church activities. But that would be a mistaken impression – he was all the time building up the core of Clubland development, extending intake, activities, and connections, writing and lecturing, publishing, canvassing support, and watching the boys grow into a senior age group and become more able to take a responsible role in club governance. The *Messenger* was itself a potent tool in creating a self-perpetuating dynamic, binding the members to each other and to their Club. In printing a diary of events of the immediate past and future, in all of which either some part, or the whole, of Club membership had participated – and by including many reports by the boys themselves of activities in which they had taken part, as well as running competitions for member entry – the periodical established club identity and loyalty. It inculcated a growing member sense of ownership in the organisation. In the absence of unity between Club and Chapel these binding qualities, growing ever stronger, were an essential foundation for what was to come.

It would be incorrect to portray the Circuit, or the worthies of the Walworth chapel, as being opposed to the revitalisation of their church. They welcomed the increased profile which the energetic new minister was creating for Walworth in the community, and they were not hostile to a swelling congregation, or even to the introduction of increasing numbers of young people. They could identify no lack of spiritual advocacy in his delivery of the gospels, or in the consequences for church membership of his leadership. James administered Communion to boys joining the Church – he reports using 'the same Communion set which Professor Moulton used for the wounded and dying in France', and more than once records his pleasure in the numbers who responded to his preaching by committing themselves in this way. On 12 December 1926, after delivering a sermon on Simeon in which he had urged his congregation to identify the element missing from their Christian lives, James noted in his bible his amazement when 161 congregation members walked down the aisle towards him to declare themselves communicants. It does seem that his pulpit presentation was both more evangelical, and centred on biblical text, in the earlier days at Walworth – whereas his notes for later sermon content were based more upon general moral principles and behaviour. There is some reason to think that over time James became ambivalent in respect of the worth of the heightened emotional and directive approach taken by evangelism, preferring to bring young people into the church through more moderate and gradual routes. How far this reflected a personal withdrawal of commitment to its methodological principles, as opposed to the pragmatic adoption of a measured presentation which he believed to be more appealing to his youthful congregation, is moot – certainly he acknowledged some distaste for overblown performance.

In the revamped Messenger of January 1925 James reports a visit from Reverend Dunning and a group of Cliff College evangelists

– involving street processions lit by Chinese lanterns – and describes one of the sermons as 'evangeobabble'. And in a *South London Press* article – 'Church or Central Hall' – in 1925 the interviewer states: 'I gathered from Mr. Butterworth that he left College a red-hot gospeller and Mission man, but that his experience at Walworth had upset all his preconceptions and theories.' The article describes him as 'iconoclastic'. James was an affecting preacher, but his views on how boys were best approached and won over involved neither distanced religiosity nor the dramatic crescendo of sudden evangelical conversion. Instead he favoured the low key overtures of a welcoming friend. There had been a great burgeoning in boys' clubs and associations in the late nineteenth and early twentieth centuries, many with a secular base. The broadening of general education following the 1870 Education Act, the spread of the Settlement Movement led by Oxbridge and the public schools, intervening wars with their destruction of life and meaning, the rootlessness of industrial communities, widespread poverty, and the egalitarianism of new political systems had all weakened previous totemic beliefs. It may be that in order to win any following from youths who had no strong religious orientation or commitment, the worship within a youth club co-existent with a church needed to be tempered in the manner of its pursuit, even whilst remaining devout in its nature.

Jimmy Butterworth was all his life, and above all else, a master communicator, whether speaking or writing. At Walworth he was always in print, from Clubland stationery – cards, programmes, tickets, subscription forms and envelopes, all with the usual exhortations and appeals for funds – to periodic reviews, illustrated pamphlets, flyers and advertisements, constant generation of newspaper and periodical articles, special reports of the numerous club activities, camp literature and instructions. And, if insufficient printing ink was being utilised by all those, then he produced his own books and publications – proceeds, always, to Clubland. He was a networker on behalf of his clubs long before modern communication technology facilitated contact for the entire population. He travelled to lecture, and to spread the word of his Clubland church – making time to go home to preach at Oswaldtwistle, and return to visit the workers and members at the Beech Road Mission. At both places he always received a prodigal's welcome – in February 1923 the Mission periodical reported its welcome to 'our old friend and leader, the Reverend J. Butterworth, who preached to a packed hall, and whose visit has been the sole topic of conversation for weeks.'[12] And on a home visit to Lancashire a Green Haworth churchgoer anticipated that 'If little Jimmy Butterworth is preaching tonight we shall fill the chapel.'[13]

He was an equally prolific correspondent, as his vast archive of replies attests, and remained in frequent contact with his many friends and allies from earlier periods. John Holgate wrote often from Lancashire, as did his close friend from Oswaldtwistle, Alec Shaw Wildman – later famous as a fashion journalist and illustrator – and his old mentor Reverend John Bennetts. Arthur Sculthorpe, the young miscreant from Holmes Chapel, whom James had likened to a piece of silver waiting to be found, made his way to a sound life, and wrote frequently from his military postings in Europe, and then the East, announcing from China his success in his nursing exams, and his plans to return to marry his sweetheart in Liverpool. And JB's 'Fathers in God', Rev. William Moulton at Cliff, Rev. Thomas H. Barratt from Didsbury College, and the Didsbury Principal Rev. Wilfred J. Moulton, all wrote offering him their sympathetic encouragement. Upon the latter's sudden and unexpected death in December 1924 James wrote that 'I have lost my best friend and guide.'[14]

The *Messengers* continued to be full of the events he was so skilled in creating, but what does not appear in print is the niggling resistance, repeated minor setbacks, and reluctance to recognise any independence in membership activity, which were constantly placed in the way of Club progress. The new probationer had been faced with the enormous task of rescuing a dying chapel. James later wrote with some exasperation that 'Clubland was not an intrusion into a flourishing church, but an alternative to dereliction'.[15] James knew how to light the church up again – he had served a similar apprenticeship at Beech Road – but although the Walworth establishment applauded church revitalisation they had different ideas about what should be done to accomplish it. Reverend Barratt's negotiations at Didsbury that James should be given a free hand were not honoured, causing him later to regret the waste of his energy in disputes over trivia during his first decade at Walworth.

There was dissent in the Circuit, and at Walworth, around the extent to which youth work should be an intrinsic element in the work of the church. James had made the introduction of a young church membership significant from the beginning, and worked towards making it a more substantial proportion of the whole – and ultimately co-extensive with it. Many of the Walworth establishment could go with him part of the way, and applauded his early efforts, although his discouragement of the suburban Sunday worshippers caused some initial dismay and friction.

But – with what James described as 'complacent churchianity' – fewer of the circuit 'elders' would tolerate his increasing close focus upon young people at the expense of other groups, and James was daunted by their 'apparent preference for extinction over survival through youth clubs'. When he wanted to put in showers and changing facilities, to service the extended range of sports activities, there was unyielding resistance from the trustees and circuit officials. When he begged and borrowed sufficient funds to obtain boxing gloves, and other equipment necessary to club activities, these were physically confiscated and locked away by caretakers governed by circuit officialdom. His provision of a Club strip for the matches, gym kit for PE, and academic gowns for special church occasions, was not welcomed. There was great resistance both to any expansion of the clubs, and to any use of the *Clubland* title in church affairs, as well as a blank refusal to acknowledge the young people who attended the church clubs as having the status of members of the Walworth Chapel. Most of all there was a prolonged battle over the extension of James' ministry there.

At the end of his first Walworth year James was 'cordially invited' to remain at Walworth for a further year, and each year this same invitation was extended by the Circuit meeting, and appreciation of his work recorded. But the minutes do not record the arguments and submissions from James' allies on the church and Circuit committees which had needed to take place previously in order to secure the invitation. The District Synod of 16 September 1925 – attended by Reverend J. Holland Ritson, MA, DD, that year's President of Conference, as well as by the prominent Methodist Theologian Reverend Scott Lidgett, known for his youth initiatives – recorded that 'The Synod gladly recognised the splendid work done by Mr. Butterworth at Walworth'. Walter Hawkins, beloved by the Club boys as their 'Bishop', argued repeatedly on James' behalf against the three-year-rule, with the fervent support of Sir Ernest Lamb, both submitting that the circumstances were exceptional.

James reported that: 'There were three powerful forces against Clubland's unpopular schemes, namely – the chapel trustees who wanted no change, the Circuit which wanted its survival on their lines only, and the Connexional authorities who desired so strategic a site for a central hall.'[16] The opinions of lay church officials, permanently resident in the district and used to influencing the activities of their church, carried conservative weight and potency against the schemes of a young and enthusiastic probationary minister, who would shortly be moving on to another circuit. The Clubs were finally permitted – albeit with restrictions – although the club leader was already aware that a probationer would not be able to do anything of real importance in the couple of years of his tenancy, and that 'if any impact was to be made on the district at all, it meant living in it a lifetime, and dying there.'

The Stormy Petrel of Methodism

Leonard Barnett, writing about James Butterworth in his book *The Church Youth Club*, says that Butterworth's epic work took shape 'in days when the churches, for the most part, had scarcely begun to develop a sensitive conscience on the score of the vast masses of boys and girls quite outside the range of their organizations and activities.' This church insensitivity meant that 'for years he spoke bluntly to his own church, neither giving quarter nor desiring it. Like most men of his calibre, he had to stand a great deal of misunderstanding and acrimony, and was for a long time the stormy petrel of Methodist youth work', whose 'unconquerable determination' was an inspiration to many who came after.[17]

Despite the constant barriers to club progress from the local Methodist bureaucracy, and the pressure to re-direct his ministry along traditional lines, James continued to pour all his efforts into drawing the undirected youth of Walworth into his church, to join the clubs and activity groups he was developing for them there. At Beech Road he had begun to exercise a consummate skill in fundraising – acquiring equipment and furnishings, and securing rebuilding of a substantial part of the old premises. Before that he had watched his family and church mentors at Green Haworth raising support for their chapel throughout his formative years. Once he had caught his breath in the London air he lost no time in seeking support and funds for his church and the club he was building within it. His efforts to attract contributions from within the church were repaid with modest returns from members in the voluntary envelopes he supplied, but he also travelled frequently to lecture and address other congregations and audiences, with the plate or collection going to Walworth. The life of his ministry developed some regularity. Each summer boys – and later girls also – went to camp. Church anniversaries and festivals were celebrated, and the parliamentary system developed. *The Messenger* took on youthful writers, plays and reviews were produced, and the membership increased. The Walworth church clubs were full of event and activity, and the local press and *Methodist Recorder* took note in their columns that there was an exciting new venture for the young in South London, giving it a welcome profile. But a crisis was coming, and not merely from the growing antipathy between the probationary minister and the old guard among his church officials. The church buildings had remained dilapidated for decades, and rebuilding was now desperately needed – but the Church Trust was in deficit and it seemed that what could be secured was barely a drop in the ocean of what was needed to prevent abandonment of the building.

Because James Butterworth's life from end to end was so closely bound and enmeshed with Methodism and Clubland, it is barely possible to make any meaningful separation between on the one hand his friends, and on the other allies of his cause within Methodism, some of whom had the wherewithal to sponsor and further his club endeavours. Once in London he made firm and lasting friendships and alliances with those of like mind within the Circuit and District, as well as mutually supportive contact with individuals in other Methodist organisations, such as the Methodist schools and colleges. He found a warm friend in Basil Henriques, Oxford graduate and war hero of Cambrai, who set up a progressive Jewish youth organisation – the Oxford and St. George's Jewish Lads Club – in neighbouring Bermondsey, the two of them not infrequently attending each other's clubs as visiting speakers. Another loyal comrade and ally was Reverend John (Jack) Leale, of St. Sampson's, Guernsey, also a Didsbury man, who wrote to James as to a kindred spirit having read his 1925 book *Byways in Boyland*. Jack Leale's St. Sampson's Boys' Club hosted the Walworth Club members at annual camps on Guernsey from 1926 onwards for many years, until the outbreak of World War Two. Leale later became a Jurat of the island, as well as President of the Controlling Committee during the years of the German occupation, from December 1940 to August 1945. A lifetime later his good friend Jimmy Butterworth presented the funeral address following Jurat Leale's death in 1969.

Of course there were also deep comradeships formed at the Club. Besides 'Bishop' Walter Hawkins, and the devoted Miss Gay, there was Reg Turtle, an accountant who volunteered to help in 1922, and remained Treasurer and a loyal friend for the rest of his long life. Ted Bowyer was an early member and helper, playing Caractacus in one of the first dramatic productions, and remaining within the Club until the war years. At the start of the thirties Alec Reed, a publishing and media expert, joined the club enterprise as a committed helper, and when Gordon Lyle – the son of friends who had provided welcome hospitality in James' early days – qualified in dentistry, he offered his dental services free of charge to the Club members. Eventually these three – Reg Turtle, Alec Reed, and Gordon Lyle – formed a core of committed governors, making a practical contribution to club life, supporting the club and its leader through thick and thin, and meeting at the club premises every Wednesday evening to discuss Clubland finances and projects. Beyond these stalwarts over the years there also grew a small army of voluntary helpers to organise, supervise, coach, serve in the canteen, accompany trips and outings, make theatre costumes, and accomplish a vast range of other tasks and duties. But in the first few years of James' ministry Walworth Church was a much lonelier and more isolating place for him than it thereafter became.

From the tone of his dealings with his boys, his colleagues, his friends and allies, and from written correspondence, it becomes clear that James inspired warm affection and personal loyalty, which went far beyond simple respect and admiration. He reached out in love and friendship to the young members of his congregation, as he sought to promote both their spiritual welfare and physical well-being. An observer of a sermon he delivered during a Guernsey camp in 1926 wrote 'Their Minister holds them with cords of love. His simple yet profound, quiet and yet emphatic style, was so striking that even children forgot to fidget as he preached.' But he was no pushover; Clubland grew from his uncompromising drive – nothing less would have attained the desired end – and his personality and leadership were not compatible with a laisser-faire attitude. He was exacting in respect of permissible conduct within the Club, and his key principles of behaviour – such as 'partners not passengers', and 'pride in premises' – were firmly applied.

Len Neal and his brother Frank joined the boys' club in the mid-twenties, when Len was thirteen, and both became leading club members during the twenties and thirties. Len – later knighted for his services to trade unionism – recalled the strict moral attitudes which prevailed within the club, as well as its spotless cleanliness. He remembered the Head as a great man whom he would follow anywhere – but confirmed that he had been uncompromising about 'getting rid of the church people from any influence in the club'. Len Neal wrote in December 2000, aged 87, that Clubland and Jimmy Butterworth deserved a prominent place in London history for what had been done for the youth of Walworth. The goal James had set for himself was demanding, but all at Walworth, and on the Circuit, were impressed by his initiative and achievement, even those who recognised with dismay that his ambitions for the Church were proving to be in stark contrast with their own.

Most crucial in view of the pressing circumstances, were the early allies James found within the church, friends of Methodism with local church influence who were also sympathetic towards his work at Walworth – Sir Ernest Lamb was foremost among these champions, but there were important others such as George Shrubshall, J.P., Mr. Edmund S. Lamplough, Mr Joseph Rank, and his son J. Arthur Rank, who were also substantial benefactors of Methodism.[18] In James' first decade at Walworth it was crucial that he secured support from individuals whose views carried weight with the trustees and stewards, and at the Circuit and District meetings – and found benefactors who were themselves able to offer financial assistance or had influence with potential sponsors. The difficulties seemed insurmountable, with the 'diehards' continuing to resist all club progress – there were neither any funds available for rebuilding, nor any willingness to redesign in the way James wanted even if the finance could be found.

Words of encouragement came from supporters: Wilfred Moulton wrote with a cheque representing collected contributions from Didsbury on 3 November 1924, commiserating with him over the hard task that he faced; George Prior, lay Circuit member, wrote on 14 November after a meeting, 'I am heart and soul with you in the fight you are being compelled to make', assuring James that despite a few opponents who found petty faults there were large numbers who, like himself, could see the great work he was doing; Sir Ernest Lamb assured James on 12 December the same year that he should not 'worry about the "passage of arms" at a Walworth Committee meeting between the Chairman of the District and myself. It doesn't worry me one iota'; and Walter Hawkins advised tactically on 23 May 1925 that 'to win over the man in question you have to play him, not use frontal attack'.

More than once, in the atmosphere of low-key but continuous resistance from his church elders, James considered the possibility of resigning, of leaving what seemed like a hopeless impasse. But Reverend Hawkins counselled patience and persistence, and in the end he knew he could never abandon the movement he had started, or the boys and girls at its centre. He wrote later that his lifelong devotion to Clubland had narrowed his entire focus: 'This of course has meant turning aside from all the things I wished to do. It has been impossible to do anything or go anywhere without wondering how my club members could share in everything. I take no credit for this – it just happens to be that way – an inability to do anything else except put Clubland first, whatever it may mean to myself.' Of those first club members, whose corner he was fighting, he wrote: 'The general idea seemed to be that the first crowd of lads would stand by me and I by them through thick and thin, until we had built a college for youth in Walworth.'[19]

James had also met, and struck an affinity with, a man whose professional expertise was to be of enormous importance in the history of Clubland. He had considered various plans and designs for rebuilding at Walworth, should sufficient money – a seeming impossibility – become available, but despite battles with denominational committees whose architects had very different ideas, he could find nothing which satisfied the images he had cherished for years. Eventually Maurice Webb, President of the Architectural Association, suggested Edward Maufe, a Yorkshireman and great-nephew of Titus Salt, the founder of Saltaire. Maufe had attended school in Ilkley, but his family had moved south, and Edward had graduated from Oxford in 1908 before studying design at the Architectural Association School of Architecture. He had served in Salonika during the War – leaving his wife Prudence, a designer and interior decorator, in charge of their baby son. In 1922 he had designed the church of St. Bede's, Clapham, followed by St. Saviour's in Acton in 1924 – and attracted notice by winning a silver medal at the Paris Exhibition in 1925. Later, in 1932, Maufe won a competition to design Guildford Cathedral, with his hallmark building features of tall lines and austere simplicity of style, productive of an atmosphere of worship. Edward Maufe and James Butterworth discovered in each other a meeting of minds in respect of a new church design for Walworth, and Maufe was sympathetic to James' ideas. But the costing of the building – an estimate of £25,000 even with Maufe's best attempts to make the price attainable – seemed beyond anything that James might reasonably hope to approach, however many farthing boxes, member envelopes, lectures, and special appeals he organised.

This was a daunting period, with discouraging church committee meetings, when feelings ran high and it seemed as though resolution and lasting accord would be difficult to achieve. Jack Leale wrote from Guernsey agreeing that 'anyone who wants to shift things [in Methodism] finds themselves confronted with "a dull obstinacy"';[20] and several people close to James – Lady Dorothy Lamb, Walter Hawkins, Arthur Sculthorpe, John Holgate – frequently expressed their concerns that his health was suffering from overwork, and the endless pressure to raise substantial funds.

It was almost unimaginable that any miraculous transformation of the situation would occur, but at the end of 1926 there was a sea change in events, a succession of upheavals of such dimension that the upshot was nothing short of a metamorphosis. The first small advance had been a Circuit missive from Circuit official Henry Shrinkfield, dated 6 October 1924, informing James that he has 'sincere pleasure in conveying the wish of the Invitation Committee that you will remain in the Circuit as long as possible, that is up to your Ordination.' The writer also expresses his appreciation for the 'splendid work and your influence for good in the Circuit' and says that it is 'a personal joy to have your friendship.' Early in 1926, his Ordination year, there was an encouraging letter from Rev. John Ritson – President of Conference that year, and also a native of Lancashire – saying that a speech James had given at Blackheath 'warmed us to you' and that 'after all we want the same things. Lancashire forever!' A few months afterwards Ritson wrote a foreword for James' forthcoming book – the second in two years – declaring that 'this young minister is a master-builder.'[21]

James was duly presented as a candidate for ordination by the Rev. W. Hodson Smith as part of that year's York Conference, on 27 July. It was a big event in the life of any Probationer, and in church terms, the culmination of a lifetime's ambitions, but James had his eye on another impossible peak. After the ceremony Treasurer Reg Turtle wrote his congratulations and vowed his help with the 'great dream', asking: 'Do you really think you can raise £20,000?' He said the idea made him gasp, even though everyone would give their support.[22] The next month Frank Renton, Circuit trustee, wrote from hospital to say that he has read *Adventures in Boyland* – then newly published and intended to swell the church fund – from cover to cover, and that he and his wife wish to help as club officers one evening a week, and to donate £50 to club expenses.[23] Renton does, however, caution the minister, perhaps a little too late, against his comment that the working of boys' clubs is hindered by lay circuit officials, as such words will cause hostilities, 'and surely you have enough of these to satisfy the most pugnacious Lancastrian.' The year wore on with James upbeat in terms of club and church events, but privately greatly worried over Walworth's future.

And then, in the middle of the Christmas preparations, the ground shifted. On 10 December Sir Ernest Lamb amazed and overwhelmed James – who reported that he could only fall to his knees in silent thankful prayer – by announcing that he had compiled a list of sponsors who were willing to contribute sufficient funds to cover all but £5,000 of the money required for rebuilding. Sir Ernest wrote it out for James, on his monogrammed notepaper, in his drawing room, as follows:-

Walworth Wesleyan Methodist Church, 10. XII.26: New building scheme, on plans to be approved by the London Mission & Extension Fund Committee and to include demolishing the present Chapel and basement club rooms, and replacing same by a new Chapel with ancillary premises; together with the provision of requisite accommodation for the Clubland work associated with the name of Walworth and the Rev. J. Butterworth's ministry there; estimated total cost £28,000. In addition to a possible contribution of £250 from the Wesleyan Methodist Trust Association ltd., the following definite promises have been made *conditionally* upon five thousand pounds of the balance required for the above scheme being raised, in grants or subscription, before the 31st May.

Arthur Rank	500
Lord Marshall	1000
Sir Chas. Wakefield	1000
F.R. Ferens	1000
Geo. Shrubsall	2000
Sundry others	5106
Ernest Lamb	5000
Joseph Rank	5000
	————
	£ 20.856
	————

Instructions were written for the Shrubsall, Sundry others, and Ernest Lamb amounts 'to be grouped together and entered as a number of anonymous donors "in memoriam". Joseph Rank's donation to be labelled "A friend of Missionaries".'

These magnificent donations clearly anticipated that James Butterworth would remain in post. Rev. Hawkins, who had known what was afoot, wrote on a note, 'Jimmy Beloved, Verily your tides have turned. Congrats no end. Have you succeeded in exacting a Methodist undertaking that you can stay in the Walworth job always?'

At the Circuit meeting of 20 September 1926, chaired by the Circuit Superintendent Rev. Arthur Walters, Reverend Butterworth had been invited to remain for a sixth year. The minutes record: 'The Superintendent referred to the unique success which had attended the Rev. J. Butterworth's ministry at Walworth, and said that he was peculiarly fitted for that work and it was undoubtedly in the interest of Walworth that Mr. Butterworth should continue for a 6th year'.

At the next quarterly Circuit meeting at Barry Road on 20 December there were 53 persons present, and the meeting was attended as usual by the stewards and trustees of Walworth Church – these typically included Rev. Hawkins, Miss Gay, Mr. W. Vogel Goad (Steward), Mr. S.H. Panther (Senior Steward), Mr. F. Renton (Trustee) and Mr. Edward Conisbee (Steward) – as well as the ministers and officials of other churches of the Mostyn Road Circuit. The church and Circuit officials praised God for his beneficence, and gave their thanks to Sir Ernest and the other benefactors, and a nod of appreciation to the Walworth minister. The tone of the discussion seemed to be that the right course had been taken – the possibility of Reverend Butterworth's indefinitely extended ministry at Walworth was not directly addressed, but must have constituted a sizeable elephant in the room as plans for the church's future were considered. The minutes record:

> The chairman (Rev. Walters) made a short statement with regard to the future of Walworth and said that the question had for some time past been a source of considerable anxiety to those responsible, and explained how in a most unexpected way the rebuilding of Walworth had become a glorious possibility. Reference was made to the wonderful consecration service conducted by the Rev. J. Butterworth on the Sunday evening of the announcement of the possibilities of rebuilding.'

The Meeting passed a resolution that:

> This quarterly meeting hears with great gratitude to God of the generous gift made towards the rebuilding of the Walworth Church, and adaptation of the premises at the back of the Church for boys and girls club work. It prays for the guidance of God on the deliberations of the Trustees and Joint Committee of the Synod, Circuit, and London Mission Committee.

The Chairman also informed the meeting that, through Sir Ernest's generosity, there was to be a Lay Assistant at Walworth, at no cost to the Circuit, with the appointment being left in the hands of the Superintendent and Mr. Butterworth. A resolution was accordingly passed – its wording is of much significance:

> This quarterly meeting hears with great thankfulness of the promise of Sir Ernest Lamb to provide for lay assistance at Walworth. It notes it is for a period of at least five years provided that the Rev. J. Butterworth continues his ministry at Walworth.

James Butterworth had gained in confidence and authority in consequence of these undertakings for the future of the Walworth youth clubs. He was no longer the untried probationer with big dreams who had arrived at Walworth in 1922, but an ordained minister, five years in post – he was at home on his territory, and knew his allies, and most of all he had the sure loyalty of his members. He saw his way forward. He set about raising the balance which the sponsors required by the end of the following May, and made preparations for a transformed future.

Master Builder

During the years of the great struggle, and throughout the rubble and dust of demolition in 1928, the enforced Club occupation of make-do temporary accommodation elsewhere in the church buildings, and the excitement of the influx of designers and builders, there had nevertheless been no pause in the intensity of internal Club activity. The Club leader's boundless energy and drive ensured that disruption and changing surroundings remained extraneous to the central life of Clubland. The *Walworth Messengers* of earlier in the decade had given way to the *Clubland Reviews*, brimming with descriptions of engagements, talks, money-raising ideas, visiting preachers and speakers, bands, music, celebratory events, dedications and special services, presentation of cups and medals, awards of titles, parliamentary reports, sports matches and

competitions – and, always, comments from their Head, sometimes serious in tone, sometimes pithy and witty, instructing or comforting, always seeking to involve and encourage the Club members. A stone-laying service takes place, attended by many luminaries of the Circuit, with all the activity clubs and sections represented by their captains, the young people in their formal academic Club gowns for the occasion; Reg Turtle reports for the Boys' Club noting a third successful annual camp at Burton-in-Lonsdale; there are urgent bulletins detailing the state of the 'opening fund'; current affairs columns contain news from Queenswood and The Leys Schools, with plans for future visits and meetings; and there are exhortations to attend forthcoming fund-raising events such as the Daffodil Bazaar. With his particular talent their Editor and Leader is able to present each item and topic in a way which shows forth the value he places upon it, and creates that value for others. Clarity and efficiency define his approach to organised and structured Club events – the activities are appealing, schedules are reliable, the provision of supervision and coaching is reassuring – everything put before the members is sound and solid.

The main Club Review had even spawned a junior edition – *The Young Adventurer* – edited in the late twenties by L. Butcher, aged 15, who showed considerable talent and enterprise in putting the periodical together. This *Junior Review* also reports matters of particular interest to the young readers – such as amounts of money raised by particular Junior projects – and publishes articles by Club luminaries. In 1928 Editor Butcher secures a correspondence with Edward Maufe, architect of the New Clubland Church, as well as providing a page of 'Boys' Camp Instructions', and he confides the members' plan to present Reverend Butterworth with an engraved plate which is to be fixed to his desk. He produces a clear and informative evaluation of the house system, now in its second year – in 'What the House System means to Walworth' Butcher writes that it provides 'inestimable help in Club administration. Each House has its chairman or captain, and these possess complete control over their Houses, and are at liberty to arrange inter-house tournaments and events, subject, of course, to the approval of the Section Captain or Chairman and of the officers.'

The Clubland Head's pride in his new chapel, and its elegant grace, would soon give the lie to the Duke of York's earlier view that Walworth was 'without one touch of beauty.' There were many reports in the local – and national – press, the Times declaring that the architect had 'risen to it with originality, sympathy and refinement' giving it a 'slightly

Swedish flavour' with its 'warm lavender-grey bricks and Portland Stone dressings.' The building was to have a garden court beside the church, with planted trees, and the club premises housed below the chapel. The architect had provided for integral accommodation for the minister, and Miss Gay generously relinquished her maid Ethel Evans, who moved with James as his housekeeper, and remained with him in that role for many years – in fact for the rest of her life.

James Butterworth's written output had always been prolific, but increasingly, through the twenties and his struggle to create and build Clubland, he found himself the subject of articles as well as their author. Stories about his work at Walworth appeared regularly in the local *Accrington Observer* – which recorded all the achievements in the life of this increasingly famous native son of Lancashire – and also in the *Methodist Recorder*, the latter frequently printing their correspondent John Holgate's loyal accounts of James' progress. In addition Clubland accounted for many column inches in various other newspapers, most

Last days of the old Walworth Chapel

constantly the *South London Press* – Reverend Butterworth himself was well aware of the advantage of putting his views in print, and provided copy willingly and often. In an interview with the *Daily Telegraph* in 1928, with £28,000 raised and banked for the building project, James explained: 'Our idea is that religion must not be cheapened because it is planted in a poor district ...'. When demolition of the old church was imminent the *South London Press* reported in 'Tears and Smiles in a Church' that 'On Sunday night the church was crowded and people were standing outside when Rev. J. Butterworth preached his last sermon.'

The last service in the old Chapel was the Sunday of August Bank Holiday 1928, and the Clublanders took flowers from the Communion table to lay at the Cenotaph in Whitehall. In 1929 *Pearsons Weekly* described the new chapel as the 'World's Most Wonderful Church' – and on 6 February 1930 the *Methodist Recorder* reports a Clubland Church meeting where the Leader was 'presented with a gold wristlet watch which the rank and file of the church had subscribed to as a token of their affection for him and the splendid work he did in opening Clubland Church last year.' It was beyond doubt that there had all along been much interest and respect for the energy and vision James had demonstrated at Walworth – if not always unmitigated approval in Methodist circles.

As the beautiful Clubland Church went up, the Club itself grew busier, reaching a crescendo of planning and anticipation through the summer of 1929. The Clubland Review of 1930 reports in detail the events of the previous Autumn, describing the church buildings and Club rooms. The Opening Ceremony on Tuesday 1 October was conducted by the Lord Mayor of London, Sir Kynaston Studd, accompanied by the Lady Mayoress and the Sheriffs of the City. Many of Clubland's benefactors were present – Edmund Lamplough, and George Shrubsall, with Sir Ernest Lamb presiding, and the President of the 1929 Methodist Conference, the Reverend Dr. William F. Lofthouse, M.A., performing the Dedicatory Service. The President of the Primitive Methodist Conference, and President of the United Methodist Conference, the Right Reverend Lord Bishop of Southwark, and his Worship the Mayor of Southwark also spoke.

In a church context it was a star-studded occasion, and nor was it the last – the entire month of October was full of celebratory events and services of thanks and dedication. There was a Queenswood Night, a Kingswood Night, a Girls' Night, and a Boys' Night, besides the special service for the first Sunday after the opening, and a congratulatory visit from the Bowes Park Wesleyan Choir, which had supported the

Edward Maufe's Chapel: the First Clubland Church

The interior, looking towards the gallery, and showing the open timber roof, of tie-beam pattern, which is painted blue and green, with gold stars and other decorations. The floor is raked, and the gallery, which projects a fourth into the interior, is stepped. The pews are of natural oak and wax polished.

Nave and balcony

Starred ceiling
and altar

New club
room below
the church
with Cabinet
benches

Small games
room –
snooker and
table tennis

Clubland movement from the beginning. On the last night of the month Mr. & Mrs. Vogel Goad provided a big Clubland family gathering with tea. Clubland still needed £1,200 and a new organ to open without debt, and James reported that 'the Minister had not a penny up his sleeve and not more than 6d in his pocket'. There was a great ovation for the Club's loyal patrons – Edward Maufe presented the gold keys of the Boys' Club Rooms to Mr. Shrubsall, and Prudence Maufe gave the gold Girls' Club keys to Mrs. Shrubsall. The Shrubsalls, Mr. Lamplough, and Sir Ernest had each quietly made extra funds available as the overall building bill crept up from £28,000 to £34,000. The Service Sheet for the service of 31 October, 1929 contains a final appeal slip detailing the cost of the entire scheme – which George Shrubsall endorsed, writing on it: 'We want you to have a clean start, so my wife and I will be responsible for the clearing of the debt, excluding the organ, after getting all the premises in order.' In the end even the organ was gifted, with substantial assistance from Edmund Lamplough and Reverend Wiseman, and James' mantra of being 'free from debt' was realised, at least for the time being.

Within days of the grand opening James' health broke down, forcing his absence from Clubland for two months. It was an ever-recurring theme – his outpouring of impossible sustained levels of energy and effort followed by mental and physical exhaustion and collapse. He did his best to downplay the seriousness of these episodes, disguising them with anodyne descriptions which fooled nobody. Those around him were witness to the inevitable cost to his constitution of the reckless spending of inner resources, and were constantly concerned for him, cautioning him against excess. There had been a period of exhaustion at Beech Road when a colleague observed 'I fear you overdo things' and through the turbulent twenties at Walworth friends had written warning him to slow down – John Holgate was constantly anxious, telling him to ease up, and had advised him not to extend his Walworth ministry beyond ordination because 'I don't think you would stand the strain without a break'; and his friend Alec had written 'Don't work too hard Jim'. Lady Lamb sent her condolences during an earlier bout of ill health, and George Shrubsall had expressed misgivings more than once, writing 'I'm sorry you are getting overdone again' and later 'I'm afraid your zeal will overrun your strength, you cannot carry all Walworth on your shoulders.' During James' campaign to raise finances to rebuild, Jack Leale wrote from Guernsey that he was enclosing a cheque 'even though you don't deserve it as you're not visiting us, and I expect most of it will have to be spent getting people to do your work when you break down through having no rest ... this pig-headedness is associated with Lancashire rather than Heaven.'

The breakdown of health after the opening was a serious one requiring months of convalescence rather than weeks. Walter Hawkins, who James described as being like a father to him through the years at Walworth, wrote reassuringly during his absence: 'I got your witty schedule, but read into it a rotten time. You will regain good health and command', and a couple of weeks later 'Beloved Jacobus, off to stay with my daughter in Colchester for Christmas – when I wake at night I say God bless Jimmie as I turn over.' In December Prudence Maufe wrote that 'we were all praying for your speedy return to health and Clubland last night – it was like Hamlet without the Prince.' Even the *Methodist Recorder* commiserated with him for this bout of illness, alerting others who wrote to wish him a speedy recovery.

The years of his taxing crusade for Clubland, together with James' unremitting focus on the progress and well-being of the Club, had taken a heavy toll – and there was another dimension of uncertainty and disappointment that James had had to endure. He had had several romantic encounters through the years – he had been sweethearts with the young daughter of a Methodist minister in Oswaldtwistle, who left with her family for America in 1912, and correspondence suggests a likely affair of the heart during his time billeted with a local family in Étaples during the War, as well as a passing involvement in his early twenties. Then, in Guernsey for the first time at the 1926 Club Camp, he met Brenda Bird, a relation by marriage of Jack Leale, and was smitten. Matters progressed; an engagement was announced in the *Young Adventurer* (its staff triumphant because they had met Miss Bird first before the Minister had arrived at Camp), and in Oswaldtwistle John Holgate – a jeweller in his everyday professional life – prepared a display of gemstones and ring styles for Brenda to choose her engagement ring. In October 1927 she visited Walworth for the first time, and it seemed that there would be a marriage at the Club in the Autumn of 1928. Two of James' younger siblings had married in the course of the decade – Florrie in 1923 to Albert Stirzaker's younger brother Cyril, and, unexpectedly, his brother Billie had fallen in love with and married John Holgate's sister Emma Lena, who was ten years Billie's senior – so it was maybe time for the older brother to settle down as well.

Sadly the wedding was not to be – perhaps Miss Bird got cold feet when she realised the extent to which married life would be dominated by Clubland – and for whatever reason the romance faltered and was finally called off early in 1928. James was undoubtedly wounded by the affair – coming as it did during the critical years for Clubland's future, when he would have to hold fast to his focus and nerve to make the crucial decisions which would affect so many lives – although his reaction was perhaps more akin to disappointment than heartbreak. He had shared his plans with colleagues, friends, and club members, and received congratulations from all his acquaintance – and hence needed to make all aware of the reversal. Reg Turtle wrote in March 1928 that he 'cannot yet believe your startling news – surely consolation will come', and Walter Hawkins, comforting as ever, wrote the next month: 'My Dear Jacobus, Better a monk than a fettered swain … friends are there to mourn with you.' They did mourn with him – but for the time being Clubland affairs demanded everyone's full attention, and there were to be many years and another war before James found the happy ending in his personal life.

Going it alone 1930

The bound annual edition of the *Clubland Review* for 1927 begins with 'The Great Adventure' – an historical account in several short chapters of the old church and the start of Clubland, from the pen of J. Butterworth, Editor, describing the recent crossroads and the opportunity which has been offered. Through the first half of 1927 fund-raising work to raise the balance for the necessary rebuilding and refurbishment occupies minister, members, colleagues and friends of Walworth, and many fund-raising projects are detailed in the club periodicals, as well as extra gifts from sponsors to help the new church on its way. £5,000 was still a massive sum, but James' resourcefulness was equal to the challenge, giving lectures, writing articles, organising fund-raising ventures, and penning a flurry of letters to supporters over the next few months. These drew forth many pledges of assistance, such as Harris Martin's response from Beech Road – 'of which thou art the Bishop for life'– stating the Mission's willingness to contribute to the rebuilding fund. The Clubland Church would not be allowed to fail at this point for want of support. At the next quarterly Circuit meeting on 21 March 1927, in the week of the minister's birthday, a further unanimous invitation to remain in the Circuit for the next year was extended, and in September, when the meeting was held at Walworth, he was invited to stay for a seventh year 'in view of the special work he is doing there in the development of the Clubs for Boys and Girls, and the success that has attended it, his exceptional gifts for that work, and also in consequence of the scheme now in hand for rebuilding the premises.'

In between these two meetings James called a special meeting of his own which was of profound and far-reaching effect. The Club Enrolment and Dedication Service was held on Monday 30 May, 1927 – the day before the outcome of the rebuilding fund was to be declared. The tone of the meeting was solemn – it was to consider the significance of the new movement coming into being. This was the inaugural meeting of Clubland, and the Minister directed that it should be held privately within the Church for Club members only, stating in advance that only those who answered to their names at the service would be enrolled as members of Clubland. In his letter announcing the importance of this meeting to the 250 current members James stated that : 'It is a most responsible membership, as our whole Church is watching and waiting to see if our Loyalty and Service is real ... We are meeting before the Last Anniversary Meeting in our old Church to inaugurate Clubland officially and revise our membership. We want those who cannot keep our Loyalties to resign.'

It was a request for an 'all or nothing' undertaking to the Club, and an upgrading of membership status of which he wished all to be aware. As part of the proceedings the Officers answered the oath of allegiance and received their books of office and record – JB also professed his allegiance to Clubland and made a promise to remain as its leader for the next ten years. The four College Presidents, who were attending for the purpose, formally named the Club houses Richmond, Didsbury, Handsworth, and Cambridge, and all members – first the Juniors, and in a later separate service, the Seniors, came one by one to the Communion rail to make their vows of loyalty and service to Clubland and receive their house badges. James later wrote of how deeply he was moved at witnessing how each Senior – moving on from Junior years in the Club – came to take the Sacrament from Reverend Moulton's wartime Communion Plate, and at the peace within the church, and the quiet of his young members as they left at the end of the service.

Each member's declaration of commitment to Clubland represented a meaningful personal undertaking – but alongside this demonstration of devout spirit, JB also wished to clarify and redefine the practical and administrative terms within which the Clubland Church would operate. He wished – as he put it in a *Clubland Review* early in 1928 – to 'put our house in order' specifying that: 'With the new Clubland Church, Clubland's Policy must be unrestricted. The demolition of the

Old Church must mean a complete departure from the old ruts. We must close the book on the five years of misunderstandings and hindrances to Clubland's Policy. Clubland has presented an alternative to dereliction. We cannot be tied down again to methods, organisations and machinery as out of date in a Down Town Church as a hand loom in a weaving shed.'

He demanded that Walworth must centralise its finance into one unified Church Fund, rather than its previous many disparate financial compartments, and it must also unify its efforts. With a 'strong body of Clubland enthusiasts added to the Trustees' Meeting' the interests of Church and Club were to operate as one. Clubland was to consist of two clubs, girls and boys, each with two sections, Junior and Senior, and each section divided into the four Methodist College houses. Each club, section, and house was to have its own staff council and committee – the enrolment books were to constitute 'a complete clerical system' in their organisation, detail, and formality. In the new regime there was to be no casual membership, and members were asked henceforth to belong wholeheartedly to the club which belonged so wholeheartedly to them.

It was little short of a coup. The new First Clubland Church, which would rise from the ashes of the old Walworth Wesleyan Chapel, would be a unified organisation led by James Butterworth, and its senior members were henceforth to have a presence and a voice on any committee which influenced its finances and future activities. James had carried the day for Clubland's authority – but some who had begun by wishing the Walworth Boys' Club well, even working within it, found that the wave of its advance left them behind. James sought the specific withdrawal of club officers representative of church headquarters, explaining that the Club must henceforth become self-managing. And others who had been his colleagues and supporters from the beginning – such as Circuit Steward Edward Conisbee, one time leader of the Walworth Church Choir – left the project. Conisbee wrote that, even though he welcomed a new church and increased youth activity, 'You have never been in any doubt as to my views on the proposed scheme for Walworth ... I cannot consistently throw in my lot with those who enthusiastically support the scheme.' Conisbee assured James that he had no feeling of bitterness and valued their old friendship. Later he wrote again from Abergavenny that he is still saddened by the 'parting of the ways' at Walworth, but wants to come and see the new building in the future. [24]

Later in the year the Circuit Finance Committee increased James' stipend by £20 per annum, with another £20 increase specified for September 1928. It was acknowledged that inevitable changes in

Walworth's ministerial staff should be anticipated, and resolved that the Circuit Superintendent should confer with the District Chairman, as well as the Home Mission and London Mission as to future Walworth arrangements. At that point officials were chiefly concerned with whether, and at which chapel, another probationer might be installed, but there was clearly an atmosphere of uncertainty around the subterranean movement in the Circuit, and a growing awareness that a paradigm was shifting. 1928 was to be the year of demolition and rebuilding, but there was further turbulence in store beyond that of bricks and mortar.

The District Synod had noted: 'The great progress made with the Walworth Scheme for a Club and Church' and had instituted a special committee to consider Walworth church affairs, whose members included Mostyn Road Circuit ministers and stewards such as Sir Ernest Lamb, Mr. Vogel Goad, Mr. E.S. Lamplough, Reverend Walter Hawkins, Mr. George Shrubsall, and Mr. J. Arthur Rank. All were influential in both the Mostyn Road Circuit, and the District – that year George Shrubsall and Arthur Rank were to be among the lay representatives going from the District to the annual Conference – and there is little doubt that behind the scenes there was growing contemplation of an independent, or at least autonomous, future for Clubland.

At a Quarterly Meeting of the Circuit on Monday 19 March 1928 the exhibited plans for the New Clubland Church were approved and James' invitation was extended for a further year. It was resolved that the Trustees of the new buildings should undertake the provision of a house for the Walworth Minister, now a fully ordained man – but although an increase was voted to the Minister's stipend, as well as an additional amount to be paid in rent to Miss Gay, a year passed with nothing done to obtain a house. The reasons for the inaction became evident when Chairman Walters reminded the Circuit in the Spring of 1929 that the new church building was to be opened on October 1st that year, and also referred to the possibility of Walworth being separated from the Circuit at the Annual Conference of 1930. In mid-1929 this could only be a possibility since such a great matter certainly required a vote. The Quarterly Meeting of Monday 16 December 1929 was held in the newly-opened Clubland Church – the Chairman declared the Circuit's pleasure and satisfaction in meeting on the new premises, but also its great regret that Reverend Butterworth was prevented from attending by illness. 'They resolved to send Reverend Butterworth a message of love and sympathy, and also congratulations on the wonderful consummation of the great Clubland Church scheme.' At the next Quarterly

Circuit Meeting at Barry Road on Monday 17 March 1930 Chairman Arthur Walters reported that there had been 'a request from the Trustees and Leaders meetings of the Walworth Clubland Church that it should be separated from the Circuit next Conference'. It could not escape notice that these meetings were the very ones where the strong voice which James had secured for his Clubland members at the Enrolment and Dedication Service in May 1927 was finally heard and acknowledged. Reverend Walters accordingly supervised a vote by the 73 members present – which included the Walworth Minister and his assistant Reverend J.R. Penistan. A majority of 58 in favour and 12 against – with 7 remaining neutral – confirmed that Walworth should become a 'single station' outside the Circuit. Fittingly, it was Reverend James Butterworth's thirty-third birthday.

Two months later the District Synod recommended that 'in view of the nature of the work at Walworth it be separated from the Mostyn Road Circuit, and become part of the London Mission.'[25] In June the Circuit said goodbye to Reverend Walters – James' comrade in his project for the previous five years – who told the meeting that its recommendation for Walworth's separation had now gone through the necessary Committees and needed only to be sanctioned by Conference. The 187th Methodist Conference, of July 1930, was held at Rylands – there are several names familiar from London District Three on the attendee list, and many members of the prestigious yearly gathering were well known to each other. No doubt Mr. Lamplough, Mr. Rank, Sir Ernest Lamb and others were all extremely attentive to the Conference Direction at para.3 of Section V: Alterations, Divisions, or Amalgamations of Circuits, which states : 'That Walworth (Clubland Church) be separated from the London (Mostyn Road) Circuit and become a separate station under the London Mission as London Mission (Walworth) with one minister.'

At a later point in the Conference Minutes for 1930, Standing Order 68, dealing with 'Extended Appointments' states that these must be checked more carefully after three years, and that circuit stewards must give notice of impending extended invitations and their justifying reasons after the Spring meeting for consideration the following September. Of course this is merely an incidental footnote, and unconnected to his history at Walworth, although there may be some irony in the fact that James Butterworth was currently half way through his tenth invited year.

There were, of course, no further invitations. James was not present for the next Mostyn Road Quarterly Circuit Meeting of 15 September 1930, nor ever again – he had his own Circuit business to attend to. The Meeting resolved to send a letter of congratulation to Sir Ernest – now Lord Rochester – who had just been appointed Paymaster General. It was also resolved to 'send fraternal greetings to the new Walworth Circuit Quarterly Meeting from this, the first Quarterly Meeting since the separation.' Walter Hawkins gave James a copy of a letter he had received from a reverend friend William Butcher, who had spoken at Clubland's Easter Service, which declared with admiration: 'It is a wonderful bit of work – indeed it is the most plucky thing in Methodism. So daring a plan, so successful an issue.'

Notes

1 *The Story of Walworth* Mary Boast Pub Council of the London Borough of Southwark, 2005, 1976, 1993).

2 Butterworth, J. *Walworth Monthly Messenger,* vol. no.1. November 1922.

3 Ibid.

4 *Clubland Review* 1928.

5 Eagar, W: *Making Men: The History of Boys Clubs and Related Movements in Great Britain. University* of London Press. (1953) p.376.

6 *Letters of a Clublander* Part 7 Section 31.

7 In the UK there are 375 circuits and 31 districts.

8 In 1940 he returned to live with his daughter in his native Peterborough, and was described by the *Methodist Recorder* in November 1949 as dying there 'in triumph' on 22.11.1949 aged 92.

9 Dawes, Frank: *A Cry From the Streets: The Boys' Club Movement in Britain from the 1850s to the Present Day.* Wayland Publishers 1975, p.136.

10 Tom Pelham, son of the Earl of Chichester, wrote a *Handbook to Youths' Institutes and Working Boys' Clubs* in 1889.

11 *Clubland Review,* 1927. Chapter 3: 'The Great Adventure'.

12 *Beech Road Messenger,* 1923; anon.

13 Mr Dodgson, 30 April, 1975.

14 Comment in Cuttings Book Catalogue Archive ref. 79.

15 *Letters of a Clublander,* Ch.31.

16 Ibid Ch.33.

17 Barnett, Leonard P. *The Church Youth Club.* The Epworth Press (1951) Chapter 4.

18 The Joseph Rank Benevolent Trust continued to sponsor Clubland into the sixties, making possible its development as a unified island site with hostel accommodation

19 *Letters of a Clublander,* Ch.40.

20 Letter from Jack Leale: 28 July, 1926 Ref. 142.06.

21 Rev. John Ritson. Letters ref. 132 01 and 148.06.

22 Letter from Reg Turtle 28 July,1926, Ref. 147.16.

23 Letter from Frank Renton 15 August,1926, Ref. 147.14.

24 Letters from E. Conisbee: 10 December, 1926 ref 144.18; 13 May,1927, Ref. 148.15

25 District Synod Minutes, 13 May, 1930 Section 33, Division of Circuits].

CHAPTER FIVE

The Glory Years

The Temple of Youth

The Clubland Church had been built in under a year, and officially opened in October 1929. JB's pride in the new buildings is manifest in his glowing descriptions:

> The tall tinted windows so delicately prepared ... The great height suggests spaciousness so necessary for the uplifting of those in overcrowded areas ... Clubland, our Girls' and Boys' Clubs – our 'Public School', our training centre, runs the whole length of the ground floor underneath the Church ... the rooms are in silver grey and cream with the Club colours, red and green, as border lines.

Edward Maufe had created far more than a church: the floor below contained numerous other rooms and offices – the Ministers and Stewards' vestries, women's and men's assembly rooms, a gymnasium and lecture hall, modern kitchens, storerooms, and cloakrooms, a senior boys lounge and workshop, a large games room, and a council room for Captains and Chairmen with lockers and drawers for those in office. The Girls' Club was a virtual replica of the Boys' Club, but approached from the other end of the Clubland corridor. There was also accommodation for the Head, a church garden, and a roof playground – the latter accessible up 'a most wonderful stairway with dome lighting'. But even with all these wonders it was only the beginning. Another decade of fund-raising and building was to take place before Queen Mary's grand opening of the completed Clubland premises in May 1939.

Throughout this decade JB's continuing battle to raise sufficient finances to enable his architect to go on building was a constant backcloth to the thriving life of the club. In his book *The Needs of Youth* A.E. Morgan singled James Butterworth out as being one of only a few club leaders to realise that 'a properly equipped building, a light and beautiful environment, and furniture and pictures to satisfy the eye' were essential to the design of a youth club.[1] Morgan praised the Clubland leader for his unwavering insistence that such surroundings were no less necessary for those who lived in South London slums than they were for university students. Not everybody shared this view – Jimmy himself related that as the buildings went up he would find epithets such as 'the Communist hide-out' and 'Butterworth's folly' daubed onto the walls. This did nothing to dent his determination, or hinder Clubland's expansion and popularity. At the beginning of the thirties the membership lists had to be briefly paused when the flood of new members into the newly-independent organisation overwhelmed its current capacity, but the growing club premises soon caught up, and within ten years membership increased from a few hundred at the beginning of the decade to nearer 1000 before its end.

Word of the facilities and activities offered to members at Walworth Clubland Church spread throughout the neighbourhood, drawing queues of young people through its doors. Newspapers publicised the pioneering youth work taking place there, and in 1933 Clubland's public profile took a leap when Sir Ernest Lamb – from 1931 Baron Rochester, and Paymaster-General in Ramsay MacDonald's National Government – gave a speech in the House of Lords in which he advocated spending Government money on building clubs for young people, and told their Lordships the story of the First Clubland Church in glowing terms.

> Its purpose is to minister more adequately to those in the surrounding over-crowded district. This Clubland, the exact address of which is 54 Camberwell Road, is a home of friendship for boys and girls previously outside any Church. With ideals of all-round fitness it trains members to realise the best in life. In clubs open every night it provides for the development of mind, body and spirit, with emphasis on the spirit because the spiritual completes the whole. The entire premises have cost £34,000, every penny of which has been raised by voluntary contribution, and now the young people themselves, some 500 in number, ranging in ages from ten to twenty-five years, are contributing no less than £1000 a year in weekly sums and varied efforts for upkeep. It is open every night, and I invite your Lordships to see the place for yourselves, for, as an example of what can be done by voluntary effort, it will well repay a visit. [2]

The Head set store by the view that the external design of Clubland should reflect the value he placed upon the entitlement of its members to equality and opportunity. The corollary to this was his insistence that those within should show respect for their surroundings. 'Pride in Premises' was a principle soon applied as assiduously by the Clubland Parliament as by the club leader. He saw the rooms of the club as models for the future homes of the members and wrote that 'they must never suggest the chaos of jumble sales or filthy back kitchens.' He also insisted upon due contribution to club upkeep – 'Partners not Passengers' – stating bluntly that 'the club does not exist to subsidise poverty.' He understood well that the young membership would most truly own a Club which they could feel they had made, rather than merely been given: just as he understood that self-government in the Club – in itself a valuable exercise in taking responsibility – would produce greater commitment to decisions concerning Club affairs. JB was always present at the meetings of the Parliament, although he rarely did more than hold a 'watching brief' unless requested. And whilst he was unapologetic in his expectation of silver for the collection plate, it was also true that unrestricted assistance was quietly provided to those in need of it. It was to be 'a Home of Friendship, not club only, not church only, but both as one, and something more than either.'[3]

The First Clubland Church was ambitious in its aim of equipping members with an entirely new attitude to life, and at its heart was the role of the Clublanders themselves in running Club affairs. When the King visited he was received by a Cabinet of boys rather than the usual committee of Governors. The range of Clubland activities was fourfold: recreational, educational, social, and spiritual – although JB commented that he found distinctions such as these 'somewhat invidious', since there were no hard and fast exclusions and boundaries between the categories. He did not consider traditional church patterns and groups to warrant an exclusive position simply because they had always been given one. For instance he took the view that 'Sunday school bores people and does not form part of Club life – Club chapel every night is of greater value than an hour on Sunday.' The latter position was one that he modified after the second world war by giving greater emphasis to the Sunday evening fellowship. Unafraid to state his view clearly JB told the *Methodist Recorder* a few years later that Sunday schools had no future, declaring that 'If Robert Raikes were alive today there is not a Sunday school in the land where he would be welcome'; and shortly afterwards the *New*

Chronicle of Christian Education reported this as an 'Amazing Attack on the Sunday School'.

He was determined that the spiritual dimension of Clubland life should not be distanced from members' physical and social pursuits, and should be indivisible from ordinary pastimes – it was not something separate and beyond those activities but intrinsic to the fellowship within them. The girls' and boys' private chapels at Clubland were constructed to lead directly off the games rooms – which JB put forward 'as a silent witness that religion is not something separate or remote, not something added or dragged in, but central to Club and related to life.'[4] He held one service in the Chapel on Sundays – but every night of the week the Club was open to its members, providing access to music, art, handicrafts, drama, games and sport, with voluntary helpers supervising Club activity, often at a professional level. Clifford Bastin and Reg Stockill, both of Arsenal Football Club – Bastin also played for England – were regularly in attendance to provide the boys with football training, and Bastin was made Sports President at the end of 1931. As soon as he was medically qualified Gordon Lyle became Clubland's honorary dental surgeon, equipping a dental surgery at no cost to the Club.

Honourable Members

The developed Clubland parliamentary process was an object lesson in creating a frame of activity which involves and stimulates the participants, promotes the development of responsibility and loyalty, and binds and unifies the entire membership. It was the most engaging and compelling of club structures, and in the illustrated Club handbook JB described the Parliament's duties and functions in sufficient detail to demonstrate both its appeal, and its usefulness as an instrument of Club government.

> The Cabinet consists of 20 Chairmen, age 15 to 18, who are in charge of 'houses' or departments and work with their respective officer. Each chairman is received into office at the annual meeting and receives a log book in which he keeps records of events, criticisms, and suggestions relating to his duties. The log book report is read at monthly Cabinets and weekly Parliaments. The Parliament assembles for one hour each week with all club members attending. The Head Boy is the Prime Minister, the Parliament Chairman is Mr. Speaker. Chairmen of Houses, and Chairmen of Dramatics, Sports, Gym, Athletics, Games, Handicrafts, Library, Art, Medical, and Chapel, complete the Cabinet.

Boys in office ... face the whole Club each week with "Honourable Members of the House, herewith my weekly report." The private members may also ask questions. In the hour the leader is able to pick up everything that is going on without needing many meetings and notices – the members also all find out what has been happening in Club. No fixtures clash, no activity becomes a loose limb independent of the whole, all work from the centre as a team.'[5]

JB adds that the chairmanships are held for one year, and the names of all who have held office are inscribed on the Honours Board in the main games room.

The Junior Captains, aged 13–14, also have a responsible role in charge of a Junior House or Department, and must write up a Log Book report each week. The Head Junior – the section captain – is senior to all the other captains, and appoints them to take church collections. House captains deal with membership and all house affairs, whilst Department captains have distinctive duties particular to their departmental activities – the Chapel Captain appoints captains in turn to read the lessons in the Club Chapel, whilst the Handicraft Captain deals with workshop affairs, the rota of classes, the care of materials etc. Once monthly on Cabinet night the supervising Club Officers meet the Captains (Juniors) at 7 p.m., the Chairmen (Seniors) at 8 p.m., and each other at 9 p.m., to confirm all the Senior and Junior business.

Girls' Parliament

Boys' Parliament

Senior Parliament

In his book *Clubland*, JB related a few of the more novel suggestions made to Parliament from time to time: a chapel captain advocates a slower bell rhythm so that boys 'stroll, not rush like hell into chapel', and a music captain asks for greater discipline as 'It's time something was done with them what uses the piano as if it was a tin can.' The Speaker may reprimand Honourable Members on the use of inappropriate language – 'blinkin', or 'shut your trap' – or call them to order for other offensive remarks, but all members are able to question the Cabinet on any Club matter, or state their case in respect of it. Club business is deliberated in order, and private members bills are discussed and voted on at the end of the sitting. Sometimes distinguished guests are invited to address the House on sports, music, art, etc., but JB emphasises that there are no other activities on Parliament nights as the general assembly of all Clubland members is given precedence over everything else.

James' friend and fellow pioneer Basil Henriques wrote a comparable book entitled *Club Leadership* the next year,[6] in much the same spirit of championing those who had little. Henriques had high praise for *Clubland* – describing it as 'far and away the best book that has been written on boys' clubs' – and drew attention to the Clubland parliamentary system in particular, writing in his own book that 'probably in no club is it so highly developed as in that one.'

Parliament was certainly the supportive backbone of Clubland structure – but there were many other limbs of activity and enterprise. JB always sought to avoid 'churchianity', and any form of religious expression – such as overt evangelism – which would prove too intrusive upon the trust of the boys he sought to draw close, but that did not mean that he neglected matters of the spirit. Instead he sought to bring an intrinsic spiritual dimension to Clubland life which did not require distance or formality. The *Methodist Recorder* called it a 'daring experiment in modern evangelical work' merging the religious with the secular interests of the members.[7]

If Parliament was Clubland's backbone then the Sunday Service, Clubland's Angelus, lay at its heart. Each Club – junior and senior, boys' and girls' – had its own Chapel, and there were separate short services after club activities each night, with the whole membership uniting for worship on Sunday evenings. All members were involved in the Clubland Service, and although it was usually the Head who gave the Sermon on Sundays – occasionally old club members took their turn at the lectern – there were gowned senior boys and girls reading the lessons, whilst the Juniors sang the anthems and took the collections. The form of the Service itself was the result of discussions and deliberations in Parliament, and JB wrote that although the atmosphere was 'quiet and reverent', with members kneeling upon entering, and whilst praying, it was never suggestive of 'the dim religious air of churches.'[8]

Beyond the dimension of self-government which lay at its core this was a decade of growth and expansion in many directions: Clubland's

Clubland's Sunday congregation with the Juniors at the front

Art studio and workshop

premises and buildings; the size of its membership; its public profile and stature; celebrity interest in Club affairs; fund-raising projects; broadening sponsorship and support; extended recreational facilities, and a range of Clubland publications. Not least, during these years the Juniors of the Walworth Methodist Church clubs matured into the Seniors of Clubland, raised in the Club, informed by its spirit, trained by its leaders, and able to take on valuable work within it.

The movement of high octane energy within Clubland during this period generated a ceaseless and impressive level of event and activity. The June *Clubland Review* of 1930 is produced entirely by the Junior Captains, who cover all the Club events, outings, and celebrations. The new Parliament Captain declares his pride in his appointment, and reports a Club visit to Lyons that month. There are plans for the Girls' Club to go on its annual trip north to the Yorkshire Dales later in the summer, and for the Boys' Club to camp on Guernsey straight afterwards. That year 64 girls camped at Burton-in-Lonsdale, and 80 boys endured a 'gruelling crossing' for their Guernsey adventure – the boys' camp report in the *Review* catches the flavour of the visit:

Junior boys in Guernsey

Girls' camp with leader Laurie Lowe (back row right). JB in his
signature camp top hat

Arriving at Beaucamps

There is a particular and strict Camp routine until 10 a.m. then the Camp is free for the rest of the day, and Campers may go where they choose. Eighteen of the twenty Captains came to Camp, so the organisation and order was outstanding, and a good tone given to the whole camp. There were walks, visits to Petit Bot, and free cinema in the evenings. We had excellent weather and generous hosts. There was a calm return crossing, and the boys were given reserved compartments on the train, and cool drinks. They slept on the journey and came back to Club by 8 p.m. to a Guard of Honour of the Girls' Club in comic dress. The Head told the parents how well-behaved everybody had been.

The Clubland Theatre flourished with productions of *Journey's End* and *Abraham Lincoln* and a continuous roll of line-up shows was presented – in the games rooms there were constant competitions and championships, and outdoors the teams had a full list of football and games fixtures. At the beginning of October there was a Harvest Festival supper and thanksgiving services. The annual Club enrolments took place mid-month together with the dissolution and re-assembly of Parliament – the incoming officers swearing the loyalties, the new Captains receiving their Books of Office from the Head, and the appointment of Head Junior and Head Senior. Club cups were awarded, and received by the outgoing Captains, with all Club Officers listed in the reviews. Later in the month the first anniversary celebrations took place, along with the opening and dedication ceremonies for the new organ. There were four services, each with a preceding organ recital featuring Clubland's accomplished musicians Mr. Edmund Lamplough and Rev. F.L. Wiseman. In December a 'magnificent' Christmas Bazaar was held, raising a total of £350 – a large sum in 1930.

And so it continued – JB never took time out from thinking up projects and enterprises, getting them off the ground, publicising them, and raising money to fund them. He organised endless outings, teams, club rallies, engagements and activities, and visits and talks to and from other associations and individuals. And when they had taken place he circulated written accounts of them to all who might be interested, or who might contribute to Clubland's upkeep and building work. New rooms were opened in the Club, new shower baths were installed, a Guernsey activity room was funded by friends on the island, and the proceeds of JB's constant lecture engagements yielded additional funds for Club amenities.

The energy and ability of the club leader were recognised, and his reputation grew with that of Clubland. The Duke of Gloucester, visiting

Clubland in March 1934, praised the Minister for putting 'his whole heart and soul into the job', and a visiting Australian minister, Rev. Frank Wheaton, was quoted in *The Congregationalist* the same month saying: 'The Head is a genius with boys and girls ... I would rather be invited to preach at Clubland Church than at Westminster Abbey.'[9] The *Times Educational Supplement* of 4 August that year offered a commendation:

> Last Tuesday I saw depart from Clubland, that unique organization of boys' and girls' clubs which has been built up in Camberwell by a Methodist minister, a party of 120 girls for a 10 days' holiday camp in Guernsey. At a glance one could tell that the camp would be a success. Everything had been organized down to the last haversack button, yet without the slightest loss of the genuine camping spirit: arrangements moved swiftly and smoothly in an atmosphere of jolly friendship and ready service.'

Jimmy Butterworth had realised his dream: his Great Adventure had come to pass, and Clubland prospered.

The Home of Friendship

As a young probationer ten years previously JB had arrived in Walworth untried, to join an unfamiliar and frequently unsympathetic church community, in which he was often isolated by his driving determination to revolutionise his church, transform his congregation, and offer a home to youth. By the time he had secured Clubland's separation from the Mostyn Road Circuit and established its path he had many staunch friends – sponsors and allies, visitors and supporters, and not least his members and helpers – all moved by a wish to promote and be part of the Clubland enterprise.

Old friends were still with him – John Holgate wrote from his new home in Sevenoaks that he has been 'surprised and delighted to hear your name mentioned and your words quoted so often – there is no doubt whatever, my Lad from Lancashire, that your work at Clubland has stamped you for all time as a pioneer. You richly deserve the praise.'[10] Clubland's 'Bishop' Walter Hawkins was a loyal presence and confidant from the day JB arrived in Walworth until Hawkins' retirement to Peterborough in 1940, writing then to JB: 'Our friendship has always been outside Troy measure'. Basil Henriques, supported by the philanthropist Bernhard Baron in his Jewish boys club in Berners Street – now Henriques Street – had become a firm friend of both JB and Clubland,

and one who was closely aware of the pressures of club leadership. And on Guernsey another club leader, Rev. Jack Leale, welcomed the Clublanders to annual camps, offering moral support and personal hospitality to JB on many occasions.

There were also the supporters who had stood with him, backing their faith in him and his project with hard cash – men such as Lord Rochester, George Shrubsall, and Edmund Lamplough. As Ernest Lamb, Lord Rochester had been Clubland's earliest influential supportive voice, and author of the miracle that paid for Edward Maufe's vision for the church in 1928. Edward and Prudence Maufe themselves, as well as staying in constant contact throughout the thirties on matters of design and refurbishment – whilst Edward was also working on the design of Guildford Cathedral – were frequently present at Club events. Near the close of a fifty year association JB wrote to Edward Maufe: 'I have never got around to telling you how much your comradeship has meant to me.'[11] Joseph Rank, a Methodist benefactor who had contributed to financing the new church, and whose charitable family trust was to prove a crucial ally to Clubland in later expansion, began to attend Clubland gatherings – and Dr. F.L. Wiseman, a Methodist leader, first admired by JB when he preached in Accrington and visited Steiner's dye works, had also smiled benignly upon the great enterprise, jointly donating the organ with Edmund Lamplough. The two – a past Conference President and a future Conference Deputy President – presented a 'Song and Story' night on Tuesday 24 November 1931, with musical illustrations of bible stories for members and their parents. As the Clubland edifice went up JB acknowledged his great financial debt to the Shrubsalls by giving their name to major club appointments, such as the new theatre, and when George Shrubsall died, aged 68, in February 1935, JB wrote a heartfelt tribute to his generous patron and 'Father in the Club'. For the rest of her life his widow, Alice, continued to provide substantial financial support and personal concern, writing that JB should now consider himself a son to her.[12]

The list of close friends of Clubland who had provided other church necessaries is a long one – the Kingswood and Queenswood schools donated the stalls, whilst the four Methodist colleges – Didsbury, Richmond, Handsworth, and Cambridge gave the little altar. The Communion Cabinet and Plate had come from JB's 'father in God' Reverend Wilfred Moulton several years earlier, the Communion chairs were from Walter Hawkins and Hannah Gay, and the font chairs from Rev. T.H. Barratt and Rev. Dr. W.F. Lofthouse. Numerous church items and fittings were given by Walworth officials, Messrs. William Vogel Goad and Sam Panther, the Leales, Prudence Maufe, Penrhos College, and Rev. Penistan; and JB's pulpit – a 'box for him to preach in' – was provided by his Officers and Junior and Senior club members.

Besides Clubland's tried and trusted friends the First Clubland Church was also attracting the notice of more illustrious individuals. Henry, Duke of Gloucester, noted the publication of JB's 1932 publication *Clubland*, and had visited in the Spring of 1934 – a visit which was shortly followed by the Lord Chamberlain's invitation to a Buckingham Palace garden party in the following July. On 3 December 1935 the Duke's brother, the Prince of Wales, also paid Clubland a visit, accompanied by Lord Rochester. Prince Edward sat in on Parliament, visited all the Club activities in progress, saw the boxing in the gym, and shook hands with the Senior and Junior Heads. Predictably this visit – after which the Prince's private secretary Godfrey Thomas thanked JB fulsomely for his careful hospitality – was widely reported, with press coverage in dozens of leading newspapers and national dailies as well as the usual pieces in Accrington and South London, and the Methodist periodicals.[13] Walter Hawkins wrote to JB that 'Clubland has more than a *Recorder* constituency now. And enquirers multiply ... it has pierced its way into the general mind as a fact of significance ... Your life work will not fail now for lack of the dibs.'[14]

This visit from the Prince of Wales was not his last contact with JB, as is evident from further correspondence, including a letter from Auteuil following Edward's abdication and marriage, congratulating JB on the completion of Clubland.[15] In December 1936 a recent Clubland assistant, Rev. H.C. Dent, recalled in respect of the 'late King' how 'you had talked with him intimately and formed a high opinion of his humanity'.[16]

'Bishop' Hawkins was right about increased interest in Clubland – bequests and donations beyond the Clubland community were significantly generated by the heightened level of publicity. A newspaper vendor announced a gift of £5,000, another benefactor left a legacy of £8,000, and there were many smaller gifts. For the Clubland Head every penny he could raise was crucial. He knew that the building work – which lurched along through the thirties in accordance with what could be afforded – would require a very large sum of money. The final estimate was in excess of £100,000. Further houses on the envisaged Clubland site had been purchased for clearing in 1933, and the burden of financial stress alongside the chaos of rebuilding was taking its toll on JB's endurance. The greater public profile reached a celebrity

readership, and the resultant interest and generosity towards Clubland –
from visitors as diverse as the composer Sir Henry Wood, Stanley Rous
(President of The Football Association) and the actress Sybil Thorndyke
– itself prompted further newspaper articles.

Clubland was not a one-man show however. JB was its formidable
frontman, but from the first days the administration, governance, and
servicing, went far beyond what one man could accomplish, however
unstintingly he worked. During the twenties and thirties, as the
membership increased, the buildings grew, the activities available to Club
members multiplied, and the premises offered vastly greater material
facilities than previously, it became crystal clear that JB needed support
from a burgeoning army of helpers. This army was not an invisible
one, but it was essential that it be unpaid – none of the precious funds
for building the Temple of Youth could go to paid help, and Clubland
was not in receipt of any government grants. In consequence all the
valuable practical assistance which JB received within the Club was
necessarily voluntary. That was how it began, and remained, throughout
his ministry. The Clubland canteen was staffed by a willing rota of
helpers – usually the mothers of members, known as 'the Mams' – and
the activities were all supervised by volunteers, some of them with a
high level of expertise, such as Arsenal footballer Clifford Bastin, who
continued to come regularly to train the Clubland teams, and Andy

Cliff Bastin, Arsenal and England, awarding cups to the winning Clubland houses

Burton, a Clubland member and gifted painter, who took charge of the art classes. He is representative of the huge contribution to Clubland's voluntary strength made by many of its talented maturing members.

By the start of the thirties JB had many Seniors who were able to help with club duties, take a supervisory role in Club activities, or in the canteen and office, and who were eager to put something back into the Club which had given them so much. Stan Emmanuel, a keen football and drama member during the thirties, later returned to Clubland after seven years of desert warfare and internment as a prisoner of war. He was a constant presence there during the late forties and fifties, often managing the Club during the Head's absence, and ensuring the wheels turned smoothly. Stan reported in an interview many years after that it had been he who had first coined the abbreviation 'JB', broadly adopted by Clubland members and friends from the thirties onwards. He emphasised, however, that the Head insisted upon respect and it was always 'Sir' to his face.

In addition to the Officers of the Club Parliament, who took on responsibilities for various aspects of Club organisation, Clubland nurtured impressive levels of talent. Andy Burton, in addition to running the art group, also drew sketches for many *Clubland Review* covers, as well as the cartoons featured within them, and was the subject of a *Methodist Times and Leader* article on 18 November, 1937, which declared 'Clubland finds a poster artist in Walworth and gives him his chance to develop.' His work was later hung in the Royal Academy. He produced the artwork necessary for the Clubland stage presentations. The productions themselves were directed by member John Blatchley – who went on from Clubland to the Old Vic, acting and then producing. Blatchley was leader of the breakaway group which founded The Drama Centre – later part of Central St. Martins College – in 1963, the first 'Method' drama school in the UK. A third creative talent was Max Benedict, who edited the Clubland films before going on to an impressive film career with several major studios.

Other Clubland members came to prominence for their profile of competence and responsibility in Clubland affairs, in later years progressing to responsible positions in public life. Frank Neal, who had joined in the mid-twenties, became Head Senior of Clubland, and a key Club officer, trusted with meeting and greeting the dignitaries who visited Clubland for special services and ceremonies. Frank's younger brother Len became the Club's first lay preacher in 1934. In an article in the *Methodist Recorder* in January 1971 Len acknowledged JB as being the mentor of his Christian faith and development. Following several years of impassioned work for trade unionism Len won a three-year scholarship to read economics at Cambridge. Through the thirties JB was assisted at Clubland by a succession of ministerial candidates, with all of whom he kept in close touch during following years. The earliest was Rev. Penistan, whose appointment had been funded by Lord Rochester as an assistant to JB. When Rev. Penistan moved on to Llanelly Rev. H.C. Dent stepped into his shoes, followed in turn by Rev. Gordon Davies. In 1937 Gordon Davies left when he was appointed to the Ambleside Methodist Circuit, but he returned to help take care of Clubland during the war years – until he himself enlisted as a chaplain with the British forces. Upon JB's death many years later, and nearing the close of his own distinguished ministerial career, it was Gordon Davies who delivered a moving memorial address for his old mentor, commenting affectionately that during his years in the Club he had often failed to notice JB's presence in a group of boys until he saw that one of them was smoking a pipe.

Many Clubland voluntary helpers brought lay professional skills and qualifications to their work there. Alec Reed worked at Odhams Press, and helped with the publicity for cinematic and drama productions. Dr. W.H. (Billy) Whiles became a medical officer at the Club, for a while envisaging a future for himself in boys' club work, but eventually moving away to marry and begin a hospital career. He wrote to JB in November 1936 that 'I can never express all that your friendship has meant to me throughout the years I have been in London.'[17] Dr. Gordon Lyle began to provide dental help during these years, the start of a lifetime of involvement in Clubland management; and Reg Turtle, accountant and Treasurer to Clubland from 1922, continued his many years of devoted assistance.

In *Clubland* JB pays tribute to particular individuals – unnamed yet well known within the Club – describing them as the 'unexpected workers who pop up to share in the Club toil'. He captures their spontaneous actions in a few telling descriptions.

> The man who is just now struggling to turn off the hot water because rowdy boys using the club shower baths haven't the sense to regulate the taps is an All-England captain. In a dingy room in a dismal court a brilliant university scholar is sitting out the last hours with a dying club boy. The man waiting outside the prison with his collar turned up in the rain for the discharge of a Tiddler is a knight, and an MP celebrating

Dr. Billy Whiles and JB conducting a pre-Camp medical inspection

success is checking an official function room to room to ensure that the two club invitees have all they want.

JB was not idle in spreading the word of Clubland's programme and aims. He constantly publicised its needs and requirements, and made it his business to think up new schemes which would raise money, attract participation, and deliver funds. One of the most successful was the tradition of sponsored stones which he introduced. Stan Emmanuel commented when interviewed that the Head 'always had a genius for raising money' and this was demonstrated in an early project of sponsored bricks for church rebuilding in the late twenties. Upon the publication of *Clubland* in 1932 – all proceeds from which were to go to the Clubland Extension Fund – JB announced that he would send a copy for 5/- to acknowledge each sponsored Clubland brick. He also offered a copy of the Clubland Handbook and Service book together with a Letts diary in return for every further 1/- brick sponsorship.

As wall space became available around the garden courtyard area within the Clubland complex – including first the outer wall of the rebuilt church, and in the mid-thirties the external theatre wall opposite – the offer was extended to cover more handsome items of masonry: stones with the donor's chosen details engraved on the surface. The stones were first designated 'Foundation Stones', to indicate the architectural beginning of the new venture. Then as the decade wore on and the building work gathered pace, the dilapidated adjacent dwellings on Grosvenor Terrace – whose backyards blocked the courtyard – were demolished. Clubland buildings were erected in their place and the sponsored masonry items became 'Restoration Stones'. Finally the buildings were complete and there was a garden quadrangle contained within the four walls of the Head's house, the Church, the theatre, and the club room wing – after which the postwar stones took on their final characterisation as Commemorative, sponsored at £100 each donation. They constituted then, and now, a lasting memorial to all those who wished to demonstrate their acknowledgement and support for Clubland in this way. To walk around the walls of the quadrangle is to witness a parade of fame in many fields from the thirties onwards. Many leading contemporary figures – dignitaries, stars, royalty, and celebrities as well as long-term faithful friends of Clubland – funded these stones, which were often unveiled amid great ceremony and publicity.

The Campaign in Print

Publicity and communication were the life-blood of funding, and were happily coincident with JB's excellence in the dimension of written and spoken words. Even within Clubland, and exclusively for internal use and reference, there was a constant proliferation of printed material – but many items were designed to attract financial contributions. There were the *Clubland Service Books* – which JB produced and often sent to subscribers as souvenirs – which contained the dedication 'To all whose prayers, gifts, and service have helped create and build Clubland, from the days when it commenced with six boys until now, and to all who in the years to come will make it a home of friendship for those who need it most'. The 1938 version of the Service Book had been 'designed and printed by Ron Moulder, an ex-head of the Seniors, who is employed locally at Wightman and Co. Ltd., Printers.' There were Clubland service sheets with instructions – 'All repeat this meditation' and 'Stand as Prefects enter' – and many printed flyers, entrance tickets, gift envelopes, invitation cards.[18]

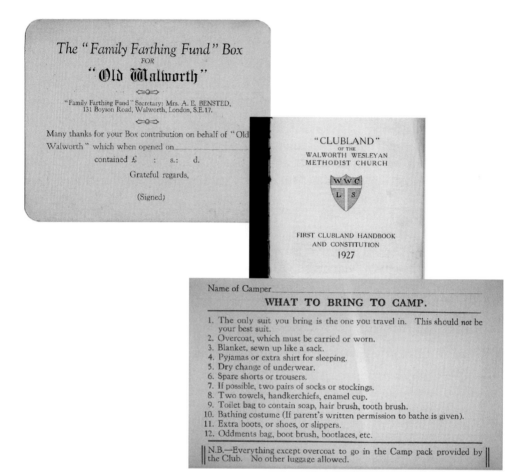

The "Family Farthing Fund" Box
FOR
"Old Walworth"

"Family Farthing Fund" Secretary: Mrs. A. E. BENSTED,
131 Boyson Road, Walworth, London, S.E.17.

Many thanks for your Box contribution on behalf of "Old
Walworth" which when opened on ___

contained £   :   s.:   d.

Grateful regards,

(Signed)

"CLUBLAND"
OF THE
WALWORTH WESLEYAN
METHODIST CHURCH

W W C
L   S

FIRST CLUBLAND HANDBOOK
AND CONSTITUTION
1927

Name of Camper ___
WHAT TO BRING TO CAMP.

1. The only suit you bring is the one you travel in. This should *not* be your best suit.
2. Overcoat, which must be carried or worn.
3. Blanket, sewn up like a sack.
4. Pyjamas or extra shirt for sleeping.
5. Dry change of underwear.
6. Spare shorts or trousers.
7. If possible, two pairs of socks or stockings.
8. Two towels, handkerchiefs, enamel cup.
9. Toilet bag to contain soap, hair brush, tooth brush.
10. Bathing costume (If parent's written permission to bathe is given).
11. Extra boots, or shoes, or slippers.
12. Oddments bag, boot brush, bootlaces, etc.

N.B.—Everything except overcoat to go in the Camp pack provided by the Club. No other luggage allowed.

In addition the printed material included copies of the *Handbook and Constitution*, instructions for Club Camp, receipts, and acknowledgement and thanks slips for farthing boxes. There were Share Holder forms and reports – interspersed with brief written texts such as 'Clubland is a fence at the top of the cliff instead of an ambulance at the bottom' – Clubland shilling shares cards, the Holy Communion Service Book, certificates of office for those who have completed their year of office and whose names have been inscribed on the Club Honours Board, concert tickets, announcements of forthcoming events, and of the successful conclusion of past ones. Any individual event might spawn a multitude of associated printed notifications. Sometimes these latter appear in the *Clubland Reviews* continuously produced for over fifty years – both monthly, with their distinctive Clubland colours of red and green stripes running across the front, and annually, bound in hardback – or on other occasions news items are published separately. 'Settlement Stonelaying at the Club – Miss Fowler (who has given £1000) will preside'. Mrs. Shrubsall is laying a stone for the Church and Honorary members – Miss. E.M. Trew for Queenswood and the Girls' Club, the Senior Prefect for Kingswood and the Boys' Club will attend, and the proceedings are to include the Dedication Ceremony. The Clubs will be open for inspection, with a sale, refreshments, and suppers.

Through the thirties JB was the author of many lengthier publications – a succession of books, pamphlets, and illustrated brochures, all designed to spread word of Clubland's work, raise its profile, and increase the pool of interested supporters and sponsors. A 1936 booklet, Clubland: The Temple of Youth, was reviewed in glowing terms in The Boy – the periodical publication of the National Association of Boys' Club. The Editor writes in the leading article

> I think it is the best thing yet produced in print by the club movement.
> I am certain that some of the pages ... will be constantly quoted as
> the best things said on their particular subject. I remember that when
> someone first told me of Butterworth he described him as "a sort of
> parson down in Walworth" and that I replied, "the sort of parson who'll
> go down in Walworth hasn't yet been invented" ... I already knew three
> or four parsons who would go down in Walworth, but none of them
> ever filled a Church with boys. Butterworth has, because he has got the
> boys of London into his heart and has got himself into the minds of the
> London boys ... I am not recommending the Clubland booklet simply
> because it is so right on the religion of the club boy, but because it is also
> dead right on the meaning and consequences of Leadership.

Nor did the campaign in print cause JB to pause in his personal correspondence, and he kept up a continuous stream of letters to friends and associates – retaining thousands of replies which now occupy a substantial file in his official archive. There was an ongoing exchange throughout with the Clubland architect Edward Maufe – to share ideas and advance the building project both in its minutiae and *a propos* of grander schemes – as well as with the parents of his members whose queries ranged over a variety of Club matters. Mrs. Moore complains of her son's loss of office due to his poor behaviour; the Olivers have concerns about the forthcoming camp arrangements; Percy has moved away but wishes to continue to contribute to the Club. JB answers them all, and promptly – advising, explaining, warning, thanking, enquiring or encouraging, as appropriate. His responses reveal that he will not brook breaches of discipline, or Club rules, but nevertheless provides a well of kindness to the needy.

Alongside the print generated by Clubland and its head, there was a parallel volume of newspaper coverage, the press cuttings for the decade running to many hundreds. Clubland had enjoyed early press coverage in the *Methodist Recorder, South London Press,* and *Accrington Observer,* and Clubland's regular press base had expanded to include national and regional daily papers and periodicals such as the *Evening News, The Times, The Listener,* and *The Northern Daily Telegraph,* as well as *The Guernsey Evening Press.*

Despite the exponential increase in profile and interest, none of these building years was easy for Clubland's leader, bearing the myriad tasks and responsibilities which fell upon his shoulders. In the Winter *Review* of 1932 JB announced, whilst urging the members to get their subs envelopes in before Christmas, that 'The Head, alas, must go out on tour if Clubland doors are to be kept open this Winter ... He will lecture anywhere if the collection goes to Clubland Funds.' And in *Clubland*[19] he acknowledged: 'I have never been able to escape from my vision or to turn aside from the call to put Clubland first whatever it involved.' There were times when he felt he had made errors, or feared that he would not be equal to the best that Clubland deserved, but he could never seriously contemplate doing anything other than continue the great campaign that he had launched.

Many commentators and reviewers have sought to capture the essence of Jimmy Butterworth's crusade – what it was that drove him to demand so much of himself so unremittingly and for so long. When he was fundraising for Maufe's work through the thirties he was not yet halfway through his ministry. He never ceased seeking and hoping to establish the elusive strong and stable financial base for Clubland – but nothing ever got any easier in the decades which lay ahead. He himself commented with some understatement that 'buying a slum court bit by bit is an experience' – owners sometimes insisted on pricing their businesses along with the premises, and multi-occupation landlords drove hard bargains. He wrote of the wide diversity of the buildings and businesses which surrounded Clubland – a milk depot, a laundry, a corset shop, stables of stamping horses, lorries loading, hammering and shouting, a variety of smells, tenements of thirty families using one entrance, illness, crowding, dirt, and squalor – and pondered ruefully how much just a few crumbs from rich tables might accomplish for those raised in such a setting. 'Hundreds might go to camp for the amount spent upon a banquet or a cruise.'[20] Yet although he fought for egalitarian entitlement for the boys and girls of Clubland he did not promote radical socialism, and declares in *Clubland:* 'It is not necessary to hate the duke to love the dustman.' His stated focus is not political but the enabling of Club members: 'Club is where the boy's own personality is directed along the lines of fullest self-realization.'[21]

Various news organs offered thumb-nail sketches of JB's venture at Clubland. *The People*[22] offered a straightforward simplistic account of extending his own self-betterment to others like him. 'Jimmy did not feel it was right for a boy to want so much out of life and to get so little. And then it was that he made a mighty vow to himself that if ever the chance came his way he would see to it that other poor boys and girls would not suffer as he had done.' Eagar, in his review of *Clubland* as his 'book of the month', acknowledges the bond its author shares with his membership, observing that 'A parson who knows what boys think of parsons must be no end of a parson and a bit of a boy himself.' Both have something of the truth, but not the whole. If improving the position of underprivileged young people were the entire story then JB might have thrown in his lot with the National Association of Boys Clubs – supported by Henriques – which had also been growing in strength since its foundation. But his entire history and identity – and the enduring rock of his impoverished and fatherless young life – had been founded in his church, and his own growing voice within it. It was an essential element of his vision that his pioneering enterprise for youth should be shaped within his ministry, and that it not be subject to any external authority.

It is a risky and presumptuous endeavour to seek to define a complex personality and psyche – in this case there is at least JB's confirmation of the importance to him of a church context. In his own words, 'Clubland hopefully clings to the church, because no other institution in the world has such a gospel of transforming power that can mean so much to youth.'[23] Elsewhere in a handbook article 'To the Unprivileged Boy' he writes: 'I can claim close kinship with you because I have passed your way and was much poorer than most of you ... Now let me tell you my simple creed. I believe in the nobility of unprivileged boys who, with opportunity, guidance and friendship can take their place anywhere with true dignity and self-respect.'[24] JB often referred to the spirit of Clubland, titling another article in the handbook: 'Club is not a Building only but a Spirit'. During the enrolment of Club members he told them his hope was that they might 'enrich the spirit of this place',[25] and in his book *Clubland* he wrote that 'The danger to movements outside the Church is the tendency to leave out the spiritual ... but the Church has the opposite danger of fettering the spirit by organizations too strongly wedded to traditions.'[26]

The domain of the spirit is, so to speak, a broad church, and the term is meaningfully used across a variety of contexts and individual situations, which may bring wonder, delight, and understanding without any necessary connection to the objects of conventional religious belief. JB clearly did not consider the term synonymous with 'religious', and he is indeed wary of the distancing consequences of 'religious' pronouncements and regulations. Yet by 'the spirit of Clubland' he wanted to transmit more than simply a value given to virtues such as loyalty, egalitarian treatment, honourable behaviour, just decisions, appreciation of beautiful surroundings, mental purity, or even the fellowship to be found within Clubland's walls, which he often referred to as an instantiation of that ineffable spirit. Clublanders' regular and respectful attendance in church on Sundays, as well as in their Club chapels, was so fundamental a necessary principle as scarcely to require stating – its contravention would speedily bring down the Head's wrath upon the offender. The Clubland 'Angelus' – the Sunday Service – was the high point of weekly worship in which the entire Club participated. It was conducted 'by youth for youth' and its constitution perhaps departed from conventional structure – 'The Clubland Service contains a little Catholic ritual, a bit of Quaker silence, a measure of Nonconformist freedom'.[27] JB revered Communion, and the willingness of those who were of age to give themselves to the 'Lord of all Good Life' in this way. Despite his many negative remarks concerning the infelicities of evangelism, and those who employed it clumsily, he told the *Methodist Times* and Leader in October 1938 that he remained of evangelical persuasion, even though many thought him 'more like a headmaster' than a minister. It is unnecessary to seek an answer to the question of whether faith or education dominated his approach – he would have seen both as enlightenment – and perhaps the essence of what he believed in was the holiness of his Clubland work.

In his Memorial Address of 8 May 1977 Reverend Gordon Davies – a key contributor and presence in thirties Clubland – paid affectionate tribute to his old leader, speaking 'for all those boys and girls whose lives have been literally transformed because of Clubland':

I've never known a man so feared and so respected, so hated and so loved, so stern and so friendly, so ruthless and so forgiving, so impossible and so understanding, so small and so big all at the same time. He really was unique; a genius who captivated anyone who so much as glimpsed what he was after, but was hard to work with for the same reason and had to do all the hard slogging himself because he outstripped any normal understanding. He dreamed dreams, and made them come true.

Trial and Travel

In addition to his 'hard slogging' within and on behalf of Clubland JB remained faithful to his roots, and there were frequent trips north to preach at Green Haworth Methodist Chapel, and to visit Beech Road and Didsbury, where he was always welcomed with great enthusiasm. He addressed the congregation many times at Green Haworth anniversaries, and the *Methodist Recorder* and *Methodist Times and Leader* reported that for the special anniversary of 1936 'Reverend Butterworth successfully piloted the centenary celebrations, published the history of the Chapel, and through services and friends secured over £150 to clear all debts and start the village cause without anxieties on its second century.' Photographs appeared in the *Accrington Observer*, with this 'most famous member of the Chapel' kneeling in the midst of the congregation. During the course of his ministry he gave the address at the Chapel and Sunday School on many occasions both before and after the centenary celebrations. But eight years after the close of his ministry his childhood Chapel met its own sad end, holding its last anniversary service in 1985, prior to its closure and sale. 'The Chapel on the Hill' a booklet written for the occasion by John Crook – descendant of Farmer Jacob Crook who used to provide the Whitsun Treat field for Jimmy Butterworth and his Sunday School peers in times past – told the story of the Chapel's heyday of packed congregations, before the mines and mills closed, and the population shrank.

Gordon Davies, deputising as Clubland leader during the second world war, said of JB's *modus operandi* in the thirties that 'he never seemed to need sleep. He never stopped working, and rarely stopped talking. He could write with inspiration, and raise money faster than inflation.' All these things were without doubt true – but each time JB would in the end overreach himself, outrun the dynamo, and collapse needing total rest. This happened again in 1935 amid the financial stress and chaos of demolition and rebuilding. Clubland stalwart Edmund Lamplough wrote to him on 5 January 1935: 'It is clear that you must go North or risk serious health breakdown', and George Shrubsall's widow, ever mindful of JB's well-being, wrote in March 1935 also fearful that his health was suffering. The next month, on 18 April, the *Methodist Recorder* confirmed 'Clubland's Pioneer to rest', continuing: 'The specialist who recently examined Mr. Butterworth gave a very serious report on his condition, and emphasised that a complete and prolonged rest was necessary so that he might be restored to health and strength … for thirteen years he has laboured in Camberwell without a single holiday.' On that occasion JB was back in Walworth by the end of May 1935, and Mrs. Shrubsall was able to write 'My Dear Jimmie, so glad to hear that all is well with you after your rest at Whitby.' But draining though these interludes were, and accompanied by the additional anxiety of a break in Clubland receipts, nobody could have foreseen the magnitude or consequences of the next emotional trial.

JB's brother Billie, who was a butcher in Oswaldtwistle, wrote to him in January 1937 that 'History has repeated itself'. Their sister Florrie, younger than Jimmy by three years, had attempted to commit suicide. 'Florrie has had what some would term a nervous breakdown but what in reality is a mental derangement and this morning tried to take her life. Mother has been down this last day or two but fortunately did not see the actual happening … Florrie turned the gas on and jumped through the bedroom window.' There had been some injuries – a blow to the back of Florrie's head – and she was in the Infirmary, waiting to be moved to Queen's Park Hospital. Her son David was with his grandmother. He finished: 'Jim, I cannot tell you what to do or anything else but God will perhaps show what is best for Mother. It is her I am thinking of always. Please do what you think best. God be with you. Love, Billie.'

This was a blow of huge dimensions. His sister Florrie had married Cyril Stirzaker, younger brother of Albert Stirzaker – Jimmy's fellow Methodist protégé under Rev. John Bennetts in Oswaldtwistle, and at Didsbury – fourteen years previously. Two years earlier than her suicide attempt she had given birth to David, a sickly baby troubled by a disabling medical condition, and had fallen victim to a prolonged episode of post-natal depression. In Jimmy's absence Billie kept a watchful eye on family members and particularly his mother, who still lived at Robert Street. An organist at Green Haworth Chapel and bass with the Accrington Male Voice Choir, Billie was married to Emma Lena, ten years his senior, and sister of John Holgate – who had supported

Jimmy from adolescence onwards with careful advice and guidance. Their daughter Ruth was six years old.

The family pulled together: Ann Butterworth took her grandson David for a while whilst Florrie underwent hospital treatment and counselling before being released to home supervisory care. But Florrie remained intent upon ending her life, and some weeks later she escaped the watch of her carer and made her way up the hill to the field beyond her childhood home at Rough Hey, where she drowned herself in Jacob Lodge, the same dark lake in which her father had taken his life many years previously. He had been thirty-seven years of age, as was Florrie.

In the aftermath of Florrie's dreadful death, when Jimmy was back in London, he was too disturbed by events to settle again into his Clubland life. This was not his typical pattern of occasional exhaustion from overwork, but the shock and distress of his sister's mirror repetition of their father's act made it impossible for him to continue as before. He wrote something of this to his close acquaintance the Head of Kingswood, A.B. Sacketh, who replied: 'My Dear Butterworth, My mind is aghast at the load you must have been under – even the worry and difficulty of Clubland seem negligible by comparison.'[28]

There are no records of what specifically prompted JB's decision to undertake a lecture tour of the United States. Contemporaneous Clubland publications make no mention of medical reasons for the Head's absence – and the *South London Observer* reported both that JB had cancelled a tour arranged the previous year, and presently been persuaded to take a holiday in America prior to the Clubland building programme.[29] Nevertheless, upon his return after four months away the *Methodist Times and Leader* of 2 September 1937 reported his plain acknowledgement that the trip was made necessary by troubled health: 'I just had to get away. It was purely and simply for health reasons.' This was his longest absence from Clubland since its inception – there were no Club camps for the first time for fifteen years, but his team of assistants and helpers led by Gordon Davies held the fort. His Head Senior, Frank Neal, made sure that the membership remembered its obligations, reminding them via the *Review* that 'when the Head returns from America the first thing he will say will be: "How have the weekly envelopes kept up?"'

The 1937 American trip turned out to be something of a dress rehearsal for the many transatlantic tours JB undertook throughout the fifties – but this was seen only in the light of hindsight, and there was no reason to anticipate a repeat at the time. In 1937 JB went first to New York, where he was in contact with Eddie Eagan, then an assistant attorney, who was greatly interested in youth work. Eagan, who had been at Denver University before serving in the US army as an artillery officer in the First World War, afterwards attended Yale where he became the national amateur heavyweight of the US in 1919 – a year later he won his first Olympic gold medal as a light heavyweight boxer at the 1920 Olympic Games. Eddie offered JB hospitality at his home at Happy Harbour, where he lived with his wife Peggy – a daughter of the Colgate family – and their children Caroline and Sidney, and put him into contact with business acquaintances and potential sponsors. JB was invited to speak at Eddie Eagan's boys' club and told the *South London Press* in July that Eagan's club was 'different from all other American boys' clubs. It is a republic, with boys as mayors and councillors – like our Cabinet and Parliament.'

The South London papers kept up with JB's travels – the *South London Observer* reporting on 23 April that the Clubland leader had undertaken an American tour, addressing the American Conference of Club Leaders soon after his arrival in New York, and attending a banquet where he sat next to ex-president Hoover and first met Eddie Eagan, before travelling on to Canada. In Toronto he was received by the Lieutenant Governor,

JB at the high table for the Conference banquet

and afterwards stayed with Reverend Ray McCleary, who had visited Clubland two years previously, and was building up a Clubland Church. In August a *Methodist Times and Leader* article, entitled 'Rev. James Butterworth in the Far West',[30] describes JB going to camp with 400 boys in Indiana, then being taken 2000 miles by a Mr. L. Valentine to stay in the Colorado Rockies – Mr. Valentine having discovered his link with Rev. Samuel Chadwick of Cliff College. JB had also visited Maniton in Oklahoma, where he was introduced to cowboys, native Indians, and riding horses. After leaving Yosemite in Colorado JB headed East to Boston before preparing for the journey back to England. Eventually the *Methodist Times and Leader* – one of many newspapers which carried stories of his return – was able to report JB's 'Home-coming to the Clubland Church' at the end of August, where he found all the members waiting with flags and banners to make him a presentation of a new Communion set.

The USA travel had blown away many cobwebs and JB returned able to resume his labours, although close friends had not given up their anxieties and exhortations on his behalf. Jack Leale urged him to go to stay with them on Guernsey for a break that Winter writing: 'I expect you are preaching "keep fit" to your Club, so practise what you preach.' And Mrs. Shrubsall continued to worry into the next Summer, coaxing him to see a specialist she knew before setting off anywhere else: 'I want you to have the best advice available. Jimmy Mackay says you have had to carry a terrific job for years with very little recognition.'

'God Bless Our Club'

In the mid-thirties, after much heartbreak and fundraising – and endless brick dust – the old buildings were finally demolished, and the rebuilt and extended Clubland at last went up, with its club rooms, workshops, art room, theatre, gymnasium, open air playground, hostel, and Head's residence. By 1939 two years of final building and rebuilding were drawing to a close and the completed Temple of Youth, wrought at a final cost in excess of £100,000 – raised entirely by Jimmy's endless fundraising projects, his lecturing and publications, and his canvassing of Clubland sponsors – neared completion.

The grand opening of the new buildings was to take place on 20 May. At the beginning of the year Queen Mary had given her consent to perform the opening ceremony, bringing true the Accrington newspaper vendor's long-ago prophecy. The main event was prefigured by a stone-laying ceremony at the beginning of April – a 'Youth of All Nations' meeting attended by the children of Ambassadors to Britain, who dedicated commemorative stones on behalf of their countries. Frank Neal, Head Clubland Senior presided as host to the young people; Doris Tan, niece of the Chinese ambassador, represented China; the daughter of Viscount Kano of Japan laid the Japanese commemoration stone; representatives of Germany were present and expressed their good wishes; Amar Sindhu Mallick attended for India; the son of the Belgian Consul, Leclerq, gave a speech; and the daughters of the Norwegian and Swiss Ministers were there. Jean Daladier, son of the ill-fated French prime minister, was unable to attend. Also present was Bobby Kennedy, son of the American Ambassador Joseph Kennedy, making his first public speech aged 13 at Clubland, where his name is inscribed on the 'Youth of All Nations' stone.

The 1939 Opening was timetabled and choreographed in minute detail. The Programme, produced by the Head with his usual meticulous care, included a detailed breakdown of the day's events, together with instructions to members, Clubland's thanks to Queen Mary, and acknowledgement of the gift of the 'Shrubsall Memorial Hall'. A plan of the premises was provided – Her Majesty was to be received by Lord Rochester, the Head, Mrs. Shrubsall, Edward and Prudence Maufe, the Head Boy Frank Neal, and the Head Girl Margaret Jones. Club Seniors

Bobby Kennedy, younger brother of the future president JFK,
laying his stone at the Club in April 1939

only were to stand in the forecourt – all to be gowned in their Club and House colours – and the Juniors were to wear the red and green Club ties, and new gym tunics. The commemorative tablet is described and a list of the stones and their donors given – Queen Mary had consented to commemorative stones for the Duke of Windsor and the Duke of Gloucester being laid in advance. Following the royal arrival Edward Maufe, the Clubland Architect, presented her with a golden Clubland key, and he and his wife were complimented by Her Majesty for their work in designing and furbishing the premises. Of course, it was too much to hope for that there would be no hitches. Sure enough, the ceremonial key that Queen Mary had been given failed to open the balcony door and the main party had to retrace its steps to find another way into the Chapel. She took it all in good part however and later sent her thanks for the way she had been received, saying that she had greatly enjoyed her visit and wished Clubland prosperity and success.

The great event was, of course, widely covered by the national press. Thousands had flocked to the Camberwell Road to watch the spectacle – the arrival of the Queen and other notables, the band, and the hundreds of young people in their Club colours. There were many expressions of congratulation – the Queen's lady-in-waiting wrote privately 'to say how immensely impressed we were by all we saw', and Lady Rochester added her congratulations on the way the Club Seniors had carried out their roles in the occasion. The big daily papers carried numerous photographs, and histories of JB and Clubland – whilst local papers took a more homely approach, the *Sunday Dispatch* repeating JB's interview comments about his boyhood, and the *Haslingden Observer* reporting that Queen Mary had asked the Head's mother if she had come all the way from Lancashire for the day.[31]

It was a crescendo of excitement and achievement – the fulfilment of Reverend Jimmy Butterworth's lifetime plan for the magnificent buildings of his Club, and truly the product of blood, sweat, and tears. Even then, with the official opening past, there were further minor appointments outstanding – some electrics and windows, a room or two yet to be furnished. But, overall, it was finished – and the preparations underway for the first Guernsey Camp for some two years, to take place that August, added a celebratory dimension after a decade of building. Within weeks of the opening the organisation of Club camps began, attended as usual by a multitude of forms, instructions, planning, and keen anticipation. Peggy Rees, daughter of Herbert Rees of Holmes Chapel, and Anna Costain, of the Manx building family, from Caldy,

Wirral – both ex-pupils of Penrhos College, a Methodist girls' boarding school in Colwyn Bay – had been invited to attend as helpers. Peggy wrote at the end of June that she was greatly looking forward to helping at the Club camp, and for both young women it was to be the start of a long involvement with Clubland affairs. But in July, as anticipation heightened and Camp plans neared fruition, there was devastating news from Guernsey – Paul Leale, the eighteen-year-old son of Jack and Leonie, and the older of their two children, had lost his life in a boating accident. JB, who had known Paul since his early childhood, and to whom Paul had spoken relatively recently, was one of the few close friends with whom Jack Leale shared his grief.

At that late stage arrangements for the Club Camp went ahead despite the tragedy. The camp had been arranged for the whole of August – planned both as respite following Clubland's completion, and to give the decorators a chance to come in and add finishing touches to the premises. JB wrote later: 'Every section of that generous community went out of their way to give Clublanders the time of their lives', and no doubt the kindly locals sought to shield the young people from the sadness engulfing their host's family on the island, and to divert them with holiday activities. Even so the proximity and enormity of this family tragedy would naturally mute the wholehearted pleasure of both visitors and hosts. The young campers enjoyed a happy time on Guernsey – but in hindsight this backcloth to their Summer presaged the disruption and conflict which lay ahead.

As the Clubland campers returned to London from Guernsey shopkeepers were already sandbagging their premises. In the unfinished account of his life begun during the course of the War JB wrote with pathos: 'We returned for London's first blackout to rooms that we were never to use, and to modern lighting we were never to switch on.'[32] As the last batch of homecoming Clublanders arrived: 'There was not the usual crowd of mothers lining the streets or gaily lit club rooms for welcome reunions.' Instead there were crowded trains and soldiers everywhere. In the midst of the preparations for war JB described the chaos around him, as well as his natural dismay at the impact of the declaration of war upon the newly opened Club complex after a decade of stinting and saving, of demolition and building.

> We could have saved thousands of pounds if we had only left over the decorations, electric fittings and final touches. All that was done whilst we were in camp was dismantled or disfigured within a few weeks …

During the week buses and trains took away children, when the anguish of mothers was a pathetic contrast to seeing them off to camp. Our Juniors were evacuated, many Seniors moved with their firms to safety zones, others joined the Forces. How we had talked about our return when at last we could do our work without building worries. '

Her Majesty Queen Mary

ROYAL OPENING. May 1939.

Royal opening May 20. 1939

JB knew about war – his exit from the previous conflagration had been a mere twenty years earlier – and he knew that the consequences of war are to be counted in losses beyond the material. It goes without saying that he immediately offered Clubland to aid peaceful community support

> Everybody must know that war means destruction and massacre. It won't be just buildings that will be in ruins, for it takes such a long time to climb back into sanity after killing games. We shall offer our premises for any humanitarian service, but refuse our pulpit for any military propaganda. If the clubs are wiped out those of us who are left will have to begin all over again to minister to an embittered remnant.[33]

Most of all there was the heartbreak he felt for his members, lost to the war effort. 'I have always known that these lads mean more to me than anything else in life, but I never realised until now how much they are part of my life.' Frank Neal had already decided to join up and had written on 15 August: 'My Dear JB, Club and you have been my guiding influences and meant everything to me.'[34] Max Benedict wrote early in September: 'We remain firm and serene in the ideas you've told to the attendants of your services, and I feel I have met one of those knights without armour'; [35]and at the end of the month S. Loosely, newly enlisted as a Royal Corps Signals Officer, wrote telling 'Dear JB' that he was full of despair that war had come. He was being sent overseas and wanted JB to know all that Clubland had meant to him, the privilege of having been a Club member, and how he treasured the 'happy memory' of gatherings and talks in JB's study.[36] On the same day Margaret Thorn, an evacuated member of the Girls' Club, wrote: 'Dear Mr. Butterworth, I am living with nice people in a house at Windsor.' Margaret says that her family is planning to visit her but that she misses home and Clubland. She ends, 'God bless our Club'.[37]

It had been a triumphant decade – the crowning decade of JB's life – but at the moment of Clubland's completion it had been brought to a tragic halt.

Notes

1 Morgan, A.E. *The Needs of Youth* Oxford University Press, 1939.
2 Official Report of Parliamentary Debates, Feb. 28th, 1933.
3 *Letters of a Clublander,* Introduction.
4 *Clubland: The Temple of Youth* (Illustrated Handbook) p.25.
5 Ibid, p.21.
6 Henriques, Sir Basil H Q. *Club Leadership.* Oxford University Press (1933) pp.92–3.

7 *Methodist Recorder* 30 April 1936.

8 *Clubland: Temple of Youth,* p.27.

9 *The Congregationalist* 21 March 1934.

10 Letter from John Holgate: 15 Nov. 1936.

11 Letter from Butterworth to Edward Maufe.

12 Letter from Mrs A Shrubsall, 3 March 1935, Ref 144.46.

13 These included the *Daily Sketch,* the *Accrington Observer, Morning Post, Star, Birmingham Post, Evening News, Evening Express, Times, Leeds Mercury, Nottingham Guardian, Methodist Recorder, Manchester Guardian, South London Observer, Nottingham Evening Post, Cambridge Daily News, Northern Daily Telegraph, Christian World, Methodist Times and Leader,* and the *South London Press.*

14 Letter from Rev. Walter Hawkins, 11 April 1933, Ref. 136.22.

15 Letter from Edward, Duke of Windsor, 15 Feb. 1939 from 24 Boulevard Suchet.

16 Letter from H.C. Dent, Berkhamstead, 22 Dec. 1936, Ref. 123.08.

17 Letter from Dr W.H. Whiles: 14 Nov. 1936, Ref. 142.52.

18 'For a happy New Year the Reverend J Butterworth and the Reverend J.Penistan request the pleasure of the company of ... at the Annual Social and Supper of THE JUNIOR BOYS on Wednesday January 1st, 1930,at 6 p.m. in the Lecture Hall.'

19 *Clubland* p.17.

20 *Letters of a Clublander*: Enlarging the Premises.

21 *Clubland,* p.27.

22 *The People.* 2nd June 1935.

23 *Clubland,* Ch.5.

24 *Clubland: The Temple of Youth Handbook.*

25 *Letters of a Clublander.*

26 *Clubland,* Ch.5

27 *Letters of a Clublander.* Ch.24.

28 Letter from A.B. Sacketh, 1 March, 1937.

29 *South London Observer,* 23 April, 1937.

30 *Methodist Times and Leader.* 13 August,1937.

31 *Sunday Dispatch*; *Haslingdon Obse*rver, 21 May, 1939.

32 *Letters of a Clublander,* Ch.45 'Sunsets and Blackouts'.

33 Ibid.

34 Letter from Frank Neal, 15 August1939 Ref. 130.02.

35 Letter from Max Benedict, 10 September, 1939; Ref. 157.06.

36 Letter from S. Loosely: 26 Sept. 1939 Ref. 128.16.

37 Letter from M. Thorn, 26 September, 1939; Ref. 157.06.

CHAPTER SIX

Crucible, 1939–1945

Exodus

In May 1939, in a fanfare of publicity and celebration, Queen Mary had opened the completed Clubland premises. All those present who had striven for so many years towards that day had looked forward confidently to a fulfilling future for Clubland. One in which its work could progress within the beautiful new buildings, untrammelled by the constant necessity of raising funds to build. But at the end of the Summer the Clublanders returned from their Summer camp in Guernsey to a London reeling from the shock of being again at war.

Tommy Walker (Chelsea and Scotland international) with Clubland's First XI. Most of the team were in uniform soon afterwards

In commentary written during the war years JB described the chilling onset of the conflict: 'The Blackout descended, and there began the era of gas masks, barrage balloons, wailing sirens, street shelters, dug-outs, and decontamination centres. Humanity seemed to lose its identity – no commandments need be kept when a main one must be broken.'[1]

Of the many trials which the war brought there was one which particularly affected those who had invested their lives in youth work, and which left them bereft in its wake: namely the enforced dispersion of the young, either to places of relative safety, or – for those old enough for military service – to places of greatly increased danger. Boys' clubs provided thousands of recruits into the armed forces, and although many hundreds of clubs remained open – as did Clubland – there was an immediate depletion in senior membership. As they came of age the Seniors who had grown up in Clubland, and were taking over supervision of its self-government as its Officers and Cabinet, were called up and sent off to training centres to prepare for military action abroad. In the months following the declaration that the country was once again at war Jimmy Butterworth lost the best strength of his Senior Boys' Club and Parliament to soldiery in one of the armed forces. He knew what war meant, having gone to fight in France at a similar age: he knew the dangers to body and mind to which the young membership he had nurtured would inevitably be exposed, and the confrontation with mortality that they must face. In his journal he wrote, 'Only a little while ago camps and clubs rang with the music and laughter of many more who will not return. They were all so full of life and promise.'[2]

The Junior Club also suffered immediate depletion as the British evacuation initiative – *Operation Pied Piper* – moved into action from September 1, 1939. London was thought to be most at risk from bombing by the German Luftwaffe, and evacuation trains moved the capital's children out to the greater safety of the countryside in large numbers. In fact in the course of the war the children were evacuated in waves, the biggest following the onset of the Blitz in September 1940. In between these waves many children were brought back home by their families, but hundreds of thousands remained outside London for the duration of the war. JB regretfully observed that 'the time came when few were left who had grown up in Clubland'. By 1942 it seems that only ten of the original 800 members were left and there can be no doubt of JB's desolation at the loss of the membership he had so carefully developed and tended. He did not seek to restore the Junior Club until the next decade – but straightaway, and throughout the years of war, he worked constantly to replace the Senior membership, recruiting from air-raid shelters and evacuation centres.

Clubland itself was soon requisitioned by the authorities as a rest centre – as were hundreds of club premises – although JB preserved areas such as the theatre and other rooms for continuing Club activities. There is no disguising that he felt extremely bitter at the insensitivity with which this displacement was effected, and at the apparent disregard of his youth work and dedicated premises, even whilst official lip service was paid to the importance of preserving organisations for young people.

> It's considered a very little thing what becomes of clubs even if it did take a lifetime to build them. A Clubland built for youth work now housed ARP, Rest Centres, Day Nursery, and School Meals. It counted for nothing that 'pride in premises' had been our strongest tradition, that every brick and colour scheme, every bit of panelling and furnishing represented the shillings and designings of members. Rooms of sacred and happy memories, oak floors and doors, were mutilated. With curtailed membership the Clubs carried on with restricted activities in improvised rooms. This at a time when press and government were pleading for youth work to be carried on at all costs. The workshops were moved next to bedrooms, the canteen went back stage because the rest centre staff wanted the new Clubland cafeteria for their lounge, the little bit of green in the quadrangle, for which we had bought and demolished half a slum court, became a coke and garbage tip. Thus with a mixed tenancy we kept to one half of the building and did our best with what we had left.' [3]

Clubland may have been depleted by the constant call-up of its Senior members, and by repeated waves of Junior evacuation, but it was a great deal more than a skeletal remnant of its former self. It was difficult to generate an income comparable to pre-war: the *South London Observer* reported on 1 May 1940 that there was a threat of Clubland closure since no contribution was made to funds by Government or any civic body, and the *Accrington Observer* repeated this stating that members aged 14–18 were maintaining the Club out of their own money. But shortly after these reports – whether in consequence of them or not – some timely financial support was received from Camberwell Borough Youth Committee, and day-to-day funding pressure eased a little.

On 7 July JB broadcast his Clubland Service on BBC at 7 p.m. for home and overseas listeners, so that members of the forces could tune in. His pre-war Head Senior, Frank Neal, who had joined the Navy, was released by his senior officers so that he could read the lesson. There was an overwhelming response from members in the forces, as well as from the general public – Alf Goldsmith, NCO, writes 'My Dear JB, Your broadcast was superb ... beautiful and clean like a breath of fresh air ... Frank was simply great, it made me cry for the first time since joining up ...' And on 16 August, 1940 both *The Guardian* and *The Times* reported that on Youth Sunday, although St. Paul's was empty, Clubland was full – then and every other Sunday.

JB was also working on further projects – some open and transparent, and others rather more clandestine. He began the Clubland Evacuation Scheme, looking for evacuation centres in the North to house the homeless of his South London Community, and took up offers of two properties available on Lord Cholmondeley's Estate, as well as two others in Whitchurch and Salop. On 17 November the *Methodist Recorder* ran an article and photographs of Club evacuees at Edgely and Barmere. He also offered accommodation at Clubland to soldiers on leave, as well as to Guernsey evacuees – the latter announced on the Forces Radio Sunday Broadcast. Another early wartime project was a special wartime edition of the *Clubland Chapel Service Book*, for circulation only to JB's members in the military services. He endorsed it with the message: 'It is for Clublanders in the forces that they may still be part of their Club Service on Sundays at seven, and Club Chapel weeknights at ten ...' This was greatly appreciated by the serving membership, who wrote to tell him how much it meant to them to be able to share in the Sunday Service, even from overseas.

Another initiative – which he did not announce widely – was a Clubland taxi service. Previously unknown to be able to drive, JB commandeered a car, and frequently drove in the darkness to meet ex-members returning home on leave to one of the ports, to ferry them to Clubland, or elsewhere to their homes and families. 'The Clubland car brought grooms in time for their weddings ... and it conveyed members to club events who would never have made it otherwise. Its charmed life was varied by work on bombed homes, evacuation journeys, furniture removing, or combing streets in the early mornings for stranded Dunkirk soldiers. None knew that this was the Head's recently acquired method for meeting new needs, which no doubt explains regrettable incidents with the police.' [4]

Throughout the war JB continued to generate press articles covering Clubland activities as well as his projects outside London. He frequently travelled to give talks to other organisations, and also to attend official functions – such as the civic reception given in his honour at the

Town Hall, Accrington, on 10 February 1940, where he received tributes from the Mayor and Councillors for his hard work and achievement in creating Clubland.

He also undertook serious wartime representation in defence of his members: in early 1940 he spoke for George Stedman, a member of Clubland for five years, and a conscientious objector, at a military tribunal in Edinburgh – and did the same for Andy Burton, resident Clubland artist. Both wrote their heartfelt thanks, and Andy Burton gave JB a painting 'as a token of my gratitude for all you have done for me.' When JB was away from Clubland and out of London Gordon Davies provided able leadership and management assisted by Laurie Lowe, who had been Girls' Club leader, and Anna Costain, who had helped at the last Guernsey camp.

Every effort was made to sustain Clubland continuity. Team training and sports fixtures continued on Saturdays – even though prey to last-minute changes due to call-up – and Parliament met, discussed, and governed Clubland affairs, each Tuesday evening as before. Sunday hikes and rambles and cycle rides carried on at weekends, and on Thursdays the Club was closed for everything but drama – when John Blatchley and John Holgate, with 100 members, put on a succession of ambitious plays. The monthly reviews were produced, uninterrupted, despite the background of disturbance and change. A postwar review offers a flavour of the persistence of Club members. 'How the producers got here during raids or the members went through rehearsals and performances with wailing sirens and crashing bombs is a mystery. We select the play *Journey's End* [5] ...as it illustrates the sheer pluck of members during that period. The whole cast was due for call-up, yet before leaving they staged, managed, and produced the whole show. The very morning after their performance most of them were off early for their first day in the Navy ...'

One of the riches available to JB's biographers in writing this book has been the wealth of correspondence from his members, which he so carefully preserved. At no time was this greater than the flood of letters sent by departing Clublanders in the months after the declaration of war in 1939, when so many were rudely plucked from their lives and sent, barely trained, to distant destinations. Frank Neal is frequently in touch – he returns to Clubland whenever he can, and otherwise writes asking for news of other Clublanders. Ted Lear writes that he is in the army but will stay in touch; Fred Marks, RAOC, sends thanks for his Christmas parcel; Stanley Emanuel describes his military camp activities at the

Tetbury Medical Corps; Howard Randall and Albert Woodall thank JB for their 'grand send-off'. Both write again – after a return visit Albert tells JB: 'I shall never forget what you did for me last weekend. It was grand to be back at Club – and the moonlight drive you and Frank made to get me back.' Howard writes from Northern Ireland on 30 June 1940 that he wishes he were near enough for the 'military member Cabinet meetings – Clubland must be so lonely – but the gang will all be back.' He relates that at evening service he has to pray with his rifle between his knees. Jimmy Anderson, Royal Welsh Fusiliers, writes at the beginning of 1940 that he is trying to get used to army life 'but from my heart I miss [Clubland] very much and wish I was back there. I know nothing and nobody here, and hope we can soon just be human again and not training to kill people.' Jimmy visits a few months later and writes: 'Thank you from the bottom of my heart for what you did for my return to Clubland on leave – I want my team to challenge Fred Wyeth's when the war is over.' Sadly, later news shows that Jimmy did not live to return to Clubland and lead his team in this challenge.

So many write in those first years with news of their new activities – Bill Smart, Eddie Wilson, Arthur Putnam in the Air Force, Harry Oliver, Lieutenant Corporal Alf Goldsmith from Iceland. As the years of conflict continue the absent members grow up, and many marry, but the tribulations of war and their changed lives bring them close to their earlier youth in Clubland. They write to thank JB for his letters, his parcels, the prodigal's welcome back to Club he provides for their leave visits, his 'taxi' transport of them. They tell JB that they are homesick, that they are humbled at the thought of what Clubland gave them – and sometimes, that they are unhappy with what they are being asked to do. A.E. Byworth tells JB in June 1940: 'This training for war, its false values, the boredom and wasted leisure, is so different from your ideals and plans when you were in the last war.'

The pathos of these hundreds of letters is undimmed across the years, and JB's emotions on receiving them, on trying to give succour and reassurance when he must himself have often been distraught by the trauma to so many young lives, may only be imagined. Unfortunately whilst he preserved his Clublanders' letters with such care, he rarely kept copies of his replies – it is clear from all the correspondence that it was his habit to reply reliably and promptly, and offer what comfort he could. How he himself drew comfort is less clear, but he remained a source of strength to his absent Seniors, and continued to lead a re-shaped Clubland through the war. His friend Howard Marshall wrote to him commiserating over 'what is happening to those grand lads of yours. We must talk about it Jimmy – we can smoke a pipe together and warm our hands at the fire of friendship. What Clubland means to those youngsters is a great consolation.'

The Burning Furnace

Following the magnificent performance of the Royal Air Force through the 'Battle of Britain' in Summer 1940, and the consequent failure of Hitler's plan to dominate the skies, bomb ships and airfields, and thereby seize control of the country, the revised German approach was the direct and intense bombing of British cities which commenced the following Autumn. The Blitz of daily bombing and night raids prompted the second wave of evacuation from London, together with the widespread use of public shelters, underground stations, and private corrugated iron shelters, as well as the imposition of nightly blackouts in an attempt to hinder the German pilots.

At Clubland the services, stage presentations, and club activities, were often punctuated by the cacophony of war in the streets and skies outside and above, and during the Blitz residents grew used to the external shocks and explosions. JB wrote later that 'The Club rocked during fierce bombing – once when it got too hot the congregation filed under the stage.'[6] There could be no preparation, however, for the devastating events of the night of 10 May 1941, when incendiary bombs scored a direct hit on the Clubland Church. Designed by Edward Maufe, and dedicated by Queen Mary almost exactly two years previously, the lovely Chapel was the crowning glory of the Clubland buildings, with its elegant tall dimensions and solid furnishings, starry ceiling, and blue and silver motif. The many friends of Clubland, its youth membership, and its sponsors, had all made special donations to chosen articles – the altar, the pulpit, the ceremonious cloths and plates, the lectern, the paintings, the organ. During the Blitz many Clubland families had moved into the Club premises for refuge and shelter, and hundreds of members were present on the night the church was bombed.

Gordon Davies, Club leader throughout the raids, witnessed the valiant efforts the young people made to save their church: 'It was the night of the worst raid, when at midnight came the alarm that the Chapel had been hit. Two parties rushed on the roof to man the hand pumps. A third group took the hose inside the building – but the mains were fractured and the fire hydrant became useless ... there was a delay whilst

Rev. Gordon Davies

water was taken from the nearby canal by the fire engine ... the fire had spread and the Church was doomed. Chains of girls and boys handed up buckets of water, but it turned to steam. Lads defied death hanging onto the parapet. Others inside the Church kept the fire confined to the roof until the rafters gave way.' The subsequent *Clubland Review* is equally heartfelt and graphic: 'Boys with bleeding hands tried in vain to pull down the paintings from the altar ... With the flames almost licking their faces, weary, scorched, and blinded by smoke they fought in what was soon to become a furnace ... Finally in the grey Sunday dawn, leaving heaps of charred destruction, crowned by twisted girders, the exhausted Clublanders fell asleep where they collapsed.'

It was an heroic fight, with the Clublanders refusing to give up until ordered away by the police, but ultimately the inferno in the Church took everything. In all the smoke, heat, and devastation just one item – the dove of peace – was rescued from the font. But that evening, at 7 p.m., the

Club member Bob Brindle's painting of the fire

Clublans Destroyed 1941 Clublans Rebuilt 1964. May, 1941 ↑
May, 1964 ↓

The bombed ruin of the beautiful Chapel

enduring spirit of Clubland prevailed in defiance of the destruction, and the Sunday Service was held as usual – amid the still smouldering ruins.

It was, of course, a cruel body blow for the man who had overcome so much over so long before so recently succeeding in building his 'Temple of Youth'. Contemplating the ruins soon afterwards JB himself acknowledged that he felt heartsick to the point of despair – but was pulled back by a timely reminder from a young member also surveying the desolation that 'you still got us, aincha?'

Charles Skinner, a Clubland Senior, used different words to send JB essentially the same message in a note he wrote the morning after the fire: 'I know how hard it will hit you. Before I looked at the ruins of our church this morning I never realised enough the comradeship and undestroyable unity of Clublanders.' Charles felt that 'all the great Clublanders I have ever known' were there with them. Many of the members came to gaze at their transformed church, sobered by the enormity of what had taken place, but nobody doubted for a moment that Clubland would get through and go on. The discovery of JB's bible, undamaged among the warm cinders, was a heartening sign. The bible, which contained lengthy penned sermon notes, and the names of many church and club colleagues, had been a gift from his staunch supporter and first Walworth landlady Hannah Gay in 1922. The elderly Miss Gay herself never recovered from the bombing of her own house during the Blitz, and died later that year in hospital, but the bible she had given JB endured and he treasured it always. Even amid the ensuing chaos JB quickly recovered his faith and fortitude, and by August was sharing with the local *South London Press* his ideas for renewed building on Blitz-cleared ground.

There was an immediate sympathetic response as the news of Clubland's damaged Chapel spread, and a spate of commiserating articles appeared across the country's newspapers. The *Methodist Recorder* led with a piece strikingly entitled 'Twenty years in twenty seconds', and all the papers reported the message of comfort and hope sent by Queen Mary, who had written to JB that 'You must take comfort in the thought that the Spirit of Clubland remains, and surely it will burn more brightly from having passed through fire.'

Clubland and its leader were resilient, a programme of fundraising for rebuilding was once more planned, and meanwhile open air services were held on the site of the ruined church for the duration of the war. Within a few months the *South London Press* was announcing that 'Clubland is not Dead',[7] and 'London Calling' – a BBC publication – featured 'South London's Temple of Youth', an article written by JB himself, detailing Clubland's history and aims, and containing several photographs.

From the beginning of the war JB had been concerned on behalf of Clubland friends on Guernsey, which was under threat of German occupation from an early point, and he offered Clubland's hospitality and shelter to all Guernsey soldiers travelling across the mainland. The Guernsey ties were close ones. St. Sampson's Boys' Club, led by JB's friend and ally of nearly 20 years, Rev. Jack Leale, had been generous hosts to Clublanders at their Summer camps on the island from 1926 until 1939. In the twenties JB had been engaged for a short period to Jack's cousin Brenda Bird, and remained in close touch with family members such as Ted and John Dorey, who called on Clubland whenever they were in England. JB's friend Jack was to play an illustrious role in Channel Island wartime history of which neither had dreamed on their many walks and talks together on the island's beaches.

Taking over chairmanship of Leale Ltd on the death of his father, Jurat John Leale in 1928, Jack was later elected People's Deputy, and in 1934 became himself Jurat of the Royal Court. He was appointed President of the States Controlling Committee at the end of 1940, 'in which office he served with absolute integrity',[8] and led Guernsey during the years of German Occupation. Throughout these years Jurat Leale refused an official car, used a tiny office, and set his standard at the level of the poorest islander refusing to permit any food in his house beyond the rations available to others. Herbert White, author of *John Leale – Our Foremost Champion*,[9] describes him as a 'frail son of the church', who was nevertheless a bastion of steel between the occupying Germans and the States and people of Guernsey. Through the long years of war JB could only watch anxiously, doing what little he could to assist, until May 1945 brought news of Guernsey's liberation. In point of fact Leale had been peremptorily summoned to the *Platzkommandantur* on 7 May to be reprimanded for his premature showing of British flags – British forces did not actually land on Guernsey until 9 May. Jack became Sir John Leale in December 1945, and was later made Acting President of the States of Guernsey. The strong bond between these two elders of their Church lasted until Leale's death in 1969, when his lifelong comrade officiated at the funeral.

Another close concern of JB's had been establishing evacuation centres for Clubland families. He had made enquiries, placing newspaper advertisements and agitating from the beginning of the bombing to secure potential premises, and the need became more pressing as increasing numbers of dispossessed in the local community sought refuge with him during the Blitz. The rest centre was also overcrowded, and Clublanders collected funds in order to provide accommodation for the homeless, sending many mothers with children, and elderly people, away to shelter. From long acquaintance JB considered Shropshire and Cheshire to be havens when he was seeking 'homes for my bombed-out Clublanders'. Harry Richards was a local council member at Whitchurch in Shropshire and later recalled that he and his wife Doris 'first met

Barmere House, christened 'Clubland Manor' by JB

The evacuation team at Barmere (Anna Costain, centre)

this human dynamo in a clerical collar when he came to our part of the country in early 1941 with one idea in his mind – to find a rest home for his friends in London who were homeless because of the Blitz ... We became so infected by his enthusiasm that we decided to do everything possible to help.'[10] To JB's great relief, and with the assistance of Harry and Doris Richards, he was finally able to set up and supervise accommodation provided by Lord Cholmondeley at Edgeley and Barmere: 'The Marquis of Cholmondeley not only loaned his Castle for a naval hospital, but loaned Barmere to Clubland rent free. His woods supplied our fuel, the gardens provided food, the Club sent a voluntary staff, so that for two years old and young were housed in safety and restored to health.'[11]

JB's brother Billie had moved with his family from Lancashire to Sevenoaks, and came to Barmere often to help with handyman tasks, and JB had also managed to secure the assistance of young Anna Costain, who had previously helped with camp and club activities. Anna was a member of the Costain building family. Her grandfather Richard Costain (1839–1902) – known in the family as 'Richey Betsy' to distinguish him as the Richard whose mother was Betsy Costain (nee Redhead) – was an ambitious Manx jobbing builder who founded the

First group of evacuees

firm in 1865 at Blundellsands, Liverpool, where he had emigrated from the Isle of Man with his building partner Richard Kneen. Richey Betsy – a 'cradle' Methodist who preached to other children as a child – married Richard Kneen's sister Margaret (1843–1914) in March 1866 and there were soon several children of their union. The couple's firstborn was Richard, in 1867, and after him Henry, William, James (AJ), and Eleanor (Nell). Anna's father, John Kneen Costain (JK), was born in 1876.

The building business went well, but the partnership broke up in 1888, when Richard Kneen returned to the Isle of Man, and Richard Costain was instead joined in business by his sons. After the first world war the Costain brothers developed housing in Liverpool, but Richard sent his son William to London, and in 1923 the separate business of Richard Costain and Sons was formed as a London Company. The London arm prospered whilst Richard's brothers, including JK, maintained the business base in Liverpool, and from the early thirties the two firms became increasingly separate. The London branch of Costains consolidated its reputation by buying, developing, and building Dolphin Square, London, in the 1930s, then the largest block of flats in Europe. The firm grew into a giant, nationally and internationally – Costain was a founder member

Miss Costain

of the Channel Tunnel joint venture, and Richard Costain, grandson of the founder, was knighted in 1954.

Anna's father, JK Costain, met and married Mary Christian Cain (known as Mickey), daughter of Robert and Anna Cain, from a well-known Manx Methodist family, and the couple emigrated to Canada, intending to pioneer a colonial branch of the Costain building enterprise. Anna was born in Peterborough, near Toronto, on 15 December 1915, the eldest of JK and Mickey's children, but her parents returned to England soon after the Great War, and she and her siblings – Richard (Dick), Mary (Kneen), and Joan – were raised at Caldy Island in the Wirral. In her birth year Anna's Uncle Jim, Rev. A.J. Costain, accepted the headship of the Methodist school at Rydal Mount, Colwyn Bay, later attended by her brother Dick. Anna herself, as well as her younger sisters, attended Penrhos, a Methodist girls' boarding school also sited at Colwyn Bay. The two schools had close ties and associations, and in 1999 eventually merged into one establishment.

The Costains were a committed Methodist family, who became acquainted with JB's work at Clubland, and who met him during his visits to the North of England. They thought highly of him and were happy for their daughter to help with Clubland projects. After the outbreak of war Anna's sister Joan became a WREN, whilst Kneen joined the Land Army. Anna, who was a keen photographer, and had been a catering student at King's College in London, stayed at home with her parents, but became increasingly involved with Clubland's evacuation work, particularly at Barmere. Anna was unofficially engaged to be married to a young man she had been seeing for some time, well matched to her in terms of age, background, and lifestyle – but as she and JB worked together tending the evacuees at Barmere the bond between them developed and deepened beyond a mere platonic partnership between the Club leader and his helper, and led to a romantic wartime proposal. Jimmy Butterworth had at last found somebody ready to love him and to share his extraordinary life.

News of the engagement and marriage caused a stir throughout the Methodist community, and a flurry of newspaper articles, photographs of the bride-to-be, and interviews, followed. JB and Clubland had a place in the national consciousness, and his surprise wedding in the midst of war was a confirmation of optimism and future promise. In June 1943 the two married amid family celebration, the great excitement of Clublanders, and their own personal joy. Queen Mary was one of hundreds of Clubland friends and sponsors who sent telegrams and messages of congratulations, and wedding presents arrived in Walworth from far and wide. On their own initiative the Clublanders compiled a souvenir booklet of the marriage, the Clubland celebratory parties, and the couple's Club homecoming, to send to their 500 fellow Clublanders in the forces, to 'convey some idea of how we tried to prove worthy of those who would also have risen to the great event had they been with us'.

The union may possibly have caused a few misgivings even amongst well-wishers. Anna was marrying a man who was almost twenty years her senior and used to the unfettered and single-minded pursuit of his vision, whose life was committed to his Clubland youth, with all the restrictions and requirements which that implied. For many the ceaseless demand for service and self-sacrifice would have been too

Wedding group – JB, Anna, and their parents

London Evening Standard cutting

Evening Standard
47 Shoe Lane, E.C.4.

Cutting from issue dated............5.–.JUN.1943

Clubland Founder Marries: Queen Mary's Message

Queen Mary has sent her "most heartfelt congratulations" to the Rev. J. Butterworth, founder of Clubland, the pioneer youth centre, Camberwell, on his marriage to his girls' club leader, Miss Costain, of West Kirby, Cheshire.

The queen's message wished Mr. and Mrs. Butterworth great happiness in their life and work together.

For the wedding celebration members of the club turned the gymnasium into a banqueting hall, pooled rations, and for four nights held a reception of hundreds of past and present members.

The honeymoon was spent in Mr. Butterworth's home town, Oswaldtwistle, Lancs, where he had been a poor newspaper boy. Though a Nonconformist, he was invited to preach at the Parish Church, where there were long queues.

Club members pooled their sweet rations for JB and Anna's reception

great, but the natural sweetness and generosity of Anna's personality, her practical skills and accomplishments, and her gift of hospitable welcome to both exalted and lowly, made her more than equal to the tremendous task. JB was supremely fortunate in his choice of bride, as Anna took on the formidable challenge of her lifetime role at Jimmy's side in Clubland.

JB's novel status in the club as a new husband soon heralded other developments with his baby son John's arrival on 24 March 1944, followed the next year by a sister, Mary, on 23 December 1945. Messages and blessings for the new babies came from all over the world as the news reached distant absent members, and the Clubland infants received a wealth of gifts and good wishes. The opening years of the war had visited greater grief and loss upon JB and his club than seemed possible to withstand. But on a personal level the last few wartime years had unexpectedly proven rich with the treasures of family and children, and a supportive home life from which to face the formidable challenges of the postwar world.

'The Lord of All Good Life'

The cover of the Clubland Review for October 1944 carries the Temple of Youth illustration, and inside the cover is the Club prayer to 'The Lord of All Good Life'. As the international turmoil continued the prayer was particularly relevant as a symbol of the sustaining faith and reassurance JB sought to transmit to his Clublanders near and far in the face of their uncertain current lives. Inside the Review JB writes that 'After the last war I was led of God to honour my pals who did not return by helping a new generation of youth to see new meaning and purpose in life.' Looking to the future he says that he intends to do the same thing this time.

Throughout that year – the fifth year of the war – the *Reviews* report Clubland's ongoing activities, and reflect the strength of its spirit of staunch reliability through the many difficulties it faced. JB sent copies of these reviews to every absent Clublander for whom he held an address, and was constantly reassured by the recipients of the value of this contact with home. The Head's supper dances on Saturday evenings continued, often attended by visiting forces members, many of whom had been promoted since their call-up to more senior ranks. JB writes with some irony that he himself had managed only private in the previous war, and that now so many of his soldier members have promotions and commissions that he feels he should stand to attention before them.

In 1944 two ex-Senior Heads, Bert Crawley and Hilda Ayling, married at Clubland at the end of January – they were just one couple of many Club members who were married by JB during the war years, often whilst home on leave, and a steady stream of babies was presented to him for christening in due course thereafter. Forces Clublanders returning on leave were frequently asked by the Head to participate in Club services, or to preach the Sunday sermon. JB commented that 'The ex-Seniors from Army, Navy, and Air Force, read lessons and prayers with a reverence and dignity which is very moving.' The record of ex-Senior members who spoke in Church included Frank Neal, Reg Suggars, George Stedman, Frank Thorn, Bill Read, Ken Randall, Bob Brindle, Albert Tolladay, Bert Crawley, and Andy Burton – but there were many others besides who returned to address the congregation of their old church. Reg later wrote movingly to JB that 'it isn't the big things in Clubland which come to mind, but little things which give hope for the future, the hush on a Sunday evening just before the Club service, or fragments from a forgotten sermon ...'

Many of the members met each other overseas – sometimes by happy accident but often going to considerable trouble to do so – and write of emotional reunions in distant places. Bill Stapleton and Laurie 'Lol' Rooney – ex-Cabinet members – send greetings to the Head from afar, saying how they are 'happy as schoolboys' to be reunited after Lol had hiked for six hours to their meeting, and reporting for how long and with what pleasure they had discussed their Clubland days. They have also heard from Charlie Gill in Algiers, and 'Nic and Chic' have sent a photo of the three of them together. In Egypt Ken Randall and Bill Darby travelled long distances to visit a hospitalised Club comrade, and the three 'just talked about the place, and the man who had meant so much to us ... thank you from the bottom of our hearts ... not just us but the hundreds of Clublanders who have found strength and happiness through Clubland and its Head.' Charles Skinner writes from his RAF posting that he yearns for the parliaments, matches, and camps, but realises that Clubland's value is deeper than a few years spent happily in a fine building and that 'chaps like Rooney and Stapleton don't cross countries to see each other just because they once played football together.' Laurie Lowe sends greetings to the Girls' Club from Cairo, where she has seen a poster of Clubland on which she recognised Bunty Coates – she writes of her wonderful memories of Club whilst adding poignantly that 'we were all so young then.'

Frank, Ken, and Bill in Egypt

Lieutenant Frank Neal from his destroyer, and Michael Tattersall from command of a submarine – both leaders in the last pre-war Guernsey camp – send their joint greetings back to Boys' Club members. Frank has started a debating society aboard which he intends to run like the Clubland Parliament. He writes that he cannot believe that Christmas 1944 will be his fifth away from home. Prior to the outbreak of war JB had increasingly relied upon Frank's dependable leadership – he deputised for JB at public events, and took responsibility for various aspects of Club management – and his enlistment had been a particularly hard loss. It's clear that the wrench of leaving had been equally strong for Frank – who after chatting about Club activities ends one letter: 'I do so miss Clubland though, dear JB'. Sergeant Jimmy Whitlock writes declaring the steadiness of his faith and promising JB that: 'One day I shall return to help build another Clubland, more beautiful than the one destroyed.' It is Sergeant Whitlock's third winter in action, moving from Africa to Sicily and Southern Italy. Squadron Leader Arthur Putnam, abroad for a fifth year, tells the Head 'I know the worthwhileness of your effort, what it has meant in every part of my life, and what my life would have been like without Clubland.' For Dennis Woolford it will be his first Christmas abroad in action, but he has been on leave in Rome and been overwhelmed by the size and beauty of St. Peters, and Reg Chary writes from HMS Enchantress that the fortitude and spirit of members abroad is the proof of the value of JB's work and effort.

As realistic hope of the end of the war became possible the scattered Clublanders could allow themselves to think of their return home. Eric Leadbetter wrote to JB that 'the Clubland reunion after the war will be greater than anyone dreamed, and then we can have our grateful say to those who kept it going.' Ted Bondy, in hospital with burned legs, describes his great joy at being able to listen through the whole of the Clubland Sunday Service – and John Dorey, Guernseyman, simply walks into Club one day after four years away in Africa.

There can be no doubt of the devastating impact of Clubland's wartime losses, or of the Head's grief and anxiety for his young congregation, torn away to fight – the prolific correspondence of the absent Clublanders together with the pathos of its content showed that they felt the loss equally keenly. The challenges and trials of its soldiers, sailors, and airmen, on their ventures abroad in the service of their country, formed a constant backcloth to Club life, even as the daily activities of the organisation continued unabated. Church services were held – Harry Whetcombe's home was destroyed shortly before he went into the Navy, but he still came to conduct the Club service; and plays and shows were staged – John Blatchley, appearing in the West End opposite John Gielgud, nevertheless returned to direct the Clubland Players on his one free night per week. Sports matches were played, Parliament and Cabinet discussed Clubland business, celebrity visitors gave talks, fund-raising projects were developed, and art and craft classes went on as before. And through it all a flow of letters from all four corners of the world reached the Club, reporting the traumas and triumphs of its absent youth.

A longing to revisit the 'good life' of Clubland is a nostalgic and optimistic undercurrent in many of the letters so carefully stored by JB, and both Leader and Services members remain positive that this may one day soon come to pass. But from the beginning, and as the years wore on, the reading grew darker and the bleak news from the fighting was often scarcely bearable. Pilot Officer Kenneth Porter,19, has fallen; cousin Maurice Duckworth's plane and everybody in it has been reported missing; and Ron Collier – whose sketches for the new Clubland lined the stairways – has also gone missing. Several members' homes and lives were lost to air raids – Albert Bowskill, Didsbury chairman and sports captain, who joined the Club aged ten, returned tragically to find that his wife, his six-week-old baby and his mother were all killed in an air raid. Bob Cutler was killed fighting in Belgium, and Jimmy Anderson – he who wrote of returning to lead his team again – was dead in India. Teddy Whitehall lost his life at sea, and his baby was in the evacuation centre. Sid Osborne – Cabinet member and Library Chairman – has fallen. Several were wounded, including Frank Neal and Ken Randall, but were able to return to action, and others were missing. Marjorie Howard wrote to JB recalling how proud she was when she was told she would be Chapel Chairman – her husband aged twenty-three has been killed in the RAF, one brother has died at the hands of the Japanese, and the other is in Italy. Her home was destroyed in an air raid. Marjorie says she was distressed when she saw the Clubland Church in ruins, but that she goes on hoping her two babies will grow up to become Club members.

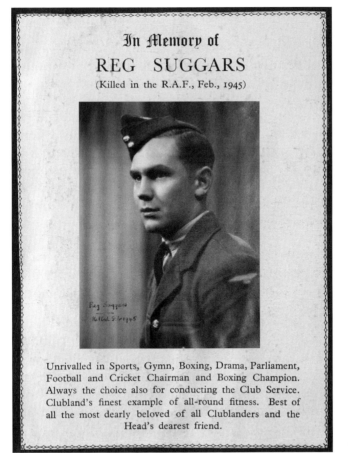

In Memory of

REG SUGGARS

(Killed in the R.A.F., Feb., 1945)

Unrivalled in Sports, Gymn, Boxing, Drama, Parliament, Football and Cricket Chairman and Boxing Champion. Always the choice also for conducting the Club Service. Clubland's finest example of all-round fitness. Best of all the most dearly beloved of all Clublanders and the Head's dearest friend.

Clubland
Review 1945

JB's lads long to be back at Clubland with their 'old gang' – but many never come home to Walworth. Ted Lear has perished, as well as Len James, a Junior Captain. As the war nears its end Reg Suggars, R.A.F., popular pre-war Club Football Captain, and Clubland's greatest sportsman is shot down in his plane, leaving a young wife and a baby son only a few weeks old. In January 1944 Reg had written to JB to tell him how much it had meant to him to be at home at Christmas, and to see all his old friends at Club. He thought that the Christmas Eve Service had been 'wonderful', and had shared with JB his gratitude for his Clubland youth, his hope for the future, and the realisation that the most profound meaning in daily living was to be found in small things. The Club grieved his loss, which seemed to symbolise for many who wrote the toll taken from Clubland by the conflict, and the immeasurable fortitude demanded of those who survived and suffered.

'Letters of a Clublander'

During these turbulent years JB began a substantial piece of work which he entitled 'Letters of a Clublander'. It remained unfinished and unpublished – save as an available archive document – perhaps because there was no time to complete it once the war ended and his energies were needed for rebuilding, and for his newly growing family at home and at Clubland. Or perhaps because it had served a purpose as an enduring expression of Club identity which was no longer necessary once peace was restored. It was conceived of by JB as a series of fifty letters, written by erstwhile Clubland members or associates, which essentially told the story of Clubland and himself – although its presentation as the product of many voices is less than convincing since it is, transparently, exclusively JB's voice throughout, sometimes unaffectedly and at other times superimposed upon quasi-fictitious or stereotypical Club members. That aside, many sections of the document provide an authentic history, and JB's unfinished autobiography has contributed significantly to the present biography.

For anyone born into an era of public and secular responsibility for youth work, a youth club created and built through the effort made, and finance raised, by one individual, and governed within a religious environment by his autocratic leadership alone, would be thought at the least to be an idiosyncratic anachronism. But the value of the Clubland structure has of necessity to be considered and weighed within its particular time and context – that of the widespread deprivation and neglect of unprivileged youth in an age which still looked predominantly to God for its salvation. Clubland was not merely, or at all, a church youth club, but a vibrant singular organisation given shape and substance by a leader whose faith was absorbed in infancy. JB's wartime book reflects the setting in which his inspirational leadership thrived, to the good and betterment of many thousands of young people. It is within this context that he can advocate Sunday evening service as 'the grand climax of the week' which 'will be remembered all over the world by members to whom it has become a very sacred Angelus.' The autobiography contains nuggets of wisdom from the mature reflections of a perceptive and very experienced and articulate Methodist youth club head concerning what is both effective and necessary to the sound development of both the organisation and its leader. It is frequently direct and apposite beyond any of JB's previous commercially published writing.

Advising aspiring leaders against allowing dilettante helpers JB writes that the leader must be a comrade first, else he will have no credence.

> It is not the swoopers arriving from a distance who redeem the situation, but the real sharers who have nothing whatever in common with charity mongers or those who like slumming. Your club is not putty for somebody's pet theories for grasping souls, bodies, and minds.

In another section entitled 'Old Man River' he writes that club leadership means

> hearing much, keeping your own council, sharing the sorrows and joys of the members who journey for a while in life on your boat, and like the old river you just go rolling, keep on rolling along ... The honours must go to members and the leader must take the rap when things go wrong – personal ambition and desire for the limelight must not creep in. There is much fun, but many heartbreaks, and a sense of humour is essential, as well as a capacity for detailed organisation and planning. You must be able to be taken for granted, always there, always available at the club, even if inside you feel lonely amid all the youthful happiness ... You must never be too busy to talk and listen to the trivial affairs of individuals, and must possess your soul in patience as it is a rare gift to just stand around laughing and talking with lads ... Many lads get lost on the road to goodness and to God.

Remembering names and faces from 'the long ago', and particularly a page-boy member who died of exhaustion, JB confirms the principle of his club work – 'I believe in your inborn nobility, and inherent goodness.' Describing the structure and business of the Club Parliament, of which all are members, he reveals its purpose: 'Parliament taught us to put thoughts into words, and take interest in much we would never have thought about. It helped to make us honourable members in other places beside Club.' And he reveals his horror of crude evangelism, warning 'Beware of evangelists who would flood the place with tracts and texts, to say nothing of saving the whole club by the barrel load.' He holds to the view that it is the business of the pulpit to offer friendship rather than bullying – and that deeply inarticulate religious meaning cannot be transmitted by anything less than friendship: 'Above all things the minister must offer friendship to all and show that the Lord of All Good Life is accessible to everybody.'

JB has reached the considered view that ordinand ministers should have a longer training period for what he considers to be a whole time vocation 'before they presume to preach to those who are already facing the music of living'. He thinks little of leaders who reserve energy for other pursuits, and cautions that: 'All this leaves no time for sitting on commissions for the saving of all London. You will walk no more in the courts of church councils nor sit in the seats of conferences, nor will your voice be heard in mass meetings.' He regards his own greatest sacrifice as giving up preaching for the sake of his Club commitment: 'Your greatest temptation will be preaching. It will be anguish to turn from that which gave you so much joy and others such real blessing. You will never pass a church without feeling that God gave you the gifts to fill it ...'

JB's instincts were always to put the spiritual interests of the members first – before creed or dogma, before externally imposed religious requirements, and certainly before his personal well-being – by offering them his own friendship and that of their fellows within a context of opportunity and advancement. And it is these principles in his idiosyncratic mix of club leadership and ministry which are made abundantly clear in this unpublished autobiography.

With the end of hostilities Clubland was able to take stock of its position. The report of Head Senior Sidney B. Harris, in 1945, described a burgeoning membership, and a Boys' Cabinet which, although formed by comparatively new members, has taken on its important duties with willing responsibility. 'The flourishing activities and the increased membership, and the excellent atmosphere in the place, show that this has been one of our happiest terms.' Sidney reports that a whole wing of club rooms – comprising space previously used for Dramatics, Art, Handicrafts, Leatherwork, Games, and the Canteen – occupied by the LCC for four years, has been de-requisitioned and restored to its original function. Cabinet is planning an Easter Camp, and 'The Head's wife and son are coming home, which will give us the chance to make the acquaintance of Master John before most of us depart for the Forces.' Sidney has himself called the Club home for some time: 'Myself and other chairmen whose homes were damaged in raids have been privileged to live at the Club ... it has given us the chance of living with and working with the Head.'

JB also wrote an article for inclusion in this *Review* describing the uses to which Clubland had been put during wartime – there had been a constant influx of homeless seeking shelter and 'Clublanders came straight from work to shepherd old folk and little children into rooms of happier memories.' The Clubs, confined to one wing, had never closed, throughout the war or during raids: 'We saw our crowded congregation go off to the forces and then recruited new members from Tube shelters ... Whilst one generation of Clublanders built our College of Youth, another kept it going in war time'. JB reported that even without publicity there had nevertheless been a waiting-list of members – and that new members and forces members had maintained the tradition of financial co-partnership never failing to raise their £1000 per year.

JB was eager to extend his fund-raising projects to obtain money for the necessary rebuilding, although neither he, nor others engaged with youth club matters, were wholeheartedly optimistic in respect of postwar restoration. Frank Dawes noted that after the flux of war, by the time it was all over, a feeling was growing that organisations outside the state-sponsored movement were becoming redundant. Funds were restricted, and NABC had to close all its residential centres due to economic difficulty – Dawes wrote that prior to 1939 the main object of boys' club work had been preventative, and afterwards became educational and a state project.[12]

Addressing the situation of returning Forces members in *Letters from a Clublander* JB compares the situation in 1945 with that of 1919, observing that: 'Those who did return in 1919 were very much like sheep without shepherds. They went from the mines, factories, and foundries ... and returned to short shifts, unemployment, and the dole.' He observes that in the meanwhile the world has moved on, and 'this time an awakening democracy is beginning to ask questions, and moreover war has been brought to almost everybody's door, and often enough inside it.' Remembering how lost he and his comrades had felt on their return from the first war, JB voices fears for the erstwhile Clublanders that it may be only their dream that they can come back to the same Club that they left. 'After the great reunions and gay celebrations you will find those days are gone forever. You will say the old club is not the same as it used to be. It is really, but you have changed from boys to men. A new crowd will not even know you, perhaps only your old Head, or the caretaker, will remember you. Launched away on reminiscences we shall become suddenly silent for John and Bert and George are no longer with us.'

The Forces Members did indeed come back to their surviving homes and families, and to their old club – and JB's misgivings soon vanished amidst the sheer relief of having his beloved absent flock back in the fold. The war had surely scattered Clublanders far and wide – during their service abroad members in the armed forces, brought up and connected in the fellowship of Clubland, grew to form an extensive loosely bound affiliation. When the war was over the returning body of services ex-members formed a substantial extra presence in Club structure.

The Head welcomed them with heartfelt thanksgiving for their survival, as they sought to re-occupy the lives from which they had been uprooted six years earlier. JB knew from his own return from military action that settling back into a previous existence was not an easy transition, and he did everything possible to smooth the path for his 'old gang' lest they now felt themselves dispossessed from their former Club. They had longed to come back, and were overjoyed to see each other and JB, and to spend time in the familiar Club rooms exchanging stories and reminiscing with their old friends and clubmates. But years had passed – for some all the years of the war – and their lives had been changed irrevocably.

They were now adults – well beyond the age at which they would have outgrown the Club in ordinary circumstances – some with their own families, and their most important concerns naturally lay outside and beyond Clubland. A number of them marked their return by taking on an officer role, or other voluntary service within the Club – but for the others it soon became plain that their ongoing interest in Clubland was essentially a social or recreational one. None of this affected JB's joy at the return of the forces members, nor did it devalue the contribution they made to Club regeneration over the postwar years. In time, however, the addition of a large adult tier of members did result in imbalances and stresses within the Club, and ultimately prompted JB to renew Clubland's earlier more exclusive focus upon its younger members.

Notes

1 *Letters of a Clublander* Ch.46 'The Great Dispersion'.
2 Ibid, 46.
3 *Letters of a Clublander* Ch.46.
4 *Letters of a Clublander* Ch.46.
5 R.C. Sherriff's play set in the trenches in 1918.
6 *Letters of a Clublander* Ch.47.
7 *South London Press*, 13 November, 1941.
8 Obituary, Methodist Minutes of Conference 1970.
9 *Guernsey Society Review*, Winter 2005–6.
10 From the script of *This is Your Life* – 'The Big Red Book'. BBC, November 1955
11 *Letters of a Clublander*, Ch.38.
12 Frank Dawes. *A Cry From the Streets*, 1975. Pt.3 Section 7 *'War Again'*.

CHAPTER SEVEN

Regeneration

Beginning Again

The immediate tasks that faced the Club, when peace and relative normality returned, were financial and material. During the Blitz the bulk of the premises had been requisitioned for 'national services', relegating the club functions to one wing of the building. Two thirds of the rooms had been turned over for rest-centre work, day nurseries, feeding schoolchildren, and the duties of air-raid wardens – for which the rooftop playground had been an obvious asset. Once the London County Council (LCC) no longer needed the facilities, they also ceased to contribute financially to its maintenance. Moreover, they left the buildings and furnishings in a state of disrepair for which there was little or no recompense, despite an estimated bill of £2000. This was before even thinking about the cost of rebuilding the ruined chapel, which towered, roofless and windowless above the quadrangle. The War Damages Commission would cover only so much, and the whole process of administration was slow and complex, with churches rightly a low priority compared with homes and essential businesses. Moreover, there were restrictions on what could be put in place. Ultimately the Chapel would be rebuilt, as the original one had been, by voluntary donation and tireless fund-raising.

The whole question of state support of any kind would remain a thorny, unresolved issue, exacerbated by a changing landscape in youth work, and the increasing involvement of government and public bodies in what had fallen in the past to voluntary organisations, charities, and churches. Part of the move to a more centralised provision was the introduction of trained and paid social workers. From the start Clubland's officers and helpers had been volunteers, who gave of their time and varied expertise freely, and who in time were replaced by ex-Seniors, anxious to repay their club for what it had given them. At the same time the building and running costs had been found from the members' subscriptions, collections, and various fundraising efforts, with major contributions from the many sponsors and donors who recognised the value of what the Club was doing. Privately, although he grumbled that Clubland had received no assistance from public funds, JB also boasted in the same breath that it had managed perfectly well without them through its own independent endeavours – and he was determined to maintain that tradition. Besides, with central funding came federation and regulation, and to the end JB would have none of either.

His other major task was restoring the Club itself, after its prolonged and profound disruption. Something less tangible but more far-reaching than bricks and mortar had been fractured by the war. Enlistment in the forces had decimated the membership and would continue to take its toll until the end of National Service in the mid-fifties. Likewise evacuation during the Blitz had effectively closed down the junior clubs which, for one reason or another, did not re-form for nearly a decade. A vibrant ongoing senior section remained, but with the debilitating effect of constant military call-up, and without the replenishing influx of trained Club Juniors year on year, there was an inevitable break in the continuity of membership.

The doors of Clubland were always open, and regular Saturday night dances were held to welcome Services members home on leave. There must have been times when the sight of so many young men and women in uniform took JB back to his days in the Scouts Hut at Étaples. Throughout the war the Club's range of activity had survived, against the odds, and in all but scale there was a sense of business as usual. The drama section had remained active, and burgeoned in the postwar years with a succession of acclaimed productions. There were concerts for families sheltering from or made homeless by the bombing; teams continued to play matches when they could; and the canteen was staffed without a break by volunteers. Services were held every Sunday without interruption throughout the war years, even after the Chapel was destroyed.

As the nation celebrated the victories in Europe and then Japan in the Spring and Summer of 1945, there was no obvious reason to doubt that Clubland would return to its pre-war state in all essential respects. In the first *Review* after VE Day JB wrote: 'Now we come to our first winter in peace, and there is going to be a long waiting list of members. To the already large membership there are added crowds of returning evacuees and forces members. Even amid our ruins we are operating in what is probably the worst bombed area in London. From wrecked and patched up homes and temporary housing come ever-increasing applicants for membership ... This is a great task to which our youthful community is committed.'[1]

It would take hindsight, however, to see how tall an order this was, as social attitudes changed in the ensuing years, and a new generation of members filled the premises. Few had recollections of the pre-war club, and they had not grown up in it – in consequence they had expectations which did not necessarily chime with those of the now returning service men and women. These, in turn, had long passed the age of senior membership, and had it not been for the war they would have moved on into adult life, or retained their connection by becoming officers, instead of which they swelled the ranks of the ex-Seniors, altering the emphasis and focus of the membership. Even without the benefit of hindsight, JB had had a sense of foreboding about what had been lost and what was to come, writing plaintively in the summer of 1945 that the returning members could not expect to find Clubland as they had left it, not because it itself was any different but because they were. No longer adolescents but men and women with adult lives ahead and world-changing experiences behind them due to the war, they could not but see things through different eyes. Many would drift away on finding a new generation of members for whom they were strangers; others would come back, if only out of nostalgia. 'An old boys association is the best possibility', JB had warned. 'After all, you have had your club.'[2]

He had been delighted at the return of his soldier members, and certainly had no wish to exclude them to make way for the new intake – especially given what they had been through. But over time it had become clear that Forces ex-members – who no longer had any clear role in Clubland – were more inclined to treat the Club as a recreation centre to relax and meet each other than anything else. But however much they had contributed to their club in the past, and to their country through the long years of war, it remained the case that Clubland had never been intended as a mere leisure amenity, and JB was as opposed to this use as he had ever been, and disinclined to offer any different arrangement from his pre-war norm. It was still true that he had built the splendid premises as part of providing to the least advantaged a better deal in life than he had had as a boy, and a necessary ingredient in that was access to fine surroundings and stimulating activity. His members were to feel entitled to the same standards of excellence as those which the more privileged young people in society took for granted – but his requirement had always been that the members gave something significant in return. Membership came with certain conditions, the primary one being that they should participate in the full life of the Club, and contribute to that life. Effectively that meant signing up to a contract which, by today's standards, would seem prescriptive and demanding.

JB was fond of saying that Clubland had no rules other than those the members chose for themselves, for the general good. This was not the whole truth. Ostensibly the running of the Club was governed by the weekly Parliament where policy was debated and determined by consensus, but only within certain well-defined parameters – the democratic process was in practice transcended by a set of unwritten basic principles. Clubland was never to be reduced to a 'drop-in centre', a term JB used with evident disdain to describe a growing number of youth institutions that allowed their members – if they could be so called – to come and go as they pleased and take or leave what was on offer in the way of activities. That approach, which became more prevalent in the post-war years, was underpinned by the assumption that restrictions and conditions tended to deter young people from attending, and thus lured fewer of them off the streets.

At Clubland, by contrast, there was actually a *requirement* to participate, and make use of the facilities for recreation and/or self-improvement for some part of the club evening. Casual attendance was not an option – nor was cherry-picking. Whilst the individual activities that the Club offered, and the excellent facilities that went with them, were a major attraction, no department was permitted to assume greater importance than the whole. Naturally some members had special interests and skills – art, drama, gymnastics, music, debating, and so on – and opportunity and encouragement were there to advance those talents, but only in the context of the communal life that embraced them all.

In his book *Making Men*, Eagar drew a distinction between clubs like Clubland – for which he used the term 'intensive' – and those that gave way to an increasingly popular open-door, come-and-go-as-you-please approach. Rightly or wrongly Clubland resisted that trend, even when criticised for not moving with the times, or for allegedly failing to reach out to those who were not just deprived but disruptive too, and unwilling or unable to make the commitments expected of a signed-up member. It was certainly true that insistence on participation, regular attendance, respectful behaviour, etc., would deter some potential members, especially perhaps those most attracted by the unruly freedom of street or gang culture.

It would be entirely wrong to suppose that Clubland had no appeal for 'bad lads', of which south-east London had more than its fair share. On the contrary, many of its long-serving members recall having been on the fringes of delinquency when they first joined. No one was turned away from Clubland, or refused second or multiple chances. But the purpose of the club was nonetheless to improve character, not to tolerate or 'pander' endlessly, and those who refused to play their part could expect no special treatment. Temporary suspension was the ultimate sanction, and JB used it to effect. Today educationalists and politicians tend to view exclusion as a sign of failure in the system, and a last resort. Yet, in Clubland's case, it is equally valid to dwell on the positive evidence of the countless members who – against their natural instincts in many cases – accepted the Clubland contract and lived to be glad that they had: rough, deprived, disaffected adolescents who wanted the benefits badly enough to swallow their pride and come back for more time after time, after walking out or being shown the door. In fact, it became something of a badge of honour to have been suspended – and many of the letters JB received later from old members took evident delight in their often turbulent early relationship with Clubland and its fiery Head. And JB in turn relished the challenge of winning round individuals who were uncooperative or hostile to his methods and style of leadership. Even when, in the early fifties, the Club suffered a serious spate of vandalism and violence from outsiders and a few trouble-makers inside, JB is on record as saying: 'After all, these are the boys and girls I am here to help.'

Clubland was by no means alone in its thinking. Basil Henriques' thriving St George's Settlement for boys and girls of Jewish faith, shared much of the same 'intensive' character. This was no coincidence since JB was a friend and lifelong admirer of Henriques, whose work had preceded his own by a few years, and the influence of his philosophy and practice is beyond doubt. Thanks to Henriques' connections the St George's Club had acquired an old school building in Berners Street, equipped for a wide range of physical and creative pursuits – and Henriques had also secured talented and committed instructors for his members. The Settlement was renowned for its sporting achievements, with teams competing at cricket, football, netball, hockey, swimming, and boxing. The showers and changing rooms, like Clubland's, were both a novelty and an important health innovation, and contributed to the members' sense of worth and access to excellence. St. George's facilities would have been a natural model for JB during the 'Dugout' days, and throughout the decade of wrestling with the elders at Walworth and seeking sponsors for his own theatre, gymnasium, playgrounds, and club rooms, and he made no secret of his debt to Henriques.

No less striking are the many similarities in the ethos of the two organisations. In the words of Rabbi Rigal,

> the (St George's) clubs were not just social. They were educational, and taught sports, acting, ballet, physical education, First Aid, etc. They helped to prepare the boys and girls to enter into the British way of life and so helped them in eventually seeking careers. At the same time they gave them a modern outlook upon Judaism and their Jewish heritage. The highlight of the year was the Annual Summer Camps. The clubs took several hundred Jewish children away for a holiday under canvas each year. For many youngsters this was the only time that they left inner city London …The clubs succeeded in creating a tremendous club spirit, which lasted long after their youth.[3]

The same basic ingredients – of fostering club fellowship and faith within a broad range of highly organised activities and outings, which trained and educated at the same time as they entertained and occupied – had come to characterise what it was to be a Clublander in the pre-war years, and there were strong parallels in practice between the two clubs. The question was whether any such organisation could survive, maintaining its physical and financial existence, as well as its founding principles, through the decades to come. If anyone was equal to the task it was James Butterworth, but the world of youth work was changing, and even for him the road which lay ahead would be a hard one and costly on many counts.

A New Jerusalem

Clubland's immediate response to the ending of the world conflict was relatively low key. In JB's own words: 'Religious Victory Services are not in our line. War is war, and to drag God into it is to make the Eternal Father of Mankind a person to be conscripted or a priority commodity for use on special occasions. We have even less sympathy with a round of merrymaking, especially when so many are still fighting, and many more have lost everything.' He added: 'It is so easy to indulge in thanksgiving services, victory demonstrations and flagwagging and then do nothing towards establishing the freedoms for which millions have died and suffered. We may dance and sing to the strains of "There will always be an England" and then wake up to find ourselves in the same old slums, temporary hutments and worse conditions than before the war.'

There was an element of *déjà vu*, as well as factual observation, in this last sentiment. The 'land fit for heroes to live in', promised in 1919, had already been a very long time coming, with memories of the poverty and unemployment of the thirties still vivid, and good quality housing still far below target in the streets and tenements around Clubland.

In the summer of 1945 between VE and VJ Day the country went to the polls and voted unexpectedly and resoundingly for Labour to replace the wartime coalition, and Clement Atlee to succeed Churchill as Prime Minister. In retrospect the result should not have been so surprising. The generation of Britons who had fought and survived one war, and so soon after had to live through a second, craved not only an end to the current austerity but a realistic promise that this time there would be no return to economic depression, glaring inequality and widespread deprivation. In 1942, with the prospect of military victory far from certain, Sir William Beveridge had published his revolutionary Report, setting out radically innovative proposals for Britain's eventual postwar reconstruction. With a Dickensian ring, the Report identified 'five giants' that stood in the way of progress on social reform: Want, Ignorance, Squalor, Disease and Idleness. Accordingly it laid out plans for wholesale changes in education, pensions, health, social security and jobs. The five giants would have been no strangers to Jimmy Butterworth when he arrived in Walworth in 1922, and within the microsphere of Clubland he had made his own response to all of them. Twenty years on, he would certainly have welcomed the spirit of Beveridge, although he might well have added: 'What kept you?'

Contrary to what is often assumed, the *Beveridge Report* met with approval from many quarters in the coalition parliament, and was not confined to the socialists at Westminster. The domestic policy of the Attlee government was strongly influenced by the *Report*, and would secure the foundations of the National Health Service, the introduction of a safety net of social security 'from cradle to grave', and the promise to build more and better homes. But in truth the manifestos of all three main parties, the Tories included, echoed many of Beveridges's aims and recommendations, whether out of natural sympathy or from political expediency in reaction to the public mood. The 1944 Education Act, which four years later would introduce compulsory free secondary education for all, was based on the work of a Conservative minister, 'Rab'

Butler. Despite this and other pledges, and despite Churchill's personal standing as a wartime leader, the electorate had good reason not to trust the Tories to deliver comprehensive social reform once victory was assured. The massive armed forces vote, in particular, swung heavily to Labour, a factor that many commentators attributed to the influence of the *Daily Mirror* – then the most popular newspaper, especially in the forces. One cartoon, published on the eve of the election, depicted a bandaged soldier holding a piece of paper announcing 'Victory and Peace in Europe', underwritten by his own words: *Here you are. Don't lose it again!*

Labour's achievements in the following five years are legendary. Under Atlee the country saw more rapid and far-reaching transformation of the economic, political, and social landscape than at any time before and possibly since. The welfare reforms in particular were groundbreaking, as was the accompanying shift, albeit impermanent, towards state control of industry. In general terms there was a significant move towards greater intervention by local and national government in the provision, and regulation, of services and amenities, such as health, housing, education, work, and leisure. Labour's most radical policies – including nationalisation, which had previously faced strenuous opposition – were broadly welcomed by an electorate not simply eager for an end to the wartime shortages but also optimistic about the ability of the new government to deliver a future programme of improved living standards for all. Moreover, what might have seemed an intolerable level of state control before the war would have been more familiar after six years of emergency legislation and government overseeing. After all, it had brought victory, and helped to develop the communal spirit that was said to have played so important a role on the Home Front.

Emboldened by its overwhelming electoral success – almost 48% of the popular vote went their way, giving Attlee an overall commons majority of 247 seats – Labour rapidly implemented a succession of major reforms. In retrospect, however, the odds were against being able to maintain the early momentum and pace of change. Writing in *The Guardian* half a century later, Derek Brown observed that

> after the clamour of victory, the peace was a drab disappointment.
> And after all the fervent promises of a new dawn, British life remained
> to a large extent grey and grim. At times, food restrictions were even
> tighter than during the war – bread was rationed for the first time. Class
> enmities flourished; social and economic inequalities remained palpable.
> Here and there were little pockets of a new prosperity: television

broadcasts were resumed, the first Morris Minors appeared, and British designers were working on the world's first commercial jet, the De Havilland Comet. But of that great universal prosperity which seemed to glow from the 1945 manifestos, there was little sign.'[4]

Labour nonetheless survived the 1950 general election, although with a reduced parliamentary majority. A year later, damaged by internal feuds, Attlee called and lost his third post war ballot. The party held on to its popular support, which in fact increased slightly and still led the field, but the British electoral system, with its first-past-the-post anomalies, and the collapse of the Liberal Party (to a mere six seats) helped to propel the Conservatives back into power and Churchill back into Downing Street.

Housing was a critical issue, and a lingering problem for government, of whichever colour. The popular joke that the Luftwaffe had done more in the way of slum clearance than successive governments in the previous half-century had more than a dark grain of truth in it. But there was nothing funny about the homelessness and temporary accommodation that were the grim reality of so many families as the months and years dragged on. Nationwide, the air raids had destroyed half a million homes, but in total three-quarters of a million new dwellings were still needed to re-house the population in 1950. Many local authorities resorted to erecting prefabricated units – or 'prefabs' as they were known. These were a familiar sight in Southwark which, as JB had observed, was one of the most heavily bombed boroughs in the capital. Not a single street in the vicinity of Clubland – Albany Road, Boundary Lane, Grosvenor Terrace, John Ruskin Street, Hillingdon Street, to name some of the closest – had escaped unscathed. Their misfortune lay in the proximity of the busy elevated railway line linking London and the South Coast – which in fact forms the western boundary of the Clubland site. Regular rubble-strewn gaps still punctuated the terraced rows of these streets well into the fifties – a favourite though dangerous playground for children, and visible evidence of the slow speed of reconstruction.

A further consequence was that the priority for new building caused postponements to the repair and improvement of surviving properties, many in serious need of attention. Labour to its credit mounted a nationwide programme to build decent council housing for low-income families; but with the state of the nation's finances, and competing demands for limited resources, the pace was not enough to satisfy demand. Ironically it was the Conservatives, aided by a recovering economy in the fifties, who would be able to accelerate the housing programme and take the credit for it historically.

Meanwhile, people continued to struggle financially. The war had bankrupted the country, and even in the years that followed Britain's defence spending remained excessively high, with a sizeable contribution to the newly formed NATO, as well as the financial support of its own ongoing military responsibilities. In consequence, the basic rate of income tax was more than twice what it is today, and rationing remained in place, due to the high cost of imports and scarcity of many essential and luxury goods. Factories and transport were hampered by fuel shortages, and homes were deprived of reliable electricity supplies. Families continued of necessity to grow food in their back gardens, and to 'make-do-and-mend' as they had done in the Blitz – food parcels from relatives living abroad were still welcomed gratefully by many.

The most positive and radical innovations of the Attlee Years were educational reform and the establishment of the Welfare State, accompanied by the nationalisation of a range of major industries and utilities: coal, gas, iron and steel, the railways and hospitals, to list the most noteworthy and most controversial. In 1948 the National Health Service came into being, providing medical and dental care for every citizen regardless of income, 'free at the point of delivery'. In the same year the school leaving age was raised to fifteen, following the recommendations of the 1944 Education Act. It was the first major educational reform for decades, and a remarkable development given the nation's preoccupation with war and want. Few can have expected education to be a priority; Churchill, for one, was characteristically dismissive, saying he had no time or wish to 'wipe children's noses and smack their behinds' whilst fighting the Nazis. Yet the conflict seems nevertheless to have inspired a campaign which was long overdue after the neglect of the interwar years.

In 1938 around 80% of children had only ever attended an all-age elementary school. Fewer than one in a hundred got to university. The legislation, drawn up in 1943 and enacted the following year, ensured for the first time that free secondary school education would be the right of every child, starting at eleven. However, rather than opting for a unitary, comprehensive system – for which many of the reformers had campaigned – a three-tier structure was put in place. This consisted of grammar schools, technical schools, and 'secondary moderns' – the latter, in the event, teaching the majority of the age group. Church schools representing the various denominations also retained their status, though funded and supervised by local authorities; and some fee-paying public schools made a proportion of places available to non-paying pupils in return for commensurate – 'direct grant' – state funding. Two notable local examples were Alleyns and Dulwich College both of which were attended by small numbers of Clublanders in following years. Finally further-education colleges were expanded for school-leavers up to the age of 18. These innovations would have significant consequences for the structure of Clubland's membership, and ultimately its role in the educational context, but initially the Senior Club was unchanged in its comprehensive provision for working boys and girls.

'A new Jerusalem' was an expression on many lips at the time, but in retrospect it had more to do with aspiration than realisation. The broad commitments of the Act were met, but legislation alone was not enough to revolutionise the educational landscape to the extent or at the speed that was needed. It took 20 years, for example, for the leaving age to rise again, to 16, and longer still for a full-scale advance towards comprehensive education, and for a national examination system to be extended to all. Against Butler's better judgement, an all-or-nothing intelligence test – the 'eleven-plus' – was instigated at the end of the primary phase to determine whether or not a child was awarded a place at grammar school. This had more than short-term consequences for future opportunity, since grammar school was practically the only pathway to university for those who could not afford private education. Even for those who passed the eleven-plus the expectation of going on to higher education was limited by social class and income. Only a small proportion of the population went to university, the majority of these having attended public schools. The availability of technical schools was also patchy, with the result that 8 out of 10 children were assigned to secondary modern schools, leaving after three or four years, with no formal qualifications, to find work. Those with sufficient luck or foresight to enter apprenticeships went on to learn a trade, but all too many had to settle for low-paid, low-skilled jobs with limited prospects. In Clubland's original formulation the Senior Club had provided its members with the secondary education that they were denied – as JB had been denied – by starting work so young. The new secondary phase of education, as implemented under the 1944 act, did little to displace that Senior Club function for some years. It was with strong justification that JB continued to refer to Clubland as a 'youth college' and, with the same conviction as before, continued to run it like one.

The regular established exodus of Clublanders into the armed forces did not end in 1945, and in many cases it still involved perilous active service overseas. At the upper end of the Senior Club age-range military conscription for National Service awaited the majority of boys when they reached 17 or 18 – there were four times as many men in uniform in 1950 as there are today. Many of the members, after only four years in the Club, found themselves deployed for two years in areas of conflict such as Aden and Palestine, in occupied territory including West Germany, in the remaining outposts of the Empire, and from 1950 in Korea also. The Korean war cost 750 British lives, with many more injured or captured.

In short, as its twenty-fifth anniversary approached, Clubland's natural constituency was little changed. The rising prosperity that would mark the coming decades was yet to make itself felt – and by the same token, the need for Clubland, and for the opportunities it held out to its members, was undiminished for some time to come. Despite the austerity – or perhaps because of it – the Club grew and flourished in these postwar years.

Restoration

Every Clubland member and officer of the early postwar years remembered ever after the instruction 'bring a brick', which JB routinely issued to anyone entering the club at the time, including visitors. In general it was a catch-phrase for any effort, however small, that could be made toward the restorations; but it had a literal meaning too, as the rubble was cleared from the ruins and surrounding areas, and bricks were used for general repairs throughout. A great deal of the manual work was done by the members, as Alec Reed recorded cinematically for *The Clubland Story*,[5] albeit with some evident choreography. In the summer *Review*, 1947, JB reported that for a significant period every senior member had been frequently engaged in carting away tons of bricks and rubble from the ruins.

The first major tasks were to make good the basement clubrooms under the chapel, and to create a Garden of Remembrance in the quadrangle, but in fact extensive renovation was needed right through the premises, due to the aftermath of requisitioning as well as to the Blitz. The shell of the Chapel itself was also cleared of the debris from the fallen roof, and the floor tarmacked to be used for outdoor activities and memorial services – until it was demolished for rebuilding in the sixties. One joyful pastime it facilitated, especially after the Juniors were

Queen Mary arriving
for service in the
ruined Chapel

Restoration Service in the Ruins

re-formed, was roller-skating, despite the sloping floor. It is diverting to speculate on what Health and Safety officials today would make of the sight of the horde of young children charging up the ramp and careering down it, and of the grazes and bruises they took home to show for it. Current regulations would be likely to have closed Clubland down on the spot, together with the vast majority of similar voluntary organisations who were liberal in allowing such activities in an earlier era.

A spur to the work taking place on the Club premises, as well as a testament to it, was the temporary transformation that had been undertaken in time for the return of Queen Mary, on 18 May 1946, a week after the fifth anniversary of the bombing. An altar was constructed, and decorated; the two head Seniors, Vera Burroughs and Mac Phillips, took the service. Queen Mary, wife of one wartime king and mother of a second, spoke movingly of her confidence that the Club would 'rise from the ashes' and continue its renowned work for London's youth. The Accrington Male Voice Choir journeyed down from JB's birthplace for the occasion, and a fledgling Clubland band played the national anthem with energy, if not accuracy. The Queen, responding afterwards to an apology for a few missed notes remarked that any band can play 'God Save the Queen', but only the Clubland band could simultaneously prompt the congregation to sing 'O God our Help in Ages Past'.

Making good the premises for present use, meeting maintenance bills, and starting to save for extensive and essential rebuilding work were major preoccupations. In 1946 members' subscriptions, Sunday collections, sales of handicrafts, and door money from several drama and music productions raised over £1500. The sum was matched by a contribution from the Lord Mayor's fund, and money raised from Restoration Stones on the walls of the quadrangle each engraved with the benefactor's name. These stones became an important feature of JB's postwar fundraising drive, particularly during his later tours of America. A stone could be named for £100, and a brick purchased for 2/6 (12.5 pence) – and many sponsors took the opportunity of having their names engraved for posterity.

Through relentless striving and hard work Clubland had freed itself from current account debt, and actually managed to establish a small surplus, as early as 1947 – but this hard-won and minimal financial achievement brought with it a cruel irony. In the 1947 *Review* JB wrote:

> Our appeals against the withdrawal of grants, which other youth

centres receive, have failed. It is a poor reward for our years of sacrificial pioneering. The reason for this injustice is that we show a balance in hand. Of course we do. Since the war ended, we have fired girls and boys in the adventure of restoring their destroyed Church. Their response was magnificent and deserving of encouragement. Their first task was to get the place out of debt. They have done so, and lose all their grants after almost superhuman achievements. Well may they ask in all their rejoicings was it worth the effort and the sacrifice? From the first we have held it as vital that youth must be trained to serve and support its own clubs. Our tradition is to make partners not passengers. Must we now go back on that and tell youth to give and do as little as it can? Is sacrifice, personal effort and enterprise to be penalized? The State, clubs, and members would all benefit if grants were given to stimulate and not to discourage the efforts of youth.

What had been withdrawn was actually the recompense for the requisitioning and wartime use of the premises, rather than finance for the running of Clubland itself – and of course JB had never seriously courted or relied upon state support. He was wedded to the ideals of self-help and self-sufficiency, and his long-ago Chapel upbringing had instilled in him the twin attitudes of sacrifice and pride – silver not copper in the collection plate, and an abiding abhorrence of debt. In the 'Dugout' days when he began his ministry, it was just possible to run the club on a manageable budget, with small subscriptions, voluntary helpers, and a few financial sponsors who saw the value of what he was doing and gave to it generously, but without seeking to interfere or control. Acceptance of government grants would certainly have compromised that basis and led inevitably to friction. It was a fair point that denying financial encouragement to those who have made great efforts to help themselves, whilst rewarding others who rely on grants and do little, is both short-sighted and unjust. Ultimately, though, it is also fair to say that it arose as much from choice on JB's part as from discrimination against Clubland.

Nonetheless the looming expense of rebuilding and extending the premises defined the next decade and beyond. As well as running the Club and continuing his demanding ministry to young people, JB was increasingly burdened by the need to establish a reliable source of income that would outlive him and secure the future of his Club for generations to come. He was already forming the idea of an adult community, or 'settlement' – affordably housed in and around the existing club – which would provide both income and youth-leadership for as long as they were needed. Such accommodation could help former members who were in need of decent homes – close to their Club where they could meet and maintain old friendships – but it also looked forward pragmatically to a time when the Club would have to run and fund itself without his undivided attention.

In March 1947 he celebrated his fiftieth birthday, and in September Clubland's twenty-fifth. He was not as young as he had been and was secretive about the true state of his health and the effect his work had upon it. Moreover he was now a married man with a young wife and two very young children. But above all his generational relationship to the members was entering a new phase. Although he would still be at his post for the best part of three more decades, he was already becoming aware of the need for contingency planning if his creation was to endure. The idea of a Clubland 'island site', served by hostels which housed volunteers, remained for the time being the germ of a grand plan for the future. In the present he still had a club to run, a ministry to provide, and a family to raise – or rather two families: a small one and a very large one.

John and Mary

Back to business

On 8 May 1945 – VE Day – the Club closed and an altar was erected in the theatre, decked with flowers in memory of those who had fallen. On either side were placed the crosses from the wreckage of the Girls' and Boys' Chapels, and the log books of Cabinet members who would not return. It was a day of remembrance and sadness. A special tribute was made to Gordon Davis, who was still serving in Holland, in recognition of all that he had done to hold Clubland together through the war years. On the following Sunday the same treasured objects were moved into the ruins of the church where a Service of Remembrance was conducted by the Head, his two Head Seniors, Gladys Brown and Sid Harris, and former ones, Frank Neal and Kathleen Coates.

The new team of Chairmen included Jock Surtees, Ken Le Blond, Alf Morbin, Dave Shuard, John Lane, John White, Ernie Power, Ron Enston; and on the girls' side Elsie Darby, Iris White, Marg Harmsworth, Edna Churchill, Joyce Waller, Joan Tipper, Edna Copperdale, and Doris Clark. With these names on the logbooks, the new generation of Clubland got underway. It was a beginning, but it was also a continuation: in those first months after the war ceased, it might have seemed that nothing had changed, on the surface at any rate. Ordinary club nights resumed on Mondays to Thursdays from 7 until 10, designated 'for the youth of the district, aged 14–18'. The middle hour of each night was for 'study or service' – namely a class or activity from a list that included art, drama, handcrafts, ballet, boxing, gymnastics, and a newcomer known as 'basic movement' – with an hour either side for lighter pursuits and relaxation in the form of dancing, games, singing, use of the canteen, and so on. The exception was Tuesday, when at 9 o'clock, all senior members were required to attend the Club Parliament, an opportunity to share responsibility for running their own club, as well as to practise the arts of public speaking and debating. On Friday the club was closed except for special activities such as rehearsals. Saturday was theatre night, when shows or plays were staged for audiences of members, parents, friends, and visitors – and/or dances held. Finally, on Sunday at 7, there was the Clubland Service. Repeating once more what he had always avowed, JB wrote: 'This is Clubland – its centre and inspiration.' The service was followed most Sundays by the Union under the colourful presidency of Alec Reed, when distinguished speakers were invited from the world of sport or the arts or entertainment, or films shown in the theatre – which was equipped with a screen and fully functioning projection room.

It was an 'intensive' programme by any standards. The Clubland ethos of the forties and fifties, as in the pre-war days, offered no apology for the expectations it placed on members to commit a significant proportion of the time they spent on the premises to some rewarding activity, and to contribute to the communal spirit of the Club with the effort and enthusiasm that gave expression to it. 'Spirit', in this sense, meant more than simply religious observance, although that was an essential ingredient, complementing the secular life of the club and bringing together its creative and recreational aspects.

Attendance at the weekly services was all but compulsory, although without any requirement to profess a religious belief – the flip-side of which was that professing non-belief was no excuse for non-attendance! JB had always seen the purpose of Clubland as serving the physical, intellectual, and spiritual needs of boys and girls 'outside any church'. He was not interested in preaching to the converted; nor, more interestingly, in preaching in order to convert – which in its crudest sense he saw as a kind of arrogance. True enough, many of the members did acquire or deepen their religious faith as a result of their time at Clubland and its Chapel. But, even amongst those who did not, many recall that JB's sermons on practical virtue as exemplified by Jesus Christ, and their own participation in the simple services which marked the close of each week, had a profound and enduring influence on their lives. For JB the Chapel was the epicentre of the whole Clubland experience, but it was not presented with a heavy hand. He chose with care the words which expressed its role so as to maintain its inclusiveness and relevance: the Chapel gave the club its 'tone', he wrote, and had a transformative effect on the personal lives of the members, whether or not they embraced the doctrines. The services were simple but were conducted with reverence and respect for the conventions of religious worship in the Methodist tradition – they never patronised the young congregations or attempted to appeal with novelty or mere entertainment.

These notions of 'all round fitness', 'loyalty and service', and 'fellowship' would inevitably lose some of their currency in the years to come, to the point where even the language itself began to sound arcane. The spirit of an era is often captured most permanently and evocatively in pictures: Andy Burton's paintings and posters – those opposite and a mural in the Parliament room, now sadly painted over – are also stylistically dated, which is precisely why they reflect so well the ideas and sentiments they express. The mood of cooperative enterprise, of forging forward to a brighter future is perfectly preserved. Burton's paintings also represent

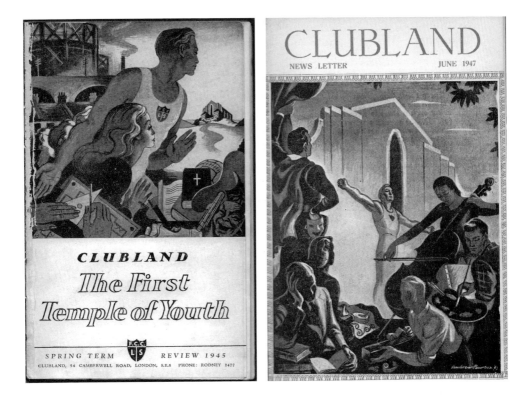

the fusion of physical fitness with intellectual and artistic expression, each underwritten by the spiritual: the essentially holistic character of Clubland that was JB's vision.

Of course, it was not the case that all of the members, all of the time, responded in the same rounded way, embracing all facilities equally. There were those who were simply more physically or creatively inclined than others, who had a narrower and more individual focus upon the opportunities which the Club offered – they were drawn to the sports teams, or to the art room, or to the theatre stage. There were others, too, who had no special motivation: who wanted nothing more than to use the Club for the extremely attractive meeting place that it was, and who saw the activity hour and the Parliament as an unwelcome intrusion on their leisure – or in some cases just a price worth paying for the luxury of it. Most of the Seniors above the age of 14 were in work, and many would have had enough of being told what to do during their long day. JB was not closed to these needs and natural preferences, but nor did he hide his intolerance of time wasting, or his dislike of group monopolisation of a facility to the exclusion of newcomers and aspiring youngsters. There was always a hard balance to strike between the pursuit of excellence – which JB unreservedly encouraged – and the nurturing of lesser talents, which could reduce the strength of a team, or the quality of a performance, or even be a nuisance and distraction. Nonetheless, maintaining the balance was vital to the notion of the Home of Friendship, and over the years JB had vigorously defended the rights of all members to have their turn and their chance.

As for those who frittered their time, he had a number of uncomplimentary labels: they were the 'loungers', 'slackers', and above all 'passengers', that were not infrequently mentioned on the pages of the *Reviews*, and were not long left in peace if they persisted. There were, as every member recalls, rows and fallings, walkings out – or even chuckings out. JB was often harsh in his criticism of those who did not toe the line, yet he had a remarkable way of winning over even the most recalcitrant of members, not always politely but usually without lasting resentment. Indeed, some of those with the fondest memories of their Club days were those whose interactions with the Head were the most turbulent.

JB's determination and strength of leadership were undiminished as he set about rebuilding the Club and establishing the new order, but there was no escaping the fact that he was getting older – now in his fifties he had for many years been inclined to periodic bouts ill of health, and nervous exhaustion bordering on depression. He had always earned both respect and deep fondness from the bulk of members, but he could not hope to achieve the same natural rapport with the hundreds of headstrong adolescents who joined the Club after the war, as he had enjoyed as a younger man in the heady years that ran up to it. For those past days he felt and expressed a deep and understandable nostalgia. The war had eroded the makeup of the membership at both ends of the age-range: there was no longer a Junior section to feed the Seniors with trained youngsters, and his older Seniors were endlessly being called up for National Service just as they reached the age when they were ready for leadership roles themselves. In all outward respects it was business as usual, and the Club was alive with activity and achievement despite these difficulties – but difficulties there were, and undercurrents which would eventually break the surface, and force changes.

One change of direction which resulted directly from the war was the expansion of the ex-Seniors and their recognition as a distinct new section. It was formed around the returned forces members, now demobilised, and also extended to those returning from their eighteen months of military service. In the 1947 *Review* he wrote, with unfeigned delight: 'A rather wonderful thing has happened to me. Not for many years has anything made me so happy and hopeful as the unpremeditated revival of the ex-Seniors.'

> I had grown so weary of seeing the Seniors empty into the forces and each year beginning again with new members until their call-up. There seems to be nothing behind them and nothing in front. No past, no future, just a floating club with an uncertain present. Traditions were gradually being lost because none was left to transmit them except a tired old Head.
>
> Then in my twenty-fifth year at Clubland a group of ex-Seniors wanted to meet. As so many on whom we had relied had faded out there was not so much encouragement given to this new group. They were given the whole premises one night a week (Wednesday). Within a month the group grew to fifty. It was so good to be alive again, to see the old training and traditions counting for so much. The past twenty-five years had not been in vain after all. Here was a fellowship far too deep to be even talked about, a fellowship, silent, understood, appreciated. Anna Padbury and Bernard Bailey were elected as temporary ex-Senior Presidents. Alf Goldsmith takes gym, Bill Hows and Len Clements in music. Chic Childs and Elsie Darby in drama ... Crowds of new ideas are springing up.[6]

JB reported in 1947 that the Wednesday Club – known as the Over Twenties – was a 'merry crowd, alive with memories, atmosphere and spirit. They know the Club will remain there for them after their "forces wanderings" ... Many of them have children of their own, so I can't boss them around any more'. It was observed by others that JB was rarely deterred from bossing anyone, whatever their age or status. Meanwhile the Senior section, now defined as 14–19 but subdivided into under- and over-16s and doing without one of their previous club nights, continued to attract new members and reached 120 by the middle of 1947.

There was considerable – mostly amicable – rivalry between these sections, not only in sports but in artistic output as well, particularly theatre productions. The presentations from the dramatics groups were especially impressive at the time, thanks in large part to the work and expertise of Tony Jackman, and supported by an excellent stage crew run by Denis Appleton and others. The theatre had been part of the last wing to be completed before the royal opening in 1939, and had fortunately survived the bombing. With its underground workshops for scenery construction, its lights tower, projection room, green room, and ever growing wardrobe, it was truly a mouth-watering facility for anyone drawn to the stage. All the club sections competed for rehearsal time and opportunities to perform and produce. Music concerts, ballet, and light opera, also added to the repertoire. Last but not least the theatre's sprung and polished floor doubled as a fine dance hall: regular Saturday dances were interspersed with the shows and events which the different sections put on.

In the Spring of 1947, for example, the *Clubland Review* advertised the following, fairly typical programme for the month of May, on top of the four weekday club nights, and Sundays:

> Saturday May 3rd – Play *Night Must Fall* 7
> Saturday May 17th – ex-Seniors concert
> Saturday May 24th and 31st – All sections dance.
> *8 pm start. Price 2/-. Bring your friends.*

In the same year the Clubland Players staged J B Priestley's *I Have Been Here Before*, Stanley Houghton's comedy, *Hindle Wakes, The Crooked Billet* (Dion Titheradge), and *Catherine the Great* (Biro and Lengyel), along with a number of concerts.

Nor was there any let up in the volume of dramatic output in 1948. The ex-Seniors performed *Pygmalion* and the Seniors *R.U.R* – the initials stand for Rossum's Universal Robots – a work of science fiction by the Czech playwright Karel Čapek which has the distinction of having introduced the word 'robot' into the English language. The Clubland performance had the further distinction of being the first stage appearance by one of the country's most celebrated actors, Sir Michael Caine (then Maurice Micklewhite), as one of the five robots. He was fifteen, having joined Clubland just after the war, enticed – in characteristic fashion and on his own admission – by a pretty girl. He remembers it as 'a joyous place with loads of things to do'. One of them, to his good fortune, was acting. The play was produced and directed by ex-Senior, Stuart Ready. The cast included Helena Glory and Ken Moir in the lead roles, with Alan Thomson, Ivy Warner, Arthur Jarman, and Les Etheridge among the supporting roles. Staging the play, particularly with such a youthful and inexperienced cast, was an ambitious venture. As Michael Caine observes in his autobiography it was intellectually as well as artistically challenging. The official report in the 1948 *Review* was glowing in its praise of the performances, including Caine's, but he

The Clubland Players in *R.U.R.*, 1948

recalls a notice, written by a fellow member in the alternative *Clubland Magazine*, which he ruefully quotes in his autobiography, along with his own postscript: "'Maurice Micklewhite played the Robot, who spoke in a dull, mechanical, monotonous voice to perfection.' Bastard!'[8] He claims that it laid the ground for a lifelong dislike of critics, but it did not diminish his awakened passion for acting. For the next two or three years, before his call up for national service he was, he remembers, 'always in a play'.

He also describes being 'taken under the wing' of Alec Reed, long serving Clubland governor and President of the Sunday Union. Alec worked in publishing, but was also an avid film buff, and regularly brought films from his own collection to show after the Sunday service. Sir Michael warmly acknowledges his debt to Alec:

> Not only did [he] teach me everything he knew about the history of film, he also introduced me to the technical side of moviemaking. Every summer the whole club would go on holiday to the island of Guernsey, off the south coast of England, and Alec would make a documentary of the trip. It was a proud moment for me when my name came up on the credits for the first time – "Maurice Micklewhite director". Once again the audience laughed. Bastards. But I realised they were right. When I made it to the big screen it would have to be under a different name.[9]

The run of plays and shows extended into the following year starting with two productions from the ex-Seniors – *Arsenic and Old Lace*, and *Sixteen* – directed by Stan Emanuel and Ken Randall respectively. Stan's personal achievement was especially gratifying. The reviewer reminded readers: 'It doesn't seem long since Stan was languishing in a German prison camp and once we thought he would never recover from the effects.' Clubland's reputation in the performing arts continued to grow, and was clearly enjoying a golden period that lasted into the fifties, venturing into dance, musicals, cabaret, and light opera as well as straight drama. Many of the participants in this and other shows, would go on to serve as officers in the Club for years to come and pass on what they had learned to future generations of members.

The other major attractions of the Club were in art, crafts, and a range of sports. A thriving art department developed thanks to ex-senior Ron Lawrence, and the gymnasium was in constant use, under the tutelage of Charlie Carroll. Boxing was also popular, though more on a recreational basis than a seriously competitive one. South London was home to a plethora of famous boxing clubs and gyms, and Clubland was never a contender at the top level. Still, a number of accomplished boxers, such as Arthur Russell and George Slark, served in the club at the time as voluntary instructors. The Club also regained some of its former strength at football and netball, competing in local leagues and regular friendly fixtures further afield, against schools or colleges with which the Club was associated. The footballers had the enormous benefit of classes by Ronnie Rooke the Arsenal centre forward and in 1948–9 had their best ever season, following one of their worst the previous year. They ended top of the Southwark League winning 20 of the 23 matches, as well as every friendly match bar one. Sid Grossmith and Ron Tizzard were the leading scorers, and Charlie Carroll the captain. Many looked set for higher honours in the game. In May the Chelsea Football Club manager Mr. Tirrell, and captain John Harris, came and spoke at the Sunday Union and met the Clubland team afterwards. The possibility of a match with a Chelsea youth team was discussed, as were 'trials for one or two of the [Clubland] lads'. There is no record of the anticipated matches and trials, but Charlie Carroll did sign up with First Division Charlton Athletic shortly afterwards.

As successful as Clubland was in competitive games, it faced a significant obstacle which JB constantly lamented in the years after the war. Its facilities were almost exclusively indoors, and in consequence in order to play matches it was necessary to get permits to use public amenities – which were in short supply in an area so built up and so badly affected by war damage. Football permits were hard enough to obtain; cricket, not surprisingly was practically impossible. The only alternative was to appeal to organisations blessed with playing fields to take on Clubland teams between league fixtures. Merstham Youth Club in Surrey obliged from time to time; so did Westminster Training College and Alleyns School: the *quid pro quo* was a return visit to Clubland for a dinner and dance.

Like all sports club managers what JB longed for was for his teams to have a ground of their own. For a time in the early fifties, JB was optimistic that if a benefactor could be found Clubland could buy the Peckham Centre, a small estate less than a mile away which was then temporarily up for sale. The Peckham Centre housed a community engaged in social and medical welfare, and had both residential property and grounds. It would have offered a solution to two of Clubland's long-term needs – affordable housing for ex-members committed to working in and for the Club, and the outdoor recreational facilities that the site in Walworth so badly lacked. Finally, the rent from the properties would have provided a steady income, replacing or reducing the need for endless fund-raising and appeals. It was a brilliant concept, and with the current low property prices in that part of London there was a window during which it might just have been achievable. What was more, had it materialised, it would soon have become a massively valuable asset. However, in the event the local authority Southwark Council moved first, requisitioning the site for a new school, and JB's dream faded into the realms of the might-have-been. One of the few projects for Clubland that he did not succeed in translating into reality.

Return to the Channel Islands

In the gloriously hot summer of 1947 the annual Guernsey camps were reinstated, to JB's unconcealed delight. They had always been the culminating event of the Club year, and were now a sure sign to him that Clubland was back on track. 'The Guernsey States' he wrote, 'have loaned us the huts at Beaucamps again, for which we are deeply grateful'. Jack (Sir John) Leale, as before, was strongly influential in securing the camp, along with the Dorey family's assistance with the local arrangements and hospitality. During the occupation of the Channel Islands the Germans had adopted Beaucamps as a barracks, and JB warned the members that 'the Germans have made rather a mess of our old camp quarters and all the equipment has gone'. Consequently there would be work to do as well as a holiday. Actually the camps had never been referred to as 'holidays' – like all Clubland activities they

Sir John Leale (2nd from left) welcomes the first postwar camp after the liberation of the Channel Islands

were organised and regulated, with communal meals and scheduled activities, and epitomised the corporate nature of the Club. Today people tend to disparage such regimentation, even though structured adventure packages still have considerable appeal. In the late forties it was more readily accepted as the norm for organised camping trips, as is shown by the popularity of the Scouts and Guides movements – or on a commercial scale by the success of Billy Butlins' holiday camps.

All the same, it is significant that JB saw the need to spell out the conditions of camp attendance in the most explicit terms, possibly recognising that attitudes and expectations of what a camp should be were beginning to shift. In the May Review, along with the good news that the camps would start in July, he wrote: 'Now read carefully: Don't come if you think it's a private holiday where you do what you like. It's a camp – not a hotel. You go with the camp, live with it, stay with it. Keep its rules and hours and help in the work. We don't just provide for those who want to go off on their own.' Nor were the campers to expect luxury: the huts were basic, and there was no bedding or equipment: 'You bring a blanket sewn like a sack as a sleeping bag. Also knife, fork, spoon, enamel plates and mugs, towel and soap. Bring as little as you can. All you bring must go in one suitcase.' In another sign of the times the campers were told that they must bring their rations books. The meals were provided, but with rationing still in force the ingredients could only be obtained if the members pooled their individual allowances.

Nevertheless, from all accounts the Clubland camps of the late forties were wonderful. For many of the members they were the only affordable opportunity to travel beyond England during their early years. Members contributed to the travel costs, but everything else was found – raised by efforts and concerts as well as donations throughout the whole year. Some had never seen the sea, even less crossed it and swum in it off rocky headlands or sandy coves, like those that ringed the island. The camps ran through the months of July and August, each group staying for ten days; the ex-Seniors first and the Seniors following in the school holidays, for the benefit of the youngest. The beaches were beautiful; the nearest, at Vazon Bay, was only a short walk from Beaucamps, but in the course of each camp the members would visit most of them, either by charabanc or on the long cliff-top walks organised for them.

Beaucamps itself is now a high-school by the same name. Then it was nothing more than a collection of huts beside a large cinder parade ground – a natural playing field as well as the location for the kit inspections and roll-calls that were the order of the day. These surroundings did not detract from its perfection as a camp, and the members loved it always. On each Sunday there was a 'church parade' involving a walk to one of the Methodist chapels where JB was typically invited to preach and the members to take the service. Afterwards families in the congregation took small groups of campers home to Sunday lunch: an opportunity for them to meet some of the islanders, and the islanders to meet the Walworth boys and girls. For some it was the start of friendships that lasted far into adulthood. Much of the footage of the *Clubland Story* consists of scenes of the Guernsey camps, with shots of the boys and girls on the deck of the boat leaving Weymouth and arriving in St Peter Port, parading on the square, scrambling on the cliffs, diving off the rocks, and – with seemingly obsessive determination – building massive human pyramids on the beach. Of course, few such activities would be permitted on a youth camp now without all kinds of regulation and overseeing which were entirely absent then – the miracle of the Guernsey camp days was that they were organised to the hilt, yet at the same time provided the campers with an extraordinary level of freedom and self-reliance.

The cannon on the parade
ground at Beaucamps

Sun and sand

A large part of the success of the forties camps was down to Mrs. JB,
Anna, who had also been a helper in Guernsey at the last camp prior
to the outbreak of war in 1939. Anna brought many talents with her to
Clubland, and utilised them unstintingly for the benefit of Club members.
She had a wealth of artistic, creative and practical skills – dress-making,
costume design, accounting and budgeting, amongst others. Above all
she was a wonderful cook with formal training as well as natural talent,
equally at ease catering in bulk for large numbers as she was for smaller-
scale or special occasions. She took on the management of the voluntary

Senior Camp 1948. Back row far right, Alec Reed.
Second row far left, Michel Caine.

team that cooked and served up meals to a hundred ravenous campers three times each day, despite the problems of rationing and a scantily equipped kitchen. She was also a gifted and enthusiastic photographer – had she been free to choose a profession it would certainly have been photography. Her own appearances on screen are quite rare since she was usually on the other side of the camera – adding extensively to Clubland's film archive with some beautiful and nostalgic footage of Guernsey, latterly much of it in colour, in the last years of the camps. Over the years Alec Reed and Anna between them put together an evocative collection of 16mm films, and in 1949 a copy of the footage was requested by the States of Guernsey as one of the 'best scenic stories of their Island ever taken'.[10]

The 1947 camps were repeated in the Summer of '48 and '49 with similar success. In 1950 they were cancelled because JB was away in America on the first of his many fund-raising tours – and thereafter with the continuity broken it was a struggle to revive the tradition on a sustainable basis. The costs of fares and other expenses were becoming prohibitive, coupled with the fall off in donations and subscriptions that had necessitated the American trip. Moreover, there were the first signs of improving social prosperity which, though neither great nor uniformly distributed, did put more money in the pockets of many of the working members and their families. Rather ruefully JB wrote that it was unjustified to ask supporters to subsidise the camps when, 'often enough the recipients are better off than the givers'. Whilst that may have been an exaggeration, the fact was that JB's priority had to be keeping the Club premises open and in good repair all year round – in time rebuilding what had been destroyed. One more visit to the island took place in 1951, though with little of the fanfare that had accompanied those past. A single retrospective entry appears in the October *Review*:

> After 28 years we end the glorious history of Clubland Guernsey camps. Despite the wet August, our last camp was a very happy one. There was, of course, unutterable sadness in doing things for the last time, the last look at Vazon Bay, the final locking up of the huts on leaving, a lingering look at our home for so many years. There were a million memories at every turn of the road ... The Vale Chapel was crowded for our last service, at which His Excellency the Lieutenant Governor, read the lessons in honour of our farewell. In a moving address he paid a gracious tribute to Clubland and its long association with the Island. Then on August 31, the mail boat sailed away with the last group of Clublanders and so ended our Guernsey camps with sadness too deep for words.

The last Guernsey camp: 'A sadness too deep for words'

After the first postwar visit JB wrote in a newsletter: 'If only someone would buy us a camp so that there would be a bit of Guernsey that is forever Clubland'. Sadly, though unsurprisingly, no one did. However, in 1952 a headline in the *South London Press* announced: 'Clubland may buy a castle – holiday camp plan'. It continued:

> South London children who are members of Clubland, Camberwell road, may spend their holidays in historic castle in Hampshire. Clubland's head the Rev J Butterworth has inspected the castle with a view to its purchase. The building is Highcliffe Castle, at Christchurch. Mr Butterworth considers it would make an ideal holiday home for the boys and girls of Clubland. At present they spend their holidays in Guernsey. He said: we want a real holiday camp for Clublanders and I thought I should investigate the possibility of acquiring the castle. But no negotiations have been started yet.

Never guilty of setting his sights too low, JB did pursue the idea seriously for some time and came close to signing the deal, with help from its former resident, the Hon. Mrs Stuart Wortley who was an enthusiastic patron of the Club. However, like the Peckham estate, it was not to reach fruition, whether from insufficient funds or simply losing out to a higher bidder is not recorded.

The Silver Jubilee and beyond

In October 1947, Clubland celebrated its 25th anniversary. It was a protracted affair spanning almost a fortnight starting with the first of two Sunday services led by a hundred-strong choir of Seniors and ex-Seniors. Since the Club had no organ or chapel – at least not one with a roof – the services were held at Kingsway Hall, at the invitation of its famous minister Dr Donald (later Baron) Soper. In certain respects Butterworth and Soper had followed similar paths and these would have crossed on many occasions. They were driven by the same desire to combat poverty and inequality: the Kingsway Mission catered, like Clubland, to the needs of the least advantaged in society – though without the same exclusive focus on youth – and both men stayed in their respective posts for decades rather than moving around from circuit to circuit in the customary Methodist way.

Arguably they shared the honour of being the two most notorious Methodist clerics of the twentieth century, in Soper's case for his strident left wing views and politicised preaching – he was an active member of the

Labour Party and as committed a socialist as he was a Methodist. Crowds gathered at Speakers' Corner in Hyde Park on Sunday mornings to hear Soper's acclaimed oratory, JB often among them. How they felt about each other personally is hard to say: mutual respect no doubt for each other's efforts to improve the lives of those at the bottom of the social ladder, but less approvingly perhaps with regard to lifestyle. They certainly had very different origins – Donald Soper was educated at Haberdashers' Aske's and Cambridge, with a doctorate from the London School of Economics. He remained committed to evangelism and temperance and was known to be critical of JB for his more nuanced attitudes to both of these in later life. JB, for his part, took a sceptical view of Soper's elevation to the peerage in 1965, having refused to accept any state honours for himself. However, such tensions, if they were tensions, came later. In 1947 Dr Soper's offer of his chapel as the venue for Clubland's Jubilee was a gracious one, and was graciously accepted. It was packed on both Sundays.

On the two Tuesdays Clubland held 'Open Parliaments' with the Head Seniors – Ricky Elliott and Betty Kirrage – presiding, and visitors and parents, exceptionally, invited to come in and see what went on, and some of them to speak. The two Saturdays were taken up with theatre events – extracts from recent productions and films of the Guernsey camps, followed as always by dancing. Among the guests were ex-member John Blatchley, who was in London playing at His Majesty's Theatre in the West End; the Scottish international and Chelsea player, Tommy Walker; Leslie Compton of the Arsenal, and his brother Denis, the England all-rounder, not long back from the first postwar Ashes tour and a summer series at home against South Africa. Representing Guernsey was the Tottenham centre-forward Len Duquemain. Born at Cobo he used to deliver telegrams to Beaucamps as a boy during the pre-war camps. All made speeches, met the Clubland teams, and stayed for the party afterwards. As a follow-up the visitors promised members of the Clubland teams tickets for the forthcoming Chelsea-Arsenal fixture, and for players from both teams to come back afterwards with their wives and girl-friends to a 'gala dance' at the Club.

Clubland's links to the top echelons of the world of sport seem remarkable now. The Jubilee guest-list was not a one-off event. Regular contacts with top-ranking athletes had started before the war and continued long after it. The relationship with the Arsenal Football Club had an especially long history, dating back to the days of Herbert Chapman (the manager during the early thirties) and Cliff Bastin's contribution as a voluntary part-time coach at Clubland. The connections continued after the war, not only with Arsenal but with Chelsea too, and with the Football Association itself. The late J W Mears, Chelsea Chairman, and Stanley Rous when he was the Secretary of the FA, both became Clubland Governors. Later still Denis Follows laid a stone on behalf of the FA, and the Hill-Woods (Denis and his son Peter) kept alive Clubland's close ties with Arsenal.

JB himself was a fanatical follower of football and rarely missed a game at either Highbury or Stamford Bridge, often as a guest. The passion dated from the days when his father took him as a small boy to watch Blackburn Rovers, a ten mile walk there and back as he was fond of telling people when, much later, he was sitting in the comfort of the stands or the directors' tea room. He never wavered in his attachment to Blackburn but strangely never developed any links with the club, and rarely saw them play, except for the occasional away matches in London. The rest of the time he was a neutral spectator who simply loved football, and would watch the games intently, pipe in mouth, applauding good play by either side, but never cheering or rising from his seat even when a goal was scored.

The Clubland connections did not end with football. At Christmas in 1948, Col Eddie Eagan, former Olympic Boxing gold medallist flew to London with a gift of boxing gloves, accompanied by Lee Savard,

From left Lee Savard, Wally Ruel, and Eddie Eagan

a leading heavyweight contender in the forties and fifties and well known to the boxing enthusiasts at Clubland. In 1950 Savard won the British and European version of the world championship. Wally Ruel, the boxing chairman, received the gloves on behalf of the Club, and Savard autographed them. JB had met Eagan during his 1937 visit to the States, and the latter would play a significant part in his future tours. Eagan had also encouraged his friend Thomas Dewey, the Governor of New York, to pay a visit to Clubland; and in 1949 he arrived there unexpectedly with the express purpose of seeing what the place was like on a normal occasion. He wrote a month or two later to tell JB: 'You have a wonderful story to tell backed up by a great achievement, and I would like it told to our people'[11] – and was instrumental in persuading JB to do just that in 1950. In November 1951, the legendary Freddie Brown came to the Club to lay a stone on behalf of Cricket. A photograph in the *South London Press* recorded the visit with the caption: 'Former

Anna with Sybil Thorndyke

England skipper Freddie Brown meets Clublander Denis Appleton from Brunswick Park, Camberwell.'

Clubland also benefited from a growing number of supporters in the entertainment world, resulting in a series of visits from well known celebrities of stage and screen. Sybil Thorndyke had preached on more than one occasion in the club chapel, and in JB's words 'inspired new interests in drama'. Another regular visitor and active ally was Richard Attenborough who, together with his wife Sheila Sim, developed a close and lasting friendship with Jimmy and Anna, as well as being admirers and benefactors of the Club. Their association began in 1949 with an inspiring talk on drama to the Sunday Union, during the high point of Club theatrical output, and gained strength from then onwards – Sir Richard became a Clubland governor, and when he was the subject of *This Is Your Life* in 1962, JB and a group of Clublanders appeared on the programme.[12] They also met with great regularity in the stands at Stamford Bridge where they had practically adjacent seats – Attenborough was a passionate Chelsea fan and a director in the Joe Mears era. Another close neighbour in the Chelsea stands was friend and fellow Methodist minister Bill Motson, accompanied by his young son John who grew up to be one of the most familiar voices in football in his long career as a commentator.

In the coming years a trail of illustrious guests would come to Clubland to unveil stones and remain to meet and talk to the members. Already there had been numerous visits from royalty and nobility as well as many from the ranks of sport and show business. In the fifties the list was extended to include Eamonn Andrews, Laurence Olivier and Vivien Leigh – and most famously and publicly, Bob Hope, although that is a another tale for later pages. On 9 May 1953 another famous friend, Gracie Fields – almost royalty herself – paid a widely reported visit to Clubland, to unveil a commemorative stone, which she followed by singing her signature song 'Sally' on a small stage in the quadrangle, with JB and his mother Ann, lifelong fan and fellow Lancastrian.

In retrospect it might be asked how far such visits resulted in real and lasting benefit to the Club. Celebrity endorsement might lead to direct or indirect financial support – it certainly raised the profile of the club in the press and elsewhere, and brought publicity which might encourage others to support and sponsor in like manner. However the old adage that all publicity is good publicity is not necessarily true for every organisation, and even good publicity might have created the impression that Clubland was doing very nicely and needed no further help. Whilst this

News of Gracie's visit attracted huge crowds who blocked the Walworth Road bringing traffic to a standstill. Gracie sang to them from the balcony of the ruined Chapel. The conductor and passengers on the stranded bus (top edge of the picture) enjoyed an unexpected bonus for the price of their tickets!

Gracie singing 'Sally' for the Club members in the quad.

was far from the case it was not always obvious to observers. Clubland's premises never looked poor or in need of repair, least of all when decked out for special occasions and visits – but there was some irony in this because the cost of furnishing and maintaining it so well was the reason why additional funds were always so urgently needed. There was also the possibility that publicity might bring the wrong sort of attention – not everyone looked on Clubland favourably, and the regular exposure that came with celebrity sometimes led to negative responses of envy and resentment. But all these were far outweighed by the positive influence of famous guests. It was certainly the case that the celebrity of its visitors broadened the experience and horizons of the Club's young members, as well as deepening their confidence in the worth of their membership, and endorsing the widespread respect and regard for the work which was done there.

Faultlines

In 1949 there was an unprecedentedly large turnover of members: part of a pattern that was becoming the norm, exacerbated by the absence of Juniors, and by the wholesale departure of established older members at 18. The February *Review* begins: 'The new Head Seniors are Alan Venier and Gladys Baker. We wish them and their new Cabinet of twenty a happy year in Club management. They have to deal with loads of new members.' At the same time he added: 'We shall greatly miss the stalwarts who have graduated to the ex-Seniors. Especially the ex-Head Seniors Bill Ryan and Ivy Walker, and great chairmen like Roy Barrett and Arthur Jarman. They have served the Seniors with great distinction, and they will now strengthen the ex-Seniors. It is a devastating thought that half the present Seniors will be in the forces before camp (July) and a sad fact that but for call-ups there would have been 500 Seniors.'

The expansion of the ex-Seniors – which had so pleased JB when introduced – was intended to reinforce the membership from above and, by example, to have a stabilising effect on the fluctuating senior sections. But as the fifties got underway, and the adult contingent grew in numbers, it became something of a mixed blessing. On the one hand it represented a reservoir for mature leadership, ready and willing to take on responsibility. Many individual members went on to become long-serving officers, not only for the existing Senior Club but on into the mid-fifties when the Junior Clubs were reinstated – requiring a small army of adult volunteers to run the activities and lead the reformed

Houses. Stan Emanuel, Ken and Bunty Randal, Len and Lily Clements, Ted Cutler, Jim and Topsy Stow, Len and Rene Dobbs, Lily Simpson and Les Harris (later married), Laurie Massey, Arthur and Margaret Jarman, Jean Hall and John Langton, Iris and Bernard Bailey ... are just some of the names without which there could have been no revival of the old Clubland, or anything remotely like it. But there were others who understandably simply wanted to use the premises of which they had such fond memories – to attend the Saturday dances; play table-tennis and snooker, make friends, meet partners; or in some cases to pursue their own special interests in sport, drama, art etc. – without necessarily being encumbered with nurturing the next generation of adolescents. This was not an unreasonable desire: after all, they had 'done their bit' in no uncertain terms, had had their share of obeying orders and answering calls of duty, and were no longer so ready to be bidden.

Moreover, as time went on and the austerity of the forties began to ease, there were other competing attractions around the corner, and a little more money to spend on them. For some the Club still remained the centrepiece of their lives, as much for the adults they had become as it had been when they were younger. Dozens were married by JB in the Club and their children in due course baptised there, some of whom later enrolling as Juniors – Frances Cooper, Lynn Clements, Anne and June Harris, Nicky Barrett, Gillian and Judith Stow, Peter Hindmarsh, Georgina Fraser, Pamela Webb ... to name a few. But for others, the affiliation was less strong, and whilst the Club was a great amenity, it was becoming one amongst others. When JB said sincerely that the Club was there for the returning members, he had not meant it in the casual terms that some understood it, and he made no secret of his impatience with those he considered to be interested only in their own pursuits and unwilling to play any useful role in the life of the Club. It was inevitable that tensions would arise around the issues of Club use and obligation – and these led eventually to the disbanding of the Wednesday Club, and its replacement with a 'Service Club', restricted to those who were prepared to play an active role in serving the next generation.

The growing-pains of the renewed clubs were not confined to the ex-Seniors. There were unruly elements in the Seniors, due to the volume of newcomers unfamiliar with Clubland's traditions and exacting standards. There was nothing new in this; there had always been a minority of the membership that chafed at the discipline, or rebelled. But with the fluctuating population, and influences and pressures from outside the Club, there was an identifiable shift in attitude among some of the Senior membership. One of these pressures came from the very lessening of poverty that the fifties brought – not for all, but for many. One of the changes that JB sensed, and complained of volubly, was a resentment some of the members showed at having to pay, or in other ways put themselves out, for the amenities Clubland offered. He wrote: 'Youth has money. Employers will tell you what the wages are, and parents will tell you that much of it doesn't find its way home.' (It was still customary in the fifties for working children to hand some or all of their wages over to their mothers until they left home.) 'Do you remember the member who couldn't pay his Club sub because cinemas, cigs, speedway etc. cost so much! And the member who complained at the Club shilling because of the income tax demand ... yet bought a television set. Or couldn't afford Club camp at £1, yet cheerfully paid £8 at a Butlin's Camp. Come! Cut out the humbug and give your club a square deal or look for a better shillingsworth elsewhere.'

Matters were not helped by the fact that many more public youth amenities were now free, in line with the rapidly expanding welfare state.

Sunday morning, East Lane Market.

Andy Burton cartoon in the Clubland Review

There could not have been a greater irony than this for Clubland, or its founder: the man who had fought for social reforms, battled inequality and the exploitation of youth, now found that the very policies and social changes that vindicated his struggle also threatened the values which had underpinned his ministry, and clashed with his belief that nothing is achieved by providing young people with something for nothing, however well intentioned. 'Youth', he concluded, 'must learn that life is giving as well as receiving.'[13] But youth, he was finding, was showing less of an appetite for learning such lessons, especially if they had to pay for them as well, and more especially when there were plenty of less demanding amusements around to spend hard-earned money on, or enjoy for nothing.

Despite such challenges, the full and thriving life and activities of Clubland nevertheless continued unabated through the postwar years and into the fifties. Yet it did so against the muted background of the Head's growing concerns lest the quality of Clubland fellowship might, at some level, be compromised the new attitudes of an element of his Senior membership. However the more pressing and immediate need was always finding funds to meet rising costs and essential maintenance. These weighed upon JB interminably, with the great shell of Maufe's chapel a daily reminder that sooner or later the money would have to be found for rebuilding. Subscriptions and regular donations were no longer sufficient to meet even the costs of keeping the Clubland doors open for the foreseeable future. The situation required extraordinary action – a course of action different from anything previously undertaken to raise the necessary finance.

Notes

1 *Clubland Review,* May 1945.
2 Ibid. (and see in full above ...)
3 http://www.exploringeastlondon.co.uk/stepney/settlement/ostg.htm. This site will remain available but will no longer be updated. For further information about Lawrence Rigal, and the long term future of his websites, please visit Rabbi Rigal's Website.
4 *The Guardian,* 14 Mar 2001.
5 DVD versions of the *Clubland Story,* originally 16 mm, are available from Southwark Local History Library*** (see appendix).
6 Clubland review, 1947.
7 A psychological thriller written by Emlyn Williams.
8 Michael Caine, *The Autobiography: From the Elephant to Hollywood.* Hodder and Stoughton, 2010.
9 Ibid.
10 December Newsletter in the 1949 *Clubland Review.*
11 *Clubland Review,* March 1950.
12 See below 1962, and letter.
13 *Clubland Review.*

CHAPTER EIGHT

Clubland at the Crossroads

Through a Glass Darkly

As the second half of the century got underway the optimism which had underpinned the Club during its vibrant postwar revival became increasingly difficult to sustain, along with JB's own positive mood. His anxieties over the balance sheet were never far out of his mind, fuelled by his lifelong phobia of debt. In the early Summer of 1950, encouraged by his American contacts, he made the major and unprecedented decision that Clubland's best hope of raising finance lay in lecture tours to the United States. In June he made the first of five tours during the decade, to raise money for immediate needs, and with the hope of securing one or more wealthy sponsors. He returned in the autumn with £1000[1], and even better, a promise from the comedian and film star Bob Hope to come to London and give the proceeds of a run in the West End to the Club – both of which he did the next year.

The welcome back JB received from the members was huge and heart-warming, but there were troubles below the surface which had started before he left and had not gone away during his absence. Numbers were falling, and the membership itself was becoming less united; the atmosphere less congenial. Clubland's established core of loyal members was for the first time shrinking in relation to the whole. The demographic of South London was beginning to change, too, with the result that some of the long-standing ex-Seniors were moving out to the suburbs as their incomes improved, and fewer of the newer intake were stepping up to fill the gaps in the depleted ranks of officers. As always the constant shadow of National Service also hung over the Club, continually stripping it of what JB called the 'top enders', without whom there was less strength to deal with any minority intent on disruption.

The enrolled members, however, were only partly accountable for the growing tension. There were intrusions, too, by outsiders looking for mischief or gate-crashing dances, or waiting outside to intimidate or attack boys and girls as they arrived or left. The latter did not always take this meekly, and fights would ensue, bringing the Club unwanted attention and perpetuating the slide in numbers. Some who sought a safe and amiable environment, where they could meet their friends and pursue their interests, began to stay away – further reducing much needed income as a result. Writing of such disturbances in a Club newsletter even as early as 1950 JB observed that: 'Situated where we are we have not escaped the menace'. It marked the start of a series of intermittent disturbances that went unreported at the time. JB had no desire to broadcast Clubland's internal problems and risk alarming either parents or patrons, or to advertise what he feared would look like his own or Clubland's failures.

The monthly *Reviews* make no mention of specific incidents and in fact continue to give an upbeat account of the Club's many positive achievements and major events. One in particular was the third return visit of Bob Hope, on 3 October, 1953. He arrived from Madrid for a Saturday appearance in Clubland, once again accompanied by his friend Jerry Desmonde. All traffic was stopped by the police due to the crowds outside on Camberwell Road through which the visitors had to thread their way, whilst inside there was standing room only. The football team in their club strip chaired Hope into the theatre, recently redecorated in its green and gold livery for the first time since the war. The event was also marked by the opening of the newly created Bob Hope Lounge, and the unveiling of a new plaque. That evening Hope travelled with JB to Manchester for two packed houses at Bellevue. The whistle-stop tour finished with a dash to Southampton to catch the SS United States. Only after a final party on board came the news that the whole weekend had been for Clubland's benefit, confirmed in a broadcast commentary by Raymond Glendenning on the Paramount newsreels, worldwide radio, and the BBC Light Programme.

Yet, notwithstanding its publicised successes, the backcloth of growing disquiet in the heart of the Club persisted. The truth was that there were bad apples within the membership as well as outside it, and the episodes of disruption could not be contained indefinitely. Pressures grew until, over the winter of 1953–4, the dam broke. That February Clubland was the scene of an evening of wanton destruction as one or more gangs of youths went on the rampage with knives and razors, slashing furniture and smashing fittings and causing several hundred pounds worth of damage in a single evening. To JB's horror this was not exclusively a matter of invasion by violent and destructive outsiders. Mercifully the anger of the perpetrators was vented mostly on property rather than persons, though some injuries were also reported. A single police officer arrived, but not before the damage was well and truly done. No arrests were made since there were no witnesses willing to identify the offenders. JB naturally declined to press charges – he had gone to court too many times in his life to speak up for lads who had fallen foul of the law to start prosecuting them now. He also kept the story from the press for as long as he could, especially the local press who were not averse to criticising or stoking controversy about the Club.

However, in the first week of March he wrote a full-page article in the *Methodist Recorder* – entitled 'Clubland at the Crossroads' – in which he weighed in on the current national debate about youth conduct and a perceived rising tide of widespread gang violence and hooliganism. In breach of his own cautious judgement he included, by way of example, a reference to the recent troubles at Clubland. He revealed that 'the crowds which poured into it are now halted by outside intimidations and insults,' with the consequence that a policeman was on duty at the Club most nights, and asked 'How comes it that its exquisite furnishings are now destroyed, its settees and chairs ripped to pieces and razor-slashed beyond repair? He despaired that the vandals were 'stealing, bursting pipes and flooding the place' and carrying out 'a host of meaningless acts of destruction.' He could not believe that this was happening in the sanctuary for youth he had created at Clubland, or even worse, that some offenders were within his membership, and that 'rival gangs in great achievement are now competing with each other in destruction'.[2]

Within hours the story was making headlines in the national press, in part due to the enhanced profile Clubland had again enjoyed in the wake of Bob Hope's visits, but equally because of the intense public interest and alarm over escalating youth violence. It was a testing time for JB and the Club, but judging by the volume of column inches devoted to the subject, it was not merely Clubland but the whole country that was at the crossroads. Quoting the *Methodist Recorder*, the *Times* reported: 'Destruction at youth centre. Contests between rival gangs.' The same day *The Daily Herald* posted the headline: 'Stilettos wreck a dream' (referring to the long thin knives that were popular accessories with some gangs at the time, along with razors) with the subheading: 'Hooligans have wrecked Britain's finest youth club'. The *Evening News* called it, 'A

London tragedy.' The *Sketch* led with: 'These mad dogs' and together with the *Daily Mail*, warned of gang warfare and hooliganism on the increase. The fullest account of the incident was by Jeffrey Goodman of the *News Chronicle*, who came to see the wreckage for himself.

> 'Nothing will ever completely shatter the vision of the Rev James Butterworth, creator of the hundred thousand pound Clubland youth centre, that symbol of dignity and order in London's tough Camberwell. But today his faith is shaken – by vandalism. Fine furnishings have been destroyed settees and chairs ripped to pieces and razor-slashed beyond repair. Rival gangs of "cosh boys" and "razor lads" competing in vandalism and desecration.
>
> Wearily he walked with me through the fine halls and club rooms of this great experiment. He pointed to the long green curtains in the main hall slashed completely. 'We had about 30 easy chairs, beautifully upholstered. Brand-new – all destroyed by razors. Six pianos – keys ripped out of them. A library of 200 records snapped and strewn over the floor. Broken pictures of stars: a clubroom with its walls covered by pictures of celebrities who have donated to Clubland – almost every picture had its glass broken and frame smashed. The toilets have been locked against youths who dragged water cisterns from the walls, broken pipes and smashed basins …'[3]

Clubland was by no means the only target. The Warden of The Robert Browning Settlement, a stone's throw away on the Walworth Road, reported a similar outbreak of vandalism resulting in an £800 bill for repairs. Other clubs up and down the country, especially in inner cities, had the same tale to tell – as did a number of cinemas, dance halls, and coffee bars in the following months and years. Arguments abounded about the causes of what many saw as an epidemic of violent crime, and the press were quick to pick up on the idea that the problems at Clubland and elsewhere were 'gang related'. Even the usually restrained *Methodist Recorder* had seized on the phrase: 'Rival gangs compete in destruction' for its headline, and others slanted their versions of the story in similar fashion.

In doing so, however, they blurred an important distinction. There was a world of difference between the premeditated operations of the criminal gangs – which certainly existed in and around Walworth – and the random, apparently motiveless acts of violence and disorder that were starting to make the headlines in the early 1950s. The 'spivs' and 'wide boys' of the wartime years were vindictive if they were crossed, and often violent in protection of their 'turf' and their interests, as were the serious underworld mobs. But neither of these was in the juvenile business of breaking up youth clubs or coffee bars or ripping out cinema seats, seemingly for the sheer hell of it. On the contrary, criminal gangs had no wish to draw attention to themselves, for obvious reasons; it was bad for business. The new phenomenon, of which Clubland's difficulties were a symptom, was not 'gang warfare' in any classic sense, despite the more lurid headlines. It was something more difficult to contain and more difficult to explain.

Much as JB might have preferred the disruption to be characterised as a purely external menace, a broader account was already in the public arena. A week after the worst of the violence, one local paper, the *South London Observer*, openly queried the source of the damage, suggesting that some of the so called 'gangsters' were in fact club members. It quoted a CID spokesman from the nearby Manor Place Police Station who was also sceptical about the extent of gang involvement, and who revealed that there had been some problems with anti-social behaviour amongst some of the Clubland youth for some time, worsening after Christmas 1953. This was uncomfortable reading, but clearly reflected the truth, and JB was forced to acknowledge to the *Observer* that a minority of lads in the district, some of whom were Clubland members, had been causing trouble. Playing it down, JB insisted: 'It's just a phase that will die out. Walworth is as good a place as anywhere. Most of our members are grand lads and they are a pleasure to work with.'

The impression given by the national press was that the vandalism seemed to have sprung up overnight. But the reality was rather different as JB finally admitted in the April *Review* article – 'Notes on Recent Set-backs' – explaining his previous silence and stating his determination to carry on without lowering standards:

> Those who work and visit here know that for about two years we have had some very bad patches through destructive gangs. The ever-helpful police, who have had a patrol here most nights, have made it possible to carry on, for they know and we know just what we have to contend with and what has happened. That the recent publicity has come as a surprise to our readers is because no reference has been made to trouble in our monthly publications. This is because we have always tried to keep out of the press and for that reason do not write articles about our work.
>
> When the *Methodist Recorder* at long last persuaded us to write an article on youth problems we were distressed, and protested when it handed out our comments to the general press. Then came a swarm of reporters

who will all agree that we did not wish to publicise our trouble. We did at any rate succeed in preventing photographs and newsreels.

Our 33 years here of disinterested service, shunning pulpits, platforms and publicity is our answer to any charge of desire for notice, and also a reply to what we really think of the youth of the district, which is the finest anywhere when they get in the right gangs.

Our faith in God and lads is not disturbed because a minority busts up the place from time to time. Heartbreaking though these set-backs are they are nothing compared to the achievements of the lads of the district who helped create Clubland, who fought to save it throughout the blitz, who cared for so many homeless in its premises during the war and restored it after destruction.

This is the answer to what we think of the youth of the district and why we have given a lifetime to its welfare. A few gangs can't rob us of the love and trust and friendship of so many others. Our standards are high and we won't lower them for anyone. So there are bound to be clashes. But in an age when youth tends to resent discipline from any source it is all the more necessary not to pander, for without discipline and ideals youth gets nowhere. We have no intention of escaping into either religious emotionalism or negative pastimes. Our troubles have emphasised a need and revealed that we are in the right place. There would be no need to be here if it were plain sailing.

JB put a brave face on events – but was still at a loss as to how to respond to the level of disaffection and hostility which he saw exhibited, not only outside and around the Club, but sometimes inside it as well. In the *Methodist Recorder* he had written: 'This is no success story. Clubland like everything else has not got the answer to present-day youth problems. The ten closed churches around us are grim reminders that conventional methods won't work [and] the many social clubs which have fallen by the way don't inspire much enthusiasm for modern methods.'

'Youth on the Loose'

If JB was unsure about solutions he was not short of theories about the causes, and was critical of those he felt to be responsible, whether wilfully or through negligence. First and foremost he blamed conscription. There was no surprise in this: he had seen the effects of call-up at first hand, not only on individuals but on the structure of family and Club life. He was convinced that National Service hung like a cloud over the senior members, and disrupted their normal progress into adulthood. In his view it was particularly harmful for working boys, because it got in the way of their planning and preparing for a rewarding career – the anticipated absence in the forces made later job prospects seem too far in the future to be a priority for them. For those privileged enough to stay on in school through their teenage years the path was much smoother and the incentives clearer, but for the majority of his members post-14 schooling was not an option. 'Somewhere about the age of 16', JB wrote, 'boys become conscious in a vague way that whatever they do it's just marking time until conscription at 18. Work, effort, jobs with a future, club activities don't seem to matter anymore. Easy money for the least work tends to become a way of life in the most formative years. "Let's try everything while the going is good, for we shall soon be in the forces!"'

His was not a lone voice: many social commentators, teachers, youth workers, and educationalists were of the same view. One was the warden at the Browning Institute, whose club had undergone the same experience, and who publicly endorsed JB's view that call-up had much to answer for. Another ally spoke out on the pages of *The Daily Worker*, which presented JB's case under the headline: 'Call-up blights life from 16 onwards'. It should be said that there were as many, especially from older generations, who argued to the contrary, saying that national service, far from causing bad behaviour, actually gave youth a taste of the discipline and tough training that was lacking in their lives; and that this was the best antidote to the desultory lifestyle and disruptive behaviour which was making so much news. JB's counter-argument was that the problems were arising in the years between school and call-up, which meant that any positive training that might come from national service at 18 came too late. Training, however given, was needed earlier, in the early and mid teens, when habits were being formed, temptations were freshest, and behaviour most volatile. JB considered it of great significance that during those same formative years, families and youth organisations were being deprived of the influence of their 'Big Brothers', who were being sent off into the forces where the younger ones knew they would soon have to follow.

Who was right remains a moot point even today. Whether an earlier end to conscription would have prevented or reduced youth problems in the fifties cannot be tested. Besides, there were other forces impinging on the lives of young people at the time which may have been equally, or even more, influential. One of the most potent was cinema, which was enjoying massive popularity, especially with the young, and a number of films were beginning to appear which were blatantly targeted at youth audiences. A notable example was *Cosh Boy*, released in America as *The Slasher*, and subtitled: 'Youth on the loose', which was showing in local cinemas in the week in which the Club was vandalised. It was a British *film noir*, made in 1953, directed by Lewis Gilbert and starring James Kenny and Joan Collins. The plot was eerily apt. It featured a youth gang that progresses from mugging old ladies to other more sophisticated offences, until eventually they are caught and convicted. They escape with a lenient sentence on condition they join a youth club, where by intimidating others they expand their operations. Meanwhile the leader of the gang (played by Kenny) – whose widowed, doting mother has no control over him – seduces the female lead (Collins) whilst her boyfriend is being beaten up. The film is set among the bombsites and dark streets of postwar London, and includes scenes featuring the language, tools and techniques used by the gang in the conduct of their crimes which, critics of the film claimed, were soon being imitated on the streets.

By today's standards the details of the film would be considered quite innocuous – Gilbert himself claimed in 2000 that it would currently be shown to 10 year olds – but in its time it was deeply controversial and was the first British film to be 'X rated' (prohibited to under 16s), adding of course to its rebellious appeal. JB was well aware of the film and its content, even if he did not go to see it. Like many others in his line of work he must have wondered how much more could take place to make his job more difficult than it already was. He wrote bitterly:

> Without parental control or any sort of discipline and with films
> showing every technique of glamorised wide-boys, a new youth, with
> money to spend, has now assumed the self-importance which allows no
> criticism. While Clubland was being smashed up *Cosh Boy* was being
> shown at the local cinema.[4]

Interestingly, in 1970 at the start of the skinhead cult, the film of Anthony Burgess's book, *A Clockwork Orange* had a run at the Odeon, Camberwell Green, with observable negative consequences that were noticed in the locality by teachers and social workers – again awakening the familiar public outcry that once more cinema violence was leading directly to actual violence. This time the evidence was sufficiently strong to cause action – the film was later withdrawn from general release on the decision of the director, Stanley Kubrick.

JB also blamed money for deteriorating behaviour, claiming that 'some of these youngsters have more to spend than their fathers used to earn'. The wages that 15 to 18 year-olds could earn in 1954 were not great by any stretch of the imagination, but in relative terms even modest spending power was a novelty, coming after the austerity with which most of them had grown up. It was an added inducement to many to opt for unskilled work rather than learning a trade via the apprenticeship route, which in the short term paid less well. JB also saw increased spending power as encouraging a take-it-or-leave it attitude to facilities like youth clubs, to which members resorted only when the money for pricier amusements ran out. There was a knock-on effect, too, on the way in which many youth organisations were beginning to adjust their methods of dealing with difficult adolescents – treating them with a lighter touch, and making generous allowances for disruptive tendencies, or dignifying such behaviour with terms like 'self-expression'. Needless to say JB looked on such trends as deeply flawed: he considered that the great mistake the organisations concerned were making was in aggrandising youth – spelling the word with a capital Y – and in the process giving young people an inflated and unhealthy sense of their own importance. There was no contradiction here. JB had always sought to instil and promote in his members a sense of their own value and potential – but the discipline and ethic he required within Clubland, and his egalitarian approach to member entitlement, were fundamentally incompatible with any illusion of self-importance, whether in an individual or a group.

The Teddy Boys

One way in which increased spending money manifested itself was in the way teenagers dressed. The comparatively drab suits, worn as their best by working lads in the immediate postwar years, began to change markedly after 1950. South London youths, with a bit more to spare, looked for ways to sharpen their image. Some found what they wanted in a fashion that had already become known as 'New Edwardian', promoted by a group of Savile Row tailors and harking back to a style popular among the upper class at start of the century. The fashion had resurfaced amongst their wealthy, elegant clientele in the 1940s – but was swiftly abandoned when the tight trousers and long 'drape' coats were suddenly adopted by hundreds of upstart teenagers from *south* of the River. In their history of the Teddy Boys, Ray Ferris and Julian Lord describe it as 'a great social irony' that Britain's working class youth stole the sharp Edwardian look away from the upper class elite and made it their own.[5]

It is usually claimed that the first Teddy Boys came from the Elephant and Castle. Certainly the first reports of the New Edwardian craze emanated from the Elephant in or around 1952. The abbreviation of Edwardian to 'Teddy' or 'Ted' did not catch on universally until the following September when the *Daily Express* became the first contemporary newspaper to use the phrase in print, although it had probably been used before by the Edwardians themselves. The fear and loathing they are known to have aroused in some sectors of the public was probably an over-reaction to the real danger they posed. The belief that a national wave of serious crime had followed directly on their heels had no statistical basis,[6] but there was a rise in street violence and menacing behaviour. In the eyes of many, they were a scourge and a symbol of moral corruption.

The public's most familiar image was of groups of Teddy Boys hanging about on street corners, jeering at passers-by, catcalling and wolf-whistling at girls, and looking for a reaction to their provocative appearance. Many parents feared for their children and habitually warned them to keep away from the Teds, by crossing the road or avoiding places where they were known to congregate – Camberwell Green was one such gathering spot. It would not do to walk through a group of them, or risk bumping into one, or even making eye-contact, since the wrong look could start a fight. It was generally understood that all Teddy Boys carried weapons, as fashion accessories or to be used for fighting: razors, flick-knives, knuckle dusters, coshes – and most famously, bicycle chains. Brawls did occur in public venues; dance halls were particularly prone to outbreaks of fighting or hooliganism. So, too, were cinemas and, of course, youth clubs.

In many cases, and probably the majority, the bad behaviour went little further than asserting an identity or striking a pose, albeit an arrogant one and one that got up the public nose. In a phrase that had yet to be invented, the Teddy Boys were 'in yer face', and evidently pleased by the reaction of those who were irritated or intimidated by them. For the media they provided a seemingly bottomless supply of news stories and features, most though not all condemnatory. Some commentators argued that, setting aside the worst excesses, the Teds were simply out for a good time. Unlike the spivs and cosh boys, with whom they were often inaccurately compared, they were not career criminals because they didn't need to be. They had money and enjoyed spending it on clothes, cinemas, music, and dancing – and why not?

Some apologists went even further, dignifying the Teddy Boy phenomenon as a class movement, a product of social change that was long overdue, and a celebration of it – if a somewhat eccentric one. Behaving badly, like high fashion, had been the entitled prerogative of the upper classes, and for the first time working-class boys and girls were enjoying a taste of both, in their own style. Some youth leaders, too, took the line that the way to relate to the Teds was to accommodate their tastes and attitudes rather than criticise or seek to change their behaviour, a foretaste of the 'hug a hoody' approach of more recent times. The premise was that to engage with disruptive youngsters, you had to let them into clubs on their terms or they would not come. Well-intentioned as it may have been it had one obvious drawback in that, for a sizeable minority, a popular pastime was wrecking places, with no exceptions for the ones that had welcomed them in.

The emergence of the Teddy Boys coincided with the period when Clubland was experiencing its worst troubles. Given that they appeared early and numerously around the Elephant and Castle, it was more or less inevitable that the senior membership would be affected to some degree – some would have said *infected* – by the Teds. But there is no documentary evidence that they were responsible for, or even connected with, the mayhem in the Club in the winter of 1953–4, beyond being another expression of the pervasive undercurrent of youth rebellion in society. It was not until after the press got hold of the story that JB made any explicit reference to gang problems, and later still before he linked it in any way to the New Edwardian cult. When he did he was not sympathetic – nor did he express approval towards those who condoned or encouraged hooligans by setting up clubs specially for them, in the naive belief that thanks would be forthcoming.

One example was Rev. Douglas Griffiths, a fellow Methodist and minister of Friendship House, part of the South Lambeth Mission who, as the *South London Press* put it, 'tramped around South London's gangland looking to contact Edwardian youths. He wanted to open a club for them where they could meet in decent surroundings and separate the stigma of violence from the "uniforms".' Under the headline 'Clubland attack on the Teddy Padre', the reporter quotes JB's evaluation of the project, and others like it:

> Edwardian seems a silly term unless it means Edwardian manners and discipline as well as the modern travesty of dress. The publicity given to such gangs only adds to a false sense of importance. To perpetuate the

name by organisations for them would only give further opportunities for undesirable rivalry. These gangs have no intention of staying in any one club, cafe, cinema or dance hall. They would find club interests very tame and would not be subject to any discipline or activities. There is no crime in wanting to make the grade and be self-respecting and those who do make such efforts should be protected from having their club bust up by irresponsible birds of passage. There would be no club for Edwardians or anybody else if all were allowed to do as they please and act as they are not allowed to act anywhere else. It's also fantastic that those who can afford such weird and expensive displays in dress, should destroy the purpose and spirit of youth clubs for which others work and sacrifice so much. Many Clublanders would now be in Edwardian rig-out if we had tolerated such exhibitionism, and what a club that would be in which to introduce Junior members. [7]

The last line of the paragraph leaves little doubt about JB's own response to the Teddy Boy phenomenon, whether to those who tried to join the Club, or to existing members who turned up in the Edwardian garb. The Edwardian dress-code was not something incidental to who the Teddy Boys were: it defined them, so that any attempt to regulate what they could wear would be certain to antagonise them. Since, as JB says, 'such exhibitionism' would not be tolerated, the only alternative was to exclude them. But as many organisations were finding to their cost, banning Teddy Boys was likely to result in no less serious consequences than letting them in, with gangs coming back in strength to take revenge, or with the violence spilling out into the surrounding streets. Two months after the rampage at Clubland the *Daily Mail* reported that: 'Cinemas, Dance halls and other places of entertainment in South-East London are closing their doors to youths in Edwardian suits because of gang hooliganism. The ban, which week by week is becoming more generally applied, is believed by Police to be one of the main reasons for the extension of the area in which fights with knuckle dusters, coshes, and similar weapons between bands of teenagers can now be anticipated. In Cinemas, seats have been slashed with razors and had dozens of meat skewers stuck into them."[8]

The Teddy Boys were anathema to JB. He was deeply offended by them, as were a great many of the generation that had fought or lived through two wars, and who were now confronted by a new brand of youth with more prosperity than they had ever had, throwing it away contemptuously on worthless things. Though JB had insisted often enough that these were the boys and girls that he and Clubland were 'here to help' he could see no purpose or value in help that meant giving way unconditionally to youth's basest and most selfish instincts. Clubland existed to provide the underprivileged with a training for a better life. If that ethos had to be abandoned or significantly diluted just to make up the numbers coming through the doors, then unthinkable as it was the time might have come for those doors to close.

There was, however, another idea which was becoming ever *more* thinkable to JB. This was that he should admit defeat with all but a core of Seniors and Officers, and start again with younger children – tens to fourteens – with the aim of introducing them to Clubland's ideals and values whilst they were still at a receptive and more amenable age. In the Spring of 1954 this idea progressed from thinkable to irresistible, and finally into reality – defining Clubland's positive and successful future for the next two decades.

The Writing on the Wall

'Clubland Invites the Juniors': this was the headline in the *Evening Standard* in May 1954[9], for an article announcing the reopening of Clubland to a junior age group.

> Clubland, the Camberwell youth centre ravaged by hooligans a few months ago, is being reorganised by the 56-year-old head, the Rev James Butterworth …

> The £100,000 centre is to open its doors for the first time since the war to 10-year-olds. They will join a Jr section and graduate to become senior Clublanders. Older members are being asked to help run the junior section. Mr Butterworth believes his plan will mean the beginning of the end of hooliganism and will restore Clubland's reputation as Britain's finest youth centre.

> "Already I have enrolled about 200 junior boys and (200) girls and they are going to bring about a complete change of atmosphere," he said. "For a long time I have felt that Clubland was not doing the job it used to. It has been in danger of becoming a kind of cheap dance hall. I believe the only answer is to take youngsters off the streets before they learn the ways of the razor gangs and cosh boys."

> Since the war and evacuation Clubland has been open only to Seniors aged 15 to 18.

The *South London Press* added a more colourful touch to the story: 'A few days ago the Head found six small boys chalking on a Clubland wall, and demanded an explanation.' The outside of the Club was a regular target for graffiti of various kinds, often derogatory, and he had asked them angrily what they thought they were doing. They said they had nothing else to do and nowhere else to play, and in the course of the ensuing conversation JB invited them to come in and look round the club. They did, and after they had seen the theatre and the gymnasium and Parliament and games room and roof playground, and all the rest, they had asked if they could join and bring their friends. 'That' concluded the *SLP* reporter, 'decided Mr Butterworth (who thereupon) announced a complete reorganisation of Clubland.'

The story delighted JB. The number six had a particular resonance for him – the very first Club in 1922 had famously started with 'six boys in one room', and history was now repeating itself and in its turn entering Clubland folk-lore. JB told and retold the tale for many years afterwards, with some variations in the detail, but with a core that was never in dispute. The incident did take place more or less as described in the *SLP* article, but the decision to start the Juniors was almost certainly one that had been coming to slow fruition in JB's mind, rather than a sudden epiphany – as the *Press* report implied. It is also unbelievable that it was any kind of revelation to JB to learn that there were children in the streets nearby who had nowhere stimulating to play. He knew it only too well, and had worried over Club's neglect of the younger age group ever since wartime evacuation had interrupted junior membership. In JB's plainest version of the story,[10] he asked the boys if they would like to come back with their friends on the following Monday to discuss forming a Club with themselves as the founding members.

Not surprisingly the boys took up the challenge, and considerably more than six turned up the next evening. JB told the *SLP* that he had truly been 'astounded by the response', which continued unabated until the premises were at capacity. The first activities to get going for the new recruits were art, gymnastics, badminton, and table tennis, but others quickly followed: boxing, five-a-side football (then a relatively new concept), cricket, roller-skating on the rooftop playground or in the chapel ruins, drama, music, chess, handicrafts, carpentry. Within the first month the boys were given a second night on Wednesdays, and at the same time a Junior Girls' club was restarted on Tuesdays and Thursdays, with the addition of netball and ballet and dressmaking to the range of activities – in those days girls didn't play football or box! Like the boys', the girls' Club reached capacity within a matter of weeks, as news spread across the district and around the school playgrounds.

A waiting list had to be started. Members who were absent for four consecutive club nights had to give a good reason why, or make way for the next in the queue.

Such was the eagerness of Walworth and Camberwell children to come to the Club that in retrospect it is puzzling that the change had not happened sooner. It was now nine years since the first summer of peacetime, and the streets and bombsites around the Club had been playgrounds for hundreds of youngsters with nowhere else to go after school except home – and many homes had remained substandard from war damage. There were two main reasons for the delay. First, there had been no spare nights in the week, nor spare facilities for new members. The Senior and ex-Senior clubs of the late forties and early fifties had grown and thrived, at least until the twin effects of improving wages and outside influences began to shrink numbers. It had taken all JB's energy to revive and fund the existing clubs, resume the Guernsey camps, and find enough officers and helpers to run the activities and maintain the facilities. The Senior Club had endured throughout the war, and had been the priority, but JB had also felt a special responsibility – as well as a deep affinity – for the returning Forces members at the end of the war, and had given a lot of time to helping them readjust and rebuild their lives.

A second reason for caution was the sheer enormity of the challenge of finding enough volunteers with the right qualities and dedication to staff a large intake of boisterous, demanding children. As the steady drift southward to the suburbs began to quicken, and many families left the district forever, there was an inevitable strain on the pool of potential officers living close by. It would be a tall order for people to travel in after a day's work from districts like Nunhead, Sydenham, Norwood, and Bromley to lead and supervise Junior Club activities. When JB expressed the worry that he and Anna might one day have 200 rowdy children to entertain on their own, he was only half joking. In the event, they need not have feared – the response from ex-Seniors, and some older Seniors, was as astounding as that of the Juniors. More than enough were ready to sign up for an evening or two a week, including many who had moved away from the district but kept up their attachment to the Club. What is more, some of those volunteers would still be giving Clubland their time and talent twenty years on. The value of their commitment and ability can scarcely be overstated.

It was Stan Emanuel who had reputedly urged JB to revolutionise the top-heavy and unproductive postwar membership to make way for a new Junior Club. He recalled this himself in an interview he gave to the authors in 2000 just before he died. If anyone could have persuaded JB it was Stan – himself an ex-Senior and Junior too – whose only absence from Clubland had been due to active service, and then captivity, during the war. JB now formally closed the Senior and ex-Senior clubs, save for the members who had kept the sporting and cultural activities going and performed the multitude of tasks on which the running of the Club as a whole depended – those who made up the stage crew, wardrobe, maintenance, catering, publications, and administrative teams, in addition to coaching and instructing younger members. This had remained a strong and loyal section, and with the advent of the Juniors, it had a new *raison d'être*.

The influx of so many noisy and excited children, when there had been practically no time to plan and organise in advance, would have brought chaos to most organisations. But with so many willing and capable hands, and such wonderful amenities, the transition was remarkably smooth, and brought with it a groundswell of renewed enthusiasm. For JB, and some of the older officers who had been pre-war Juniors themselves, it was like turning back the clock to a more receptive era – and as for the children, they settled into the clubs with great ease and enthusiasm, just as though Clubland had been theirs from the beginning. Which, of course, it had.

Cabinet and Members

The Parliamentary and House systems had always been a fundamental part of Clubland, and the Junior dimension of its original structures of organisation and self-government were revitalised in the new Club. As soon as the Junior membership reached the hundred mark, the four houses of pre-war Clubland were re-formed. They were, however, named more prosaically Green, Red, Blue, and Brown, rather than identified with the four Methodist theological colleges as previously, of which the new young members would have no knowledge. Each house had an Officer in charge, whose primary role was to get to know all the children of that house, and to be responsible for their welfare, making sure that they got the most out of their membership. The officer also appointed a House Captain and Vice Captain to help with organisation, and to form a bridge of communication with other house members.

As well as their pastoral function the houses also served to channel competitive energy, of which there was an abundant supply. The Captains picked the teams for inter-house matches in advance of each club night, and read them out in the Parliament, along with match reports and other house related notices. Rivalry between the four houses was intense,

Junior Girls' assembly, c. 1955

and no less on the girls' side than the boys' – and performance was rewarded by the awarding of house points, not just for competitive sports but also for achievement in art, craft, drama, music, debating, writing for the *Junior Review*, and more. The prize for the winning house at the end of each term was to have its colours pinned on the *Guernsey Shield* – a trophy presented to Clubland by the Guernsey Board of Administration in commemoration of the camps, to mark the ending of the long association in 1951.

In addition to the house representatives, each activity also had an Officer in charge, assisted by a Captain who showed a particular interest or skill for that activity. Each of them was called upon to give a regular update to the Parliament on the work going on in his or her department – both in order to promote the activity and to give a sense of cohesion to what was going on in the Club as a whole. It was excellent training for the young Captains themselves in reporting and speaking publicly. The house and activity captains made up the Junior Cabinet – and as the Head of the Club JB also appointed a Head Junior, who took turns with him at chairing the Parliament and reporting on how the Club was doing generally. One Sunday in each month, the captains met in the Head's house for tea and a cabinet meeting, after which they attended and officiated in the Chapel service, wearing their gowns of office – which due to their age often trailed on the ground as they took the collection, or stepped up to read a lesson.

It was sometimes asked whether this new Junior Club was not simply replicating school – without the academic lessons, but with the same underlying character – houses, badges, prefects (or monitors), competitive games, assemblies, discipline, and so on. On the surface, perhaps it did. The model for the new Juniors was very much that of earlier years, when most of the members – indeed all but the very youngest – had left school and started work. At that time Clubland had had a more overtly educational function but, after the 1944 Education Act came into force, the need for such compensatory provision was less acute. The new Junior Club ran roughly in parallel with the last year of primary and the first three years of secondary education, so in that sense there was some degree of duplication that had not existed in the original clubs.

As well as the similarities there were, however, some obvious differences. Perhaps the most obvious was that the children were there because they chose to be, and for the most part doing things they liked doing. Since the only sanction if they misbehaved was to be given back their money and sent home early – or suspended for a week for more serious misconduct – there was a strong incentive to play by the rules. If they didn't like it, they didn't have to be there, so that by natural selection the majority of members were more accepting of the rules and regulations than they might have been at school, where their presence was obligatory. This by no means implies that the Junior members of 1954 were little angels, biddable and respectful. Many came from broken or dysfunctional homes, and had parents who could not control them or had given up trying. They played out and played rough in the street, caused and got into trouble, used coarse language and were disruptive and insolent at school. Yet, from the start the new Juniors seemed to accept Clubland's uncompromising code of conduct without objection, and to take a pleasure in the many formalities and traditions that went with it.

Clubland was truly a special place for its young members. If it resembled school at all, it was not the kind of school most of these youngsters were ever likely to attend. With its splendid premises, houses, captains in gowns, and Parliament, it bore more outward resemblance to a public school than to a typical state primary or secondary modern school. These features gave the Club a kind of solemnity and dignity, particularly in its distinctive Parliament, which characterised it. But at the same time it was also great fun to be a member – the diversity of the activities meant that there was something to appeal to practically everyone, with freedom to sample a different class each time, or to specialise and seek to excel at one pursuit. The nightly programme required close organisation: the doors opened at six with a long queue out into Grosvenor Terrace waiting to be registered. The first half-hour was free time and small games – there was always a comically fast (no running) walk down to the limited number of table-tennis tables in the games room. Formal activities ran from 6.30 to 7.30, with a changeover bell at 7.00 for classes with limited numbers or scheduled house matches. To an observer it might have looked like chaos, but for those involved it all ran like clockwork.

After activities – and showers for some – queues formed again in the canteen for squash and biscuits, and a Club speciality, bread-pudding, followed by the Parliament. Full parliaments took place on Wednesdays and Thursdays, when members filed into the theatre house by house, the Captain leading, to take their seats for the Parliament. After the reports and notices, there was an opportunity for members to ask questions or raise issues, or for a debate on a chosen topic. Anyone wishing to speak had to stand up and address the House as: 'Cabinet and Members'. One of the enduring memories that former members recall is the roar of 'Chair', whenever a speaker forgot the protocol, especially if it was an Officer – the other favourite memory is the cheer and drumming of feet by the house leading on points. Shorter non-parliamentary assemblies were held on Mondays and Tuesdays, followed by a film show – mostly cartoons, and usually rounded off by the inveterate pugilist, *Popeye*, who was for some reason always the most popular.

Strange as it may seem in a new century, this formula was an outstanding success. Even then it was quite traditional in its methods, but children are often conservative creatures and they loved it. This was no accident since, like everything in Club, it was informed by JB's many years of experience and developed insights on the mentality and motivations of young people, especially boys. He had been an early champion of girls' clubs – beginning these as a student in Manchester, and later at Walworth only a year or so after his arrival in 1922 – but it was his own grim experience of boyhood that had driven him, and it was with boys that he more naturally empathised. What he and so many of his class had been denied, through poverty, shortened education and child labour, was the fun and adventure that boys had craved during their last pre-adolescent years, and he had never forgotten it. He referred to those years in his early writing – in parallel with the Greek categorisation – as the 'heroic age', and he had spent most of his early working life analysing that boyhood psyche. For example, in his 1925 book, *Byways in Boyland*, he wrote: 'The heroic age ... is the age of the gang spirit, when boys love to be in groups or cliques, have secret societies and codes, etc.' These years have often been called the *romantic* age, with roughly the same sense. The most successful children's adventure authors and screen-writers have understood this age group well, and played to it unreservedly: Enid Blyton, Arthur Ransome, Roald Dahl, J.K. Rowling. Clubland, in its era, simply did the same, and with the same success. Being a Clubland Junior *was* romantic and heroic, as well as fun. With resounding popularity JB transposed the ideas of gangs and secret societies and codes, into houses, captains, arcane parliamentary procedures, and incantations like 'Cabinet and Members' – and his Pied Piper genius once again fired young imaginations and secured a lasting membership as it had for the First Clubland Church.

And then the Premiers

As Christmas approached a series of special celebratory events took place, setting a precedent that would continue for the duration of the Club. Starting with Advent there was a run of carol services for the different sections, and parties likewise, culminating in the Christmas Eve Dinner, dance, and midnight mass for the remaining older Seniors, ex-Seniors and the officers. Another annual event was also started: an afternoon outing on 24 December for the junior boys and girls – all 500 – to Harringay Circus, due to 'the great kindness' of a mysterious Group Captain Walter Wilson. A fleet of coaches arrived in Grosvenor Terrace to transport them to the north London arena. When the Club re-opened in January 1955, a year on from the dark days of razor attacks, smashed furnishings, and mixed messages in the local and national press, JB was able to write that 'A House of Chaos [had again] become a Home of Friendship'. It was also a house of high activity: Monday to Thursday full-on club nights, Saturday concerts, parents evenings, dances, sales and craft fairs to raise revenue.

Ultimately, no matter how successful and vibrant the new Junior Club was, it also had obvious limitations. It was only part of the Clubland mission – the preparatory part – whose real function was to instil the training that would underpin the Seniors. Also, for the Juniors, the Club was finite: within a year or so the older members, including the first set of captains, would already be reaching 13 – some approaching 14 – and beginning to look and feel out of place in a club that started with ten-year olds. House points, children's parties, and noisy assemblies were bound to pall with time. Those that became captains had something to retain their interests, and the year they spent in office was for many of them a memorable and rewarding experience, and one that gave them a real sense of responsibility and lessons in leadership. But when their year was up, and others awaited their turn – they couldn't return to the ranks and needed a new challenge, or else they would leave and find it elsewhere. At the other end of the scale, the diminished Senior section was significantly older – they were young men, a number of them serving as officers in the Juniors. There was therefore a void resulting from the culling of the mid-adolescent sector during the troubles of the previous year, and this meant that there was no existing group into which the older Juniors and retiring captains could feasibly graduate and feel comfortable. The fracture in continuity that the war and its aftermath had brought was still a problem.

The dilemma for JB was that if he re-admitted Seniors who had not been Juniors, recent history might simply be repeated. He had seen how a small dissenting faction could poison the atmosphere, and drive away those who wanted to take advantage of Club benefits without fear of violence or intimidation. Clubland's tough and deprived neighbourhood had always produced an element of trouble-makers in the membership mix – and to some degree this was still the case. In the past it had been the older members themselves who had stood up to the bullies and wreckers, and provided a good influence on the rising Juniors – to preserve the balance there needed to be a critical mass of members who were on the side of order, otherwise there would always be the danger of indiscipline and disruption. On the other hand, there were not yet enough of the older Juniors to form a viable Senior Club on their own.

During the summer of 1955, as the first anniversary of the Juniors came and went, JB came up with the idea of a fifth house. It consisted of the retiring Cabinet and other members of similar age. They could attend the Junior Parliament, sitting to one side, and help to add some maturity to the proceedings – in return they could then use the premises for a further hour or so of activities and leisure. This was to be called the Premier House (then just the Premiers) and formed the core of what very soon evolved into a home grown Senior section – one of the most successful ventures in the Club's postwar history.

The two Premier Houses, girls' and boys' respectively, eventually dropped their connection to the Juniors and had the run of the premises from 8.00 until 10.00 or 10.30, later merging – by act of Parliament – to form a mixed club on two nights and finally on all four. They had the same range of activities, minus the more child-oriented ones, and their own Parliament one night a week, held in the temporary chapel. They were also invited – and soon after expected – to attend on Sundays, an obligation that was not placed on the Juniors. The Premiers swelled the Sunday congregation beyond a hundred, and by more year on year. Some of the members protested about the requirement, but JB would not give ground. He insisted, as ever, that the short Sunday service was the spiritual centre of the Club and bound the disparate parts into one, just as the Parliament bound together the secular elements. To be a senior member was to embrace the complex whole, not selected preferences. Besides, most of the Premiers, with or without religious backgrounds, found the Sunday evenings an enjoyable contrast to the more energised club nights.

As the first batch of Premiers headed into their mid-teens and a second tier of Juniors added to the numbers, some of them brought friends from school or work. Others heard of the Club by word of mouth and applied to join. Gradually a balance was established of ex-Juniors, new members, and Premiers, without encountering any of the ugliness that had almost closed the Club down in 1954. JB rejoiced in the return of his Home of Friendship, and justifiably. It was a happy membership, and for the most part an appreciative one. Of course there were plenty of headstrong and wilful individuals among the members – none more so than JB himself – and the usual pattern of spats, walkouts, and reconciliations was resumed. But heated though relations often were there was respect on both sides, each putting up spirited arguments.

There were, however, some weighty perennial battles. As the members grew older, dancing naturally became one of the most popular pastimes. There were regular Saturday night dances attended by all the sections of the Club, except the Juniors. There were also dancing classes – strictly ballroom – and sometimes half-an-hour of dancing to round off a club evening. But the members weren't allowed to jive – discouragement or prohibition of jiving was commonplace in the mid-fifties due to its association in the public perception with the Teddy Boys, and with Rock 'n' Roll. The relations between these two is often blurred since the Teddy Boys, uniquely British, predated American Rock 'n' Roll by some years – and jive dancing, which went back to the 1920s and 30s, predated them both. It was better known then as Swing, or Swing Jazz, and evolved with Big Band music in the US, arriving in Britain with the G.I.s during the war. Jiving quickly gained popularity among the young, whilst the older generation remained wedded to their quicksteps, foxtrots, and waltzes. The rhythm of the quickstep was a close enough match to the new style of dancing for the two to co-exist, so that it was not unusual in dance halls – provided it was tolerated – to see the young people in the middle of the floor jiving away whilst older others quickstepped around them.

So it might have been at Clubland dances, had it not been for the arrival of Rock 'n' Roll in 1955 and its almost instant adoption by the Teddy Boys and Girls, leading to a spate of riots in cinemas around the country. Possibly the most notorious, and certainly the closest to home, was the mayhem that broke out in the historic Trocadero Cinema at the Elephant & Castle (New Kent Road) after the screening of *Rock around the Clock*. The stewards and 'usherettes' tried to stop the customers jiving in the aisles and on the stage, and the latter retaliated with the by-then familiar orgy of vandalism, inside and outside in the street. The music, the dance, and the violence became inseparable, and for people like JB, jiving was little short of an abomination. Naturally enough the Premiers, being of their age and generation, wanted to jive, and two of the most frequent questions raised in the Parliament at the time, were 'Can we ...?' and if not 'Why can't we ...?' JB and some of the older officers, being equally of their time, were just as naturally implacable, genuinely believing the dance to have malign influence.

The Premiers found various ways round this embargo. One was to post a lookout at the entrance to the theatre dance hall, so they could switch seamlessly into a quickstep if JB made an unwanted appearance. They were unaware of the nice irony of JB's having warned the members of the early clubs – when any dancing at all was frowned upon by the Walworth Chapel elders – to switch to 'a-hunting we will go' should one of the old guard approach. Another remedy the Premiers had was to adapt the quickstep itself to suit the music. Thus the Clubland quickstep evolved into an idiosyncratic dance form all of its own, with jiving almost sedate in comparison. As it turned out, they need not have gone to any such lengths. With an innocence that was quite often surprising, JB would not have realised his members were jiving if they had done it in front of him – he had no television and had never knowingly seen it. When he eventually saw the Premiers jiving he told one of them it looked rather good and asked why he had never seen them doing it before!

The introduction of the Premiers completed the postwar revival of JB's Clubland, a decade after the end of war and the return of the forces members. JB, with his unquenchable persistence and perseverance, had

Football Association (F.A.) Chairman Sir Stanley Rous meeting
Premier Boys' Football Team

Clubland Premier Team 1959 wearing England shirts presented
to the Club by the F.A. From the left – Back row: Roy Gamble, Bob Allen, Pete
Gennery, Allen Sparksman, Dave Evens, Alan Wren, – Front row: Laurie Williams,
Jim Lunn, Ted Masters, Frank Jupp, Doug Laithwaite.

Gene Tunney meeting the boxing class 1958

forged his way through the challenges and pitfalls of the postwar years. He had come to a dangerous crossroads, but negotiated it successfully, setting Clubland onto a course that would maintain its character for decades to come.

Notes

1 Current monetary value approximately £24,000.
2 *Methodist Recorder*, 4 March, 1954.
3 *News Chronicle*, 4 March, 1954.
4 *Methodist Recorder*, 4 March, 1954.
5 Ray Ferris and Julian Lord. *Teddy Boys: a Concise History*. Milo Books, 2012. Chapter 1.
6 Ibid.
7 *South London Press*, 6 July 1954.
8 *Daily Mail*, 12 April 1954.
9 *Evening Standard*, May 1954 (no date).
10 See *Review*, July 1954 for a slightly more romanticised account. The same *Review* entry also adds that, by a happy coincidence, JB had a phone call the day after the Junior Club started from the SS United States to invite two ten-year-olds to visit the ship by tender from Southampton, tour the decks, and be the first boys to go to the top of the funnel. JB chose two of the miscreant 'six': Ronnie Hunter, who lived next door to the Club, and Terry Judge.

CHAPTER NINE

To America With £5!

Fundraising tours of the fifties

The Clubland fifties were repeatedly punctuated by JB's trips to the USA to attempt to raise finance to rebuild, and to fund expansion. Jimmy Butterworth's ambitions and aspirations to reach and help young people had driven him onward like an arrow from early childhood. In his pioneering youth club venture at Didsbury, and even before that at the chapel in Oswaldtwistle, he had learned that the church could achieve none of its aims without financial backing. Everything had to be paid for – and JB's intentions for the long term had never included making do with run-down rooms and second-hand equipment in dingy premises. He aimed always to provide for his members the very best equipment, furnishings, and buildings money could buy.

Once he reached Walworth and became an ordained minister his access to the great and the good within Methodism meant that the names of canvassed supporters became illustrious – featuring nobility and royalty, and celebrities from the worlds of sport, stage, and screen. Neither he nor Clubland could have progressed without the strong web of sponsorship which underlay his work for youth. In the early days of childhood and chapel the Methodist backcloth of his family, and the endorsement and encouragement of the worthies of his local church, provided Jimmy with an unshakeable confidence in the rightness of his commitment, and in the appropriateness of supporting it by seeking funds from sponsors, however much or little they might gift to his project. A central tenet of his conviction and experience was the belief that the intrinsic and self-evident moral worth of his enterprise was so compelling as to justify entirely the constant canvassing of financial contribution.

JB's practical views on redistribution of wealth speak clearly from his diary records. His ethical stance is that those who have material plenty, status, or celebrity, may legitimately be approached for support, and that he was entitled to seek Clubland's benefit through the finances and fame of sponsors. He took account of the wherewithal of the potential subscriber: his etiquette when preaching in other UK churches to raise funds – a frequent practice during the thirties – was to avoid making any direct appeal for Clubland funds, and in fact to decline offers from impoverished churches or individuals. But if the hosting minister otherwise invited a collection he would accept the contribution with grace. The acceptance of funds was often accompanied by receiving substantial hospitality from supporters, particularly when travelling away from London. This was certainly a prominent feature of JB's American tours – one which might easily be found discomfiting or even compromising – and his diary accounts show that he was not insensitive to the awkwardness which was a hazard of canvassing and accepting gifts, both monetary and in kind. But from his earliest days within Methodism he had absorbed his mother's principle of 'silver, not copper, in the plate', and unhesitatingly considered the justification of entitlement to assistance, based upon the need and rightness of cause and principle, to be beyond question.

Clubland had been from its beginnings wholly dependent upon the fundraising activities of its founder and leader. He took sole responsibility for generating its upkeep and income, as well as expansion, and the list of his sponsors and financial supporters is very long indeed – from Lord Rochester and the Shrubsalls in the twenties, to Lord Rank's sponsorship of the Clubland island site and hostel in the sixties and seventies. The impressive lists of those who funded and supported Clubland, and the influence and publicity generated by Clubland's famous friends, certainly underlay the funding of major building and extension projects, without which its history and reputation would have been very different. These substantial contributions are nevertheless best regarded as peaks of Clubland sponsorship achievement – they stood upon a solid rock of many levels of enduring support.

There was the firm basis of the extensive voluntary staffing of Clubland, and the many benefits in kind provided to it – the members' 'Mams' constant reliable presence to serve refreshments and help prepare for special events; the activity leaders, who offered regular, dependable, often highly-skilled, assistance – actors, football players, painters; the many services given freely by professionally qualified friends and supporters;

the skill and vision offered as affordably as possible by the Clubland architect and his wife; the organ recitals and performances of musicians from within the church or the membership; the loyal attendance and attention of his Clubland governors for all the decades of his Walworth tenure: and the practical contributions of the Clubland officers and workers – not least his wife Anna – for all manner of administrative and creative assistance.

Everyone was busy – and in the foreground of all the activity JB's own labour was the busiest and most unstinting: his ceaseless organisation of fetes and fairs, concerts and competitions, Christmas bazaars and jumble sales; the constant small contributions from well-wishers; the response to his endless exhortations in the *Reviews* and newsletters for outside help to purchase engraved foundation stones; his promotion of tickets for various special Clubland productions; his writing and sale of handbooks and publications with proceeds to the Club; his plea for prompt payment within the Club of money for outings, and visits, and special projects – and, always, the reminders to pay membership subs on time and in full.

Throughout his life JB was an assiduous recorder of his experiences, and his archive provides a treasure trove of closely handwritten annual diaries from 1913 onwards. In these annals he recorded his thoughts, the sermons he would preach, ideas for talks, his travels, engagements and contact details, and comments and ponderings upon the small and large events in his life. Sometimes the contents seem to go proxy for conversations he might envisage taking place – at others, evidently dissatisfied with a page of script, he might score out and re-write the page in its entirety. Some years the diaries are small – the Football Association diaries he received over several years contain tiny notes which spill over the lines, or note engagements only briefly in the limited space. But most years the volumes are larger, and this is particularly so during the nineteen fifties, the decade of his five major fundraising trips to the United States.

JB was a gifted fundraiser, bringing to his persuasive interpersonal rhetoric the same talent which informed his pulpit performance. After the destruction which had been visited upon the Club by World War II, he needed all his charm, skill, and innovation to secure the backing required to rebuild Clubland and place it on a firm financial basis. However postwar Britain was not overflowing with surplus funds and there was far more potential wealth on the other side of the Atlantic, as JB had discovered during his 1937 visit. He therefore went westwards

– despite the long absences from Walworth and family which this required. There is no doubt that these tours of America were exhausting to both body and spirit. They may have been rich adventures for a lad from Lancashire, but they demanded enormous physical energy and mental resolve – and travelling cap in hand also compromised JB's ability to say what he really thought. Through the decade his aim was increasingly to buy up the properties around Clubland to make it an island site, and in addition to build hostels to provide the Club with a future income. His sixtieth birthday was looming and he foresaw the time when his energies would be depleted and Clubland must become self-supporting. Whilst JB acknowledged with gratitude the flow of funds he was able to garner in America, without which the Club could not have survived, it is also true that the touring and talking sometimes entailed being more than amenable to a lot of people whose companionship JB might not otherwise have sought, or whose outlook and views he did not share. But for JB it was a given that the needs of Clubland were paramount, and must take precedence over all else.

The first American Tour: 8 June–1 October, 1950

Finding money to keep the Club going and growing was always, even at the best of times, a driving issue from which there could be little rest or relief. Even when Clubland prospered with full clubs, and rewarding activities which ran smoothly and received positive publicity, there was still the constant underlying need to produce ongoing income.

The war ended, the forces members came home amid rejoicing, and Club life continued to flourish as new members lined up to be part of its life and activity. The dedication of Club on Wednesdays for the exclusive use of the returning forces contingent was recorded as a great success in the 1947 *Review*. Neither was the Club short of formidable sponsors and supporters. Queen Mary continued her frequent donations to Clubland, and communication with JB – paying a deliberately low-key and informal visit to the Head and his Seniors on Saturday 18 May, 1946 – and the first contact was made between Clubland and a widowed Scottish noblewoman whose three sons had died in the early years of the war. Lady MacRobert, of Dounside, Tarland, went on to establish memorials to all three, setting up trusts to honour the interests of her late husband, and in particular 'fostering in young people the best traditional ideas and spirit.'[1] Her official representative, Murray Scrimgeour, was himself a supporter and frequent visitor. But although

Lady McRobert unveiling the restoration stone in memory of her three sons

Lady MacRobert's sponsorship was substantial and welcome it was a drop in the ocean of Clubland's requirements. The great rebuilding and developing programme which was necessary to restore Clubland to its pre-war ascent, and equip it for the future on a self-supporting basis, required an inordinately large injection of hard cash.

The main event which propelled JB into his first fund-raising tour of the United States, and a decade of trans-Atlantic canvassing, was a visit in 1949 from New York Governor Thomas E. Dewey – a friend of Eddie Eagan's whom he had first met in 1937 – and from then onwards there was correspondence between them discussing the possibility of a trip. Governor Dewey – a New York lawyer, Republican nominee for President in 1944 and 1948, and influential 1952 supporter of Dwight Eisenhower – also anticipated the possibility of a meeting with Fulton Ousler, Senior Editor of *Reader's Digest*, and a feature on Clubland. The *Reader's Digest* article did indeed come to pass – although several years later – and a long article entitled 'His Miracle for London Boys' was published in 1957. Dewey held out the offer of logistical support for his trip, which was described by JB as a 'crucial inspiration'. In the *Reviews* of 1949 and 1950 JB stated that the end of an era was upon them, with the financial position of the Clubs 'serious and desperate', even in respect of day-to-day running. He remained saddened by the broken continuity of membership – an inevitable consequence of World War II losses and ongoing national service, which had taken the generation of members raised within Clubland to run their clubs when of age, and replaced them with a different postwar youth which was spending much of its money casually in other ways. But the enormous input of finance of which Clubland now stood in need was immeasurably greater than any sum which might be garnered from membership subs and contributions. JB was between a rock and a hard place: he knew that Clubland's future would be riding on a risky outcome if he went, but to do nothing was unthinkable.

Although the tour was inspired by Dewey's 1949 visit there was no firm plan in place until Eddie Eagan also visited the UK in the Spring of 1950 and offered JB hospitality, contacts, and a round-trip ticket. The offer was irresistible – and off he went. Eddie Patrick Francis Eagan was born in Denver in 1897 – the same year that Jimmy Butterworth was born in Oswaldtwistle – and was, as Jimmy had been, raised from childhood by his mother, taking on odd jobs to help fund his college fees at Denver, including playing the organ at the Congregational Church. His academic success at Denver enabled him to transfer to Yale, where he was captain of the boxing team, and afterwards he studied law at Harvard, and came to England as a Rhodes Scholar at Oxford, later pursuing a legal career. He was an outstanding athlete. In 1920 he won the Olympic Championship as a heavyweight boxer, and repeated this success for the American Olympic team in 1924, in 1932 matching his Olympic boxing gold with another gold medal as a member of the United States four-man bobsled team in the Winter Olympic Games. In 1945 Governor Dewey made Eddie head of the State Athletic Commission – he later headed President Eisenhower's People to People Sports Committee, and was inducted into the Colorado Sports Hall of Fame in 1966. In 1927 Eddie had married Margaret (Peggy) Colgate, of the wealthy toothpaste family, and they lived with their children Caroline and Sydney at 'Happy Harbour' on Long Island Sound, Rye, New York – where they provided a base, contacts, and sometimes engagements for JB on all his American trips during the fifties.

The *Clubland Review* reports for Summer Term 1950 that 'with hardly a word of warning, or a moment to say goodbye, 8 June saw the sudden departure of the Head for America.' The tour itself was cobbled together

The Eagan family at
Happy Harbour

at the last moment, Governor Dewey laid on an official car to ferry JB
around, and Eddie Eagan provided an ongoing pass to the Yale Club
where JB could entertain any guest for free on Eagan's account. After an
initial drama when the outbound flight from Heathrow (then London
Airport) turned back with engine trouble – the clouds of black smoke
billowing from the starboard engine clearly visible to his anxious family
watching from the airport roof – the journey proceeded smoothly, and
once in America JB sent back long informative letters for display on the
Clubland notice board for the duration of his tour.

JB's 1950 diary has a Cunard White Star 'to Europe' label affixed,
and inside the front cover a tour plan for 12/16 weeks: the exchange
rate appears as three dollars to the pound. JB left London Airport for
New York via Shannon, Newfoundland on 8 June, arriving 7 hours late
on Friday 9 June. The New York lifestyle was a far cry from that of the
Walworth Road – as hinted by JB's souvenir menu from the Stork Club on
East 53rd Street, hangout of the rich and famous, movie stars and business
moguls – and the scope of his far-flung engagements set a precedent for

future tours. In June and July he travelled to St. Louis, Dallas, Sherman, and Gainsville. In Early August he was in Colorado and gave addresses in Denver and Boulder; and in Nebraska he travelled to see the Boys Club, run by promoter Nicholas Wegner, which was the subject of a commercial film. Back in New York Eddie Eagan told him that a contact, John Considine, Beverley Hills film producer, was interested in making a film of Clubland, and an initial meeting took place on 17 August at the Plaza Hotel to discuss the possibility. Ultimately, although JB saw more of Considine, he turned down the Clubland film venture because of misgivings about possible exploitation if the film were made.

On 20 August JB visited Los Angeles – it proved an auspicious day for Clubland fortunes. In LA he was given permission by Cecil B. de Mille to enter Paramount Studios, where he met the famous comedy film star who became a major sponsor and friend of Clubland through many years. Pausing in a group of spectators on set, JB heard Bob Hope ask who would like to see him shoot *The Lemon Drop Kid* – to which JB replied that he certainly would not, as his business was helping kids and not shooting them. Bob Hope – who was born in Eltham, Kent but always joked that he had left England when he was two because he 'wasn't getting anywhere' – was intrigued to discover more about the 'little English minister' who had spoken back to him, and this encounter marked the start of a long association between the two.

Another celebrity figure JB encountered in Hollywood was Sir Laurence Olivier, who promised him that 'the next time we meet will be in Clubland.' Two years later the *Daily Mirror* ran a story under the headline 'They Kept Their Word', with a photograph of Olivier and his wife, Vivienne Leigh, sharing the dance floor in the Clubland Theatre with a crowd of senior members in 1952. The article states that they had previously met Reverend Butterworth 'when he was on a hitchhiking tour of America to raise funds to rebuild the centre' – but this description of JB's mode of transport should not be taken literally, despite his lack of funds during the tour.

JB's stay in the United States gave him the opportunity to find out more about the youth organisations pioneered by his colleagues in the American church. In September, having completed his programme of meetings, sermons, and arranged speaking engagements, JB travelled to Oklahoma City to meet Reverend Bill Alexander at the First Christian Church – where he found a very similar vision of church function – and a few days later he visited again the boys' club in Toronto, founded and led by his fellow pioneer of church-based youth work, Ray McCleary.

'They kept their word'

On the afternoon of Thursday 21st Sept. JB embarked on his voyage home on the Queen Elizabeth, scheduled to arrive in Southampton on the following Wednesday. The Cunard royal ships, Elizabeth and Mary, had both been in service as troop ships during WW2, carrying up to 18,000 troops at a time into the European theatre of war, but had since returned to commercial services. In financial terms the trip had been a successful venture for JB. He liked to say that he had been permitted to take only £5 to the States with him, although in fact there was no such restriction on travellers' cheque amounts. The actual allowance was £5 in notes, and that was supposed to be a backstop for emergency return funds. In 1952 £1 had the same value as £24.34 today, so the five pound allowance was something below £125 at present rates – and was then the equivalent of 15 dollars. On this calculation the $3,000 (£1,000) JB took home to Clubland with him from his first American tour therefore represented over £24,000 at today's rates – perhaps not the millionaire investment he always hoped for, but certainly a very reasonable return on his four months touring and talking.

There is a curious postscript to the tour in a letter from Alby Gaynor – husband of Eddie's daughter Caroline – after JB's return hoping that 'your next visit is more enjoyable.' [2] There is little to suggest anything negative in the diaries – beyond a pace that was sometimes breathless, or the disorientation of a long trip away from home in unfamiliar territory. Certainly he met many individuals whose work was of interest to him, or who became his friends – although on later trips JB's diary notes concerning the people and events he encountered became more outspoken. The significance of Gaynor's remark remains a mystery, and there perhaps is no reason to connect the fact that it was four years before JB was willing to leave Clubland for another transatlantic adventure.

The Second American Tour: 17 June–5 October, 1954

Back home JB confided that he did not really expect anything to come of Bob Hope's promise to donate performance takings to Clubland. An entertainer on the other side of the Atlantic had made a generous gesture in the grip of the bonhomie of their exchange, but it could not be viewed as a serious undertaking. Then the press reported Hope's announcement in Hollywood that he intended to donate a fortnight's takings from a Prince of Wales booking in April 1951 to Clubland, and the very next day JB received a telegram from the actor confirming the reports, immediately commenting in response that the donation would save the Clubland Church, ruined since its bombing in May 1941.

True to his word to JB Bob Hope visited London in 1951 and performed for two weeks at the Prince of Wales Theatre, between 23 April and 5 May, 1951, donating the full fee to JB and Clubland. JB was there for a performance, laughing at Hope's joke that he had come to the theatre just to 'count the house – he doesn't trust me!' The amounts were subsequently variously reported – but the actual sum was in excess of £14,000. When Bob Hope visited Clubland a young Michael Caine (Maurice Micklewhite) – a postwar Clublander and an aspiring Thespian in the drama section – was one of a group of members chosen to meet and talk to him, a moment which was, as Michael Caine records in his autobiography (*From the Elephant to Hollywood*), was his first introduction to a well-known star. He recalls the great impression Bob Hope made on him at that meeting, but had no expectation that the famous visitor 'had even noticed the gangly teenager hanging on his every word'. It seems he had, however, as he discovered years later when he met Hope again, at a show during the publicity for the film *Alfie*. No mention of the Clubland connection was made at the time, but a short while after Michael's agent telephoned to ask if the fee for his appearance

Bob Hope, wearing his 'ten-gallon hat' borne aloft by Senior footballers

had gone straight to him. 'It hadn't' Caine continues. 'A week later I got a call from Bob himself. He had sent the money straight to Jimmy Butterworth at Clubland. "You owe them," he said. And I do.'[3]

In September 1952 the papers reported Bob Hope's second visit to London – to star at the London Palladium and pay a further visit to Clubland. Bing Crosby came too, and the pair topped the bill in an all-star show which Hope arranged at the Stoll Theatre as a fundraiser for Clubland, and other organisations. This was not Hope's last fifties visit, and at a concert at Belle Vue, Manchester, Bob Hope again committed his takings to Clubland. In an interview with the *Daily Dispatch* on 6 October 1953 – one of a dozen or so national and local papers to report the visit – JB described his American sponsor as 'the greatest man I have ever met.' JB's FA diary that year – which also gives space to the important observation that Preston North End has finished second in Division 1, equal on points to Arsenal, but losing on goal difference – contains the first mention of a potential Bob Hope room at Clubland. Later a reality, the Bob Hope Lounge and its photographs became a permanent feature of the Clubland building, familiar to decades of Club

Bob Hope and Bing Crosby backstage with JB

Bob and JB interviewed by famous BBC commentator Raymond Glendenning

members. JB fully acknowledged his debt to Hope for 'visits and benefits which restored the premises and saved Clubland from closing'.

November entries for 1952 contain the first mention of another enduring show business friendship. The note reads: 'Attenborough Grand Theatre Leeds' and 'Queens Hotel'. A very young Richard Attenborough was starring in *The Mousetrap* at the Grand in 1952. Richard Attenborough and his wife Sheila Sim became lifelong close friends and supporters of JB and Clubland. The following Spring Gracie Fields' visit took place, attracting a huge crowd of fans outside in the Walworth Road as well as the members who made up the audience inside. Gracie brought her husband Boris and shortly afterwards JB travelled to their home in Capri at their invitation.

At the beginning of 1954 came the spate of vandalism and damage which broke out at Clubland – with chairs ripped and razored during a farewell party for forces members. This prompted the shocked *Methodist Recorder* article of 4 March, 1954 – entitled 'Clubland at the Crossroads' – reporting JB's anger and grief that such violence and intimidation

JB met James Cagney when he was starring with Bob Hope in the Vaudeville film 'The Seven Little Foys'

The Eighth Little Foy

could take place in the Club. The attacks could have presaged a damaging downhill trend in Club fortunes, or prompted despondency in its leadership – but in a typically inspired and innovative move JB instead brought about a sea-change, resolving with new determination and optimism to counter the membership imbalance by re-establishing the Junior Club. The *Evening Standard* in May 1954 recounted the new plan in some detail, reporting JB's intention to reorganise Clubland from bottom to top and welcome in boys and girls aged 10–14 for the first time since 1939, who in due course would move up to form a Senior section. 'Once again it is to become a "university of citizenship" for boys and girls where they can learn to become useful members of society instead of joining street gangs.'

In an upsurge of vitality JB undertook his second American tour in June 1954, again staying with the Eagans, as well as at the Waldorf Astoria – courtesy of Harvey Firestone, CEO of Firestone Tyres – visiting Peggy Eagan's family, the Colgates, and meeting up again with Bob Hope several times. He was introduced to a great many well-known people including James Cagney, Jack Dempsey, Cecil B. de Mille, Jane Russell's family, and Carey Grant, as well as prelates of the church, politicians, and businessmen. He travelled widely throughout the towns of New

JB with Hitchcock and Cary Grant on the set of 'To Catch a Thief'

York State, Texas, California, Pennsylvania, Virginia, and Colorado – and before leaving in October he again visited his friend Ray McCleary in Toronto, Ontario, where Rev. McCleary had successfully established support organisations for the socially excluded and needy.

This tour is distinct in flavour from JB's first visit. He knows now what he's aiming for and there is a far greater dimension of bread-and-butter engagements, rather than merely meeting suggested contacts and hoping there will be some follow-up. There is plenty of small news coverage of his tour, and visits to diverse organisations, and JB speaks at rallies, addresses community groups, gives sermons, and attends other meetings. The biggest difference in audience is the emergence of Rotary Clubs, with their wealthy contacts, as a lucrative source of sponsorship – there were none mentioned during the 1950 tour, but from 1954 they are a constant feature of JB's American engagement lists, and result in a significant increase in the total of funds raised. Of course there is a parallel increase in the number of occasions when JB must repeat his story, and the story of Clubland, and all his tales re-emerge somewhat polished and tweaked in the telling, but they are not yet permanently crystallised, and JB is not yet staled by their repetition. When he embarks for his return voyage home on the SS United States at the beginning of October, JB's diary records that he has raised £4,200 – well over £100,000 at today's currency value. And on reaching home there is more encouragement from discussions with J. Arthur Rank who promises to match Clubland fundraising projects £ for £ up to £10,000 from the Joseph Rank Benevolent Fund.

The Third American Tour: 16 June–30 September, 1955

By now JB knew the ropes – the US tours had proven lucrative fund-raisers, but the gilt of the transatlantic adventure was off the gingerbread, and JB was dispirited very much of the time he was away on the 1955 tour. Grief was a factor in this despondency. A month before he left London, his mother, Ann Butterworth, had died aged 82, and there had been minimal time to come to terms with their shared past life and sad parting. The Rev. George H. Maskell wrote of her that 'undaunted and tireless she moved between her family, the loom, and her church.'[4] She had lived in Coventry with her daughter Nellie and son-in-law Hargreaves for the last fifteen years of her life, coming frequently to London to spend time with her son and his family, and there is no doubt of the influence of her values upon him, during his childhood in Oswaldtwistle and beyond.

JB sailed over on the SS United States once again where, despite his appreciation of the warm welcome extended to him, he chafed at the extent of idle table time he must spend on the voyage. Chief Purser Henry Moreno had written to JB earlier expressing his hope that he would join the ship's company again, and regretting his absence at Easter when the Duke and Duchess of Windsor had been aboard – and prior to sailing JB was joined aboard by Anna, John, and Mary for a luxury dinner laid on by the officers. During the voyage JB bumped into members of the fabulously wealthy Moncrief family, and although this led nowhere in terms of Clubland sponsorship he began to think ruefully how all the Club's financial problems could easily be solved by just one 'silver bullet' millionaire donation. As it was, a number of potential advance engagements had been cancelled, the diary was empty of commitments, and when he reached New York no replacement appointments awaited. JB writes of sitting dejectedly in his hotel room with 1000 Clubland booklets, wondering whether anything positive would ever materialise since none of the churches he had written to had replied.

Bob Hope's brother Jack Hope, instigator of the tour, had not succeeded in putting together the envisaged itinerary of Rotaries and other associations, and no engagements were forthcoming from other contacts.

Eventually Bob Hope took JB to a premiere taking place in Philadelphia, with the object of securing introductions at the celebrations and parties which accompanied it. JB was mortified by what he felt to be Hope's coolness and lack of interest during the trip, and anxious lest he had asked too much of the star – in the event there was a poor turn-out and no positive outcome or contacts resulted. JB's diary suggests that he had become more dubious about the nature of Bob Hope's support and assistance, although Hope reassured him that the efforts he was making would produce results, and ultimately further contacts were set up. But through the first months JB writes that he is suffering in the relentless heat, missing his home and family, and failing to raise the anticipated funds for Clubland's future.

Back in New York JB confirmed his refusal of John Considine's Clubland film project, despite Considine's view that such a film would 'make millions'. He was somewhat dismayed to find that his friend Thomas Dewey, whom he admired and respected greatly, disagreed with him about the Considine film, taking the view that although it might be made for profit or contain an element of misrepresentation, the film would raise Clubland's profile and general capital to a degree that made the project acceptable. JB did not, however, alter his decision, and continued to regard any plan to make money out of the Clubland enterprise as a potential compromise of its integrity.

As before JB stayed for some of the time with Eddie and Peggy Eagan, but had become disenchanted with the domestic situation at their home, and the necessity of spending significant periods there. In his diary he records upsets and altercations at Rye, not least between the Eagans and their son Sidney, whose behaviour and lifestyle was sometimes disturbed and unsettled. The scenes he witnessed caused him to record privately that he would be unsurprised by eventual family crisis at Happy Harbour.

However despite the low mood of many of the earlier diary entries matters did improve as the summer wore on and JB became busier – there were even moments of buoyant elation and thankfulness following successful TV appearances, talks on *Coast-to-Coast Radio*, or an appreciative reception of a church address. And there were several productive arranged forays outside New York – Buffalo, Niagara Falls, and Washington – as well as impromptu trips and introductions. Peggy Eagan took him to Greenwich and introduced him to Gene Tunney – who became a generous Clubland supporter and signed up for a commemorative stone. Whilst back in New York he also met Beverley Bogert, then 90, for whom he developed great affection – Bogert purchased a restoration stone, and introduced JB to 'a raft of wealthy Americans'. By the Autumn the diary records positive rewards for the Clubland building fund, but along the way JB was also becoming painfully aware of the frustrations and potential mortification of his position. He h ad grown weary of having to repeat his 'story' on innumerable occasions, spend substantial amounts of time in company he did not enjoy, and attend evenings of society and entertainment – such as the revues frequented by Eddie – which made him uncomfortable.

In America it was, of course, effectively a truism that somebody seeking donations of large sums of money would be much in the company of successful capitalists – and for a man who had decades earlier professed to regard Keir Hardie as his idol, this may suggest difficult demands upon personal consistency and integrity of attitude. JB was not much stirred by political ideologies in their narrow interpretations, but it was always definitive of his stance that he did not seek charity for Clubland and its members, but rather the support to which he considered they had an inalienable moral entitlement. This principle, however, could not be demanded of everyone who gave, who might be more likely to think of themselves – if they sought a definition at all – as simply giving money in a charitable cause. Neither could all sources of sponsorship by any means be guaranteed to enjoy wealth acquired in accordance with ethical transparency. JB's response to such criticism was to cite William Booth, Salvation Army founder and sometime worshipper at Walworth Methodist Church, who, when criticised for accepting donations from non-believers, responded that he would 'wash it in the tears of the widows and orphans and lay it on the altar of humanity.' An updated version of this would probably have been that JB could think of nobody better than himself and Clubland to clean up any dubious donations that came his way.

In August Peggy Eagan – always solicitous of JB's comfort – saw him off to Texas securing him a roomette on the train. JB did not meet any hoped-for oil kings, who would solve all Clubland's sponsorship requirements with a single signature on a cheque, but he did make a significant contact with the Webster family in Houston. Mrs. Webster, nee Wilkinson, was the sister of JB's childhood sweetheart Maria, who moved out to the US with her Methodist minister father in 1912. This is a bright spot in his summer – although the diary also records many hours in his hotel room at the Shamrock, Houston, hoping for contact, calls, or letters. Disillusioned and despairing, JB noted with some resentment how the 'feeblest of preachers' was able to hold down a lucrative job with paid staff, when he could not raise money for his ruined church, and felt his work to be 'belittled, and undervalued'.[5] But casting self-pity aside JB continued with the sermons, rallies, rotaries, talks, and interviews, accepting that his millionaire donor would not materialise, but instead seeking to settle on 'a stone for many'.

In September, when JB was back again in New York tying up loose ends for the journey home, there were several late engagements. A promised Bob Hope contact in Topeka set up an exhausting three-day series of meetings – at which JB felt he had to deliver more of a blatant business pitch than a sermon, although the compensation was a Clubland gain of $1000. Back on SS United States, Henry Moreno passed on donations of $200 for JB's sermons, in return for which he placed a stone and dedication in Clubland's American Wing – Moreno later sent to Clubland a personal donation of $500 from himself and his wife.

The overall total of funds raised on this tour recorded in the diary reached £12,200 at 1955 currency value. A detailed breakdown of the accounting shows that rotary club meetings were again more frequent than in 1954, and there was also a significant increase in the number of radio talks and interviews. The tour had, after all, been a success, raising a very substantial sum for Clubland – three times as much as the previous year – as a result of JB's efforts. But it had also frequently brought disillusion and despair. Safely on board and homeward bound on 4 October JB wrote emphatically in his diary that he was 'tired of selling my story.'

The Fourth American Tour: 28 June–28 September, 1956

JB returned to the usual busy Autumn and Christmas at Clubland – including an appearance on *This is Your Life* on Sunday 20 November 1955, which took him more by surprise even than most of its subjects since he had never previously heard of the programme. His appearance spawned a rash of brief reports in dozens of papers and a wave of correspondence from old acquaintance, as well as new interest. He also noted in his diary that Chelsea had finished at the top of Division 1 again, as well as recording a fourth Club visit from Bob Hope, accompanied by Alma Cogan, the following Spring. There were other visits from Harvey Firestone, as well as from Beverley Bogert who put up £1,100 following his visit to see Clubland for himself.

Bob Hope and Alma Cogan in the Bob Hope Lounge

By then, despite the trials of the previous year, the next American tour was already on the horizon. There had been many reports of JB's fund-raising project in the American press, and other American supporters had offered contributions to travelling expenses – although in the event JB did not take on any sponsorship, and travelled instead with the intention of securing a restoration stone from every state he visited, clearly feeling it incumbent upon him to strike whilst the iron was hot, and his US profile was high. For JB and Clubland this was a positive and optimistic period. At home the establishment of a Premier Club section, stepping stone between the Juniors and a new Senior Club, was a brilliant solution to what had been a complicated and unsatisfactory senior structure, whilst in the restored Junior Club itself membership had flourished. And in America his audience awaited him. The Club threw a celebratory farewell party for its Head, and he left the builders demolishing the remains of the bombed church, in anticipation of the re-building which was at last on the approaching horizon.

On board the United States again JB was welcomed as 'the ship's chaplain', with Purser Moreno unabashed in his devoted pursuit of JB's fundraising pitch. JB still hoped against the odds for a magical

The officers of the S.S. United States: they christened JB 'The Ship's Chaplain'

millionaire sponsor, but none materialised on the voyage, although he did make contacts with several supporters whom he met again when he got to New York. One of these was Ted Hilton – whose invitation to his Moodus Holiday Resort included crowning a beauty queen, and left JB returning with his pockets full of cash feeling 'like a gangster' – and another was Paramount boss Stanton Griffiths who also offered a contribution. He even discovered on the voyage that ex-President and Mrs. Truman were in the cabin opposite his. All in all, notwithstanding the few inevitable dramas and untoward events, the tenor of the 1956 American Tour was much more positive than the previous year's trip – it was as busy as JB could wish it to be, with many established well-wishers.

JB's diary describes further drama with his hosts at Rye – reporting that a few days after his arrival Peggy called emergency services out to look for Sidney in his boat against the advice of both Eddie and himself, when 'the ensuing row could be heard in Texas.' JB was relieved to quit Happy Harbour for the peace of Contentment Island with Peggy's brother Byard Colgate and his wife Beatrice for Independence Day. He then trod the by-now familiar paths between Hotel Statler and the New Yorker, comparing the steady flow of calls and letters to the drought of his previous trip. He revisited his elderly friend, Beverley Bogert, who had found three more $100 contributors for Clubland – and discovered a new one: Albert Bradley, Vice President then CEO of General Motors had been born in Blackburn, and the two were delighted to share stories of sneaking onto the Blackburn Rovers ground without paying as children. At Rye Peggy had offered JB an open cheque for Clubland, which he had refused, but a few days later she telephoned specifying a specific substantial donation. JB records his view that Peggy was in fact frequently more supportive of Clubland than Eddie appeared to be.

In the city JB received a standing ovation from the New York Rotary meeting on 12 July, and the next week was taken by friends to watch the ballgame at the Yankee Stadium, and to meet top broadcaster Red Barber, with whom he got on very well. He also met some big business moguls – Lorenz 'Ivy' Iverson, renowned engineer and inventor, president of Mesta Machinery, as well as Pittsburgh builder Edward Crump Jnr – kings of industry whom he found to be 'plain and ordinary folks' behind all the trimmings. Wealth, however, by no means implied that any generous contribution would be forthcoming – Iverson got on well with JB, but showed no signs of making any financial commitment to Clubland.

JB's disenchantment with 'telling his story', which had plagued him at the end of his tour the previous year, did not in fact prevent his intercourse with the wealthy people who were in a position to help him, and who were all accessible resources for Clubland support. There is every reason to suppose that JB – skilful at reading the responses of others – was also fully aware of his own charisma and influence, as well as the leverage provided by his clerical collar. JB's grandson of the same name, who did much of the diary research for this book, remarked guilelessly: 'I wish I could have seen my grandfather work a room.' It would be deliberately disingenuous to deny that JB was an accomplished and inveterate performer, who was well able to play his audience.

In Texas Methodist Lewis Decker, a contact from 1955, arranged a series of sermons, press meetings, and talks, with moderate financial success. JB also met up with Bill Moncrief Jnr. again, and through him other very rich individuals – powerful men of huge influence both in the state and more widely. Barely half way through his tour – a month shorter than those of previous years – JB had cause to be pleased that he had already raised $8000, and was looking forward to his next

Coast-to-Coast TV appearance, which could be relied upon to generate further interest.

The diary record indicates that there was no let-up in the ongoing family drama of the Eagans – Peggy's Clubland donations seemed to be an additional bone of contention – however JB and Eddie later appeared together on a TV show which raised $1000. JB also visited Bob Hope and his brother Jack, who was still talking of meetings first suggested two years previously. JB continued to feel uncertain of Bob Hope's interest in Clubland, which seemed to wax and wane, sometimes making him feel a nuisance. He had formed the view that Bob Hope's home, and perhaps the performer himself, were not as relaxed and content as his wealth and presentation might imply. Later that month JB was stung by his treatment from a contact to whom Hope had referred him – a chief at New York Yankees – who declined to speak directly with JB instead sending him to an employee who 'deals with charity.' Subsequently JB reported a mischievous pleasure when he later considered that Hope had been effortlessly out-talked by Jack Benny at a lunch all three attended.

Meeting Cecil B. de Mille unexpectedly one evening whilst dining out JB responded to de Mille's mistakenly calling him Father Butterfield by quipping that he is 'Buttercup on Mondays, Butterfly on Tuesdays, Butterfield on Wednesdays, Butterscotch on Thursdays, Buttermilk on Fridays' and then came into his own as Butterworth at the weekends. The great man was amused, and JB followed up the encounter with a Clubland pitch by letter thinking he had a head start – but de Mille's daughter merely replied on behalf of the filmmaker's Trust, saying that his request would be considered further when the profits of *The Ten Commandments* filtered through, but that the Trust was presently fully committed.

On 18 August JB took a body blow when he discovered via LA newspapers that the British *Daily Mail* was seeking his comments on an article in a Church of England newspaper accusing him of scrounging from the Americans to finance Clubland. JB writes in the diary of his despair at this type of coverage, and suggests that there is gross hypocrisy at play. The *Daily Mail* article of 18 August 1956 was bluntly entitled 'Clergy Scrounge Money in US'. From Pasadena JB commented on request stating: 'I am in California as a guest of Bob Hope and other friends who have visited our London club. I am not going around scrounging money in America. I have never made an appeal either from the pulpit or any social clubs I have addressed.' He also wonders why a Church of England newspaper is commenting on activities within Methodism. JB's response here, although understandable, is undeniably something less than transparent. It is no doubt true that he never made an unvarnished or crudely phrased appeal for money – there is also no doubt that JB was in America to raise money, and that that is made clear to everybody he encounters. Contemporaneous USA articles describe him as attempting to help teenagers by selling stones to raise funds. It is reported that 'Fifty stones are needed to complete the American wing, and Rev. Mr Butterworth said yesterday he would remain in this country until he sold that many. Each stone bears the name of the donor.' The *Methodist Recorder*, ever full of praise, had added to the picture by reporting in England on 2 August: 'Once more the magic word 'Clubland' opens American hearts. Connecticut Campers hear Walworth Story and the Dollars Rain Down.' In September JB returned to the turbulent atmosphere at Rye, where Sidney reportedly considered it acceptable to ask him during dinner: 'Why do you come scrounging for money for brats in England?'

Later in the month JB was at a loose end, having been asked by the Hopes to keep the time clear so that they could book him up, he had little to do save for desultory meetings and appointments, such as baptising his friend Keith Glenn's latest child, and being interviewed by Mayfair Magazine. The latter led to publication of an article entitled 'Phoenix in the East End' in February 1957 of which JB says: 'So much of this glamorised write-up is untrue that I wouldn't know where to begin to correct it. It's not even in the East End and so much else I never even said or dreamed.' Otherwise he had to endure the background of constant quarrels at Rye until he could return with relief to the SS United States on 28 September for his voyage home. On board there was a good turn-out of passengers to hear him preach, and afterwards a lady on his table donated her Bingo winnings to Clubland – and four Catholic priests sent JB a bottle of wine. He reported being startled by the realisation of the kind thoughtfulness around him – and moved to thank God again for his success and his health for the duration of the tour, which has raised $24,000.

The Premier House welcomes JB back from America, 1956

The Fifth American Tour: 10 June–13 October, 1959

In the end, despite his protestations, there was one further American fund-raising tour through the Summer months of 1959, although that did at last prove to be the final venture of its kind. The years in between these last two tours were eventful ones during which the new chapel rose on the blitzed site, and many visitors from America – including Douglas Fairbanks, Gene Tunney, and John Hay Whitney the US Ambassador – prompted JB to consider one more foray in the United States. Clubland was even beneficiary of a film that year; *Jet Storm*, starring celebrity friends such as Richard Attenborough, Dame Sybil Thorndike, and many other well-known actors, had its world-wide premiere in aid of Clubland at the Regal Cinema, Old Kent Road, Bermondsey.

JB resolved to cross the ocean one last time – but when the day of departure arrived his mood was far from optimistic, and the first entry in his tour diary – 19 June 1959 – is little short of heartbreaking. He had left Clubland without the usual farewell party, having fallen out with members and leaders over the contribution they were making to the new building. He writes that he cried himself to sleep, feeling more hated than loved, and speaks of the futility of his life, his fears for the tour ahead, and of feeling ill and without energy. Totally disheartened JB preached on board as usual, but wrote that 'I feel weary of these wanderings for money for other people.' At 62 a tour such as he had undertaken was an exhausting physical enterprise, but the demoralising effect of his Clubland farewell threatened to sap his spirit before he began. Reaching New York he was somewhat cheered by Keith Glenn's reliable warm welcome and visits to old friends of previous tours, and by 17 June he was able to rally for the first board meeting of the newly formed *Friends of Clubland* organisation. Eddie Eagan was appointed President, and James Adams – a committed supporter who was to prove a valuable friend and ally of JB – was elected Treasurer. Unfortunately there was more acrimony developing at Rye over Peggy's wish to give Colgate stock to Clubland, and not to Eddie's charitable project *People for People* – both Jim Adams and JB came to feel that this sporting charity had become Eddie's greatest priority and his main fund-raising project.

Many of the same people and places who featured on tours earlier in the decade are again significant – but now the states and cities are familiar to JB, and previous acquaintance has in many instances become genuine friendship. Keith Glenn, the Eagans, the Colgates, Harvey Firestone,

Bob Hope, Barney Cooper, Bishops Frank and Kennedy, Beverley Bogert's son, Harold Clarkin, Lorenz Iverson, Cedric Hardwick, Rev. Dick Cain, Douglas Fairbanks, and many others, people the landscapes of New York, Pittsburgh, Fall River, St. Louis, Rhode Island, Greenwich, Tucson, Chicago, Phoenix, Los Angeles, Pasadena, San Diego, and San Francisco, as before.

On 18 June JB was taken to dine and to be installed in a Waldorf Towers suite by Harvey Firestone Jr., where he was set up with staff and a free table in a luxurious penthouse. Firestone later pledged $5000 to Clubland, and also offered JB some sound advice to locate potential big funders rather than the less economical and more exhausting round of lecturing and local TV appearances. Byard Colgate approved that approach, and Beverley Bogert's son – his father having sadly died the previous year – was also interested, although there is no record of any larger donation than the generous $5000 Firestone contribution following JB's talk at the huge Firestone factory in July.

JB continued with his Rotary Club talks – through the five tours they had proved the most effective method of making contacts productive of substantial donations. He also visited Ivor Hope, the eldest of Bob Hope's seven brothers – a visit salutary for its discovery of how far they all relied upon their famous sibling for their personal funding. He also self-funded an 800 mile round trip to Pittsburgh to see the Iversens – JB entertained the hope that after such a journey Iversen, who had never made a Clubland donation, might move towards sponsorship, or provide introductions to associates, but despite his hospitable welcome there is no indication that either of these resulted.

On 22 July Anna, John, and Mary arrived in New York for a reunion holiday, also moving into the Waldorf suite provided by Harvey Firestone. It was an optimum time for family solidarity. JB was away the week they arrived preaching to a huge congregation in Tucson Arizona, where he received the very sad news of the death of his favourite Aunt Minnie (Lavinia) who had married his mother's younger brother Jack Duckworth from Rough Hey when JB was a boy there in 1910. Although Jack senior was 'Uncle Jack', he and JB were not a generation distant in age, and he and Minnie had always been close to JB and supportive of him. Their son Jack, JB's cousin, worked unstintingly for the Methodist Church in Huncoat, near Accrington, and he and his wife Audrey were frequent visitors to Clubland. He was reunited with the family on 30 July, his frame of mind since the start of the tour having improved substantially, and they moved to stay with friends in California, where

Barney Cooper took them to the Hollywood Bowl. Later they visited Los Angeles and toured Paramount Studios before going to stay on Bob Hope's ranch, and afterwards with Peggy Eagan's sister Caroline Weston.

JB enjoyed seeing America through their eyes – going on a visit to the Empire State Building, and taking John to see a baseball game – although their presence did mean that he was less free to follow up contacts or commit himself to engagements. He did keep an undertaking to go and see Sidney Eagan in LA, but described regretfully finding him in a shabby rented room the worse for alcohol. After a brief stop with Bishop Frank and his family in St. Louis, Anna and the children travelled north to stay with her sister in Ottawa, and JB – whose fundraising fixtures in Chicago had fallen through – returned to New York to salvage what he could in the remaining weeks.

The situation at Rye got no easier – the diary reports that Eddie was resisting the release of cheques to Clubland, and JB and Jim Adams were perturbed by what they considered to be his preferential treatment of his own charitable organisation in the light of his leading role in *Friends of Clubland*. JB would certainly have preferred to spend his last days in America in the tranquillity of the Colgates' home at Darien, but the family was committed to staying at Rye on return from Canada. It was a sad note of dissent in what had been an enduring and friendly relationship, and so near to the end of his last US trip. But Peggy came to wish them an affectionate bon voyage for their crossing from the quayside – and in Clubland's history there can be no doubt of the great benefit of JB's American fundraising tours of the fifties, and the enormous positive influence of Eddie Eagan in bringing them about. Crossing for the last time on the *United States* JB again declared that his transatlantic tours had come to an end. He wrote in his diary: 'This four months out of my life has taught me never again to play the role of beggar. It has made me far too sensitive to go fundraising.'

JB's return to Clubland on 14 October was an emotional occasion. The theatre had been filled with flowers, and the welcoming ceremony was attended by all the captains and leaders turned out in their formal Club regalia. Bill Barnes, the new assistant minister from the US, gave a welcome back speech. JB, lifelong wordsmith and orator, was overwhelmed by the sentiment of the occasion and lost for words. He could say nothing beyond 'I love you all very much and I won't ever go away again.' For the first service the following Sunday 18 October chairs for 200 were set out, but more than 250 queued to get in for

JB's homecoming message. On this occasion he was equal to it: 'I have placed my trust in film stars, financiers and fund raising tours but in peace and confidence I now trust in the purposes of God for my life and this place called Clubland.' Afterwards he confirmed that it was 'one of the happiest evenings I have had for many a long year and there was no mistaking the affection of my members and their parents who came. If this is the start of real understanding friendship then our work and worship together is going to be the richest fellowship any minister could desire.'

In a newspaper report the following year the *Evening News* (17 October, 1960) announced 'Clubland Rises from the Ruins' – and the *South London Press* declared 'No more US Money Begging for Clubland's Head'. In the latter article JB was reported as stating: 'America – I never wanted to go there in the first place. It was humiliating. But after building up Clubland in the prewar years having it almost immediately destroyed by bombs was a dreadful blow. There was no money in Britain in the early postwar days so America was the only place to turn to. I went there five times. The last tour took a lot of out me ... afterwards I was very run down. I'm 63 now and I've got to retire from my day-to-day running of Clubland: I reckon that without those American tours I would have had five more years here.' JB has written 'rubbish' on the cutting of this article – but it does seem to contain more than a grain of authenticity – and the transatlantic trips bore undoubted positive rewards even whilst they proved a mixed blessing in other ways. It is also true that JB showed little sign of stepping back from hands-on Clubland management for many years afterwards.

Notes

1 Letter from Lady MacRobert: 11 May, 1946.
2 Letter from Gaynor, A: 8 Oct. 1950. Ref. 155.011.
3 Caine. Michael. *The Autobiography: the Elephant to Hollywood*, p.347.
4 Durrant's Press Cuttings re 16.5.1955.
5 JB's Personal Diary, Summer 1955.

CHAPTER TEN

The Rock 'N' Roll Years

This is Your Life

In June 1955 JB again left Clubland on his third US tour, leaving Ken and Bunty Randall in charge of the clubs until his return at the beginning of October. Whilst he was away a new television show, imported from America and heavily trailed, arrived on UK screens. It was *This is Your Life*, hosted by Eamonn Andrews. The format is now very familiar: each episode tells the life story of a well-known or celebrated individual by bringing friends and family, some from distant times and places, to provide the biographical profile of the subject. This had made the programme a hit in the States and would keep it so in Britain for decades to come. But the real hook for viewers, in those days, was the shock and surprise of each guest as he or she walked unsuspectingly on to stage, to be met with the words '…This is Your Life'. To this end a huge amount of preparation and collusion was needed, under a cloak of strict secrecy. If the subject found out, the episode would be cancelled, as it sometimes was. Indeed that is exactly what happened in the run-up to the very first show. The intended victim was the football legend Stanley Matthews, but his name was leaked to the press. Instead of cancelling the programme altogether, the producers turned the tables on Andrews himself, and made him the first unsuspecting guest.

The first scheduled subject was Yvonne Bailey, better known by her Special Operations Service code name, 'Odette', during the second world war, when she was parachuted into occupied territory for undercover action. She was followed on the show a month later by the band leader, Ted Ray. Then around the beginning of November, Anna Butterworth, and Reg Turtle the Clubland Treasurer, were approached by the producers to set JB up for the fourth episode on Sunday the 20th, and to assist with the job of contacting the acquaintances who would step out to greet him.

The invitation presented Anna with something of a dilemma. As she well knew, Jimmy had an ambivalent attitude towards the media, and there was no way of predicting exactly how he would react if and when he found himself in front of the cameras. Although he welcomed any opportunity to maximise financial support for the Club, he dreaded publicity that might be interpreted as commercialising Clubland or exploiting its members, and had turned down at least one offer of a feature film about the Club for that reason.[1] However it became clear to Anna that the television proposal held great potential for attracting donations, of which the Club was endlessly and desperately in need. The problem was that the arguments for and against were fairly equally balanced – how an unwitting JB might respond to being put into the spotlight was anybody's guess. Much would depend, too, on how the press reacted to the event, especially the local south London papers which could not always be relied upon for support in Clubland matters. It was true that JB had been feted for his appearances on quizzes and talk shows in the States, but that was far away from home, and the culture was different there.

There were also logistical problems. A major one was that the programme went out live at 7 p.m. on a Sunday, just when JB would be starting the evening service – so there was a big question around how he might be got to the studio without telling him why. That was one of the toughest obstacles, but after a consultation with governors Gordon Lyle and Reg Turtle, the three decided it could be done and gave the producers the go-ahead to start preparing the script. A period of subterfuge and outright lies followed. Nobody but those chosen to be on the show were permitted to know the secret. Ricky Elliott was primed to take the service on the night without being told why, other than that JB would be 'away' for that evening. Meanwhile it fell to Reg Turtle to find some way to persuade his old friend to abandon his pulpit when the time came, and to go with him to the studio. Anna and Reg had to contrive ways to meet almost daily to organise the details. Since JB was always at the Club, they resorted to passing notes arranging times to meet, and were fearful that suspicions of a rather different sort might be aroused if one of these should be intercepted.

Despite some tense moments, the lid was kept on until the last minute. Reg's rather flimsy ruse was to arrive at the Club around 6 p.m. and tell JB that his help was needed over some life-or-death problem that he would explain in a car that was waiting out in the street. But instead of finding JB in his study as expected Reg discovered him in the entrance hall, talking in rather irritable tones to an understandably bemused Ricky who, like JB, had a sermon in his pocket that he was expecting to deliver around an hour later. Reg's sudden appearance – a rare occurrence on a Sunday as he lived in Orpington – caused even more perplexity. Somehow he managed to talk JB into the chauffeured car, and spin out his unlikely fiction long enough to get them to the Earl's Court venue – where Jerry Desmonde stepped out to meet them with yet another bogus tale involving Bob Hope, and on that pretext led JB into the theatre and up onto the stage.

It was at this moment of drama that the penny was supposed to drop, when the guest realised where he was and why. If still in doubt the presence of Eamonn Andrews and the Big Red Book would be enough to reveal the secret. Not for this guest, though. When Andrews pronounced the magic words 'This is Your Life', JB had no idea what he

'This is my WHAT?'

was talking about. He never watched television, and wouldn't have one at home or in the Club, and he didn't read the entertainment sections in the papers – apart from football reports. Eventually though it became evident to him that he was going to hear his own life story via a string of friends and family from his childhood to the present day. As his personal history unfolded JB was greatly moved and delighted, when one after another figure from his past came out and said their piece. As well as Jerry Desmonde, they included: Jack Blundell (a boyhood friend from Oswaldtwistle who remembered Jimmy sitting up every night until midnight, learning Greek after a day in the spinning shed); Mrs Dewhurst with her daughter Dora (whose home, Willow Cottage, was a haven to Jimmy when he was growing up, and who heard him, still in khaki, preach his trial sermon in 1919); the Reverend G.H. Simpson (fellow student at Didsbury); Ted Bowyer (one of the first 'six boys' in 1922); Billy Whiles (a medical student at Kings and one of the first Clubland officers); Harry and Doris Richards (from evacuation days in Shropshire); and Anna (looking happy and relieved). Last, wearing their gowns and symbolising the progress of Club development during the previous eighteen months, came the head girl and boy of the Premiers, Madeline Driscoll and Billy Childs.

Back on Camberwell Road, and with the Head safely spirited away, the evening service was postponed and the theatre hurriedly transformed into an auditorium. BBC technicians set up monitors so that the programme could be watched on a number of grainy screens, by the members and officers – minus Anna and the two excited Premiers who went off in a second car to make their appearances. The episode had excellent reviews – the programme was immensely popular anyway and attracted big audiences. A snowstorm of letters followed from old acquaintances and complete strangers who had seen the programme, many sending donations for the Club. There are too many to list, but one that stood out most poignantly was from Annie Morris:

My Dear Jimmy.

What a thrill to see you on This is Your Life. I thought 'that's my Jimmy'. My little pupil has climbed so high – you still have that habit of running your finger behind your ear and up into your hair. Hearty congrats and lots of love to you and yours from your old teacher of long ago..

Celebrity Clubland

Towards the end of 1954 Bob Hope had made his fourth visit to London. He was giving a Royal command performance at the London Palladium but made time to visit the Club. He appeared on the stage in front of 500 members – it was the first time he had been seen by the Juniors, some of whom also took part in a performance for him. He dedicated a stone to his family members, and another for Bing Crosby, who on this occasion could not be with him because, Hope explained, he had a bad injury caused by falling off his wallet.

The following year the Juniors and newly formed Premier House welcomed Kitty Kallen, a very popular singer at the time, best known for her hit, *Little Things Mean a Lot* (1954). The purpose of her visit was to unveil a stone donated by the American quiz show 'Strike it Rich' and its presenter Warren Hull. JB had competed on the show on his previous US tour and won a $500 prize, which had been handed to him by Miss Kallen. During her visit several newspapers ran a photograph of her kissing one of the junior boys on the cheek. The lipstick was still there when he went home at the end of the evening, vowing not to wash for a week.

Soon after a stone-laying ceremony and service was held in the ruins, attended by Mr and Mrs J. Arthur Rank. The Joseph Rank trust had agreed to match pound-for-pound whatever JB, together with the club members and friends, could raise themselves, up to a total of £10,000. This was half of what was needed for the demolition and rebuilding. Plans had already been drawn up for the new chapel by the architects Wilson and Mason, and were on show at the event. It was a much simpler and more modern design than Edward Maufe's beautiful building, with large almost square windows and a raised walkway running the length of the quadrangle, and a plan for Club rooms to again occupy the space below the chapel, with a second playground on top. Costain had been appointed as the builders – the better-known London branch of the family firm that Anna Butterworth's grandfather had founded in Liverpool.

The soon-to-be Lord Rank[2], himself a staunch Methodist, toured the Club and met the members in various activities as well as participating in the service. He and his wife had first come to Clubland in 1932, and presented cups to the winning senior houses. This visit was the start of a growing programme of financial support from the Rank Trust, reaching dimensions which eventually outstripped all other benefactors.

Preliminary sketch for proposed new chapel – in the event it was superseded by Edward Maufe's designs.

Another wealthy family that took an interest in Clubland was that of the Hon. Robin Borwick and his wife Paddy, heiress to the McAlpine construction family. JB and his family stayed with them at their Berkshire home and orchard estate, and subsequently the whole Premier House was invited to a picnic and outdoor service there, followed by a bonfire and evening of singing that many ex-members have recalled as one of their fondest memories of that period.

Bob Hope came for a fifth and last time in the autumn of 1956, soon after JB's return from his latest US tour. Hope was such a regular visitor by this time that in the *Clubland Review* that month JB lost count of the number of visits he had actually made and reported it as the fourth. This time it was the Junior football teams in their house colours who greeted him and sat behind him during his gag-studded speech. Several papers featured a photograph of Hope, with an overcoat over one arm and trilby in his hand, wrestling on the stage against one of the Juniors, the rest cheering them on. The contacts with Hollywood led to visits the next year from Carey Grant and Jack Benny, both of whom laid restoration stones in their names.

October 1958 saw a visit by Gene Tunney, world heavyweight champion in the 1920s, and friend of Eddie Eagan who had instigated JB's US tours. The *Clubland Review* quoted a glowing press tribute to Tunney, not only as a great boxer but as 'an unofficial ambassador who has advanced the reputation of his country; most important of all a ruddy good bloke'. It adds: 'To this fine tribute Clubland can add a true test of greatness, that so famous a man has the spirit to be a friend of boys, to come and spend an evening with us and give happiness to so many.' He came on a club night and saw the activities in full swing, naturally spending time in the boxing room where he met the Club boxing instructor Ted Gray. The *Evening Standard* printed the photograph with the caption: 'Gene Tunney gives punchy advice'.

As if 'unofficial ambassador' were not enough, Clubland's next guest, just four days later, was the real thing: 'His Excellency the Honourable John Hay Witney, Ambassador of the United States of America to the Court of St James', as his stone in the quadrangle read. The occasion was to honour the many Club benefactors in the US, but it also marked the formation of the trust, 'Friends of Clubland Inc.', which enabled American supporters to make tax-deductible donations in the future. The two Head Premiers and Head Juniors – Brenda Ingram and Robert Gray, Vivienne O'Connor and John Blackwell – escorted the ambassador around the activities, after which he addressed the whole Club in the theatre. He also promised to come again, bringing his wife, and sure enough he did return in April the following year and on that occasion brought with him

Head Premier Bob Gray introducing U.S. Ambassador John Hay Witney
Head Junior, John Blackwell, left

The ambassador with Douglas Fairbanks in the quad

Douglas Fairbanks Jr., who had agreed to join the board of *Friends of Clubland*. As well as Hay Witney and Fairbanks the whole illustrious US board now included: Bob Hope (Patron); Edward P Eagan (President); James S Adams; Prof Erskine Crossley (Yale); Byard S Colgate; Harvey S Firestone Jr; Bishop Eugene Frank; Dr F B Harris (Senate Chaplain); Bishop Gerald Kennedy; Gene Tunney; and Jack Hope.

Clubland's own board of governors was hardly less well connected – famous visitors were very familiar in Walworth as the 1950s drew to a close and Clubland's 40th anniversary approached. Richard Attenborough continued to be a regular visitor and supporter, and his friend John Mills with his wife Mary Hayley Bell, and their teenage star daughter Hayley, also attended a remembrance service and mingled with the members. JB had met them in the Lancashire village of Downham where Hayley was filming *Whistle Down the Wind,* co-produced by Attenborough. Max Benedict, who had attended the pre-war Guernsey camps as a youth, was the film's editor. On the football front Joe Mears, the Chelsea Chairman joined the governors, soon to be followed in the sixties by Denis Hill Wood of the Arsenal. The Burnley Chairman, Bob Lord, also became

JB with Richard Attenborough and Hayley Mills on location for the film
'Whistle Down the Wind' in Lancashire

a benefactor, and professed friend – an unusual liaison perhaps for a
boyhood Blackburn Rovers fan.

Such prestigious visitors as these certainly raised and maintained
awareness of Clubland's existence, as well as bringing a splash of glamour
to its publicity – and there were the obvious immediate benefits of
financial contributions and sponsorship, as well as the wider support
which accompanied a raised profile. Clubland probably had more than
its share of famous friends, although it was not uncommon for youth
clubs to form such links with celebrities for their mutual benefit. The
singer Frankie Vaughan was well known for the interest he took in many
institutions, including the nearby St Paul's Church club in Lorrimore
Square, around the time when Bob Hope was helping Clubland. Taxi
drivers directed to Clubland – if they could be persuaded to go south
of the River at all – would sometimes say 'Oh, that's Frankie Vaughan's
Club', confusing the two.'

Nevertheless the consequences of the media attention that followed
celebrity involvement were not invariably positive. Events surrounding the
premier of the film *Jet Storm* in September 1959 gave the lie to the benefits
of any and all publicity. On the prompting of the Variety Club of Great

Britain, it had been decided to stage the premier in the Old Kent Road, and to donate the proceeds to Clubland. This event actually took place whilst JB was away in America, but the press comments were no less daunting in his absence. The initial response from local press – the *East London Advertiser* – was celebratory enough, but shortly afterwards the editor of the *South London Press*, Mr. Eric Kinton, decided to take a challenging stance on the appropriateness of funds donated to local organisations. The following cuttings from the London newspapers speak for themselves:

East London Advertiser, 17 September, 1959:

> The little reverend – James Butterworth, founder and head of Clubland, Camberwell road – realised another ambition on Sunday when film stars in evening dress graced the Old Kent Road Regal for the premiere of *Jet Storm*.

> But the Methodist minister was not there to see and hear how the folk of the Old Kent Road area cheered Douglas Fairbanks, wolf whistled Virginia Maskell, and roared at Harry Secombe. For Mr Butterworth is now in a fundraising lecture tour of America – "my country" as Fairbanks put it in addressing the audience from the stage.

> Fairbanks is one of the governors of the International foundation of Clubland the big youth organisation whose headquarters are now being rebuilt. Money raised at the premiere is being used to help pay for the Camberwell Road project.

> Stanley Baker one of the film's main stars – the story centres around a crazed scientist, Richard Attenborough, and a bomb hidden in a passenger aircraft – was one of those introduced by Harry Secombe on the stage.

> Hermione Baddeley, Paul Carpenter, were also there. With them was British heavyweight champion Henry Cooper. The reception afterwards was held at the nearby Thomas-a-Becket public house well known to the boxing world ...

Evening News, 21 September 1959:

> A first-class row has blown up over the premiere of the Associated British film "Jet Storm" in the Old Kent Road last week. It was in aid of Clubland, the Camberwell boys and girls club run by the Rev James Butterworth.

In an article in the *South London Press* last week the editor Mr Eric Kinton, said of the premiere: "I winced at the sight of the Pearly King and Queen doing their capering cockney act for visiting film stars ... Before the welfare state the people of the Old Kent Road had to beg – but not now ... Our folk can look after themselves now and pay for their own youth clubs ... It was good advertising for the film, with jellied eels at the local to give the gossip columns a gimmick."

Mr Kinton was unrepentant when I talked to him today "If the people of that area want a youth club, they should pay for it themselves," he said. I asked Mr H R Turtle, London businessman and a governor of the club what he thought. "We are furious about this article, he replied. "There is no question of us begging. We were approached by the film company." Another broadside against the paper came from Mr David Jones of the Variety Club of Great Britain and the film company: "I have spoken to Mr Kinton and written to him in the strongest terms. Some time ago we had a letter from Mr Butterworth asking if we could help in any way with funds. We chose to hold the premiere in the Old Kent Road with two objects in mind – to give the locals a chance to see the stars and to donate the proceeds to Clubland."

Mr Butterworth's reaction: he is in America appealing for more funds. "But when he gets back I suppose he will blow up too," sighed Mr Kinton.

Kinton's attack, which was spiteful in tone and crude in expression, cast a shadow over JB's return from his final American lecture tour. Indeed the local article had been noticed by at least one national paper, and JB had felt it necessary to reply from the USA, pointing out that his lecture engagements there were exclusively by invitation, and that if audiences and organisations wished to offer sponsorship to Clubland then this was an entirely voluntary matter. The furore at home was effectively dealt with by the angry responses of his supporters, and the storm over *Jet Storm* quietened. It was crystal clear to supporters of JB's work that if the young people of the Old Kent Road, like those of the neighbouring Camberwell Road, no longer had to 'beg' – as Kinton so abrasively chose to put it – this was only because people like JB had taken on the responsibility for their welfare many decades before the welfare state came into being, raising funds so that they would have amenities and opportunities that were not provided at the time other than by such fundraising efforts and the generosity of sponsors. Moreover in Clubland's case the young members had always been required to pay what they could afford, both on principle and so that no element of condescension was present or experienced in the provision of their clubs and facilities.

In his heart however JB knew that an intimation of the future lay behind Kinton's misconceived attack. It was symptomatic of a strong underlying current in social work which would spell the end of voluntary work as JB knew it, and replace it with state-funded youth services and salaried staff. Kinton had, in fact, missed the whole point when he said that 'our folk can look after themselves now and pay for their own youth clubs'. He did not mean that the young members would contribute directly; he meant that the local authority would provide the facilities free (through taxation) and pay staff to run them. It was a political point – Ray Gunter, the Labour MP for Southwark from 1959, had reputedly stated that he wanted no private enterprise running services in the borough – and that this included Clubland. Another point missed by Kinton, but picked up by Mr. Jones of the Variety Club of GB in his response to the SLP editor, was that if glitzy film premiers had any value at all, then surely the Old Kent Road had as much entitlement to benefit from their presence as the West End or Broadway. In the same vein JB often used to cite the Old Vic Theatre, situated in the Cut in Lambeth, as 'bringing the best in theatre to South London'. It is not known whether Mr. Kinton also thought his concept of condescension applicable to the theatre in the Cut.

Soon after the new Premier Club was formed, JB also reinstated some of the long-standing contacts with schools and colleges. A favourite was the Leys, a Methodist public school in Cambridge, founded by Wiliam Fiddian Moulton – father of JB's tutor at Cliff College – and attended as a boy by Lord Rank. Another close partner and annual visitor to Clubland was Westminster Teachers Training College, also a Methodist foundation. A coach-party of Premiers and older Juniors was invited to the Leys in the summer of 1955, and regularly thereafter. They played cricket matches and went boating on the upper reach of the Cam, which runs past the school. The girls' Club had similar links to the sister school, Queenswood, and prefects from both schools made return visits to Walworth from time to time, to dances or to a Sunday service. JB valued these contacts and did all he could to maintain them. Their purpose from the early days had been twofold. Firstly that by building up a list of sports fixtures Clubland boys and girls would get access to playing fields and outdoor facilities that were non-existent in inner-city areas like Walworth. Second, repayment of the school's hospitality with invitations to the Club would enable the members to meet other young people of their age with different – often privileged – backgrounds and opportunities. This would widen their horizons and develop an ability and confidence to mix with contemporaries whose lives contrasted with their own.

Whether in the second half of the twentieth century these links were worth preserving was a live question – not least because from some standpoints the practice might be seen as patronising in a similar way to celebrity visits. The value of such contacts to a youth club for working boys and girls might be illusory. If Clubland's members were equal to any public school boys and girls – as had always been claimed – what would they gain from rubbing shoulders with the latter, or worse, being perceived as the recipients of a favour? JB's straightforward answer was that equality was not even in question, but that there was a gain for both groups in meeting on equal ground. That was the reason why Clubland's premises had to be as fine as any others, its activities as rich, its connections as prestigious, and so on. The youth of Clubland would see itself to be equal – Oxford University might have its famous union; Clubland had its Parliament, with the same objective of training future leaders and active citizens.

The contacts and exchanges had nothing of aping one's superiors, but everything of aspiration, and Clubland's alumnae have been proof of its success many times over. One of them, Daphne Williams, recalling her days in the junior and premier club, and later as an officer, said simply: 'Clubland showed you a different way of life'.[3] Many have said the same, often adding that it made them different people. Terry Barrett was one of the first Junior intake in 1954. He has no hesitation in attributing his choices and successes to his time in the Club, which he says, 'played a pivotal role in changing my view of the world and the possibilities therein'.[4] Without the Club, in which he played a significant part himself as a member and then an officer, he believes his life would have been 'mapped out for him', on the print floor of a Fleet Street newspaper. Instead he was the first of his family to go to university, leading to a career in the Probation Service and subsequently as prison governor. His wife Teresa and he were married by JB and their children were among the last that he baptised. Their lives have been rich and varied; they now live in France, where, far from retiring, they are still planning and carrying out new and ambitious projects.

JB did not deny the existence of class division, but his life was founded on the denial that it had any justification in terms of merit or desert – he wanted to see discrepancies challenged through exchange, and discourse carried out on equal ground. From the earliest days of putting his ambitions for the young into practice he faced a lack of understanding of the depths of these principles. His methods frequently met with mixed and confused responses, manifest in the opposing graffiti often found on the walls outside the club – Communist this, or Capitalist that, in more or less equal measure. There were those who never could comprehend his egalitarian principle of wanting all to have equal access to the finest.

Bricks and Mortar and Lord Rank

In June 1956 the aptly named demolition firm, Wackett Brothers, began the work of knocking down the bombed chapel. The pavement on Camberwell Road was quickly congested with pedestrians, stopping to watch as the first of the massive Portland stone blocks at the apex of the frontage was sent crashing through the tiled roof of the porch sixty feet below. Over the next few months the walls were laboriously levelled, and the floor drilled away to reveal the club rooms underneath that had survived the fire. All in all it was around two years before the buildings were flattened and excavated, and the site cleared ready for the new foundations.

A last view of the old Chapel

Demolition
begins

Shortly after demolition started, and with £10,000 still to raise for the rebuilding, JB left again for the USA. Despite unutterable sadness at the final demolition of Maufe's 'sermon in stone' he relished the start of the restoration process. Once the ground-level premises had been decommissioned he contributed gleefully by putting a brick though every remaining window pane – and also led nightly sorties onto the site to chop up the block floors and other wooden fixtures to burn on the fire in his study. That fire was legendary. It burned night and day, winter and summer, with or without the bountiful fuel from the demolitions. Whole planks and huge logs would be fed into the flames, propped on bricks and often extending half way across the room. JB's love of open fires bordered on pyromania – perhaps a legacy of the bitter winters he had endured in the cottage at Rough Hey – but this explanation could do little to appease the fire-brigade, who were more than once called out to extinguish a chimney fire. Even after Southwark imposed a smoke-free zone to tackle London's infamous 'pea-soupers' there was little noticeable reduction to the blaze in his study.

The rebuilding finally began in August 1958. The slow pace of demolition and site clearance were not the only reasons for this delay – there had been a breakdown in relations with both the builders and the architects. JB had made little secret of his dislike for the plans produced by Wilson and Mason, but there were also disagreements with Costains. Since Anna was a member of the Costain family – albeit the smaller Liverpool branch of the firm – JB had been under the impression that the Costain firm itself would be the builders, and had also anticipated some degree of preferential treatment. However, it seems that a subsidiary was contracted to do the work and it was their sign which duly appeared on the hoardings. JB felt this to be a snub to himself and to Anna, and this, together with his distaste for the plans, led him to withdraw from the contract. He had hoped to please Anna and cement family relations by choosing Costain, but inevitably his withdrawal led to a cooling between himself and the family firm. In truth there were already tensions, not least due to the understandable family fear that Anna's inheritance would eventually be swallowed whole by Clubland's voracious appetite for funds. The debacle over the re-building did nothing to help.

There is no surviving correspondence on which to base a reliable account of what happened next. The *Clubland Review* of Easter 1957 still features the artist's impression of the Wilson and Mason elevation as seen from the quadrangle. A year later, without any warning or explanation, the interior view of a totally different chapel is pictured, with familiar tall arched windows, and starred ceiling. Above it the text reads:

Clubland in the Royal Academy

Drawings of the first Clubland church were accepted by the Royal Academy and the buildings received the all London prize for the best in architecture. But what is more important, the unique conception formed the traditions of Clubland. It was a complete departure from the idea that anything is good enough for kids in poor districts. It was designed to emphasise the spiritual ministry of architecture.

The new Clubland Chapel below is also honoured in the Royal Academy by the same architect, Sir Edward Maufe, R.A. It is to be built on the ruins of his first noble creation, destroyed by bombs ... Sir Edward brings the genius of his Gilford Cathedral, his Runnymede Memorial, St John's College and St Columba's Church of Scotland and much other famous architecture to create a 'College and Cathedral' for Clubland boys and girls.

Maufe's beautiful new Chapel

Within a very short space of time, JB had evidently turned again to his old friend Edward Maufe, who had generously stepped into the breach, apparently without rancour. The whole saga remained somewhat mysterious, but by the Spring of 1959, with plans approved, Dove Brothers Builders were at work on the foundations and the drawings were again on show in the Royal Academy. Few disagreed that they were an improvement.

Meanwhile JB was working on two other major Club projects. The first was to annexe an adjacent plot of land for an outdoor playground – a facility that Clubland had always sorely lacked. The gymnasium and the netted roof space above it were too small for serious sports activities, and the one proposed for the new Chapel would not have been significantly larger. By a stroke of good fortune it was no longer needed. Directly next to Clubland, between the Chapel and Urlwin Street, was a United Dairies depot, from which milk floats laden with bottles departed before dawn each day of the week to deliver to the surrounding streets.

In Walworth's more genteel past, before the dairy had acquired the land, there had been a row of leafy gardens backing the Georgian houses on Camberwell Road. Lord Rank's father, Joseph, had suggested to

Sir Edward and Lady Maufe unveiling their restoration stone in the
Clubland foyer on completion of the Chapel

the trustees of the original Walworth Chapel that they should buy
these houses and gardens to protect the site from unwanted industrial
development – but his advice had not been taken, or could not be
afforded. The arrival of the dairy had proved him right, but now, in
1958, the premises were unexpectedly on the market once again. Joseph
Rank's son Arthur, already deeply committed to the restoration of the
Chapel, evidently took little persuasion to follow through on his father's
wisdom. He agreed to buy the land leaving JB to find the money for
demolishing the bottling sheds and loading platforms. The resulting
fenced and floodlit area, including an ample five-a-side football pitch,
transformed the Club's sports provision both for Juniors and Seniors,
and went a good way towards JB's ambition of having a complete island
site stretching between the two side streets, the railway arches, and
the main road. All that remained for that dream to be realised was to
purchase any houses which did not already belong to the Walworth
Chapel trust.

The second project, which JB had nurtured for some years, was to
build a hostel or hostels for young adults. As well as providing affordable
accommodation for students and young working adults – for whom

Edward
Maufe with
Club Cabinet
members.

housing in London was both expensive and scarce – the hostel would have two other functions directly advantageous to Clubland. On the one hand it would solve the foreseeable problem of finding leaders and helpers to serve in the Club, in an age when voluntary service was in decline, by populating the hostel predominantly with residents who were willing to play an active part in the life of the Chapel and Club. This would reflect JB's earliest notion of Clubland as a settlement, and at the same time the rental income would secure the Club's survival financially – youth clubs were increasingly being funded by local authorities, and charitable giving to support independent organisations was dwindling. It was a far sighted plan, and one that appealed to Lord Rank's business sense, as well as to his Christianity and commitment to youth work. Once again the Rank Trust[5] agreed to provide the lion's share of the substantial necessary funds, and its legal team set to work on the tortuous business of purchasing the properties and obtaining vacant possession.

The contribution that the Rank family made to Clubland was enormous. Without Joseph Rank's support before the war, and Arthur Rank's afterwards, the securing of the 'island site' – which by the end of the sixties had an estimated value of a million pounds – would probably have remained unattainable. According to the *Review* of April 1959 Lord Rank had now become Clubland's 'Restoration Patron', as his father had been the 'Foundation Patron' – an honour that was no doubt posthumous

– and in the same month Joseph Rank's grandson, Paul Bartlett Lang, laid the first brick as the rebuilding began on the Chapel. With his love of continuity JB would have found this connection, spanning three generations, very pleasing.

The chapel was completed and dedicated in 1963, with the new open-plan clubroom beneath, looking out on to the walled playground. The whole restored complex was opened by Her Majesty the Queen Mother on 12 May, 1964. Dr Ivonwy Morgan of the Methodist Home Mission led the devotions, and Lord Rank gave the speech of welcome, during which he thanked British and American sponsors for their generosity and paid tribute to JB's sustained principles:

> You can of course have discipline without freedom and in our time we have seen some horrifying examples of that. But, nevertheless, you cannot have true freedom without discipline. It is therefore our work here to try and guide this in the best of all ways.[6]

Queen Mother arriving to a Clubland guard of honour

Unveiling foyer stone with JB

The Queen Mother, in her reply, also referred to Queen Mary's visits in 1939 and 1946, and spoke of the challenges faced by young people during and following the war, praising Clubland's part in meeting those challenges. She continued:

> The companionship, opportunities for recreation, and the happy social life which young people can find here must bring added enjoyment and interest into their lives and must surely help them to become good citizens and good neighbours.
>
> It is my prayer that the wonderful work which this club has done ever since its opening, may continue to bring joy and comfort to many in the years which lie head.[7]

JB worked closely with Lord Rank for many years, and their extensive correspondence is evidence of a strong bond, as well as gratitude for the money the Trust poured into the rebuilding. In his speech at the royal opening Rank speaks of 'we', 'us', and 'our work', with the clear

Ma'am meeting the Mams: Mrs. Emanuel, Mrs. Sutherland, and Mrs. Loman:
a constant loyal presence over decades

implication that he saw himself much more as an active partner than merely a financier, and JB in turn hailed Rank as Clubland's saviour. They certainly spent a great deal of time together determining Clubland's present and future needs – and also engaging in discussions, which Rank called their 'class meetings', on religious, moral, and social issues. Their written exchanges give only the vaguest idea of what passed between them at these meetings, and the extent to which their outlooks and beliefs concurred or diverged remains a matter for conjecture, but the outcome of their relationship was a positive continuum for Clubland.

So, too, does their personal relationship, coming as they did from such markedly different backgrounds. Rank was nine years older than JB. He was born into wealth and, after a shaky start, had proceeded to amass a fortune of his own, first in his father's flour business and subsequently in the British film industry, which he greatly enriched and for which he was made a life peer. At its height the Rank Organisation owned five studios (including Pinewood) many production companies, its own distribution arm, and over six hundred cinemas, making it for a time bigger than any of its Hollywood rivals.[8] It is interesting that JB always addressed his letters, 'My Dear Lord Rank' whilst Rank began 'Dear Jimmy (or JB)' – but whether this signified a measure of deference on

JB's part towards the older, richer, more elevated man is not clear. Both were at the peak of their respective careers, both celebrated in their own fields, equals in endeavour – yet they were very differently rewarded in material terms. However strong the personal ties and mutual respect between them, there was always that inescapable asymmetry: one was the asker, the other the giver. The benevolence and largesse travelled in one direction only.

To do justice to Lord Rank, his giving came with few if any strings. He gave JB his expert advice on how to conduct the business arrangements – and corrected him when he strayed or cut corners – but he never sought to interfere with Clubland policy or practice, even if some of its methods differed from his own more conventional, evangelical brand of Methodism. He recognised JB's calibre, and the particular gift which had enabled him to influence and enhance the lives of children and young people within the Methodist church, and he was satisfied that it deserved Rank Trust money. Interestingly, Rank had a similar reputation among film makers who were backed by his company. David Lean is on record as saying: 'We can make any subject we wish ... cast any actors we choose and have no interference with the way the film is made.'[9]

All the same it would be naive to imagine that the relationship was without tensions. JB's old friend Tony Jackman, the producer of many Clubland stage plays, wrote years later in a letter: 'I remember you arguing with Lord Rank for what you believed, in spite of his moneybags'. History doesn't relate what they argued about and it is improbable that Tony witnessed any actual altercations, since their meetings were private – but whatever it was that he recalled, there is some suggestion of disquiet or disagreement that JB confided to his closest associates during the years of rebuilding. JB was never one to hide his impatience in the face of hindrances, especially those that were not of his making. He was desperate to get the hostel completed, believing it would thereafter place Clubland on a permanent, independent footing, with no more reliance on donations. His own instincts were to take the most direct route to that destination, and the circuitous path of the business arrangements and legal details were profoundly frustrating for him. Paul Lang, Rank's nephew, wrote of JB: 'He was not going to be hidebound by rules, regulations, and normal procedures if he felt those were barriers to his work'.[10] Equally, he had little time for drawn-out committee meetings. Paul Lang recalls one occasion on which he caught JB writing the minutes for a meeting of the Clubland governors – of which Lang was one – shortly before it was due to take place, so confident was he that they would endorse the decisions that he already made. But winning the governors' approval was only the first move – buying the property, obtaining possession, bargaining with tenants and lease holders, dealing with lawyers all amounted to a long and tedious process.

JB's impatience was not the only strain on the relationship. Throughout the whole protracted business, he was dependent on successive tranches of money from the Rank Trusts, and others. This was not once-off finance, and no matter how willingly and graciously the donations were made, they were the in the end the result of ongoing cap-in-hand appeals to Lord Rank, appeals that JB had to make not once but repeatedly until the work was done and the flow of income could begin. Moreover, even before the first hostel was finished came the daunting realisation that the rental from 20 rooms would not be enough to achieve the level of self-sufficiency that was the whole purpose of the exercise. The arithmetic spoke for itself, and Lord Rank was persuaded to extend his generosity to a second block, with twice the capacity of the first, although he drew the line at a possible third.

The total building bill pushed beyond six figures. For JB, approaching 70 by the time the hostels were complete, the prolonged project was both physically and mentally wearing, and it took an inevitable toll on his health. Worse, however, may have been the cost to his dignity – he had spent a lifetime fundraising and on the surface seemed almost immune to the pressure that continually securing sponsorship imposed on him, as if he were protected by his all-consuming passion to complete the job. Yet at a deeper level it also punished him, from time to time engendering feelings of resentment which were worsened by the adverse publicity which periodically rewarded his efforts. From childhood the drive to achieve an equal chance for young people like himself, who had been denied a level start to their lives, had fuelled his will. It had provided him with the justification he needed to make repeated appeals to wealthy individuals, without whose generosity and support he could not do more than dream. But his American tours had taught him that no matter how justified and necessary his fundraising campaign it was not an ennobling feeling to be forever in the role of supplicant. Naturally JB felt thankful for Rank's financial support, as he had done for the sponsorship of Clubland's other rich and powerful donors, but the position it put him in was one which prevented openness and honesty. For someone as characteristically outspoken as James Butterworth, constantly biting his lip, or saying what he believed another would wish to hear, would be an intolerable bar to authentic response. Yet the sad truth is that such a compromise inevitably became almost second nature in the context of fundraising.

The two men, although united by their goal, were not exactly kindred spirits, and JB sometimes confided that he found Rank's deeply held and often expressed religious convictions difficult to square with his hard-nosed business practices. He would regularly precede their meetings with a prayer – something JB found incongruous – before getting down to the detail of buying houses and securing vacant possession and whatever else that entailed. Although the buildings were in poor repair and due for demolition, some of them still had tenants – or small businesses on the ground floor such as a barber shop and an optician – and there were sensitive issues at stake, both social and ethical. JB wanted the same ends but found the means uncomfortable – though he was in no position to question them at the same time as accepting Rank money. His indebtedness shackled him and the burden weighed upon him even though it was securing what he believed to be God's will. The strain told, and in a letter to Lord Rank in 1966, JB described having had a blackout and needing to be carried out of the pulpit.

A period of rest secured JB's recovery, but many decades of relentless pleading, cajoling, and compromising could not easily be shrugged off. The second hostel was finished soon afterwards – both blocks were fully occupied and the island site was secured and triumphantly declared 'free of debt' – the old battle-cry. But like the proverbial fall of snow on blossoming trees, JB's health again took a sudden downward turn, and in 1969, with the club's future by no means assured, he was forced to leave London with Anna for an extensive period of convalescence.

Growing up in Clubland

JB was my father. I was born in March 1944, a week after his 47th birthday, and my sister Mary two days before Christmas, 1945. I did not know Clubland in its glory days before the war, and have only dim and partial memories of the great clubs and camps of the forties, before the fresh start with the Juniors in 1954. Mary and I lived with our parents, and a seemingly endless stream of short and long-stay guests, in the Head's House overlooking the quadrangle. The physical presence of the building was an early indelible memory: the grey brick walls and tall empty windows of the bombed chapel on one side, the theatre and gymnasium wing opposite, the roof terrace where my father took me to watch the trains. One passed every minute at peak times, and trams clattered along the Camberwell Road, in front of the Club, with similar frequency.

Until I was six or seven my bedroom looked onto Grosvenor Terrace, above the main entrance to the Club. Often, if I was awake and the window was open, I would hear the Seniors arriving or leaving. Occasionally the conversations were heated, and sometimes there were less than complimentary references to JB from members who had fallen out with him, or been chucked out for the night, which happened often enough but never seemed to stop them from coming back. Sometimes I would overhear the same story from his side. You always knew who was in his bad books because he referred to them by surname only. Mostly the altercations were minor ones, but from time to time there were more serious disturbances. I didn't see any of the violence and vandalism that took place intermittently at the Club 1953–4, but I heard it being discussed, and saw reports in the papers. It was clear that things were going badly, and that the atmosphere in the Club was being poisoned by a significant minority of disaffected members and occasional intruders. My father's moods were often dark in those days, and my mother told me later that there were times when he had serious thoughts of giving up the battle – the emotional support she gave him throughout the difficult months was undoubtedly crucial. He was also bolstered by the core of seniors and ex-seniors, some of them from the wartime years, who remained loyal and devoted to their old Club during the worst troubles, and formed the body of Officers that enabled its survival when, eventually, the new clubs started.

Clubland was once again opened to the Juniors just after my tenth birthday. It was a happy coincidence for me when suddenly, in the summer of 1954, the whole building filled with boys around my age. I was in Green House, and my house officer was Laurie Massey, who also coached cricket. The other officers included Stan Emanuel – he was the most senior – Ted Cutler, Les Harris, Arthur Jarman, Bernard Bailey, Ricky Elliott, Len Dobbs, and Jim Stow. Monday and Wednesday evenings were the high spots of my week. Mary joined the Girls' Club a short while later. She was only eight but so were quite a number of the Juniors. Some had older siblings in the Club; others just lied about their age – which wasn't an option open to Mary. I don't suppose JB was ever fooled anyway – for a man who was so strict and authoritarian in most things he was a soft touch in others, and hated turning anyone away. The Junior membership of the mid-fifties remained at capacity for around three years – as the boys and girls moved up to the Premiers their places were filled with new youngsters – and the Club rode on a crest of popularity. Club nights were full of fun and activity of all sorts as the new Juniors made the

Club their own, and reaped the benefit of the voluntary coaching, expertise and encouragement that JB had gathered and organised for them.

There were many positive reasons for the scale of Clubland's appeal in those days, and there was also one significant but invisible factor, namely the absence of early evening television, which had not yet become the ubiquitous and continuous presence that it is today. Many families could not afford a TV set, or declined to have one, and it was commonplace for children to congregate in their friends' homes to watch popular programmes. If no other option was available they had to make do with the wireless. My father was one of those who took a dim view of the invasive contraption, but in his case there was a particular reason. The hours that people watched television were strictly curtailed in the early days, and the 24-hour broadcasting which now seems unremarkable was still a long way off. In particular there was a clean break in transmission between 6 pm and 7 pm, during which no broadcasts took place. A popular myth was that this 'blackout' period was introduced to help parents to trick young children into going to bed, thinking that the programmes had finished for the evening. It was known as the 'toddlers' truce' for that reason. A more plausible explanation was that it allowed time for homework or a shared family meal. The importance for Clubland was considerable, since the doors opened at exactly the time when the screens went blank – but it was not until the early evening ban was lifted in 1957 that its full significance became clear. Just as the Junior membership had exploded upon first opening in 1954, it fell almost as suddenly with attendance dropping by half within a week of the extended transmission. It was a great shock and my dad never forgave the Postmaster General for giving way to the inevitable. He would not consider having a television set in his house, or in the Club, until well into the sixties – and only then to watch football.

Fortunately the Junior numbers soon recovered over the following weeks and months as the novelty wore off, and Clubland was once more full and lively, and a continuing challenge for its hard-working officers and helpers. Premier attendance had scarcely been affected at all by the onset of early TV since the Premiers came to Club later in the evening. The Premier section had been developed in the mid-fifties as a transition between the Juniors and a renewed Senior Club – and was relatively small, with an optimum size of around 60–80. JB usually rounded this to a hundred in the literature and in conversation, not so much to exaggerate the numbers but because he had an incurable love of round figures. He had a similar approach to counting the collection or evening's subs: if the amount came, say, to £9 7s 6d he would make it up to £10 out of his own pocket, and the reverse if it was slightly over. It gave the Club Treasurer, Reg Turtle, sleepless nights trying to construct plausible explanations for the improbably whole numbers on the balance sheets.

Another way in which JB's love of balance and symmetry surfaced was in his frequent insistence on re-arranging furniture. He would spend hours moving various items around until he was satisfied with the new formation, exhausting the patience of anyone unfortunate enough to be present when the mood took him, and who was roped in to help. Friday evening when the club was normally closed was the most dangerous time to be around, since he was at a loose end, and many were the stories of teams of dragooned assistants manoeuvring wooden cupboards or heavy pews up two or three flights of stairs, only to be directed to bring them down again because they didn't fit or didn't look right when they reached the chosen destination.

Extraordinarily this urge did not seize JB only when he was on his own property. On one famous occasion he rearranged the seating in a church off the Fulham Road, where he had a parking space on match days at Stamford Bridge. He was with two Clubland officers, one of whom had driven him in my mother's car – he no longer drove, and in any case no one would have wanted to be his passenger. They were earlier than usual for the kick-off and so JB decided to snoop around in the church hall, where he found two blocks of seating, one with more chairs per row than the other. Offended by this asymmetry he enlisted the help of his two anxious companions and set about evening the chairs up, only to be discovered in the act by the minister demanding to know what on earth the intruders thought they were doing. JB's explanation is unrecorded, but according to those who were present the good man then joined in and helped them finish the job. My father's charm was as abundant as his cheek – which it needed to be given the liberties he often took.

I was in the Junior Club for three years before going away to the Leys School in Cambridge at thirteen. The Leys is a Methodist school – it was founded by William Fidian Moulton in 1875 – and it also had a long association with Clubland. My father preached there once a year and Clubland teams went to the Leys every summer to play cricket and go boating. I settled down at the Leys, and wasn't unhappy there, but I was very sorry to leave Clubland with all its sports and activities, and sense of belonging. One of my closest friends in the Juniors was David Gray. We were the same age, and he moved up into the Premiers when I went off to the Leys. David had two older brothers in the Club, Chris and Bob. Bob was a talented athlete and a good public speaker, and JB appointed him Head Senior in 1958. Bob held this office at the time when US Ambassador John Hay Witney visited. The Grays' parents, Rose and Ted, also became closely involved with the Club and made substantial contributions to its activities – notwithstanding the intermittent ups and downs which were part of the natural rhythm of working alongside my father. For some years Ted, a former keen amateur boxer, ran the Junior boxing class, and Rose took on a succession of managerial roles working closely with Anna on the catering side.

In the August of 1964 tragedy struck the family when David was killed in a car accident whilst hitch-hiking on holiday near Ostend. JB organised his repatriation and conducted the funeral, and there was a remembrance service in the Club chapel in September. After that the two families became closer than ever: Mary and Bob began a relationship that led to their marriage in 1966, and a few years later JB's first grandchild, Simon, was born. But this is jumping ahead.

I left the Leys at Christmas 1961 for a job as a teaching assistant in South London, and became a member of the reinstated Seniors at Clubland. I was given the role of Parliament Chairman as well as helping in the Juniors. The Head Seniors then were Pamela Webb, who had been a member since 1955, and Keith McDonald, a Jamaican and a new member, and the most gifted all-round athlete the Club had known since the war, including being a formidable boxer. Some of the Juniors I had known had become Seniors, but the older Premiers were either officers, or simply ex-members who continued to come on Sundays, and to parties and reunions. The following September I left again to attend Westminster Teachers Training College. It had moved by then from its original site in Horseferry Road to North Oxford, but its links to Clubland were still maintained from that distance, as were my own.

At the end of my final year at Westminster JB used his renowned guile to persuade me to come and work for a year, to lead the Club and act as hostel warden. Assistant ministers, appointed to work in tandem with JB, and help with the enormous management burden of Clubland, had come and gone, finding it difficult to stay the course. Sometimes the turnaround was very short. My dad believed rather fancifully that he and I would have a harmonious partnership, given my having grown up in the Club, and my acquaintance with his methods. It turned out to be a roller-coaster twelve months and at the end of it even school teaching seemed like a holiday. But it was a year with many highs too, despite all the irreconcilable differences and inevitable battles. Being JB's son was no less bumpy a ride than being his assistant; being both at the same time was to say the least challenging.

The first hostel had just opened and three of the residents, more or less my age, signed up straight away as house and activity officers – Alastair Skinner, from Camberwell Art School, and Barry Street and Jim Ashley who were working in London. The energy they brought into Club was immediately perceptible, most of all because they really enjoyed being part of it. By that time Bob Gray had returned as an Officer, and my lifelong friend Terry Barrett, a former Head Junior and more recently Cabinet member in the Seniors, also joined the team. The first hostel block was all male, so the girls did not get the same influx of new helpers, but they already had the benefit of a talented and energetic set of officers, boosted by the effort and activity of several ex-Premiers.

Because my year as JB's assistant coincided with the opening of the first hostel, part of my job was hostel warden. I had the pleasure of working alongside one of Clubland's most valued pre-war members, Bert Barnes, who moved up from Brighton with his wife Ivy – also an ex-member – to be the overall hostel manager. Bert was a brilliant musician, especially on guitar. He had been the mainstay of the bands and concerts of the thirties, and now took up where he had left off, regularly joined by his son Dave who was a professional musician working in London. Together, and along with Peter Cook, the new organist and hostel resident, they revived and enriched the Club's musical life.

New talent in the Club brought fresh ideas and attitudes, especially against the backcloth of London in the swinging sixties. JB found it ever harder to adjust to the inevitable erosion of his established standards, as he perceived it to be. In fact the standards of behaviour and endeavour were still extremely high in relation to many other organisations in the changing times, but in relation to his own idea of how the Club should run, the gulf must have seemed huge. The Officers, young and old, did their utmost to preserve as much of Clubland's character as possible, whilst also appealing to the expectations of a membership that had never known the early days, and whose loyalty was harder to retain in the face of other attractions. JB often said that there was nothing more tedious than the pioneer of one generation who becomes a reactionary in the next; but living by that proved much harder for him than saying it. He never lost the respect of his core of committed officers and helpers, but his stubbornness often taxed their patience.

At Easter 1966 the Club leaders – including Bob, Terry, and myself – organised a five-day camp at a small coastal village on the French Cote d'Opal. It was not the first camp since the Guernsey days, but it was the first that JB had not arranged himself. Most of the Seniors and the junior captains signed up for it. They travelled by coach to Dover, with a minibus shuttle from Calais to Wissant. The members and young officers camped under canvas among the sand dunes – whilst the older officers stayed in the village at the Hotel Normandy, owned by a friend of Club Governor, Alec Reed. JB had not planned to come on the camp, due to an invitation to tour with the Arsenal Football Club, but at the last moment he boarded the coach instead, and to the great surprise of the advance party of Club leaders, appeared with the main group when they came off the ferry at Calais.

The Wissant camp was a great success, but in its casual and unregimented approach it was very unlike the fabled camps that JB had organised years earlier, and he must have been at every moment aware of the contrast. He spent most of the long weekend of his stay in the hotel talking to the proprietor's father, who happened to be a Great War veteran like himself. I remember him best in coat and hat standing on the windy touchline during a challenge football match on the beach between the Clublanders and local French lads – a forging of connections that would once have delighted him. He had very little to say about it, and displayed minimal enthusiasm for that or for anything else during the camp. His silence was poignant. I think that more than any other Club event, the Wissant Camp marked a gap that had opened between what he had started as a young minister over forty years before, and the current nature and direction of youthwork. It was still his Club, and object of his energetic devotion throughout his lifetime, but he seemed no longer in such easy step with the members and young officers, from whom he was now separated in age by over half a century.

Football itself had remained a passion in his life – JB went to watch Chelsea or Arsenal most Saturdays as they tended to play home games on roughly alternate weeks, and I often accompanied him. He had season tickets for both, and thanks to his close association with both clubs he was often given stand tickets for Clublanders as well – many Premiers recall going to Boxing Day and other high-day matches, sometimes in quite large parties. Stanley Rous was a Clubland governor and, whilst he was still in charge of the FA, JB occasionally received even cup final and international tickets to distribute. Gradually his attachment to Arsenal overtook his association with Chelsea, as personnel changed. The Hill-Wood family became increasingly close friends and were also generous with tickets and invitations in the latter part of the sixties, and JB regularly went abroad with the club on European tours. Outside Clubland it was his sole abiding interest – and his seat in the directors' box was certainly a far cry from crawling under the turnstile at Ewood Park to watch Blackburn sixty years before.

I loved Clubland and I revered my Dad, but neither of these emotional ties guarantees good working relations. I had neither wish nor intention to enter the ministry, and my father never exerted the least pressure upon me to do so, despite his romantic notion that I might one day take over from him and continue his work at Clubland. It was never a serious prospect, and deep down he knew it. At the end of my promised twelve months I took up a teaching post in north-east Essex, and sometime later married and moved to Canada. Three years on, however, in the summer of 1969, my father had another serious lapse in his health, and his doctor ordered complete rest away from London. I came back home with my then wife in June that year, and moved once more into the house where I had grown up, to caretake Clubland in his absence. My first son and JB's second grandson, Thomas, was born in the July and his early months were spent living at the Club. JB recovered, although weakened, and returned to Clubland in the late autumn of 1969. At 72, with uncertain health, he was beginning a sixth decade in Clubland – I was aware that his remaining years at its helm could only be finite and so took a job near home, at Peckham Manor Comprehensive School. But my father was ever a phoenix in reviving to fight another day for Clubland, and his characteristic vision and drive proved equal to presiding over several further years of prosperity in Club affairs. In 1972 he celebrated Clubland's Silver Jubilee, anticipating its future with customary exuberance. I remained a Clubland Officer until 1973 when I left Clubland for the last time to work abroad again.

Growing up at Clubland was an extraordinary experience, and being James Butterworth's son even more so. Thinking now of those years at the Club with my father, it is his wisdom that I miss most – along with his wonderful sense of humour and joy in living. The trouble with being young is that you do not recognise wisdom when it is in front of you; and then when you do, it is too late. When I think back my memories of him and of my own early life crowd into my mind; but there is perhaps one enduring picture of a summer evening in 1961 which encapsulates my father's presence through the Clubland years. It was a Sunday service in the Parliament Room, on a summer evening before the new Chapel was completed. The windows were open to the quadrangle, with the sound of birds and muffled traffic and my father's familiar voice reading John Henry Newman's beautiful benediction:

> May He support us all the day long, till the shades lengthen, and the evening comes, and the busy world is hushed, and the fever of life is over, and our work done. Then in His mercy may He give us safe lodging and a holy rest, and peace at last.

The Hard Question

The question of JB's weighting of the Clubland mix of religion and youth work is complex. There is certainly room for discussion around whether his life project at Walworth was driven throughout by religious commitment, or whether it became closer to a secular enterprise under only a light church cloak. Was fellowship the pivot upon which Clubland turned, or was it spirituality – or were the two in fact the same?

JB's gift for drawing people to him, persuading them to listen, is beyond doubt – one old member irreverently but admiring observed that he certainly knew how to put 'bums on pews' – but it would be a profound mistake to suppose that this ability necessarily excluded or diminished the spiritual element in JB's concept of Clubland. It might equally well be argued to the contrary that by insisting that every senior member attend the Sunday service he was affirming its centrality, and in particular asserting that the spiritual aspect completed the whole. Much depends, of course, on what is meant in that claim by 'spiritual', and how that concept is understood to relate to organised religion. Some commentators criticised him for prioritising Clubland's social and recreational dimension – especially and increasingly in the postwar years – and if judging simply in the quantitative terms of the amount of time spent on devotions then one might reasonably agree. Compared with most ordinary churches or even contemporary faith-based youth organisations, there were few overtly religious activities or classes over and above the Sunday gathering. But as JB argued, 'ordinary' churches were everywhere failing. With few exceptions, they were losing their congregations as the church-going population aged, and these were not being replenished from the rising generation, for whom there were so many competing attractions. By contrast his chapel was full, albeit for a single weekly service.

Some criticism came from the opposite corner, too. The more secular-minded youth workers sometimes questioned why – in an age of declining church affiliation – young people should be obliged to attend a service at all, if they saw no point to it or had no pre-existing religious belief. Fair enough that it was there for those who wanted it, but as for the participation of those who attended through obligation, or as a price to be paid for the weekday activities and amenities – was that not meaningless? There were even some of his current members who expressed this view, if they felt bold enough – but the Sunday service was a red line for JB and to the end he defended the requirement to attend. His stance was that Clubland was a community and those who belonged to it, whether members, officers, or residents, belonged to it *all*. The service every Sunday evening was a time for quiet reflection, a simple communal gathering which served to symbolise the spirit of fellowship, and the ideals of loyalty and service. On that account nonbelievers were not excluded or required to pretend to something they did not believe, but they were not excused from attending either. Besides, it was a contract and once agreed to it should be respected on both sides.

Among sceptical observers were some who, privately or publicly, took what they saw as a secular imbalance to be a sign that JB's own religious convictions had become relegated to second place. Latterly there may have been something in this: it would be no surprise if his faith in a caring God had been strained to breaking point by the accumulative effects of two wars – and he would not have been alone. The Great War, for all its horrors, had propelled him to achieve what he did. But the second conflagration, and the particular timing of its eruption at the very moment when his work seemed complete, his goals achieved, must have felt like a mockery of all his efforts. Whether or not this affected his core beliefs is difficult to say, because he kept them surprisingly private. He did not, for example, make any attempt to persuade people to take up religion or join any particular denomination, including his own family. Despite his authoritarian style of leadership, he left people free to form their own beliefs, and respected them if they were sincere, and if they in their turn were respectful of the beliefs of others. Although he grew up in the evangelical tradition, and expressly saw his role as ministering to those 'outside any church', his primary objective was not to win converts to the church but to encourage his members to be good human beings, with the skills and opportunities to live rewarding lives, and a caring attitude towards others.

His sermons, readings, and prayers reflected these wide-reaching aims. *The Clubland Service Book* that he compiled over many years and published in 1938, provided an anthology of inspirational texts by thinkers, theologians, poets, and others including himself, for every date in the year. The following is one of his own prayers:

> Grant unto us, O Lord, a renewed faith in the power of comradeship. We thank people for the strength and comfort through knowing that we are never alone, that when we do right others are glad and when we do wrong others are hurt. For the sake of those who love us, help us to live worthily. In our own happiness may we remember the friendless and the lonely and great service we can render by just being kind and gracious. Teach us how to share in the happiness and sorrows of others and give to us the ability and ease to move amongst our fellows as friends. Amen.

More than one Club member has described the sermons JB preached, and the lessons he chose to present, as concerned with ethical issues and practical living. They described positive and moral ways of living among others, and were relevant to Christianity in the sense that they reflected a Christian approach. He always appeared more moved by the everyday humanity of Jesus than by the divinity of God, or at least more conscious of its relevance to the young lives he was trying to guide.

What some may have interpreted – critically or otherwise – as a lost or wavering faith probably had more to do with JB's retreat from evangelism. He came early to realise that the boys and girls he befriended in Clubland's neighbourhood could quickly be alienated by the language too often employed by parsons. Many of a church calling showed little sensitivity to the way the words of traditional religious practice might sound to young ears unaccustomed to such expressions and imagery. He recognised that to win their trust and capture their interest he must communicate with them on their own ground and in their own terms, and teach by example, rather than by citing doctrine. He had first learned that lesson in France, observing the relations between the privates and the padres – and it was reinforced during his Didsbury years by his work at the Beech Road Mission. There were some exceptions – ministers who had taken the time and trouble to engage empathically with the young and underprivileged – but there were all too many who spoke over their heads or, worse, spoke down, or in other ways missed their target.

JB's aversion to evangelism was not simply a pragmatic development to enable him to communicate better with a young audience. At an early point in his ministry he had formed the conviction that it was a presumption, in some cases even an arrogance, to seek to plant beliefs in impressionable minds beyond providing young people with the opportunity to think deeply and reflectively.

There is evidence of his taking this position as early as the 1920s, although it is quite probable that the view was exacerbated and hardened by the aggressive style of evangelism that he witnessed on many occasions in the United States, and which was now making inroads on the British side of the Atlantic. He found the mass rallies conducted by the American evangelist Dr Billy Graham particularly distasteful, not so much for the content as for the fanfare and emotionalism that accompanied Dr Graham's appearances. During his British 'crusades', Graham regularly filled theatres and sports arenas, winning converts on a massive scale. In 1966 Sir Cliff Richard publicly declared his Christian conversion during a rally at Earl's Court, one of thousands if not millions who made similar professions over three or more decades. If JB was sceptical in his judgement of Graham's success it was because he saw the work of improving lives as prolonged and multi-faceted. An inspirational address to a packed stadium might have a profound immediate effect on some individuals, but there was more to ministry than that – and a great deal more to be done after the crusader had moved on to the next big event.

JB heard Billy Graham at Stamford Bridge in 1954, in the half time interval during Chelsea's defeat by Newcastle United. He agreed with the *Daily Mail's* reporter who disapproved of the captive nature of the audience – but more than that, he saw it as an intrusion, and just as inappropriate as it would have been to punctuate a church service with 'a kick-about in the aisle'. For JB there was a time and place for everything: the Sunday service had pride of place and a sacrosanct time, but so too did sport and art and drama and dancing, and, importantly, at Clubland none was subservient to the others.

By and large the Clubland members were content to attend the service, and to accept the rule that if they missed without good reason they could not use the Club during the ensuing week. After the war the services themselves were held in the Parliament Room until the new Chapel was built, with special festivals in the theatre or the ruins. Most found the occasion agreeable, whether or not they described themselves as religious – and even those who were not have expressed a high opinion of JB's deliberately thought-provoking addresses. They knew the hymns from school and the singing was rousing; the prayers from the *Clubland Service Book* were soothing and lyrical. Some found the services themselves revelatory or life-changing – but for many more there were simply deeply moving moments in particular sermons which in retrospect they have felt evoked the spirit of Clubland. Whatever their personal definition of the word they recognised the experience as affecting them in a way which made their life richer and more textured.

Nonetheless, striking the right balance between the religious, and the social or recreational, posed a question that grew harder rather than easier to resolve, as the century progressed, church-going declined, and more and more youth services became entirely secular. If chapel attendance were made entirely optional that might well shrink the congregation to a handful – but if it remained obligatory it might reduce the club membership anyway. Either way the dilemma was a source of growing contention: the Premiers were the last large group of members to accept the status quo cheerfully, but the sixties proved more turbulent. Other leaders debated the conundrum, but JB himself was never troubled by the slightest doubt in respect of the service – as far as he was concerned Sunday attendance remained a condition of membership and nothing would change that whilst he was in charge.

One direction in which JB moved in the latter years was towards ecumenicalism. He had always maintained informal contacts with other denominations and faiths, and had never taken a doctrinaire stance in respect of his own. The values he preached were universal ones. His close association with Basil Henriques' synagogue at Berners Street had begun very early and lasted until well after the second world war. JB loved to recount how they had spoken from each others' pulpits, the only difference being the respective wearing or removing of a hat. In the sixties and seventies a number of initiatives were mooted to share facilities and activities with the local Anglicans, but progress was limited due the disparity in the sizes and composition of the congregations. In fact many Anglican Churches had closed altogether or experienced sharply declining attendances. Another impediment emerged when it was pointed out to JB that the Clubland Chapel would have to be officially sanctified if any kind of formal union was to be established. What future had Christianity, he lamented, in the face of such self-inflicted prejudicial attitudes and requirements.

The Sixties, Students, and Succession

During the first half of the new decade the existing team of officers was augmented by the first wave of residents. The student hostel had not yet been built, but a small vanguard had moved into a converted flat next to the gym, or into temporary accommodation in one of the houses awaiting demolition. 'Student' was a generic term for any young person of around student age, and some of the incumbents were actually in employment. Alan Knowles, for example, had come to London to take up a job as a bank clerk in the City – he had failed utterly to find affordable digs and was on the point of returning home to Warrington when a colleague brought him to a dance at Clubland. His situation chimed clearly with JB's claims about a chronic shortage of accommodation for young people in London, and he offered Alan a room in the house until he could get settled. In the end he stayed for several years and was a great asset to the Club – a happy reminder for JB of the days when medical students such as Gordon Lyle and Billy Whiles had helped to found the early clubs, and a precursor of the symbiotic relationship that JB hoped for from the hostels. When Alan finally moved on, to train to become a teacher at Durham University, JB wrote in a newsletter that 'when Alan found Clubland, we also found a helper in every part of Club life and will be forever grateful for his devoted service.'

Alan was neither the first nor last to make a major contribution in this way prior to the opening of the first residential block. John Hunkin, a local preacher from Cornwall, had come to live at the Club after leaving Westminster College and taking a job at the Strand Grammar School at Tulse Hill, and Peter Cook was a music teacher who became the Club organist for many years after the chapel was rebuilt. Another was Tony Richardson, an undergraduate at Kings with plans to enter the youth service. He wrote afterwards to JB: 'I want you to know that no other period in my life was of such value as the year I spent in Clubland. It introduced me to new dimensions of standards and ideals of youth work which I shall carry with me always and constantly try to emulate in my own way. I am truly grateful to you for this.' Several came to stay from overseas: Mark Hildebrand from California; Franco and Luigi Crispini from Italy, training as waiters and unable to find rooms; Rick Aubrey, from Ottawa, who wrote after leaving: 'My stay in Clubland is now proving wondrously helpful. I am teaching on an Indian Reservation near North Vancouver. The school has only one room and I will be teaching 27 children in eight grades.' Two young women from Los Angeles, Jean Anderson and Christine Wiederanders – whom JB had met on his last US tour – also came for a year, assisting at Club by putting their impressive creative and musical skills to good use, before starting sociology studies.

These years were a period of real optimism, marked by the succession of mutually valuable partnerships – which JB described in the 1963 Review as: 'working together for the common good which has enriched life for both'. It augured well for the hostels as their foundations began to take shape, embodying the hope that a more permanent pool of young and enthusiastic assistants, and future leaders, would invigorate the Club itself, and arrest any gradual decline in numbers or range of activities. The hostel residents might also provide welcome relief to the core of older officers who by now had given unflagging service to the Juniors and Seniors for a decade or more, many travelling considerable distances two or three nights a week. As their family responsibilities grew the hours they could offer had dwindled, even though their loyalty and dedication had not. They were in need of hands to share the load – but it was becoming increasingly clear that the person most in need of relief was JB himself.

September 1962 marked the completion of JB's 40th year at Clubland, although the anniversary had actually been celebrated earlier on his 65th birthday in March. For September, secret preparations were underway for a reunion of 500 past and present members, from 1922 onwards, and these were even more impressive than the underground plans for

A group of Clubland Officers of the Sixties. From the left – back row:
Allen Sparksman, Laurie Williams, Roy Gamble, Alan Wren – middle row:
Stan Emanuel, John Wheeler, Les Harris, Brenda Ingram, Arthur Jarman,
Daphne Williams, Peggy Lyle, Anna Butterworth, Bernard Bailey – front row:
Sylvia Sparksman, Iris Bailey, Jean Langton, Anne Maggs, Flip Wheeler,
Mary O'Connor, Carrie Cooper, Lily Harris, Laurie Lowe.

This is Your Life had been. Whilst he was safely out watching football
the entire place was decorated for the grand party, for once leaving
him genuinely speechless when he returned to find the theatre packed
and so many 'old comrades' ready with reminiscences. 1962 was also
the year of Princess Alexandra's visit, followed two years later by the
royal opening of the Chapel, where the first wedding to be held was
that of two of his ex-premiers, Allen Sparksman and Sylvia Thomas.
By Clubland's standards this level of activity and celebration event was
quite normal, and outwardly JB showed every sign of cheerfulness and
enthusiasm. But the effort of keeping so many balls in the air at one time
– so far beyond most people's capacity – was at last beginning to take a
permanent toll, and behind the public persona he was hiding significant
mood swings and bouts of depression. Only those closest to him – Anna,
Reg Turtle, Gordon Lyle, and some of the older officers – began sharing
concerns. For most observers there was little indication other than more
frequent outbreaks of bad temper, but such outbursts were not unusual
and everyone expected them to pass as quickly as they arose.

Princess Alexandra with Senior welcoming party

Behind the scenes, however, the pressures were growing – not simply
the big challenges like the fundraising and organising of major events,
which he always insisted on managing himself, but the small day-to-day
maintenance of the premises. In the past the quality and stability of his
employed support team had left him free for his full-time pastoral work
and running of the clubs. Clubland's maintenance requirements were
huge – obviously the premises had to be cleaned, repaired, and kept in
working order constantly. Fuelling, stoking, raking out the vast coke
furnaces that heated the whole building was a massive commitment on
its own (until replaced with oil-fired systems during the rebuilding).
Three excellent caretakers in turn – Reg Sharie, Wally Ruel, and Fred
Marks – had maintained the club in immaculate condition, whilst Ethel
Evans and then Mrs Webb had managed the house. Laurie Lowe had
been the club secretary as well as girls' club leader. Most of the support
workers lived on the premises, or in the adjoining houses, and some
received wages, as did the cleaners who came in during the day. The
system had run like clockwork for decades, even through the war –
but one by one his old guard had retired or moved away. Mr Marks'
departure in 1955 was a serious setback – he was not only head caretaker,
but also manned the entrance-hall office on club nights – and Mrs Marks

Dancing with Junior girls

Meeting Ted Cutler and his gym class

was a pillar of the canteen. The break in efficient staffing after that was a constant headache until well into the next decade when Harry and Alice Cowan took over as caretaker and housekeeper respectively, staying with JB until he retired. Once the hostel opened there was a whole new raft of tasks to be organised and undertaken. Finding and retaining staff was an increasing burden and an ever-rising expense.

Most of all, however, it was time to take on a full time resident club leader and assistant minister – separately or combined – and to think of an eventual successor. JB had no plans to retire any time soon – quite the opposite in fact – but even he was realising that he could no longer manage on his own. He was determined to see the hostels finished and Clubland set up for the foreseeable future – and even though he sometimes made allusions to a promised land that he might never see, he had every intention of being there, and of not leaving 'until they take me out feet first'. Unfortunately the perennial problem for JB and for Clubland was that delegation did not figure among amongst his many remarkable talents. He was at best difficult to work with, at worst impossible. There had been some wonderful partnerships over the years, of which Gordon Davies was perhaps the finest example – although Gordon had the distinct advantage of being left to get on with the job for much of the time, whilst JB was distracted by his wartime evacuation work off the premises, and his budding romance. Also JB had been younger and the gap between them easier to bridge. The current dilemma was that anyone compliant enough to do JB's bidding without question would be dominated, whilst anyone wanting change would have a bruising fight on his hands – and would probably lose.

In the September *Review*, 1964, JB wrote:

> New term begins on Sunday the 6th and with it we welcome the Chaplain, Rev Geoffrey Malcolm Heath, and his wife Jean. After 42 years the Head at last comes to realise that he must have a colleague. The new chaplain trained at Westminster College as a teacher and at Richmond Ministers' College and he and his wife Jean, as a trained nurse, bring to Clubland a leadership in new enterprise.

The enterprise may have been new, but despite the expressed welcome it proved brief – and was the first of several attempts to find JB the right partner. The role was not easy to occupy; quite apart from JB's temperament, Clubland was such an esoteric and idiosyncratic organisation that to carry out and advance its work required a very particular skill-set. Moreover JB was no ordinary Methodist, and his brand was not likely to prove compatible with aspirations towards a straightforward Methodist ministry.

Although numbers had declined gradually from the previous decade there still were around a hundred junior girls, and a similar number of boys. The junior cabinet that year was a particularly strong group. JB had chosen well, with John Rowe as Head Junior and some of the most talented junior captains of the post war era, such as Jimmy Callaghan and Touker Suleyman.[11] The mixed Senior Club stood at about sixty – and although smaller than previously it also had its fair share of strong characters. They were a lively group of young people, and made a good team with the officers, who were so near to them in age.

The sixties were approaching their swinging zenith – it was an unprecedentedly exciting era of social change, and London was at the epicentre of a cultural shift in which barriers were coming down and taboos tumbling. There can hardly have been greater mixed feelings for JB than to see the Club doing well, but doing it in such different ways from those to which he was so accustomed. In fact in very many respects Clubland was still very traditional, and was certainly trailing behind the forefront of social change. But for JB the revolution must have seemed seismic – he wanted to see young people having good times in keeping with their own generation, but he must have drawn comparisons with the very different zeitgeist and goals of the era when he was building the club.

The challenge for JB was to step back and trust others to carry on the work, and to maintain an appropriate balance between the changing times and Clubland's longstanding traditions. Whilst he often looked on with pleasure and pride at the achievements of the young officers and enjoyment of the members, there were many other times when he could not countenance the loss of hands-on control and became critical, intervening and countermanding the plans of his assistants and volunteers.

Whilst on a broader scale the cultural shift permeated the country the landscape of Walworth had also seen huge changes, with the old rows of terraced houses and courtyards being replaced by high-rise flats. There was continuing demographic movement, and flight outward towards the suburbs, or to new towns and developments. The neighbourliness that had characterised the traditional terraces of houses was giving way to more isolated living, due in particular to the geography of the great tower blocks, like those on the Brandon Estate, to the west of the Walworth Road. Education was changing, and youth work was changing with it, and Clubland was facing competition from both. Educationalists

The two completed hostels at 54 Camberwell Road, adjacent to the Walworth
Methodist Church (Clubland)

were urging a greater emphasis on leisure, in anticipation of shorter
working hours and higher spending. Foreign holidays were becoming
affordable and popular, with ordinary families favouring the Coast Brava
over Margate or Southend. It was growing ever harder for Clubland to
keep pace and harder still to be its leader. Its values and principles were
as relevant as ever – as they would be today – but its management style
and behavioural requirements were dated. Finding a way to update the
latter without eroding the former was beyond JB's strength, and his
struggle was painful both for him to undergo and for his close associates
and loyal helpers to witness.

As the Seventies opened, and the generation of members that had
poured in as Juniors in 1954 had passed through, the sense of continuity
at Clubland began to weaken. For one thing the hostels were not living
up to JB's high expectations of a stable settlement of like-minded young
adults, running the clubs and the religious community. A minimum
commitment to assist in the club one night a week, and to attend the
Sunday service, was a condition of residence – in return for a very
favourable rent. Unfortunately it was both unenforceable in practice

346

and worse a source of contention from the start, seen from one side as an unreasonable imposition and from the other as having all the force of a binding contract. It was, in fact, both at the same time, but in addition it was a recipe for ill-feeling on both sides, and a more laissez-faire approach would have served better. The few residents who volunteered and willingly kept their side of the bargain were in the event worth far more than their reluctant and resentful fellows, who repeatedly avoided their Club obligations. The truth was that the hostel residents were not local boys and girls who had grown up with the Club, but outsiders starting or studying for their own careers – and even for the well-intentioned Clubland was not their first priority. Financially the hostel was an asset, but it fell short of the greater promise of JB's hopes.

By the end of the sixties the Junior Club remained active – although reduced to one night a week each for the boys and girls, whilst a comparable Senior section met on the same evenings. There were no meetings on the other evenings but the Club was open some Saturdays, and a small congregation gathered on Sundays to hear visiting speakers. As JB's seventieth year came and went his general health deteriorated to the point where friends were urging him to quit, or at least to yield more responsibility to a successor. There was still no prospect of voluntary retirement, and the Methodist hierarchy rightly hesitated to enforce it upon him after such a lifetime of achievement.

There were still triumphs and progress ahead. During JB's absence in 1969 a small delegation of parents and organisers called at the Club one evening. They were from the Freddie Mills Club, named after the famous South London boxer, and dedicated to the service of boys with muscular dystrophy, many in wheelchairs or otherwise functionally impaired. They had a sad tale to tell – the hall in which they met every Monday was needed for a badminton club, and they had been given notice to seek an alternative, and their search had brought them to Clubland. In JB's absence was there a major obstacle: he had never permitted any organisation independent of the Club to have use of the premises – every component had to be part of the whole, or had no place at all. The Freddie Mills Club leaders were not asking to join Clubland, only to be given a large space with catering and small games facilities to have to themselves each Monday.

The new canteen could have been designed for them, and there could be no question of saying No – JB's convalescence could not be disturbed by Club business, but there were anxious moments whilst awaiting his return to find that one of his most emphatic red lines had been crossed. As it turned out it was as much a restorative tonic for him as it was a godsend to the Freddie Mills Club. There had been only one reservation for them when they saw the facilities and that was the flight of stairs leading down to the Canteen from the ground floor level – but it was not enough to deter them, and for the first few weeks the helpers carried the wheelchairs bodily down the steps. As soon as JB returned he contacted builders to construct a connective ramp from the quadrangle. He christened the Freddie Mills meetings the Monday Club, and was as proud of it as of anything that had happened in Clubland since the war. From then on he never missed a Monday down in the canteen – and fifty years on the Freddie Mills Club still meets beneath the Walworth Methodist Church.

Postwar Voices

Joining
I joined in 1945 – I was 15 – I'd just got back from being evacuated

I found out about the Club from John Butterworth in 1954 – Jean brought him to a bonfire party in our garden. I was only 8 and had to fib about my age as you were supposed to be 10 to join

I joined the Club in the new term when I was 11. We went on Tuesdays and Thursdays, and that was just girls then. There were fifty of us in each house, and all the houses were full up

My wife Sylvia joined as a Junior aged 11, she lived on Love Walk, Camberwell Green. I joined at 14 in 1957 and went straight into the Seniors. I went in with Chris Gray – I came from Honour Oak and was in the same class as Chris – David Gray went in the Juniors

I joined at 14. Another member, David Ingram, had a stall on the Old Kent Road, and he told me about Clubland. I went straight into the Seniors.

I became a member when the Junior Club opened in the mid-fifties – before that there hadn't been a Junior Club since before the War. Some of the members from the thirties came back after the War and were very active officers at Clubland in the fifties – I remember Joe King, Laurie Massey, 'Sticky' Stapleton, Ricky Elliot, Roy Barrett, John and Jean Langton,

Jim Stow, Ken Randall and Bunty Coates, Len Dobbs, Les Bedson, Stan Emmanuel, Alan Thompson, Ron Moulder ... and there were others

I was in Green House – it had been Didsbury House before the War

The Club premises were impressive – central heating, marble floor, leather seats. And I had friends there. It was a great place to go – the camaraderie was wonderful. It beat the bomb craters.

My first impression was how spotless it all was. The first time I went Ted Cutler showed me round. He ran a fruit and veg stall in East Lane market and he talked to me as one cockney to another. He told me the rules in his own words: No litter anywhere; join in the activities and don't sit on your bum; the club is for partners not passengers

It was winter outside but inside it was very cosy. The furniture was beautiful with luxurious leather sofas and oak parquet floors everywhere – to me it was like a palace

When we were married it was in the beautiful church Sir Edward Maufe designed

It was wonderful to have showers. Everybody was from a rough area. JB frequently reminded us to have 'Pride in Premises'

I joined as a Junior – I was in Red House, the others were Green, Blue, and Brown. They were Junior houses – there weren't any Senior ones, but there were Club Officers. The Premier Club was the link between the Juniors and Seniors from 1955 – you had to be 14 to be a Senior

I lived in Walworth in Hillingdon Street – it was just 2 or 3 minutes from the Club. The area wasn't run down but it had been bombed a lot. Both my parents worked and we were ok materially. There was a lively market at East Lane on Sundays, and Westmorland Road Market on Saturdays was good too. There was an Odeon Cinema – and the Trocadera had a Saturday morning film club

It cost 3d to get into Clubland, or JB might just accept what you had. Anna had a red-bound ledger at the door.

Walworth was a poor area but it was nice – I had a lot of aunts and uncles in Trafalgar Street, and people stayed in their family units. A lot of property was owned by the Rolls Royce Company, and eventually the Council bought up housing. People worked in ordinary jobs – not professionals – and felt ashamed if they were out of work. Nobody claimed benefits. There were a lot of pubs at the end of Walworth Road

Walworth was a working class district – vibrant and busy. Print was the main employment. They worked in Fleet Street where print was a closed shop. There were also coal merchants' yards, as well as shops and light industry. A lot of people worked on stalls in the East Lane and Westmorland Road markets. There were churches of all denominations, and there was the Trocadera Cinema at the Elephant and Castle – which got wrecked by Teddy Boys when Rock Around the Clock was shown. They took over from the Spivs who had oiled hair and razors. There was John Ruskin School – where a lot of Clubland Juniors went – and also a lot of slum council property. There were many rough places full of ragged children – they played on the bombsites which were everywhere

****

Club Activities

We used to go on Clubland rambles – there was one officer that did them. We did become officers afterwards, Laurie and me, we were officers for the Juniors, and I helped with the art classes

At Clubland I liked football, table tennis, and boxing. We played cricket but football was the main thing – JB knew them all and we used to get in for free. We had pictures taken wearing the England Team kit.

I liked the choice of activity – there was dancing, gym, and art.

I played football on Wednesdays in the gym if I was picked for a House team, and did boxing. We played cricket on the roof in the Summer, and there was roller-skating in the ruined church. I did gymnastics every Monday in the gym – and I was in a few drama productions, usually short.

I was in the drama group, chess group, art class, and table tennis – and I did ballroom dancing – they were all general Club activities. There was Assembly first in the canteen – then an hour for activity, you got points for your House for doing well at the activities. At 7.30 you would have pop and biscuits. Then after the activities we went to the Theatre for the Parliament – the Captains would be in House colours, and announcements were made by the Head Junior. The Boys Clubs were Mondays and Wednesdays, and the Girls Clubs were Tuesdays and Thursdays. Sometimes there were reports from the House Captains and sports leaders – then JB would say a few words.

The ex-Seniors used to come to help with activities – Ricky Elliot, Ted Cutler, Joe King, Jean and John Langton, Flip and John Wheeler. All the Grays were there.

Jim Stow did Drama – and Topsy and Steve. John and Jean Langton led activities – Jean did dancing. Len Dobbs and Ted Cutler did football, and Les Harris and Jim Stow took Art. Ted Gray did boxing – and we had visits from Gene Tunney and Freddie Mills. The supervisors had mostly been Seniors – they came back and volunteered after the Army. And we had the Club Treasurers and Governors who ran things – Reg. Turtle, Gordon Lyle, and Alec Reid.

We wore cloaks at the end of the sessions, and for special events

David Ingram and Ted Cutler had stalls and were Officers in the Club. They were a club generation older than us. They would all come down four nights per week – there was Stan Cooper, Les Harris, Laurie Massey, and Arthur Jarman. Maurice Endersby was the organist at church – he was a printer. Printing was a big thing in Walworth – there were a lot of lads waiting for apprenticeships

Laurie Massey was my House Officer. Ted Cutler was football and Ted Gray did boxing – he had been a boxer, and came in as a parent. Sticky Stapleton took Drama, and Les Harris took Art – he was Lily's husband, she came to live and help at the Club when her family was bombed out. There were about 30 Officers in all, who came down every weekday evening. They came straight from work and had a cooked meal at the Club. At six o'clock the doors opened and the first in went straight to the table tennis tables – they were in the rooms under the church where the canteen was. A bell went at 6.30 and we all sat in silence in the church basement – activities officers would then say to line up for the various activities. Another bell rang at 7.00 and we went to our second chosen activity. At 7.30 there was another bell and everyone went to have orange juice and a biscuit for tuppence. JB would wander about through the activities, and would be in the canteen for the 15 minute break.

We were on the Pathé News with Gene Tunney. We did football, table-tennis, and boxing – drama came a bit later really. We would put on productions and evening shows. We did mime shows – I was a canary – Jean Langton sewed feathers onto me.

We went to the Dome in Brighton to sing in a huge service. And we used to go on outings. When I was in the Cabinet JB took us up to town to see 'Stranger in Paradise', and we sat in boxes. And there were loads of cinema first nights.

I remember Kitty Kallen visiting the Club, and Alma Cogan

Princess Alexandra came when I was in the Senior Club. And the Queen Mother was there for the opening of the new chapel in 1964

He liked the individual teams to do well, but didn't want them to form cliques within the Club

About 1956 I was in '1066 and All That', and I was in all the drama productions. Anna, Jean Langton, and Lily made all the costumes, and Jim and Topsy did costumes too. It was an era of fancy dress parties, and the Club costumes were always good. Michael Caine had been in Drama and I think he went out with a member called Amy. In the fifties there were visits from John and Hayley Mills, Gene Tunney, Richard Attenborough, Bob Hope, and the Crazy Gang with Bud Flanagan. We went to see them at the Empire Theatre.

After Club at 7.45 the Houses filed up to the Theatre, led by their Junior Captains and House Officers, and sat in ranks three to a row. The chairs were canvas in the colour of the houses, and the Captains sat at the front, facing the House, on a leather padded bench that said 'Green Captain' etc.. The Head Junior and the Vice Head Junior sat at the end of the bench on either side of the lectern, and JB sat on a bench next to the Head Junior. The House Officers all sat down one side, and the Junior activities Captains all sat down the other. This constituted the Club Parliament. JB would say 'Cabinet Members the Parliament is now open' – if those words were not used a roar of protest (that everybody enjoyed) would go up, and a shout of 'Chair', for the proper form of address. Parliament would last 15–30 minutes, but on Mondays it was shorter because there would be a film – always a cartoon ending with Popeye.

We were a very lucky group – we used to play cricket in Gordon Lyle's back garden, and Laurie and Bob Gray and a couple of others were always singing something.

I liked the football a lot, and there was always a sing-song. I still know the lads in the football team. We had a good social time together inside and outside the Club. We would go to one of our houses and share a quart between about twenty of us. We did meet girls at the Club too – one of the best things that happened to me at Clubland was finding my wife. The social side of Clubland was very good – it kept you off the streets and on the straight and narrow

My wife Joan had been at Barmere during the war when she was 12 years old. She knew Anna before she and JB were married.

We had the best times – there were outings to schools, and good days out. Sometimes we went on coaches to Ruffs Orchard, where we could pick the apples. JB knew the McAlpines, the Costains, and the Borwicks, and they all had places we could visit.

Stan Emmanuel was an old Club member who made jewels. When his baby was overdue a group of us went to the maternity unit and sang 'Oh come, oh come, Emanuel' outside the window

So many celebrities visited – there was Bob Hope, Gracie Fields, Gene Tunney, Richard Attenborough (who came several times), the Mills family, Princess Alexandra, the Queen Mother opening the new church. Before that there had been Queen Mary in 1939 and again in the forties – and the Oliviers, and Douglas Fairbanks, Bertie Mee and Stanley Rous. They read lessons, or gave an address for the Sunday Service, or just wandered about and met the members.

I remember Bob Lord from Burnley. The Arsenal Team came down for tea. We went to a Crazy Gang show at Victoria Palace with Burnley Football Club

I never went on a Club camp – there were no camps during the time I was a member

I went on some camps when I was very small, but as a family member only. Later Bob, Terry and I went to Wissant Camps which we helped organise

– but not to Guernsey again. JB ran some camps in the sixties but they were to Colwyn Bay

I went to Guernsey camps before the War. I was carrying Alec Reid's generator for filming on the boat going out and some Club joker spread the rumour it was an explosive device

There were no camps for Juniors during the time I was one.

I went to Guernsey. There were 265 Club campers and every one of us went for tea at a local home on Sundays in rotation. I went to the Doreys at Le Friquet, Woodlands

The film on Monday was one of the highlights – but I found Parliament a bit boring. I liked being in productions, and I loved roller skating in the Summer, and boxing too.

I remember visits from David Frost, Janette Scott, Princess Alexandra – as Seniors we had to get our robes on and meet them

****

The fifties Juniors
After the unsettled postwar period everything changed at Club in the early fifties. A lot of the old Seniors left and only the ones that wanted to help were kept on. As soon as people heard that the Club had re-opened for Juniors there was a huge scramble to join – both girls' and boys' clubs were full within days and there was a long waiting list. A year or so later the 'Premier House' was formed made up of the squad of ex-Captains ready to leave the Juniors – it was a Senior House, a bridge of very young Seniors, but members could also come into it from outside

I joined the Seniors at 14 – JB just decided. The older end of the Juniors formed the Premiers for a while, before it morphed into the new Seniors.

I wasn't in the Cabinet.

I went to lots of club activities and used to go to debates. I went to the Junior Parliament – at the end of the evening we'd sit in our Houses in the Theatre. It was like assembly.

I was in the Cabinet – I was Captain of Green House and Vice Junior Head, then Junior Head, and as Junior Head Boy I had a weekly report book. We had Parliament and reports every Wednesday in the Junior Club. The more formal Parliament and Cabinet structure was pre-war – after the War it was Juniors only for some time.

I was never in the Cabinet

I was very shy at Parliament and never spoke unless really stirred. JB recognised qualities in me that I never knew I had, and made me Head Junior

I did enjoy the Parliament – it was fundamental to the Junior Club in the fifties, and throughout the life of the Club. It was the essence of internal government. At the end of all the reports the Head Junior would say 'I call upon the Head' and JB would stand at the lectern and speak to the assembly. There was a shield called the Guernsey Shield which would go to the House with the most points for the term – the running total was read out at each meeting.

We were always able to challenge JB as a group about how he was running Clubland

I was in the Cabinet in 1955. There was one time we were all supposed to be going to a public event, and were all sworn to secrecy – but in the end just the Head Girl and Head Boy went because otherwise there were too many of us. Think it was 'This is Your Life.'

After the rebuilding of the new church, which opened in the early sixties, the Parliament room became an art studio, and the Senior Parliament was held downstairs in the new canteen. The Senior Parliament was held once a week on Thursday nights in the sixties – internal issues would be discussed, with occasional debates and mock trials, and there was a short informal assembly with notices at the end of each Senior Club. After those assemblies Seniors were allowed to go and dance in the theatre – ballroom dancing was a Senior activity. There were often dances for Seniors on Saturdays – Officers would attend, the canteen would open, and everybody would dress up.

JB didn't permit jiving. We DID jive – but even though he saw it JB didn't know that that was what we were doing.

****

The Head
We held JB on a pedestal

I remember stopping to gather mistletoe from a tree at Box Hill – JB said he needed it for the altar. The owner came to see what we were doing and ended up helping us

He was such a friend to everybody in Club – but I was also greatly in awe of him, in fact afraid

He always said don't accept hospitality and then not repay it. The Club made us better people – able to take the right road

He threw me out of service for coughing once

Once I was suspended when I dropped a banger in the middle of a whole box of fireworks

JB was charismatic. Part of his brilliance was making everyone feel very special. He spoke to me every time I visited the club from the time I joined

If you fell out with JB you had to write to apologise. I was thrown out of the Oklahoma production for very little – it took weeks before I capitulated, three weeks before I gave in and wrote the letter. I would never have thought of him as a friend exactly, but I would have asked him to help and advise if I was in trouble. Anna used to say to him 'Oh Jimmy' if he was impatient.

We used to say in Club that you weren't a proper member until you had been suspended five times. You'd get suspended for a week – it could be for talking in a film – and it would be read out at the end of assembly. I had a great deal of respect for JB – after a time I did see his failings, but in a way that made me think more of him. He had faults, but he had a real gift – and certainly a gift for persuading people to do things that they otherwise might not want to do.

Although we heard them in church JB's sermons were not 'churchified' – he was a good talker and orator

I thought he was amazing – he was an amazing orator

I didn't mind the church services – they used to be held in the Parliament room until everything was rebuilt. Spirit didn't come into it when we were Juniors, but when we were Seniors we had to go to service.

We had to be back from our Sunday rambles in time for service, and there were no excuses. Even when Jack Marks lost the handlebars off his bike on Gravel Hill, and he came off, he was suspended for a week. JB was uncompromising about missing service on Sunday.

My parents used to go over on Wednesday evenings, and to the service on Sundays. I remember as a child that the service was sometimes held in the bombed chapel and was very moving. I remember all the Captains filing into the service in their robes – it seemed to hold a certain gravitas

The sermons were moral lessons. I didn't come from a religious family. What he used to say gave solace

He was a marvellous preacher – the church services were not a chore

I didn't really enjoy the sermons – but he cleverly made Sunday nights quite special. He was an engaging speaker who made his message relevant for listeners. We always robed up on Sundays

I had no religious belief whilst I was a member – I was confirmed when I was in the sea cadets but it was a bit of a sham. Clubland confirmed the humanist side of things – it was more spiritual than religious

I remember a visiting preacher that was an Evangelist, and JB stopped him half way through

There was no religious content at Clubland when we were Juniors. Religion was around us in our everyday lives – it was no big thing in Club. But Seniors had to go to Sunday service without fail

I think I had some religious belief as a child, as a Junior, before the time when beliefs are questioned. I admired some of the quasi-spiritual things about Clubland practice – loyalty and service, helping others.

I learned about kindness at Clubland. I learned about not taking more than you gave, and that there is gratification in giving

****

Clubland

The fifties were busy years. JB would disappear on his tours to America and eventually return – often with celebrities

I didn't really think about the money side – I knew he wanted to build an island site and a hostel

The Club was calmer when he wasn't there – there was always some tension when he was around as he was temperamental and unpredictable. When he was away the Officers ran the Club

He used to come back from his US trips with boxes of gifts for the Club. It was better when he was there

I never knew of him being away from Club because of illness – not until it became serious and terminal. He always struck me as indomitable

I don't remember absences due to illness

I remember one service when JB was talking about his mother – he was very sombre and everybody was silent. I only found out later that she had died

I can't ever remember JB being absent from Club because he was ill

There was never much trouble from vandalism or violence at the Club when I was a member – it sometimes attracted hooligans

I remember some Teddy Boy incidents before I was old enough to be a member – also maybe sometimes late in the evening after Junior Club finished

I can't remember any vandalism

The Hostel plan didn't really work in the end. It seemed like two different units, and the Hostel members were not Club members

The Hostel was built to staff the Club with Officers. They were supposed to give their time in part payment – but except for a few, people only came to assist reluctantly.

Several Hostel residents became very good officers – maybe four or five of them. The residents actually signed a contract to say that they would attend the Sunday service, and help in the Clubs in some capacity for one night a week. But most of them either broke the contract or did the very minimum possible – it caused a great deal of bad feeling, and some were made to leave. The rent – which included breakfast and an evening meal in the canteen – was reduced to allow for their services.

The Club 'Mams' were very special. They staffed the canteen but also helped in many other ways, and particularly with making costumes for all the productions, and preparing and decorating the Club for visits and special occasions. Anna ran the voluntary domestic force, and we all helped out

I used to help with the gym activities. There were often about 30 children playing pirates, and it wouldn't be possible now with health and safety regulations. Once a girl fell over and broke her leg – I helped her to hop home and her mum wrote to thank me

JB enthused people to give up their time for no monetary award. Nobody at the club was paid – it was run entirely by volunteers and many of them had attended as Junior and Senior members

We always called the Club mams 'Mrs'. Mrs. B always had a group of mams who turned up and helped in the canteen, and with sandwiches and refreshments for special occasions

One of the mams did cookery with the Juniors

When I was in Club Dr. Gordon Lyle was the Club dentist. Fred Marks was the caretaker and Len Dobbs did football.

Nobody who worked in the Club was paid – it was all done on voluntary help. JB himself received a modest stipend and the Club cleaners had an hourly wage. The caretaker was Fred Marks, and Rose Gray became the hostel manager – but the mams who ran the Club canteen were volunteers, as were all the Officers. The Treasurer and Governors had professional occupations but were not paid for their Club activities and responsibilities.

****

The Legacy

Religion in school was just boring – but JB made sense to us

We were privileged really – being there made you a better person

Memories and standards that were inculcated by JB were deeply ingrained and in consequence not easily forgotten – JB and Anna deserved a much more prominent place in the history of pre and post War London than has been secured

We were a very privileged club – it made such a difference in our lives

He set us all on a different road. Club members learned to do good, and to help people. We all grew because of Clubland

Friendship was the best thing we had at Clubland, and being a member showed me another world

Clubland just showed you a different way of life

JB used to go up to court and plead the case for lads who got into trouble

Clubland inevitably shaped me – although in the end I needed to free myself to become an individual. I learned a lot about leadership – and I think it gave me a lifelong left wing inclination. JB and Clubland were founded on egalitarian principles

It gave individuals aspiration and self-confidence

Clubland absolutely helped me to develop as an individual. The Club was in a working class area – my Dad was a lorry driver and my mum was a cleaner – and I was down to go into print like my brothers. At Club we met a whole range of people with different ideas about the world, and I started to think about things in a more critical way. The Club 'lifted the eyes up', and I developed the ability to talk to a whole range of people. These things were not specifically taught but came in by osmosis. I was there almost twenty years from 1953 – as Head Boy I had to meet dignitaries and talk to them. I went to University instead of into print. The greatest value of Clubland was that it was open to all without any bar – it was very egalitarian. It was a wonderful atmosphere

JB liked discipline – but he wouldn't be able to insist on it in the same way now. Things have changed

If I had been in charge of Clubland there is nothing that I would have done differently

Clubland was precious to us, but also fragile – John and I would both have done a lot to keep it going. But there was no replacement for JB – the Methodists scuttled the ship

If I had been in charge I would have run it on openly secular lines – but kept all the rest. It was essentially a humanitarian enterprise, and I would replace religion with rationality as well as kindness. I would not have allowed celebrity to become so celebrated – but the relationship to the famous was bound up with the necessity of sponsorship and finance.

Long and enduring marriages seem to have been unique to Clubland – it seemed to produce a glue that kept people together. Clubland was absolutely central to the lives of the Senior group before us – and old members have always kept in contact as a group

There's a place for sanctuary which engenders the feeling of security and kindness. It could have a spiritual base – not evangelical, and not fundamentally religious. JB's sermons explained things rather than preached

Clubland couldn't have been run better.

JB was a little lad from Lancashire who did well.

Mixed voices from separate interviews with Terry, Daphne, Laurie, Jane, Ricky, John, Alan, and Len. All, in their time, young people of Clubland.

Notes

1 See previous chapter: The Third American Tour.
2 J Arthur Rank was elevated to a baronetcy In 1957.
3 From an interview with the authors and written recollections.
4 Terry Barrett (2018): *The Reverend James Butterworth – A Personal View.*
5 Full title: The Joseph Rank Benevolent Trust.
6 Transcript in the *Clubland Review*, Summer 1964.
7 Ibid.

8 *BFI Screenonline, Rank, J. Arthur (1988–1972) Biography.* www.screenonline.org/people/id/447127/index.html

9 Ibid. Ref to there as 'David Lean (1947)'.

10 Lang, P Bartlett, 1981. *Reconciliation and Grace* (self published).

11 Touker Suleyman is better known today a panellist on the BBC Two show *Dragon's Den*. He distinguished himself long before that as a Junior Captain at Clubland.

CHAPTER ELEVEN

Epilogue: The Last Years

'It was all so much fun'

In most books, including biographies, the Epilogue appears following the final chapter. But it is, sadly, true to say that in many ways JB lived his own epilogue. As the decade of the nineteen-seventies began JB was already well past the threshold of his own seventies, with a couple of extended bouts of recent illness behind him. Nervous exhaustion had always plagued him, and his way of dealing with it was never to advertise his ill health but simply to absent himself from Walworth, and return, restored to his customary vigour, some weeks or months later. A change of scene was often sufficient in itself for recharging batteries depleted by the unremitting demands of sustaining and extending the Clubland project. Ostensibly Clubland continued into the Seventies with its usual energy and output – in 1970 a special *Review* was published to mark the 50-year anniversary. In '1920–1970 Half a Century of Youthful Enterprise: Rev. J. Butterworth', JB summarises Clubland's history, and repeats the key phrases of his ministry there – 'Loyalty and Service', 'Pride in Premises', 'Partners not Passengers', 'Reverence in Worship', and 'Liberty does not mean Licence'. Whilst confirming that there shall be no compromise of the Club's foundation ideals, he also declares that his view that rebels and reformers must guard against becoming reactionaries later in life. Unfortunately this was a principle which JB himself found very hard to follow, and he struggled to relax his hold and loose the reins of Clubland.

By 1970 Clubland had a rich and eventful history – and there were so many who had lived it and could recall the epochs and events of its past. In the *Review* JB reprised Frank Neal's (pre-war Head Senior) wartime letter on meeting Ken Randall and Bill Darby in Egypt: 'We were all rather choked for a few minutes. Four years since we met last in Clubland'. The three then talked for ten hours: 'We just talked about the place and the man who had meant so much to us.' Many thought in like terms. Michael Caine – adolescent member Maurice Micklewhite of the late forties – considered of JB that although 'he always referred to himself as a little Lancashire Lad and he was only about five feet tall, in every other way he was a giant'. And an early Club member, H.G. Anton, wrote in November 1970 that having seen JB on Bob Hope's 'This Is Your Life' he felt moved to write about when he 'was one of the little demons meeting in the cleared crypt under the old church – I loved the Fretwork Room, and no boy made more Pipe Racks than I did for Dad and my uncles. The wonderful camps at St. Sampsons – I still have the little vase I won in the 100 yards – and singing 'we are the Walworth Boys'. Somewhere I've got a group photo of us with you in the middle, and another of a bathing party. It was all so much fun. I remember the tomatoes in the Guernsey house I was invited to, and my mates Jim Bowyer, and Fred Padbury, as well as Lily Bates that I had a crush on later. You gave us lads so much love and guidance so many years ago – I feel it has always influenced me. I wish you many more successful years.'

Pre-war camp bonfire

The Window Closes

The great Thanksgiving Service of 3 October 1971 had been a high point in Clubland's achievement and development, but even that early in the decade, whilst Clubland still remained vibrant, JB often felt daunted by the distance in age between himself and not only the current members but his officers and helpers, and even his own family. Writing, to a friend in September 1970 he confided – somewhat obscurely – that 'The "age gap" people talk so glibly about has been very difficult for me to communicate – not only with a membership with which I'm too old to be as I was with members I had known and trained. Even more of an age gap with me – 3 of 'em – 20 years removed from my wife then another 20 years between my children, then another 20 years between grandchildren – making up the 3 gaps. So adjustments haven't been easy and sometimes it's like being left on the sidelines – unable to fit in with and be identified with any of the 3 generations. Penalty of growing old.'

Clubland's financial future looked to be set fair by the opening of the second and larger hostel, and Club activities were running smoothly. It was scarcely believable that within three years of the celebratory peak of 1971 one of his closest and most devoted Clubland associates and officers through many decades, Dr Gordon Lyle, would be so driven by frustration and despair at JB's resistance to any delegated management of Clubland affairs to others that he would tender his resignation. Dr Lyle greatly feared that JB's recalcitrance would endanger Clubland's future, and felt that greater co-operation with both Methodism and the local authority had become essential to its survival.

The truth was that the window, which determination, faith, and sheer ability, had enabled Jimmy Butterworth to force open for his great venture so many years before, was closing. The changing postwar demographic in a migrating Walworth, the increasing involvement of the welfare state in youth affairs, as well as different social attitudes and economic expectations among young people, meant that in order to survive Clubland too needed to alter. Essentially that called for a flexibility of approach – a recognition and acceptance of new methods, and a relaxation of old ones – which JB found very difficult to countenance.

Through the seventies a succession of assistant ministers and probationers were placed at Walworth by the Methodist church, but JB stubbornly resisted innovations and alterations to his established traditions and methods. Because of this resistance, together with his age and bouts of ill-health, the Methodist hierarchy exerted pressure upon him to retire from the Walworth Church and Clubland. But although elderly and increasingly low in spirit he could not bring himself to relinquish his Clubland role, and he did not go willingly. The Reverend Norman Dawson of the London Mission – under whose aegis Clubland functioned – made a succession of offers. An Assistant Minister was welcomed by Rev. Dawson in August 1973, and in June 1975 he wrote to JB recommending acceptance of a house in nearby Herne Hill, which was being offered as retirement accommodation by the Methodists. Dawson did his level best to accomplish JB's smooth transition to retirement, but it was an uphill struggle, and he wrote again in July referring to the 'Methodist pressure for leaving Clubland'. In the following months JB's wellbeing deteriorated and he was again gripped by depression.

For the first half of the decade the Clubs continued to function in a reduced but recognisable fashion, and a loyal group of officers – Terry Barrett, Bob Gray, Ted Cutler, Les and Lily Harris, Peter Reading, David Rolfe and others – succeeded in running activities at the same standard as previously. Clubland church services went on as before, and reviews were published – although more occasionally. Special services were held to mark the fifty-year anniversary of JB's arrival in Walworth in May 1922 – the service sheet contains the usual instruction to members to 'Stand as Prefects Enter' – and JB continued to preach, publish, and conduct marriages. The same year he sent out a flyer, 'Sermons in Stones', describing the 585 Donors' Stones in the Quadrangle Garden of Remembrance at Clubland, and recalling his postwar venture of travelling to lecture in response to any invitation in exchange for the naming of a stone for £100. Characteristically – and in demonstration of the unabated zeal of his fundraising – the description ends with his reminder that 'The sad thing is that of the 585 stones, 25 are blank ... Do you know anyone who would name one of the remaining DONORS' STONES for £50?'

The leaflet also asks that every member of the ex-Clublanders bring 'another ex-Senior or friend' to the Reunion Service on the first Sunday in September, indicating increasing anticipation of falling attendance during such services. In 1973 on a Guernsey visit, JB proudly announced that he had married at least 400 of the Clublanders that he had brought out to the island to camp over the years. And he certainly also retained his lifelong enthusiasm for securing football match tickets – and was assured by Dennis Hill Wood, Chairman of Arsenal, in 1975, that he would receive ground passes as always. But Clubland membership was sadly dwindling – by the mid-Seventies there were no more than a hundred members in all, perhaps sixty Juniors and a few dozen Seniors. The Club had reduced to mixed attendance on Wednesdays and Thursdays only, and in consequence fewer supervisors and leaders were required – the Clubland profile was already merely a faint shadow of what it had previously been.

In those twilight years Clubland would have been unrecognisable to anyone who had known it in its heyday. At the last it was open just one or two nights in a week, for a handful of members; and on Sundays for a service attended for the most part by a small band of officers and ex-members, with a reunion service once monthly. Their love and respect for JB was undiminished, but his deepening depression and erratic behaviour tested the patience even of some of his oldest friends and colleagues, for whom his obstinate refusal to give up the reins and leave for a comfortable retirement almost amounted to deliberate damage to his great achievement.

By 1976, following a period of hospitalisation, his Church made JB's immediate retirement from his ministry a formal request. The existence of the wonderful buildings and their contents was solely the result of JB's unremitting work and extraordinary effort over half a century, but they had nevertheless remained the property of the Methodist Church – he had no lien upon them, nor any legal right to remain in occupation. He informed members and supporters of the imminent imposed departure in a circular letter he sent out on 15 July 1976 – shortly before leaving to live with Anna in a cottage she had bought in East Sussex – saying that he had hoped he might have stayed at Clubland but that the Methodist hierarchy required his retirement from the premises. The pathos of this bleak announcement was evident and many hundreds responded to it: Clubland members from all periods; couples JB had married; Club volunteers, helpers, and assistants; Clubland friends and well-wishers; sponsors, supporters, and fund secretaries; contributors in the broader community. Letters came from everywhere – all over the world – telling JB that they understood the 'wrench', that he and Clubland were one and the same, that it was inconceivable that Clubland could continue without him.

> *I cannot think of Clubland without your leadership and guidance and enthusiasm. I thought you would return from hospital to Camberwell and into harness. 17 September 1976*

You have had a brilliantly successful life in which church bureaucracy must have been your biggest problem. 19 September 1976

The Club has been your life for so many many years. But the dear Lord has used you so mightily. When Lord Rochester and I first knew you were so full of zeal and energy. 1 January 1977

My sister and I were there on the first night of the Girls Club, and I married one of the original six boys … 25 January 1977

All who know you are sorry and distressed to hear of your replacement – although there is nothing we can do. 9 December 1976

I read your letter with great sadness, and hope you have enough strength, after 54 years of labour, to live on the happiness of your wonderful memories. 16 October 1976

My head told me this must come some day, but my heart was not ready for the shock. Thank God for your lifetime of adding so much to the betterment of mankind. Yours as ever, for ever. 9 August 1976

JB, Dear Old Friend, Your letter of July 15th has only just reached me. I was staggered by it – the complete idiocy of thinking that there can be a Clubland without JB. Anybody who ever visited Clubland and saw it work – saw you at work and sensed your power and presence – could not do this. We are all older, but Clubland is you, it always was and has been. 12 September 1976

I am cut to the heart by your letter, and the unbelievable hurt at this time in your life. I feel as though it must be a terrible mistake – you ARE the Club … 19 August 1976

All your friends at Green Haworth and the little chapel there that you loved so much in boyhood … wish you a contented retirement. 17 August 1976

Few can be sorrier than me to think you are no longer at Clubland – Clubland and JB are synonymous. I was 15 when you came in 1922, and truly one of the underprivileged, and your concept for Clubland was an inspiration. I feel inarticulate, but I also feel very deeply what you and your work have meant to me and to so many others like me. 14 August 1976

Methodism has delivered its knockout … You lost your creation twice, but nobody can take away the memories, and the indelible imprint you made on us all. 15 August 1976

All those who write seek to offer sympathy, support, and comfort, and many are unbelieving, or furious on his behalf. A small few, seeking only to soften the blow, are perhaps not as sensitive as they might be – reminding him that 'each generation has its own norms and ideas', or advising that although it is hard to give it all up he is well past the age when most people are very glad to take things a bit easier. It is all very well meant, from people who knew JB and wanted to lessen the cost of the impending separation – but there was no way his going could be made less painful to him.

JB was not solely bent upon being obstructive in his refusal to relinquish control, although it was always typical of him to hold to a *prima facie* preference for his own methods of proceeding in the face of any innovative suggestions from others. But he was now confronted by the prospect of a profound and unwelcome tearing apart, when the simple truth was that that there could be no significant separation in fact or concept between Clubland and himself. It was, of course, customary to retire at or before his age, and for everybody concerned to recognise the appropriateness of accepting this rite of passage without demur. But it perhaps needs considering that there is no moral or logical imperative around the rightness of giving up your life's work without objection. There is no particular virtue in stifling the flow of energy which made huge achievement possible, or for exercising calmness and moderation in ceasing to be who you are. For JB the loss of Clubland was the loss of himself.

JB was already without many souls who had been comrades in his lifetime endeavour – both Jack Leale and Basil Henriques had died some years earlier, followed by the Clubland architect Edward Maufe, aged 92, in 1974 – and Alec Reed, and Reg Turtle, who had lent their constant strength and support to him at Clubland through so very many years, were gone. He was fighting on alone, and the enforced move away from Clubland inevitably soon depleted the life force which had sustained him.

The Reverend James Butterworth died on 5 April 1977, a few days after his 80th birthday, and there followed an outpouring of grief and remembrance for months – even years – afterwards. Those who had encountered Clubland and its diminutive minister paid tribute to him in letters, books, and films, for the benefits many had experienced personally during his long ministry at Clubland, and the personal calibre he had demonstrated in his unwavering commitment to his lifetime's work. Those who had written in sympathy and support the previous year, when JB was made to leave Walworth, now wrote again in grief and remembrance.

'It was both humbling and sad to meet someone so completely dedicated to his cause. MacRobert Trustees 19 April 1977

He stood like a Colossus across the site which he created. I feel his loss very deeply ... I am glad that we have so many wonderful years that we can remember. Edward MacLelland, Harley Street, 29 April 1977.

Since I heard of Jimmy's death my thoughts have taken me back through sixty years to those early days when we walked together through Green Haworth and across the high moor ... they are as fresh in my memory as if it were only yesterday ... My dear old friend, he fought the good fight with all his might and is undefeated. Alec Wildman, friend of JBs Oswaldtwistle youth, journalist and photographer. 26 April 1977

What a man, what a life. No words will ever be equal or adequate to express all the quality of his personality, and nobody will ever be able to measure the influence he has had on countless numbers of people. Rev. William (Bill) Motson, Steyn Gardens Methodist Church, 13 April 1977.

I was one of many thousands of South London children who benefited from JBs creation of Clubland ... JB himself had an enormous effect on my life ... it was a privilege to have met him. Charles Coleman, Head of Wix Junior School, Clapham Common 6 May 1977

I cherish the memory of a very great man ... I hope for one other thing out of this wonderful life and that is that someone will be commissioned to write a biography of the Rev. James Butterworth and Clubland. Frank Dawson, General Secretary, Birkenhead Council for Voluntary Service, 2 May 1977.

Dear Mrs. JB ... He was the greatest man I have ever met. The happiness and sense of purpose he created is unmatched. Ron Boost, Member.

Anna herself, JB's selfless wife, and helper since before WW2, was justly included in the high praise now flowing over JB and Clubland. John Blatchley wrote to her on 28.4.1977 of 'How much we all owe to him ... and to you too who sustained him so loyally and totally in his great work.' And Sir Leonard Neal, Clubland member in the 1920s and 1930s, writing in December 2000 with regret at being too unwell to attend Anna's own memorial service, expresses his disappointment that more has not been made of JB's life and work: 'Clubland and all its leaders, JB and Anna, deserved a much more prominent place in the history of pre and post War London than has been secured.'

The Clubland Head's death was widely reported in the newspapers, as the national press paid tribute to JB in column inches for the last time. Paul Lang, for the Rank Trust, wrote a moving memorial article in the *Methodist Recorder*, and in Lancashire the *Accrington Observer* – faithful commentator throughout JB's years in Walworth – reported of his imminent funeral at Immanuel Church, Oswaldtwistle, that 'the mortal remains of a dynamic spark will be returning to the area from which he sprang'. Several Clubland officers made the journey to Lancashire for the crowded service – including Roy and Jean Barrett, Vernon Cocking, Len Dobbs, Les and Lily Harris, Les Bedson, and Jim Stow – which was conducted by Rev. James Moorhouse, a minister in Farnworth and personal friend of JB with a shared local history.

JB's granite gravestone stands there still in the green churchyard at Immanuel Church with his ancestors, in sight of the old Methodist chapel at Green Haworth – a returning son of the moors whose life, so far distant from his Lancashire roots, had enriched so many. Clubland's alumni survived him and lived on – its unprecedented recognition and encouragement of the talents of young people was midwife to politicians, painters, actors, and public servants, many of whose names have become familiar to all. But its greatest achievement lay in the promotion of rewarding and meaningful lives for all its thousands of members – JB gave to these young people, in the fellowship of Clubland, a sense of their own ineffable value. To prioritise the exceptional and famous would be a disservice to the many thousands who remained unknown to history, but whose lives and achievements JB enhanced and valued equally – as well as to those few he reached for but could not hold in safety. His gift to so many was incalculable: a contribution to the greater good of humankind which must surely be singled out to show the magnitude of what may be accomplished, even from the poorest beginning.

Since Jimmy Butterworth left Walworth the work of the Methodist church has returned to a broader remit, although generally extended to assist the local community, first by Rev. Vic Watson, and later Rev. Norman Grigg, who developed an increased multi-cultural membership, utilising the hostel for students, refugees, and asylum seekers. It had sometimes been thought that JB's ministry had taken the church away from its first obligation to Christianity in favour of a Clubland allegiance – but in fact JB had nurtured allegiance to the 'Lord of all Good life' through the fellowship, joy, and understanding he sought to create at Clubland. He wished to discard the shallow artificiality of what he called 'churchianity', but only in order to give his young congregation something more substantial in its place. In 1947 he described the Sunday Service – the 'Angelus' – in a *Clubland Review*, saying

> This is Clubland – its centre and inspiration, the secret of its strength and usefulness. It has created its spirit, gives tone to all its club life, and transforms personal life. Its simple dignity and appealing reverence has given to generations of youth a new conception of the presence and practice of God.

This little imp of a clergyman

There have been many memorial services at Clubland since JB's death – with former members such as Alf Goldsmith, Gladys Cuthbert, Jock Surtees, Daphne Williams, Jim Stow, Judith Northwood-Stow and others gathering to read the lessons – commemorating not only his ministry and life, but also the lifelong loving and generous support of his wife Anna Butterworth, and the unstinting help she supplied to JB and to all Clubland members and officers. There have also been many Clubland reunions held for the enduring groups of Clublanders, and even now it seems of their children.

In May 2016, following an on-line post from a neighbour of Clubland who had nevertheless only recently visited the building and discovered its history, the son of a former member responded to the earlier article saying:

> My Dad was a member just after WW2 and continued his association with 'The Club' for many years until JB passed away. I used to go to reunions with Dad and met JB on many occasions. A truly wonderful and inspirational man. Dad made many friends at Clubland – friendships that lasted a lifetime. His friend's families became our lifetime friends along the way – and I've very fond memories of meeting up with them all at Clubland, particularly at the yearly carol services. I'm not a religious guy at all, but JB really left a mark on me as someone who REALLY achieved something in life, and his teachings and ethos outlasted him by many years. I really don't think that it could possibly be appreciated today, the enormity of what he achieved. Heads of state, royalty and megastars of stage, screen, and sport – all coming freely from around the world, to visit this little imp of a clergyman at his youth club in the backstreets of London – and donating generously of their time and funds.' (Luke Bedson, son of Les Bedson)

The 'little imp', although Clubland's driving force, had not been isolated in his great venture, and there were many who had shared and shaped his life along the way – champions, mentors, sponsors, and friends – without whom the Clubland story might have been very different. The enduring interest and support for a fatherless boy supplied by John Holgate in Oswaldtwistle; the encouragement and guidance of Reverend John Bennetts at Green Haworth, Reverend Samuel Chadwick at Cliff College, Reverend Thomas Barratt and Reverend Wilfred Moulton at Didsbury Methodist College; Herbert Rees at Holmes Chapel, who personified practical help for errant lads; landlady Hannah Gay and Reverend Walter Hawkins, who cherished and nurtured him when he arrived as a diminutive twenty-five-year-old in Walworth in 1922; Ernest Lamb (Lord Rochester), his first influential and devoted sponsor, and George and Alice Shrubsall who provided generous financial support for many years; generations of the Methodist Rank family who offered trust fund aid, and Bob Hope, unexpected but committed backer; Lady MacRobert, who considered JB's venture worthy of the memory of her three fallen soldier sons; his lifelong lieutenants at Walworth, Alec Reed, Reg Turtle, and Gordon Lyle; his Duckworth cousins in Lancashire. And most of all, above all others, the generations upon generations of Clubland members – the thousands of young people who filled the Clubs, from the first six small boys in the dug-outs below the Walworth Church to the faithful officers of the seventies.

Postscripts

Every word written here of the course and content of the life of Jimmy Butterworth – Oswaldtwistle orphan, Great War soldier, Methodist Minister, Pioneer of youth work, and Clubland founder and Head – makes manifest his vision and achievement, and the power and strength of his ministry. So many people loved him, and felt enduring admiration for his fight to establish an egalitarian foundation for youthful advancement, as well as gratitude towards him for his enrichment of their lives. In many ways he was not an easy man – he was demanding in terms of the standard of behaviour he expected of the young people at Clubland, and exacting in respect of the work of his colleagues. But his loving generosity towards those in need, and particularly the very young, knew no bounds at all.

In the view of his biographers and family the essence of JB's life and work cannot be better articulated than in extracts from the words of

JB reading his Methodist Recorder at Conference. He hadn't registered and so
needed to charm his way in without a pass – a skill he had perfected over the years!

three very different writers:– those of Tony and Beryl Jackman, ex-Club
pre-war members, who wrote to give him strength and reassurance when
enforced retirement was staring him in the face in 1976; the Memoriam
address of 8 May 1977, given by Reverend Gordon Davies – lifelong
friend and Clubland assistant minister and Leader during the thirties
and wartime years; and a poem quoted by JB in Clubland reviews
on many occasions entitled *The Bridge Builder*, written by Will Allen
Dromgoole, circa 1900.

i) Tony and Beryl Jackman, Loughborough, 29.9.1976.

Dear JB

Both Beryl and I were most sorry to hear of your stay in hospital. It's too
late now to send either abstract sympathy or concrete grapes, so instead
we send greetings, our congratulations on having recovered from
whatever-it-was and all our good wishes for the future.

Naturally enough, your letter came as a sad surprise since "Clubland" and "JB" have been one-and-the-same for so long, and our initial thought was that the one could not exist without the other. But after a moment's reflection we realised that this just isn't true; Clubland isn't (and never was) just a building with a minister in it. To believe that would be to denigrate all that you worked so hard and so long to achieve. Of course there's still a magnificent building, full of memories and moments that will be there long after you and I are gone, but that's only a very small part of the Clubland you created. It was a very "good box for you to preach in", a lovely place for members to work and play in, a genuine "pearl on a dungheap" before light and air were brought to Walworth, and truly it was more a home for many youngsters than the ugly terraced houses they lived in. But the real Clubland is in the hearts and souls of the myriad members who have each taken a little bit with them, wherever they are and whatever they do. And those little bits are as bright and shining as they were when the first boys tore down the dingy bricks of the old chapel, when members filled the quad to greet Queen Mary, when they burned their hands to rescue the font-cover, when they rehearsed late into the night to put on a show, when they sang on the boat as they sailed to Guernsey, when they filed out of a dancehall at midnight to return through another door to a Christmas chapel.

I remember you setting off to USA with nothing more than tuppence and a lot of hope ... I remember you arguing with Arthur Rank for what you believed ... I remember (only too well) how you constantly chucked out the stars of my shows just before the opening nights in the certainty that they would still go on. All of these things were so because you had 'fire in your belly', a burning faith that enabled you to move mountains, and somehow you managed always to do the right thing at the right time.

So do it now! It's time to relax, and God knows you've earned a rest. After all, it will always be your torch that is handed on, whoever may hold it for a season.

Cheer up and look up JB. God willing, we'll meet again before too long, and I'll expect to see you with a grin, a command to take a brick with me, and detailed instructions as to where the furniture is to go!

All our love,

Tony and Beryl.

ii) IN MEMORIAM: The Reverend James Butterworth. Died 5th April, 1977. Clubland Memoriam Service on Sunday 8th May. Rev. E. Gordon Davies (Clubland 1940–1943)

Mine is a voice from the past – yet perhaps none the worse for that. It may even be allowed to be the voice from the past, speaking for all those boys and girls whose lives have been literally transformed because of Clubland. And it must speak with undying gratitude and admiration.

I've never known a man so feared and so respected, so hated and so loved, so stern and so friendly, so ruthless and so forgiving, so impossible and so understanding, so small and so big, all at the same time. He really was unique; a genius who captivated anyone who so much as glimpsed what he was after, but was hard to work with for the same reason, and had to do all the hard slogging himself because he outstripped any normal understanding. He dreamed dreams, and made them come true: he dreamed our dreams and woke us into wonder. He 'showed us stars we never saw before' – and the fact that they were often the stars of stage, screen, and stadium is a further reminder of his magic.

He had certain unfair advantages. He never grew up, in the sense that whenever I was talking to a group of boys it was only when I realised that one of them was smoking a pipe that I found he'd joined us. He never seemed to need sleep. He never stopped working, and rarely stopped talking. He could make you believe any number of "impossible things before breakfast" and frequently did. He could write with inspiration, and raise money faster than inflation. He could knock down walls, and alter drawing plans – and instead of collapsing, the building would be all the better for it! He could throw anything onto a fire – except his principles. He had a sense of order, of beauty, of colour, of shape, that could have made him an artist. He had an awareness of God that sometimes made us aware of the devil, but always left us closer to beauty, truth, and goodness once we'd got over the first shock. We've moved loads of furniture for him: and he moved mountains for us.

This is a place of memories; a time for remembering … Names reach out to us across the years and … occasions crowd upon our thoughts.

But it is not a Memorial. This place was never planned or built as a memorial. It's a house of life, a home of friendship, a Temple of Youth. Remember how we used to sing (and had to be stopped from singing) that hymn that began 'There is joy for all the members in the sorrows of the Head'? There *is* joy. There always was. There always will be.

I've never been quite sure what is meant by 'cherubim and seraphim' but I'll bet one of them is smoking a pipe now.

iii) The Bridge Builder: Will Allen Dromgoole (1860–1936)

An old man going a lone highway,
Came, at the evening cold and gray,
To a chasm vast and deep and wide
Through which was flowing a sullen tide.
The old man crossed in the twilight dim,
The sullen stream had no fear for him;
But he turned when safe on the other side
And built a bridge to span the tide.

"Old Man" said a fellow pilgrim near,
"You are wasting your strength with building here;
Your journey will end with the ending day,
You never again will pass this way;
You've crossed the chasm, deep and wide,
Why build this bridge at evening tide?"

The builder lifted his old gray head;
"Good friend, in the path I have come," he said,
"There followed after me to-day
A youth whose feet must pass this way.
This chasm that has been naught to me
To that fair-haired youth may a pitfall be;
He, too, must cross in the twilight dim;
Good friend, I am building this bridge for him!"

**Reverend James Butterworth 17 March, 1897 – 5 April, 1977.
Head of *Clubland*, Walworth.**

Bibliography

James Butterworth: Published works

Dugout Digressions. Epworth Press, 1918
Bees Wings and Ruby Queens. Epworth Press, 1919
A Service Book of Prayers and Readings, c.1922
Byways in Boyland,. Epworth Press, 1925
Adventures in Boyland, Epworth Press, 1926
Clubland. Epworth Press, 1932
Clubland: The Temple of Youth (illustrated handbook), c.1935
The Clubland Service Book, 1938
Letters of a Clublander. Unpublished and incomplete autobiography, written
    mostly in the 1940s

JB also provided a continuous flow of articles for publication in local and national newspapers and periodicals. In particular, he was a regular contributor to – and subject matter of – *The Methodist Recorder.* These were in addition to what Clubland produced internally – the *Walworth Messenger, Clubland Review,* and numerous illustrated handbooks marking anniversaries and special occasions.

A large catalogued collection of JB's writings, together with letters, photographs and press cuttings, log books, and other items is held at Southwark Local History Library – 211 Borough High Street, London SE1 1JA

Other sources

Allinson, S. *The Bantams.* Pen & Sword Military, 2009
Aspin, Chris. *The Cotton Industry.* Shire Publications, 1981/2012

Barnett, Leonard P. *The Church Youth Club.* The Epworth Press, 1951

Barrett, Terry. *The Reverend James Butterworth – A Personal View* Unpublished, 2018

Boast Mary *The Story of Walworth.* Council of the London Borough of Southwark, 2005

Brittain, Vera. *The Testament of Youth.* first published by Victor Gollancz, 1933

Caine, Michael *The Autobiography. From the Elephant to Hollywood.* Hodder and Stoughton, 2010

Caine, Michael. *What's it all About.* Random House, 1993

Davson, Lt Col. H.M. *The History of the 35th Division in the Great War.* London. Sifton Praed, 1926

Dawes, Frank. *A Cry From the Streets. The Boys' Club Movement in Britain from the 1850s to the Present Day.* Wayland Publishers, 1975

Eagar, W. McG. *Making Men. The History of Boys Clubs and Related Movements in Great Britain.* University of London Press, 1953

Ferguson, Niall. *The Pity of War.* Penguin Books, 1999

Ferris, Ray and Julian Lord. *Teddy Boys. a Concise History.* Milo Books, 2012

Frost, Brian with Stuart Jordan. *Pioneers of Social Passion. London's Cosmopolitan Methodism.* Epworth Press, 2006.

Graves, R. *Goodbye to All That,* Penguin Modern Classics, 2000

Henriques, Sir Basil. *Club Leadership.* Oxford University Press, 1933

Holman, Bob. *Woodbine Willie.* Lion Books, 2012

Kerry Walters, (ed.). *After War is Faith Possible?'* Cambridge. Lutterworth, 2008

Lang, P Bartlett,. *Reconciliation and Grace.* Self published, 1981

Morgan, A.E. *The Needs of Youth* Oxford University Press, 1939

Nicholson, Cecil L., Maj. Gen., Sir. *The History of the East Lancashire Regiment in the Great War.* Lancashire Infantry Museum.

Owen, W. *Collected Letters.* Oxford University Press, 1967

Turner, William. *Pals. The 11ᵗʰ(Service) Battalion (Accrington) East Lancashire Regiment.* Pen and Sword Books, 1998).

Winstanley, Michael, (ed.) *Working Children in 19th Century Lancashire.* Lancashire County Books, 1995

Index of Names

Adams, James S 298, 300, 310
Alexander, Reverend Bill 280
Anderson, Jean 340
Anderson, Jimmy 182, 197
Andrews, Eamonn 239, 303, 305
Angle Wood, Somme 51-2
Anton, H G 364
Appleton, Denis 225, 239
Arras 20, 41, 49, 50-58, 62, 77
Arsenal Football Club 144, 155, 228, 236, 237, 283, 310, 332, 333, 353, 366
Ashley, Jim 331
Attenborough, Richard 239, 285, 298, 310, 311, 312, 352, 353
Aubrey, Rick 340
Ayling, Hilda 194

Bailey, Bernard 225, 242, 328, 341
Bailey, Iris 241
Bailey, Yvonne ('Odette') 303
Bainbridge, Jane (Lyle) x
Baker, Gladys 241
Bantams, The 4, 47-56
Barber, Red 294
Barmere 180, 187, 188, 190, 353
Barnes, Bert 332
Barnes, Bill 300
Barnes, John (Oswaldtwistle) 27
Barnett, Leonard 118, 139n, 380
Barratt, Reverend Thomas Hugh 3, 88, 89, 90, 93, 97-8, 100n, 116, 139, 153, 373
Barrett, Jean 371

Barrett, Nicky x, 242
Barrett, Roy 241, 348
Barrett, Teresa x
Barrett, Terry x, 315, 332, 361n, 366, 380
Bastin, Clifford 144, 155
Bedson, Les x, 349, 371, 372,
Bedson, Luke x, 372
Beech Road Mission 2, 88-100, 106-18, 134, 139n, 165, 337
Benedict, Max 156, 174, 175n, 310
Bennetts, Reverend John 35, 51, 57, 65, 78, 79, 80, 81, 84, 97, 99, 116, 166, 373
Benny, Jack 295, 308
Bigland, Alfred 49
Bird, Brenda 133, 186
Black, Padre 71
Blackburn Rovers Football Club 25, 237, 294, 311
Blackwell, John 309
Blatchley, John 156, 181, 196, 236, 370
Blundell, Jack 37, 42n, 306
Bogert, Beverley 280, 289-91, 294
Bondy, Ted 196
Booth, Charles 102
Booth, William 93, 102, 290
Bowskill, Albert 196
Bowyer, Jim 364
Bowyer, Ted 105, 119, 306,
Bradley, Albert 294
Brindle, Bob 184, 194
Brown, Derek 212

Brown, Freddie 238
Brown, Gladys 221
Burnley Football Club 310, 353
Burton, Andy 115-6, 181, 194, 244
Butlin, Billy 47
Butterworth, Ann 10, 12, 13, 16, 24,
    26, 29, 34, 37, 167, 239
Butterworth, Anna (Costain) 193,
    232-3, 238, 262, 275, 299, 300,
    303-6, 318, 348-61
Butterworth, Florrie 13, 24, 28, 34,
    98, 133, 166-7
Butterworth, John & Mary 220
Butterworth, Nellie 24, 34, 37, 288
Butterworth, Reverend Cyril 63-4,
    65
Butterworth, Ruth x, 167
Butterworth, Thomas (JB's
    father) 10, 12-13, 20-21, 23-27 if,
    33, 35
Butterworth, Tom (grandson) 334
Butterworth, William (Billy) 15, 24,
    35, 37
Byworth, A E 182

Cagney, James 285, 286
Cain, Mary 190
Cain, Reverend Dick 299
Caine, Michael vii, 118, 226, 233,
    245n, 282-3, 301n, 352, 364
Callaghan, Jimmy 345
Carroll, Charlie 228
Chadwick, Reverend fifth
    Samuel 38, 39, 46, 78, 80, 99, 169,
    373
Chary, Reg 195
Chelsea Football Club 177, 228, 236,
    237, 239, 291, 310, 333
Childs, Billy 306
Childs, Chic 225
Cholmondeley, Lord 188
Churchill, Edna 221
Clark, Doris 221

Clements, Len 225, 242
Clements, Lynn 242
Clements, Lily 242
Cliff College ix, 4, 37-40, 46, 72,
    77-80, 84, 99, 114, 169, 314, 373
Clockwork Orange, A 254
Clynes, J R 31
Coates, Bunty 194, 349
Coates, Kathleen 221
Cocking, Vernon 371
Cogan, Alma 291-2, 352
Colgate, Byard 293, 299, 310
Colgate, Peggy 278, 298
Collier, Ron 196
Compton, Denis 236
Compton, Leslie 236
Conisbee, Edwin 112, 125, of 136
Considine, John 280, 289
Contentment Island 293
Cook, Peter 332, 340
Cooper, Barney 299, 300
Cooper, Carrie 341
Cooper, Frances 242
Cooper, Stan 351
Copperdale, Edna 221
Cosh Boy (film) 254
Costain (builders) 188-90, 307, 318,
    353
Costain, Anna 171, 181, 188-90
Costain, Jim (AJ) 190
Costain, Joan 190
Costain, John (JK) 189
Costain, Mary Kneen 190
Costain, Richard (Dick) 190
Costain, Richard 189
Costain, Richey Betsy 188
Cowan, Harry & Alice 344
Cox, Reverend W R 90, 91, 94
Crawley, Bert 194
Crispini, Franco & Luigi 340
Crook, Jacob 15, 18, 34, 35, 99, 165
Crook, John x, 14, 165
Crosby, Bing 283, 284, 307

Crossley, H 76n
Crossley, Prof Erskin 310
Crump, Edward 294
Cuthbert, Gladys 372
Cutler, Ted 242, 328, 343, 349, 351, 366

Darby, Bill 194, 363
Darby, Elsie 221, 225
Davies, Reverend Gordon 157, 164, 165-7, 181-4, 344, 374, 376
Davson, Lt Colonel 55, 56, 76n
Dawes, Frank 5, 8n, 89, 107
Dawson, Frank 370
Dawson, Reverend Norman 366
de Mille, Cecil B 280, 286, 296
Decker, Lewis 294
Dempsey, Jack 286
Dent, Reverend H C 154, 157, 175n,
Derby, Lord 44, 46
Desmonde, Jerry 248, 305, 306
Dewey, Thomas 238, 277-8, 279, 289
Dewhurst (family) 37, 42n, 306
Didsbury Theological College 2, 10, 39, 77-100, 105, 112-13, 116, 119, 121, 135, 153, 165-6, 273, 306, 337, 373
Dobbs, Len 242, 328, 349, 351, 359, 371
Dobbs, Rene 242
Dorey, John 186, 196, 229
Driscoll, Madeline 306
Dromgoole, Will Allen 374, 377
Duckworth, Ann 10,
Duckworth, Aunt Minnie 299
Duckworth, Ellen (Cunliffe) 12,18
Duckworth, George 12
Duckworth, Jack 17, 34
Duckworth, Jack & Audrey 34
Duckworth, Jack (snr) 299
Duckworth, James 12
Duckworth, Maurice x
Duckworth, Peter 35
Duhamel, Mlle B 74

Eagan, Caroline 168
Eagan, Eddie 168, 237, 238, 278, 279, 280, 289 298, 300, 308, 310
Eagan, Peggy 168, 279, 289, 290, 298, 300
Eagan, Sidney 168, 300
Edgely House 188
Education Act 1870 115
Education Act, 1944 211, 214, 265
Edward VII 17, 33
Edward, Prince of Wales 154
Elephant and Castle 256, 257, 270, 350
Elizabeth, The Queen Mother 7, 322-3, 352-3
Elliott, Ricky 236, 304, 328
Emanuel, Mrs 324 +?
Emanuel, Stan 181, 227, 242, 262, 328, 341, 353
Enston, Ron 221
Etaples 4, 41, 56, 57-75
Etaples mutiny 60, 62
Etheridge, Les 226
Evans, Ethel 128, 342
Fairbanks, Douglas 298-9, 310, 312, 353
Falfemont Farm 51-2
Fields, Gracie 239, 240, 285, 253
Firestone, Harvey 286, 391, 298, 299, 310
Follows, Denis 237
Frank, Bishop Eugene 310
Fraser, Georgina 242

Gay, Hannah 105, 119, 125, 128, 137, 153, 185, 201,373
Gaynor, Albie 281, 301n
Gill, Charlie 194
Glenn, Keith 298
Glory, Helena 226
Gloucester, Duke of 151, 154, 171
Godbold, Harry 16
Goldsmith, Alf 372

Graham, Billy 337, 338
Grant, Carey 287
Gray, Chris 348,
Gray, David 330, 348
Gray, Robert (Bob) x, 309, 332, 353
Gray, Rose 330, 331, 359
Gray, Simon xi, 331
Gray, Ted 309, 351
Green Haworth Chapel x, 3, 9-40,
   77-8, 85, 99, 115, 118, 165-6, 368,
   371, 373
Griffiths, Dorothy 100n
Griffiths, Douglas 257
Griffiths, Stanton 293
Grigg, Rev. Norman 371
Grossmith, Sid 228
Guernsey Shield 264, 355
Gunter, Ray 314

Hall, Jean 242
Halstead, Reverend 79, 80, 99
Happy Harbour 168, 278, 289, 293
Hardwick, Cedric 299
Hargreaves, Peter x, 33
Harmsworth, Marg 221
Harris, Anne & June 242
Harris, Dr. F B   310
Harris, John 228
Harris, Les 328, 341, 351, 366, 371
Harris, Lily (Simpson) 242, 341, 352,
   366, 371
Harris, Sid 200, 221
Hawkins, Reverend Walter 102, 105,
   112-24
Hayley Bell, Mary 310
Henriques, Basil 119, 147, 152, 163,
   209, 210, 339, 369, 389
Hildebrand, Mark 340
Hill-Wood, Denis 237, 333
Hill-Wood, Peter 237, 333
Hilton, Ted 293
Hindle, Christopher 14, 15, 34, 35,
   41n, 99

Hindmarsh, Peter 242
Hippings Lane Infants School 16, 17
Hippings Mixed School 19
Holgate, Emma Lena 133, 166
Holgate, John 37, 86, 94, 99, 116, 132,
   133, 152, 166, 181, 337
Holmes Chapel 94-97, 99, 116, 171,
   373
Hope, Bob 7, 239, 247-8, 280-92, 295,
   296, 299, 305, 307-311, 352, 353, 373
Hope, Jack 288, 310
Horn, Reverend John 79, 80, 99n
Howard and Bullough (firm) 44,
   45
Howard, Marjorie 197
Hugill, Robert 19, 20, 84
Hull, Warren 307
Hunkin, John 340

Ingram, Brenda 309, 341
Iverson, Lorenz 294, 299

Jackman, Beryl 374
Jackman, Tony 225, 325, 374
James, Len 198
Jarman, Arthur 226, 241, 242, 328,
   341, 351
Jarman, Margaret 242
Jet Storm 298, 311, 312,313,
Joyful News, The 38-41, 72-3

Kallen, Kitty 307, 352
Kennedy, Bishop Gerald 299, 310
Kennedy, Bobby 170
Kingswood School 112, 129, 153, 161,
   167
Kirrage, Betty 236
Kitchener, Field Marshal 49
Knowles, Alan 339

Lamb, Dorothy 111, 132
Lamb, Ernest 111, 117, 121-125, 129,
   137, 138, 142, 153, 373

Lamplough, Edmund 121, 129, 132, 137, 138, 151, 153, 166
Lane, John 221
Lang, Paul Bartlett 322, 325, 362n, 371,
Langton, Jean 341, 348, 351, 352
Langton, John 242, 348, 351
Lawrence, Ron 228
Le Blond, Ken 221,
Leadbetter, Eric 196
Leale, Paul 172
Leale, Reverend John (Jack) 119, 122, 132, 133, 153, 169, 172, 186, 187, 229, 230, 369
Lear, Ted 181, 198
Leigh, Vivienne 280-1
Lemon Drop Kid, The 280
Leys School 314, 330,331
Lofthouse, William F 129, 153
Lord, Bob 353, 310
Lowe, Laurie 111, 150, 181, 194, 341, 342, 384
Lyle, Gordon x, 95, 119-20, 144, 157, 304, 339, 341, 351, 359, 365, 373
Lyle, Peggy (Rees) x, 171, 341

MacDonald, Ramsay 2, 111, 142
MacRobert, Lady 276, 277, 370
Maden, Matthew 15, 34, 99
Maden, W 34
Mams, the 155, 274, 324, 359
Marks, Fred 181, 342, 359
Marks, Jack 357
Marks, Mrs. 342
Marshall, Howard 182
Marshall, Lord 124
Martin, Florence 20
Martin, Harris 91, 98
Massey, Laurie 242, 328, 348, 351
Maufe, Edward x, 1, 30, 122, 127, 132, 141, 153, 161, 170, 171, 183, 318-21, 349, 369

Maufe, Prudence x, 122, 132-3, 153, 154, 170
McCleary, Reverend Ray 169, 280, 287
McDonald, Keith 331
McGillycuddy Eagar, William 88-9, 100n, 102, 108, 163, 208
Mears, Joe 237, 239, 310
Methodist Recorder, The 17, 98, 118, 128, 133, 139n, 143, 147, 156, 162, 165-6, 180, 185, 249-52, 285, 296, 374, 379,
Micklewhite, Maurice 102, 226-7, 227
Miller, Rev. Capt. Harry 70
Mills, Freddie 347-8
Mills, Hayley 310-11, 352
Mills, John 310
Moir, Ken 226
Moncrief family 288, 294
Morbin, Alf 221
Moreno, Henry 288, 291-2
Morgan, A E 141-2, 174n
Morgan, Rev. Dr Ivonwy 322
Morris, Annie 20, 41n, 306
Motson, John 239
Motson, Reverend William 239, 370
Moulder, Ron 159, 349
Moulton, Reverend Wilfred J 79-80, 88-9, 98, 113-4, 116, 121, 153, 373
Moulton, Reverend William Fiddian 84, 89, 99, 116, 314
Moulton, William Fiddian (Snr) 330

Neal, Frank x, 120, 156, 167, 170, 174, 179, 181, 194-97, 221
Neal, Leonard x, 120, 156, 370
Nic and Chic 194
Northwood-Stow, Judith 372

Old Vic, the 156, 314
Oliver, Harry 182
Olivier, Laurence 239, 280-1

Osborne, Sid 197
Oswaldtwistle x, 3, 10-14, 20-22,
    29-35, 37-51, 64, 72, 78-9, 84, 94-9,
    115-6, 133, 166, 273, 278, 288, 306,
    317-3
Owd Doc 18

Padbury, Fred 364
Panther, Samuel 113, 125, 154
Paramount Studios 248, 280, 293,
    300
Patrick 96
Pendle Hill 25, 88
Penistan, Reverend J R 138, 154, 157,
    175n
Pinewood Studios 324
Porter, Kenneth 196
Power, Ernie 221
Prince of Wales Theatre 282
Princess Alexandra 342, 352-4
Putnam, Arthur 182, 195

Queen Mary 1, 6, 30-1, 169-71, 177,
    183, 186, 191, 217-18, 276, 353, 375
Queenswood School 112, 127, 153,
    161, 161, 314

Randal, Bunty (Coates) 242, 303,
    349
Randall, Howard 182
Randall, Ken 194, 197, 227, 349, 363
Rank, J Arthur (Lord Rank) 7, 121,
    124, 137, 288, 307, 340, 316-27,
    361n, 375
Rank, Joseph 121, 124, 138, 139n, 153,
    288, 307
Ray, Ted 303
Read, Bill 194
Reading, Peter 366
Ready, Stuart 226
Reed, Alec 119-20, 157, 216, 221, 227,
    233, 332, 369, 373
Rees, Herbert 94-5, 300, 171, 373

Rees, Peggy 95, 171
Renton, Frank 123, 125
Richard, Cliff 337
Richards, Harry & Doris 187-88, 306
Richardson, Sydney 98
Richardson, Tony 340
Ritson, Reverend John 117, 123
Robert Browning Settlement 250
Rochester, Lord 2, 8n, 111, 139, 142,
    153-4, 157, 170-1, 274, 368, 373
Rolfe, David 366
Rooke, Ronnie 228
Rooney, Laurie 194
Rosenberg, Isaac 47
Rough Hey Farm 26-7, 33
Rough Hey Gate 10, 12-16, 24-9, 34
Rous, Stanley 155, 237, 271, 333, 353
Rowe, John 345
Ruel, Wally 237, 342
Rushton, Dennis 35, 77
Rushton, William 35
Russell, Arthur 228
Russell, Charles & Lillian 92, 100n
Ryan, Bill 241
Rydal Mount School 112, 190

Sacketh, A E 167
Savard, Lee 237-8
Scouts Hut, Étaples 63-5
Sculthorpe, Arthur 116, 122
Shrinkfield, Henry 123
Shrubsall, Alice 129, 161, 166, 169,
    170, 373
Shrubsall, George 124, 129, 132, 137,
    153, 373
Shuard, Dave 221
Simpson, Lily 242
Simpson, Rev G H 88, 306
Skinner, Alastair 331
Skinner, Charles 185, 194
Slark, George 228
Smalley, Alice 17
Smart, Bill 182

Soper, Donald 235-6
South London Press, 115, 129, 162,
 168, 185-6, 235, 238, 257, 259, 301,
 312-13
Sparksman, Allen x, 271, 341
Sparksman, Sylvia (Thomas) x, 341,
 348
SS United States 248, 272n, 287-8,
 291, 297
Stapleton, 'Sticky' 348, 351
Stapleton, Bill 194
Stedman, George 181, 194 new tab
Steiner, Frederick 33
Steiner, Jacob 21
Stirzaker, Albert 78, 97, 116, 166
Stirzaker, Cyril 98, 116
Stockill, Reg 144
Stones, Will 54
Stow, Gillian & Judith 242, 372
Stow, Jim 242, 328, 349, 351, 371-2
Stow, Topsy 242, 351, 372
Street, Barry 331
Studdert Kennedy, Geoffrey (see
 Woodbine Willie)
Suggars, Reg 194, 197-8
Suleyman, Touker 345
Surtees, Jock 372

Tattersall, Michael 195
Teddy Boys 255-8, 269, 272n, 350
The Accrington Observer 26, 44, 128,
 165, 179, 371
The Accrington Pals 44, 75-6n
This is your Life 41-2n, 100n, 239, 291,
 303-306, 341, 355, 364
Thomson, Alan 349
Thorn, Frank 194
Thorn, Margaret 174
Thorndyke, Sybil 155, 238-9
Tipper, Joan 221
Tizzard, Ron 228
Tolladay, Albert 194
Trew, Miss E M 161

Trocadero Cinema 270
Tunney, Gene 272, 289, 298, 308,
 309-10, 351-3
Turtle, Reg 119-20, 123, 127, 134, 157,
 303-4, 313, 329, 341, 351, 369

Union Street, Methodist Church,
 Accrington 14, 86

Variety Club of Great Britain 311,
 313-14
Vaughan, Frankie 311
Venier, Alan 241
Vogel Goad, William 104, 113, 125,
 132, 137, 154

Wackett Brothers 316
Wainman, Reverend Thomas 79-80
Wakefield, Sir Charles 124
Waldorf Astoria Hotel 286, 299
Walker, Ivy 241
Walker, Tommy 177, 236
Waller, Joyce 221
Walters, Kerry 76n
Walters, Reverend Arthur 124-5,
 137-8
Walton Hut 71
Walworth Wesleyan Chapel 2, 124,
 136
Warner, Ivy 226
Watson, Rev. Vic 371
Webb, Maurice 122
Webb, Mrs 342
Webb, Pamela 242, 331
Webster, Mrs 290
Wegner, Nicholas 280
Wesley, John 14, 15
Westminster College 340, 344
Whetcombe, Harry 196
Whiles, Billy 157, 158, 306, 339
Whistle Down the Wind 310-11
White, Iris 221
White, John 221

Whitehall, Teddy 197
Whitlock, Jimmy 195
Whitmore, Reverend J Wesley 10
Wiederanders, Christine 340
Wildman, Alec Shaw 116, 370
Wilkinson, M J 26
Wilkinson, Rev. Richard 18
Wilkinson, W T 41n
Williams, Daphne (Harris) x, 315, 361, 372
Wilson, Eddie 182
Wilson, Walter (Group Captain) 267
Windsor, Duke and Duchess of 171, 175n

Winstanley, Michael 22, 41n
Wiseman, Reverend F L 112, 132
Wissant 332-3, 353
Witney, Ambassador John Hay 309-10, 330
Wolstenholme, Eric & Barbara x
Wolstenholme, John 34
Wolstenholme, Margaret x
Wood, Sir Henry 155
Woodall, Albert 182
Woodbine Willie 67-9, 72
Woods, Hargreaves 11
Woolford, Dennis 195